THE
POINT
of
LAW

KT-572-379

THE
Education Act
explained RICHARD GOLD

London: The Stationery Office

Applications for reproduction should be made in writing to The Stationery Office Limited, St Crispins, Duke Street, Norwich NR3 1PD.

The information contained in this publication is believed to be correct at the time of manufacture. Whilst care has been taken to ensure that the information is accurate, the publisher can accept no responsibility for any errors or ommissions or for changes to the details given. Every effort has been made to trace copyright holders and to obtain permission for the use of copyright material. The publishers will gladly receive any information enabling them to rectify any errors or omissions in subsequent editions.

The Education Act 1998 explained is written by Richard Gold, a partner in the law firm Stone King which has an extensive education and charity law practice. Richard Gold is a member of the Executive Committee of the Education Law Association and lectures in the field of education law regularly.

Stone King
13 Queen Square
Bath BA1 2HJ

Tel 01225 337599
Fax 01225 335437

Richard Gold has asserted his moral rights under the Copyright, Designs and Patents Act 1988, to be identified as the author of this work.

Crown copyright material reproduced with permission of Her Majesty's Stationery Office

A CIP catalogue record for this book is available from the British Library

A Library of Congress CIP catalogue record has been applied for

First published 1999

ISBN 0 11 702381 7

Disclaimer

This publication is intended to be a brief commentary on the School Standards and Framework Act 1998 and should not be relied upon by any party without taking further legal advise.

Contents

Grammar schools

PART *IV* OTHER PROVISIONS ABOUT SCHOOL EDUCATION

Home-school agreements

Extension of educational opportunities for Key Stage 4 pupils

School meals

PART *V* NURSERY EDUCATION

Nursery education

General duty of local education authority

Early years development partnerships

INTRODUCTION

The School Standards and Framework Act 1998 is the legislative manifestation of the Labour Party election pledge to reform the state school system. The purpose was two-fold, to eliminate the grant-maintained sector and to provide a framework for raising standards within a context of responsibility delegated down to local education authorities, local decision-making bodies and individual schools. It is, to a very large extent, an enabling Act in that much of the detail required to implement government intentions will appear in regulations made by the Secretary of State and in guidance, in the form of Codes of Practice and Departmental Circulars, also issued by the Secretary of State. There are different levels of control over the contents of these elements. Regulations and Codes of Practice are subject to negative resolution of Parliament and there is a statutory requirement to consult on Codes of Practice. There is no similar control on Circulars although there is a well-established non-statutory consultation process. Power is thus placed very substantially in the hands of the Secretary of State not just to establish the initial process but also to change it quite substantially without coming back to Parliament for detailed scrutiny. There are good practical reasons for this: flexibility is important, particularly in untried and novel areas, and it would not be appropriate for there to be a legislative strait-jacket that would require Parliamentary time to resolve. Nevertheless, it is one of the paradoxes of the Act that the delegation of decision making away from Whitehall is accompanied by an unprecedented concentration of directive powers in the centre. In effect Government is saying that it is only appropriate for decisions to be made locally if those decisions correspond to good practice as viewed from the Department of Education and Employment.

The Act does, in fact, develop the concept of the Code of Practice which first appeared in the Education Act 1993 in relation to special educational needs. It introduces two new Codes, in relation to admissions and local education authority/school relationships. It also substantially increases the number of areas where those concerned with the implementation of particular aspects of school law are required to "have regard to" guidance issued by the Secretary of State. The judicial interpretation of that phrase, most notably in the case of R. v. Islington LBC ex p Rixon, is that there is an obligation on decision making bodies to have proper regard for guidance in Circulars and only to depart from it after due consideration and for proper reason. Given the increasing tendency for Circulars, and even more so, Codes of Practice, to be quite detailed and prescriptive in the suggested practice and procedure, this means that failure to take the "suggested" steps could lead to a court holding that due process has not been followed.

The Act is a mixture of new provision and the replacement (sometimes with major, sometimes with only minor, amendment) of provisions previously in the Education Act 1996. Where, however, no significant changes are made to a discrete area, that remains in the old legislation. Thus, it is still necessary to refer to the provisions of the Education Act 1996 in relation, for example, to the overall duties of local education authorities, to the National Curriculum and to special educational needs. The structure and detail of school inspection is still covered by the School Inspections Act 1996. Many elements of nursery education are still dealt with in the Nursery Education and Grant-Maintained Schools Act 1996. There are many necessary amendments to these Acts, but in the main these are to give effect to the new structures and terminology flowing out of the new Act. This book does not attempt to track those changes but concentrates on the substantive areas covered by the Act. No doubt, consideration will be given to a consolidating Act but for the foreseeable future it will be necessary to refer to those three Acts as well as to the School Standards and Framework Act 1998.

In summary, the Act does the following;-

Infant Class Sizes

Imposes a duty on local education authorities and all others involved to secure limits on infant class sizes – ss 1 to 4 with relevant further provisions in the sections dealing with admission arrangements and admission appeals.

Local Education Authority Duties

Requires local education authorities to promote high standards in schools – ss. 5 to 9. This includes requirements for the production of education development plans, appointment of parent governor representatives on local authority education committees and reserve powers for the Secretary of State to intervene.

Education Action Zones

Introduces the new concept of Education Action Zones consisting of a collaborative arrangement between schools under a formal structure, an Education Action Forum, which can involve agencies and organisations other than the local education authority – ss 10 to 13 and Schedule 1.

Intervention in Schools

Strengthened powers for local education authorities and the Secretary of State to intervene in schools that give cause for concern – ss 14 to 19 with relevant further provisions in the sections dealing with discipline.

Categories of Schools

Establishes new categories of schools – the heart of the Act – in place of the existing ones. For most schools this in itself will not be a significant change. Schools that were county schools become community schools and those that were voluntary controlled or voluntary aided assume the same names under the new structure. The significant change is the abolition of the grant-maintained category and the absorbing of those schools into the new structure. To facilitate this, a new category of "foundation" school is created for those grant-maintained schools that do not revert (or elect not to revert) to one or other form of voluntary status. Whatever the category, all schools will be funded on the same basis with the local education authority having responsibility for all funding other than capital funding for voluntary aided schools which, as always, remains substantially that of the governing body with central government grant – ss 20 to 23 and Schedules 2 and 3.

Local Decision Making

Sets up a framework for local school organisation committees and local adjudicators in England (with power to extend to Wales) to deal with decision making relating to the planning of school provision and admission policies – ss24 to 27 and Schedules 4 and 5 with relevant further provisions in the sections dealing with the formation and approval of admission policies.

Proposals for significant change to schools

Modifies the way in which proposals for the establishment, alteration and discontinuance of schools are to be dealt with, how the rationalisation of school places is to be dealt with and how schools are to be able to move from one category to another – ss 28 to 35 and Schedules 6, 7 and 8

The Governing Body

Re-enacts provisions relating to the way schools are to be governed. One significant change is the abolition of Articles of Government. Instead, every school will have a formal Instrument of Government which defines the type of school and the constitution of the governing body together (for schools with a religious character) with an ethos statement. Matters that were previously covered by the Articles of Government will now be covered either by the scheduled provisions in the Act or by regulations. This is a change of form rather than of substance but one which should make it easier to identify the powers of and procedures to be followed by governing bodies. Another new provision is the requirement for schools to put a complaints procedure in place – ss 36 to 44 and Schedules 9 to 13.

Funding of Schools

Re-enacts, with substantial changes in the way the budget share is to be determined, the provisions relating to the delegation of funding by local education authorities to schools – ss 45 to 53 and Schedules 14 and 15.

Staffing of Schools

Re-enacts, in substantially similar form, the provisions relating to the staffing of schools. Foundation schools are treated in a similar way to voluntary controlled schools although the governing body is the employer. Voluntary aided schools continue to employ their staff – ss 54 to 60 and Schedules 16 and 17.

Behaviour and Discipline

Re-enacts provisions relating to behaviour, discipline and exclusions in substantially similar terms save in relation to appeals against permanent exclusions. These are now to be organised by the local education authority for all schools and neither governors of the relevant school nor representatives of the local education authority may sit on the appeal panel. Relevant to this, although not included in the same sequence of sections, is the requirement for schools to put in place a home-school agreement. Ss 61 to 68 and Schedule 18 relating to discipline and exclusions, ss 110 and 111 relating to home-school agreements.

Religious Education and Worship

Re-enacts provisions relating to religious education and worship in substantially similar terms – ss 69 to 71 and Schedules 19 and 20

Admissions

Replaces the previous provisions relating to admissions. The substantive parental rights of preference and appeal are preserved as is the requirement to provide information. One major new feature is the obligation for the Secretary of State to formulate a Code of Practice relating to all aspects of admissions which all concerned must have regard to. There are new provisions for the determination of admission arrangements each year, including consultation and a right of objection to the adjudicator. There are also new restrictions on the introduction of selective admission policies and provisions for parental ballots on the retention of grammar schools – ss 84 to 109 and Schedules 23 to 25.

Work Experience

Makes minor amendments relating to work experience and education in FE colleges – ss 112 and 113.

School Lunches

Provides for a minimum nutritional standard for school lunches and the transfer of responsibility for providing lunches to governing bodies – ss 114 to 116

Nursery Education

Introduces new provisions for the planning and inspection of nursery education including the establishment of early years development partnerships and early years development plans – ss 117 to 124 and Schedule 26.

Partnership Arrangements in Wales

Enables partnership arrangements to be made in Wales between schools and FE colleges relating to the provision of school and further education – ss 125 and 126 and Schedule 27.

Local Education Authority/School Relationships

Almost as an afterthought, provides for the Secretary of State to produce a Code of Practice governing the relationship between schools and local education authorities – s. 127

Corporal Punishment

Makes a small but significant change to the law relating to corporal punishment – s. 131

Technical Provisions

Deals with a range of technical provisions, largely consequent on the change of school categories, relating amongst other things to new schools, transfers of land and staff, rating liability and trust deeds and with a number of minor and technical matters including consequential amendments of existing legislation – ss 72 to 83 and Schedules 21 and 22, ss128 to 130, 132 to 145 and Schedules 28 to 32.

Some words of warning. This is a highly technical Act and every word in it has to be given meaning. The commentary is intended to explain the particular provision in non-technical language but it is not a definitive exposition of the detail of the law and must not be relied upon without taking appropriate legal advice. Frequently, where the words of the Act are clear, no commentary is provided. In a some instances, there is no detailed commentary because the section or schedule relates only to technical aspects that have no immediate bearing on the process of running schools or local education authorities. For example, no attempt has been made to explain or track the various amendments to previous legislation made necessary as a result of changes effected by this Act.

There are many references in the Act and in the commentary to provisions that apply differently in Wales to England. Wales will not, initially at least, have a school organisation committee or adjudicators. Instead the Act provides that the Secretary of State exercises the equivalent functions and the commentary reflects this. However, executive power has been given to the National Assembly for Wales to take decisions in, amongst other areas, education under the Government of Wales Act 1998. In general terms, the functions of the Secretary of State have been transferred to the Assembly and matters which the Act says are to be dealt with by the Secretary of State will in fact fall to the Assembly to deal with.

Most of the Regulations contemplated by the Act have now been made and are in force. A notable exception relates to the introduction of complaints procedures under S. 39 which, as a gesture to the paper overload resulting from the Act, has been deferred until 1st September 2000 at the earliest. In many instances, separate regulations have been made for schools in Wales. These broadly mirror those made for schools in England but reflect the executive power that has been given to the National Assembly for Wales as mentioned above.

School Standards and Framework Act 1998

1998 c. 31

An Act to make new provision with respect to school education and the provision of nursery education otherwise than at school; to enable arrangements to be made for the provision of further education for young persons partly at schools and partly at further education institutions; to make provision with respect to the Education Assets Board; and for connected purposes.

[24th July 1998]

Be it enacted by the Queen's most Excellent Majesty, by and with the advice and consent of the Lords Spiritual and Temporal, and Commons, in this present Parliament assembled, and by the authority of the same, as follows:-

PART I MEASURES TO RAISE STANDARDS OF SCHOOL EDUCATION

CHAPTER I LIMIT ON INFANT CLASS SIZES

1.–(1) The Secretary of State shall by regulations-

(a) impose a limit on class sizes for infant classes at maintained schools; and
(b) specify the school years in relation to which any such limit is to have effect.

S. 1 (1)
The Secretary of State is required to set limits on the size of infant classes in state-maintained schools. This is to be done by regulations which will specify the school years that the limit will apply to.

(2) Any limit imposed under this section shall specify the maximum number of pupils that a class to which the limit applies may contain while an ordinary teaching session is conducted by a single qualified teacher.

S. 1 (2)
The limit is to be set by reference to the number of children being taught by a single qualified teacher and relates to ordinary teaching sessions, i.e. not events such as school assemblies. The phrases used are defined in S. 4.

(3) Subject to subsections (4) and (5), regulations under this section shall be so framed that-

(a) the maximum number specified in pursuance of subsection (2) is 30, and
(b) that limit has effect in relation to the 2001-02 school year and any subsequent year.

S. 1 (3)
The maximum number is to be 30 children per teacher and is to take effect in September 2001

(4) Regulations under this section may-

 (a) provide for any limit imposed under this section to take effect-
  (i) at the same time in the case of each of the age groups into which the pupils in infant classes fall, or
  (ii) at different times (which may be earlier than the beginning of the school year mentioned in subsection (3)) in the case of different such age groups;
 (b) provide that, in any circumstances specified in the regulations, any such limit either is not to apply or is to operate in such manner as is so specified.

S. 1 (4)
The regulations can specify different times for the limits to take effect

(5) The Secretary of State may by order amend subsection (3)-

 (a) by substituting for "30" such other number as is specified in the order; or
 (b) by substituting for the reference to the 2001-02 school year a reference to such other school year as is so specified.

S. 1 (5)
The Secretary of State can change both the limit and the year when it takes effect

(6) Where any limit imposed under this section applies to an infant class at a maintained school, the local education authority and the governing body shall exercise their functions with a view to securing that that limit is complied with in relation to that class.

S. 1 (6)
Local education authorities and school governing bodies must act so as to comply with any limits set

2.–(1) Every local education authority shall prepare a statement setting out the arrangements which the authority propose to make for the purpose of securing that any limit imposed under section 1 is complied with in relation to infant classes at schools maintained by the authority.

S. 2 (1)
The local education authority must prepare a plan for implementation of infant class size limits

(2) The statement shall-

    (a) contain such information as to the proposed arrangements, and
    (b) take such form,

as may be prescribed; and in preparing the statement the authority shall have regard to any guidance given from time to time by the Secretary of State.

S. 2 (2)
The Secretary of State may prescribe the information and the form that it will take and the local education authority must also "have regard to" any guidance that the Secretary of State may give.
N.B. This is the first of many references in the Act to "have regard to" guidance or Codes of Practice issued by the Secretary of State. The phrase imposes a duty to follow such guidance unless there are compelling reasons for not doing so. Failure to do so could lead to judicial review of the relevant decision and a court direction either to follow the guidance or to take the decision in question again with proper regard to the guidance.

(3) In the course of preparing the statement the authority shall carry out such consultation as may be prescribed.

(4) A prescribed body or person, or a body or person falling within any prescribed category, shall provide the authority-

    (a) with such documents or information, or
    (b) with such other assistance,

as the authority may reasonably request from that body or person for the purpose of enabling them to prepare the statement.

S. 2 (3) and (4)
The local education authority must consult on the preparation of the plan with whoever the Secretary of State prescribes and those consultees must supply whatever information the local education authority reasonably requires.

(5) The authority shall submit the statement to the Secretary of State for his approval-

    (a) by such date as may be prescribed, or

(b) by such later date as he may allow, where he is satisfied that it is reasonable to do so in view of any particular circumstances relating to the authority;

and different dates may be prescribed for different authorities.

(6) If the Secretary of State decides not to approve the authority's proposed arrangements-

(a) he shall notify the authority of his decision and of his reasons for it; and

(b) the authority shall prepare a revised statement under this section in respect of their proposed arrangements.

(7) Where the authority are required by subsection (6) to prepare a revised statement, the preceding provisions of this section shall apply to it as they applied to the original statement, except that-

(a) in preparing the revised statement the authority shall have regard to the Secretary of State's reasons for not approving their original proposals; and

(b) the revised statement shall be submitted to the Secretary of State by such date as he may determine.

S. 2 (5), (6) and (7)
The plan has to be approved by the Secretary of State who can specify a timetable and who can require the local education authority to revise the plan. If he does so, the local education authority must have regard to his reasons for requiring the revisions.

(8) In subsection (4) "document" includes information recorded otherwise than in legible form, and the reference to the provision of a document is, in the case of information so recorded, a reference to the provision of a copy of that information in legible form.

S. 2 (8)
This provides, effectively, for documents to be provided by electronic means which would include e-mail. There are similar provisions in several places in the Act in connection with the provision of information and consultation.

3.-(1) Regulations shall make provision for the payment by the Secretary of State of grants to local education authorities in respect of expenditure incurred or to be incurred by them for the purpose of securing that any limit imposed under section 1 is complied with in relation to infant classes at schools maintained by them.

(2) Regulations under this section shall provide for the Secretary of State-

(a) to withhold grants under the regulations from a local education authority where no proposed arrangements by that authority have been approved by him under section 2; and

(b) when determining whether any grant (and, if so, what amount) should be paid by him under the regulations to a local education authority, to have regard to their proposed arrangements as so approved.

(3) Regulations under this section may provide-

(a) for the payment of grant under the regulations to be dependent on the fulfilment of such conditions as may be determined by or in accordance with the regulations, and

(b) for requiring local education authorities to whom payments have been made under the regulations to comply with such requirements as may be so determined.

S.3

The Secretary of State has power to pay grants to local education authorities to meet the cost of complying with the infant class size limits and to make regulations relating to those grants.

4. In this Chapter-

"class" means a group in which pupils are taught in an ordinary teaching session;

"infant class" means a class containing pupils the majority of whom will attain the age of five, six or seven during the course of the school year;

"ordinary teaching session" does not include a school assembly or other school activity usually conducted with large groups of pupils;

"qualified teacher", in relation to an infant class, means-

(a) a person who is a qualified teacher in relation to that class for the purposes of section 218(1)(a) of the Education Reform Act 1988 (regulations relating to teachers' qualifications, etc.), or

(b) any other person who in accordance with regulations under that provision may be employed as a teacher of that class.

S. 4

This section defines phrases used in relation to infant class sizes.

CHAPTER II GENERAL RESPONSIBILITIES OF LOCAL EDUCATION AUTHORITIES

Duty to promote high standards of education

5. After section 13 of the (1996 c. 56.)Education Act 1996, there shall be inserted-

"13A.–(1) A local education authority shall ensure that their functions relating to the provision of education to which this section applies are (so far as they are capable of being so exercised) exercised by the authority with a view to promoting high standards.

(2) This section applies to education for-
 (a) persons of compulsory school age (whether at school or otherwise); and
 (b) persons of any age above or below that age who are registered as pupils at schools maintained by the authority;
and in subsection (1) "functions" means functions of whatever nature."

S. 5
A new duty is imposed on local education authorities. They must act so as to promote high standards in schools that they maintain. It extends also to the provision of education for children of compulsory school age who are not in a school.

Education development plans

6.–(1) Every local education authority shall prepare an education development plan for their area, and shall prepare further such plans at such intervals as may be determined by or in accordance with regulations.

S. 6 (1)
Every local education authority is required to produce an Education Development Plan.

(2) An education development plan shall consist of-
 (a) a statement of proposals, which sets out proposals by the authority for developing their provision of education for children in their area, whether by-
  (i) raising the standards of education provided for such children (whether at schools maintained by the authority or otherwise than at school), or
  (ii) improving the performance of such schools,
  or otherwise; and
 (b) annexes to that statement.

(3) In subsection (2) "children" means-
 (a) persons of compulsory school age (whether at school or otherwise), or
 (b) persons of any age above or below that age who are registered as pupils at schools maintained by the authority.

S. 6 (2) and (3)
An Education Development Plan is a statement of proposals to raise standards of education for all children (whether in school or not) and for improving the performance of schools. It includes any annexes to the statement.

(4) The statement of proposals must-

    (a) deal with such matters, and relate to such period, as may be determined by or in accordance with regulations, and

    (b) be approved by the Secretary of State under section 7.

(5) The annexes to the statement-

    (a) must contain such material as may be prescribed; and

    (b) may contain such other material as the authority consider relevant to their proposals as set out in the statement.

S. 6 (4) and (5)
The statement and the annexes must accord with the requirements of regulations. The local education authority may include other matters in the annexes.

(6) In preparing an education development plan the authority shall have regard, in particular, to the education of children (within the meaning of subsection (2)) who have special educational needs.

S. 6 (6)
The Education Development Plan must take account of children with special educational needs

(7) In the course of preparing an education development plan the authority shall consult-

    (a) the governing body and head teacher of every school maintained by the authority;

    (b) the appropriate diocesan authority for any foundation or voluntary school in their area which is a Church of England, Church in Wales or Roman Catholic Church school; and

    (c) such other persons as they consider appropriate.

S. 6 (7)
The local education authority must consult with schools and diocesan bodies of church schools as well as with others that they think appropriate.

(8) In its operation at any time before the appointed day (as defined by section 20(7)), subsection (7)(a) above shall be read as referring also to the governing body of every grant-maintained or grant-maintained special school situated in the authority's area.

(9) In performing their functions under this section the authority shall have regard to any guidance given from time to time by the Secretary of State.

S. 6 (9)
The local education authority must have regard to guidance from the Secretary of State.

7.–(1) Where a local education authority have prepared an education development plan in accordance with section 6, they shall, by such date as may be determined by or in accordance with regulations, submit the plan to the Secretary of State for him to approve the authority's statement of proposals under this section.

(2) The Secretary of State may in the case of any statement submitted to him under this section-

(a) approve the statement in any of the following ways, namely wholly or in part, for a limited period of time, or subject to conditions;

(b) require the authority to make such modifications to the statement as he may specify; or

(c) reject the statement.

(3) If the Secretary of State approves the statement-

(a) he shall notify the authority of his decision; and

(b) the authority shall implement the proposals set out in the statement, so far as approved by the Secretary of State, as from such date as he may determine.

(4) If the Secretary of State requires the authority to make modifications or rejects the statement-

(a) he shall notify the authority of his decision and of his reasons for it, and

(b) the authority shall prepare a revised statement and submit it to the Secretary of State for his approval under this section by such date as he may determine.

(5) Once the Secretary of State has approved an authority's statement of proposals under subsection (2), he shall keep under review the authority's proposals, as approved by him, and their implementation by the authority, and-

(a) where he is of the opinion that the statement should be modified (or further modified), he may withdraw his approval and require the authority to make such modifications to the statement as he may specify; and

(b) where he is of the opinion that the authority's proposals are not being properly implemented by them, he may withdraw his approval for such period as he thinks fit.

(6) If under subsection (5) the Secretary of State withdraws his approval of a statement of proposals-

(a) he shall notify the authority of his decision and of his reasons for it; and

(b) in a case falling within paragraph (a) of that subsection, the authority shall prepare a revised statement and submit it to him for his approval under this section by such date as he may determine.

(7) Section 6 shall apply to the preparation of a revised statement under subsection (4)(b) or (6)(b) above, with such modifications (if any) as the Secretary of State may determine.

(8) At any time after the Secretary of State has approved an authority's statement of proposals under subsection (2)-

   (a) the authority may submit modifications to the statement to the Secretary of State for his approval,

   (b) the Secretary of State may approve the modifications, whether in whole or in part, for a limited period of time, or subject to conditions, and

   (c) if and to the extent that he approves those modifications, he shall notify the authority of his decision and-
      (i) the statement shall have effect with the modifications, and
      (ii) the authority shall implement their proposals as modified,

as from such date as he may determine.

(9) Once the Secretary of State has approved-

   (a) an authority's statement of proposals under subsection (2), or

   (b) the modification of an authority's statement of proposals under subsection (8),

the authority shall publish their education development plan (or their plan as so modified) in such manner and by such date as may be prescribed, and shall provide such persons as may be prescribed with copies of that plan or of a summary version of that plan.

(10) In section 484 of the (1996 c. 56.) Education Act 1996 (education standards grants) references to "eligible expenditure" include expenditure for or in connection with the implementation by local education authorities of their education development plans.

S. 7

This section requires the local education authority to submit the Education Development Plan to the Secretary of State for approval. The Secretary of State has the power to require modification and the local education authority is required to implement the Education Development Plan once approved. The Secretary of State must monitor the performance of the local education authority and may withdraw approval if it is not being implemented properly. The local education authority may propose modifications to an existing Education Development Plan. Regulations provide for the mechanics of submission, approval and publication of EDPs.

Intervention by Secretary of State

8. After section 497 of the (1996 c. 56.)Education Act 1996 there shall be inserted-

"497A.–(1) This section applies to a local education authority's functions (of whatever nature) which relate to the provision of education-

    (a) for persons of compulsory school age (whether at school or otherwise), or

    (b) for persons of any age above or below that age who are registered as pupils at schools maintained by the authority.

(2) If the Secretary of State is satisfied (either on a complaint by any person interested or otherwise) that a local education authority are failing in any respect to perform any function to which this section applies to an adequate standard (or at all), he may exercise his powers under subsection (3) or (4).

(3) The Secretary of State may under this subsection direct an officer of the authority to secure that that function is performed in such a way as to achieve such objectives as are specified in the direction.

(4) The Secretary of State may under this subsection give an officer of the authority such directions as the Secretary of State thinks expedient for the purpose of securing that the function-

    (a) is performed, on behalf of the authority and at their expense, by such person as is specified in the direction, and

    (b) is so performed in such a way as to achieve such objectives as are so specified;

and such directions may require that any contract or other arrangement made by the authority with that person contains such terms and conditions as may be so specified.

(5) Where the Secretary of State considers it expedient that the person specified in directions under subsection (4) should perform other functions to which this section applies in addition to the function to which subsection (2) applies, the directions under subsection (4) may relate to the performance of those other functions as well; and in considering whether it is expedient that that person should perform any such additional functions, the Secretary of State may have regard to financial considerations.

(6) Any direction under this section may either-

    (a) have effect for an indefinite period until revoked by the Secretary of State, or

    (b) have effect until any objectives specified in the direction have been achieved (as determined in accordance with the direction).

(7) Any direction given under subsection (3) or (4) shall be enforceable, on an application made on behalf of the Secretary of State, by an order of mandamus.

497B.–(1) Where the Secretary of State gives directions under section 497A(4) to an officer of a local education authority, the person specified in those directions shall, in the performance of the function or functions specified in the directions, be entitled to exercise the powers conferred by this section.

(2) The specified person shall have at all reasonable times-

    (a) a right of entry to the premises of the authority, and

(b) a right to inspect, and take copies of, any records or other documents kept by the authority, and any other documents containing information relating to the authority, which he considers relevant to the performance of the specified function or functions.

(3) In exercising the right to inspect records or other documents under subsection (2), the specified person-

    (a) shall be entitled at any reasonable time to have access to, and inspect and check the operation of, any computer and any associated apparatus or material which is or has been in use in connection with the records or other documents in question, and

    (b) may require-

        (i) the person by whom or on whose behalf the computer is or has been so used, or

        (ii) any person having charge of, or otherwise concerned with the operation of, the computer, apparatus or material,

to afford him such assistance as he may reasonably require (including, in particular, the making of information available for inspection or copying in a legible form).

(4) Without prejudice to subsection (2), the authority shall give the specified person all assistance in connection with the performance of the specified function or functions which they are reasonably able to give.

(5) Subsection (2) shall apply in relation to any school maintained by the authority as it applies in relation to the authority; and without prejudice to that subsection (as it so applies)-

    (a) the governing body of any such school shall give the specified person all assistance in connection with the exercise of his functions which they are reasonably able to give; and

    (b) the governing body of any such school and the authority shall secure that all such assistance is also given by persons who work at the school.

(6) Any reference in this section to the specified person includes a reference to any person assisting him in the performance of the specified function or functions.

S. 8

New sections, Ss. 497A and 497B, are added to the Education Act 1996. They give the Secretary of State powers where he is satisfied that an local education authority is failing to perform its functions adequately. The Secretary of State has wide-ranging powers to give directions to any local education authority officer and to enforce those directions but he must have regard to financial considerations. The person who is directed to act is given powers to do so including powers to obtain information whether held on paper or on computer and the local education authority is required give whatever assistance it reasonably can. Any school maintained by the local education authority is also required to give such assistance.

(7) In this section "document" and "records" each include information recorded in any form."

Parent governor representatives on education committees

9. At the end of section 499 of the Education Act 1996 (power of Secretary of State to direct appointment of members of education committees) there shall be added-
"(6) Regulations may require-

  (a) any such committee as is mentioned in subsection (1) or (3), and
  (b) any sub-committee appointed by any authorities within subsection (1) or (3), or by any committee within paragraph (a) of this subsection, for the purpose mentioned in subsection (5)(b),

to include one or more persons elected, in accordance with the regulations, as representatives of parent governors at maintained schools in relation to which the committee or sub-committee acts.

(7) Regulations may make provision for-

  (a) the number of persons who are to be elected for the purposes of subsection (6) in the case of any local education authority;
  (b) the procedure to be followed in connection with the election of such persons and the persons who are entitled to vote at such an election;
  (c) the circumstances in which persons are qualified or disqualified for being so elected or for holding office once elected;
  (d) the term of office of persons so elected and their voting rights;
  (e) the application to any such committee or sub-committee, with or without any modification, of any provision made by or under any other enactment and relating to committees or (as the case may be) sub-committees of a local authority;
  (f) such other matters connected with such elections or persons so elected as the Secretary of State considers appropriate.

(8) Regulations may also make provision-

  (a) enabling the Secretary of State to determine, where he considers it expedient to do so in view of the small number of maintained schools in relation to which a committee or sub-committee acts, that the requirement imposed on the committee or sub-committee by virtue of subsection (6) is to have effect as if it referred to representatives of parents of registered pupils (rather than representatives of parent governors) at those schools;
  (b) for any regulations under subsection (7) to have effect, where the Secretary of State makes any such determination, with such modifications as may be prescribed.

(9) In subsections (6) and (8) "maintained school" and "parent governor" have the same meaning as in the School Standards and Framework Act 1998."

S. 9

S. 499 of the Education Act 1996 is amended so as to add a power for the Secretary of State to make regulations requiring that there be parent governor representation on a local authority education committee and providing for the method of electing such representatives.

CHAPTER III

Education action zones

10.–(1) If the Secretary of State considers that it is expedient to do so with a view to improving standards in the provision of education at any particular maintained schools, he may by order provide for those schools to constitute collectively an education action zone for the purposes of this Chapter.

(2) An education action zone shall be established in the first instance for three years; but the Secretary of State may, by an order made before the end of that period, provide for the zone to continue in existence for a further two years.

(3) At any time when an education action zone is in existence, the Secretary of State may by order vary the order establishing the zone by adding to the schools for the time being included in that order-

(a) any school in relation to which section 15 applies by virtue of subsection (1), (4) or (6) of that section; or

(b) with a view to enabling it to achieve improving standards in the provision of education once it becomes a maintained school, any new school which has a temporary governing body.

(4) No order shall be made by the Secretary of State under subsection (1), (2) or (3) except on an application made for the purpose with the consent of the governing body of every school which it is proposed should be a participating school.

(5) Any school which ceases to be a participating school by virtue of subsection (2) may nevertheless be included in a further order under subsection (1).

(6) In this Chapter-

(a) references to a governing body shall be read as including the temporary governing body of a new school;

(b) "participating school", in relation to an education action zone, means one of the schools for the time being included in the order under subsection (1) by which the zone is established.

(7) In this section "new school" has the meaning given by section 72(3).

(8) Unless the Secretary of State by order otherwise provides, nothing in this Chapter applies in relation to Wales.

S. 10

The Secretary of State may constitute a group of schools as an Education Action Zone if he thinks it expedient as a way to improve standards in those schools. The Education Action Zone will be established for three years with a power for the Secretary of State to extend for a further two years. The order may be varied by adding new schools or schools where the local education authority has powers of intervention – see S. 15 - but no school can be included in an Education Action Zone without its consent. The Education Action Zone provisions apply only to England unless the Secretary of State makes an order to include Wales.

11.–(1) An order establishing an education action zone under section 10(1) shall provide for the establishment of an Education Action Forum for the zone.

(2) An Education Action Forum shall be a body corporate and shall be constituted in accordance with the order under section 10(1) by which it is established.

(3) The order shall require the members of an Education Action Forum to include-

   (a) one person appointed by the governing body of each of the participating schools, unless the governing body of any such school choose not to make such an appointment; and

   (b) either one or two persons appointed by the Secretary of State.

(4) Schedule 1 has effect in relation to an Education Action Forum.

(5) The Forum established for an education action zone shall be dissolved by order of the Secretary of State with effect from the time when the zone ceases to exist in accordance with section 10(2).

(6) An order under subsection (5) may make provision for the transfer of property, staff, rights and liabilities of the Forum and for the preparation of a final statement of accounts.

S. 11

The Education Action Zone functions through an entity to be known as an Education Action Forum. An Education Action Forum is a body corporate and is an exempt charity. Schedule 1 contains the formal powers for the Education Action Forum. Every school in the Education Action Zone may appoint a member of the Education Action Forum if it wishes and the Secretary of State may appoint one or two members.

12.–(1) An Education Action Forum shall have as its main object the improvement of standards in the provision of education at each of the participating schools.

(2) A Forum may, under arrangements made by the governing body of a participating school in respect of any prescribed function of that body relating to the conduct of

the school, either-

(a) discharge that function on behalf of the governing body until such time as they may specify in a request to the Forum to cease discharging the function on their behalf; or

(b) assume full responsibility for the discharge of that function during the whole of the period for which the Forum remains in existence.

(3) Regulations may make provision-

(a) as to the circumstances in which the governing body of a participating school may make arrangements under subsection (2);

(b) for the procedure to be followed by such a governing body in connection with the making of any such arrangements;

(c) for the procedure to be followed by an Education Action Forum when discharging any function by virtue of that subsection;

(d) for statutory provisions relating to governing bodies of maintained schools to apply, with any prescribed modifications, to an Education Action Forum when discharging any function by virtue of paragraph (b) of that subsection.

S.12 (1) to (3)
The Education Action Forum exists to improve standards of education in the participating schools. The governing body of a participating school may ask the Education Action Forum to discharge any or all of its functions for a specified period or for as long as the Education Action Forum exists. Regulations will lay down the circumstances in which this may be done and the procedure to be followed.

(4) Regulations may, in relation to the discharge by an Education Action Forum of any function of a governing body under sections 54 and 57(1) to (3), Schedule 16 or paragraph 27 of Schedule 17, make any such provision as may be made by an order under section 81 (application of employment law during financial delegation).

S.12 (4)
Regulations may also provide for the Education Action Forum to discharge any employment functions that would normally be discharged by the governing body or by the local education authority under section 57, Schedule 16 (which applies to staff employed in Community, Voluntary Controlled and Community special schools) and paragraph 27 of Schedule 17 (which applies to staff employed by the local education authority to work in Foundation, Voluntary Aided and Foundation special schools).

(5) The Secretary of State may by a direction provide for any scheme under Chapter IV of Part II of this Act which relates to a participating school to have effect with

such modifications as he considers appropriate in a case where an Education Action Forum is discharging any function in relation to the school by virtue of subsection (2)(b).

(6) Before giving a direction under subsection (5) the Secretary of State shall consult the local education authority.

S. 12 (5) and (6)

The Secretary of State may make a direction to the effect that the local education authority financial delegation scheme made under Ss 45 to 53 of the Act be modified in relation to any school participating in an Education Action Forum. He must first consult the local education authority.

13. For section 3 of the (1991 c. 49.)School Teachers' Pay and Conditions Act 1991 there shall be substituted-

"3.–(1) A pay and conditions order shall not apply to the statutory conditions of employment of the school teachers in a participating school the governing body of which-

(a) have, by notice to the Secretary of State, made an application for exemption; and

(b) pursuant to that application are for the time being exempted from subsections (6) and (7) of section 2 above by virtue of an order under subsection (4) below.

(2) Before making an application under subsection (1) above, the governing body of the participating school concerned shall consult the school teachers employed at the school with respect to the proposed application.

(3) A notice of application under subsection (1) above shall specify a date, at least three months after the date of the notice, with effect from which the governing body of the participating school concerned intend to make their own provision as to the statutory conditions of employment of the school teachers employed at the school.

(4) On receipt of a notice of application under subsection (1) above the Secretary of State may, by statutory instrument, make an order-

(a) naming the school; and

(b) specifying, as the date with effect from which, by virtue of the order, subsections (6) and (7) of section 2 above are not to apply, the date specified in the notice of application or such other date as may be agreed between the governing body and the Secretary of State.

(5) Where by virtue of an order under subsection (4) above a pay and conditions order ceases to apply in relation to any school, the statutory conditions of employment of the school teachers employed at the school shall be-

(a) such as may be determined by the governing body, or

(b) so far as the governing body have not made any determination with respect to any such conditions of employment, those having effect under the order immediately before it ceased to apply;

and (so far as necessary) the local education authority shall give effect to any such determination of the governing body.

(6) In this section "participating school" means one of the schools for the time being included in an order under section 10(1) of the School Standards and Framework Act 1998 establishing an education action zone."

S.13

The School Teachers' Pay and Conditions Act 1991 is modified so that a school participating in an Education Action Forum may opt out of the statutory pay and conditions provisions. The school must apply to the Secretary of State for exemption. It must first consult with the teachers and the application must give at least three months' notice of the date it is to take effect. The Secretary of State may make an exemption order to take effect on the date specified in the application or another date agreed between the Secretary of State and the governing body. If an order is made, the governing body may determine the conditions of employment for teachers. To the extent that the governing body does not determine particular conditions, the conditions previously applying, i.e. those prescribed by the statutory pay and conditions provisions, will take effect. The local education authority must, so far as necessary, give effect to any such determination.

CHAPTER IV INTERVENTION IN SCHOOLS CAUSING CONCERN

Intervention by LEAs

14.–(1) If at any time section 15 applies to a maintained school by virtue of any of the following provisions of that section, namely-

(a) subsection (1) (school subject to formal warning),

(b) subsection (4) (school with serious weaknesses), or

(c) subsection (6) (school requiring special measures),

the provisions mentioned in subsection (2) below (which confer powers of intervention on local education authorities) shall also apply to the school at that time unless excluded by subsection (3) below (intervention by Secretary of State).

(2) Those provisions are-

(a) section 16 (power to appoint additional governors); and

(b) section 17 (power to suspend right to delegated budget).

(3) Those provisions shall not apply to a school to which section 15 applies by virtue of subsection (6) of that section (school requiring special measures) if, in connection with the same report falling within paragraph (a) of that subsection-

  (a) the Secretary of State has exercised in relation to the school his power under section 18 (power to appoint additional governors) and any additional governors appointed in the exercise of that power remain in office; or
  (b) he has exercised in relation to the school his power under section 19 (power to direct closure of school).

S. 14 (1), (2) and (3)
If S. 15 applies to a school because it is subject to formal warning, has serious weaknesses or requires special measures, the local education authority may exercise the powers to appoint additional governors under S. 16 or to suspend the delegated budget under S. 17 unless in the case of a school requiring special measures the Secretary of State has exercised his power to appoint additional governors under S. 18 or to direct closure of the school under S. 19.

(4) In this Chapter-

  (a) "Chief Inspector" and "member of the Inspectorate", and
  (b) references to special measures being, or not being, required to be taken in relation to a school,

have the same meaning as in the School Inspections Act 1996.

15.–(1) This section applies to a maintained school by virtue of this subsection if-

  (a) the local education authority have-
    (i) given the governing body a warning notice in accordance with subsection (2), and
    (ii) given the head teacher of the school a copy of the notice at the same time as the notice was given to the governing body;
  (b) the governing body have failed to comply, or secure compliance, with the notice to the authority's satisfaction within the compliance period; and
  (c) the authority have given reasonable notice in writing to the governing body that they propose to exercise their powers under either or both of sections 16 and 17 (whether or not the notice is combined with a notice under section 62(3)(c)).

(2) A local education authority may give a warning notice to the governing body of a maintained school where-

  (a) the authority are satisfied-
    (i) that the standards of performance of pupils at the school are unacceptably low and are likely to remain so unless the authority exercise their powers under either or both of sections 16 and 17, or

(ii) that there has been a serious breakdown in the way the school is managed or governed which is prejudicing, or likely to prejudice, such standards of performance, or

(iii) that the safety of pupils or staff of the school is threatened (whether by a breakdown of discipline or otherwise); and

(b) the authority have previously informed the governing body and the head teacher of the matters on which that conclusion is based; and

(c) those matters have not been remedied to the authority's satisfaction within a reasonable period.

S. 15

This section specifies three different triggers for the right to intervene under S. 14 S.15 (1) and (2)

The first trigger is if the local education authority has given the governing body and the headteacher a warning notice which has not been complied with to the local education authority's satisfaction and the local education authority has given the governing body reasonable written notice that it intends to exercise its powers. The local education authority may give a warning notice if satisfied either that the standards of performance of pupils at the school are unacceptably low and are likely to remain so unless the local education authority exercises its powers or that there has been a serious breakdown in the way the school is managed or governed which is prejudicing or likely to prejudice those standards or that the safety of pupils or staff in the school is threatened by a breakdown of discipline or otherwise. The local education authority must first have informed the governing body and the headteacher of the matters on which its conclusions are based and a reasonable period must have passed without them having been remedied.

(3) For the purposes of subsections (1) and (2) a "warning notice" is a notice in writing by the local education authority setting out-

(a) the matters referred to in subsection (2)(b);

(b) the action which they require the governing body to take in order to remedy those matters; and

(c) the period within which that action is to be taken by the governing body ("the compliance period").

S. 15 (3)

The warning notice must set out the matters on which the local education authority has based its conclusion, must specify the action that the governing body is to take and state the period for compliance.

(4) This section applies to a maintained school by virtue of this subsection if-

(a) a report of an inspection of the school has been made under Part I of the School Inspections Act 1996 in which the person making it stated that in his opinion the school had serious weaknesses; and

(b) where any subsequent report of an inspection of the school has been made under Part I of that Act, that opinion has not been superseded by the person making the report stating that in his opinion-

(i) the school no longer has serious weaknesses, or

(ii) special measures are required to be taken in relation to the school.

(5) For the purposes of subsection (4) a school has serious weaknesses if, although giving its pupils in general an acceptable standard of education, it has significant weaknesses in one or more areas of its activities.

S. 15 (4) and (5)
The second trigger is if an inspection report states that the school has serious weaknesses and that report has not been superseded by a report saying either that there were no longer serious weaknesses or that special measures are required to be taken. Serious weakness for this purpose exists if a school, although giving a generally acceptable standard of education, has significant weaknesses in one or more areas of its activities.

(6) This section applies to a maintained school by virtue of this subsection if-

(a) a report of an inspection of the school has been made under Part I of the School Inspections Act 1996 in which the person making it stated that in his opinion special measures were required to be taken in relation to the school;

(b) either that person was a member of the Inspectorate or the report stated that the Chief Inspector agreed with his opinion; and

(c) where any subsequent report of an inspection of the school has been made under Part I of that Act, the person making it did not state that in his opinion special measures were not required to be taken in relation to the school.

S. 15 (6)
The third trigger is if an inspection report has stated that special measures were required, the report was by a member of the Inspectorate (i.e. one of Her Majesty's Inspectors) or the Chief Inspector agreed with the opinion and, if there has been a subsequent report, that report did not say that special measures were not required.

16.–(1) If at any time this section applies to a maintained school in accordance with section 14(1), then (subject to subsections (2) and (3)) the local education authority may appoint such number of additional governors as they think fit.

(2) Where this section so applies in the case of a school falling within section 15(1) (school subject to formal warning), the power conferred by subsection (1) above is only exercisable within the period of two months following the end of the compliance period.

> **S. 16 (1) and (2)**
> *Where this section applies (under S. 14 (1)) the local education authority may appoint as many additional governors as it thinks fit. If it is exercising the power after serving a warning notice it can only do so within two months of the end of the period for compliance with that notice.*

(3) Where this section so applies in the case of a school falling within section 15(6) (school requiring special measures), the power conferred by subsection (1) above is only exercisable if the following conditions are satisfied, namely-

    (a) the relevant document has been sent to the Secretary of State;

    (b) the authority have received a notice in writing from the Secretary of State in which he acknowledges receipt of that document; and

    (c) a period of not less than ten days has elapsed since the date of the notice.

(4) The Secretary of State may in respect of any particular school determine that subsection (3)(c) shall have effect as if the reference to ten days were to such shorter period as he may determine.

> **S. 16 (3) and (4)**
> *Before exercising the power to appoint additional governors to a school requiring special measures the local education authority must first have submitted its "action plan" under Ss 17 or 18 of the School Inspection Act 1996, the Secretary of State must have acknowledged receipt and 10 days (or a shorter period if the Secretary of State directs) must have elapsed.*

(5) In relation to any appointment made by the local education authority by virtue of subsection (1) to the governing body of a school, the instrument of government for the school shall have effect as if (despite anything in Part II of Schedule 9) it provided for the local education authority to appoint such number of additional governors as they think fit.

(6) If at any time-

    (a) this section applies to a voluntary aided school other than one falling within section 15(6), and

    (b) the local education authority have exercised their power to appoint additional governors under subsection (1),

the appropriate appointing authority may appoint such number of additional foundation governors as is equal to the number of additional governors appointed by the authority.

(7) Any additional foundation governors appointed under subsection (6)-

    (a) shall cease to hold office at the time when the additional governors appointed by the authority cease to do so; and

    (b) shall not be eligible for re-appointment except where, and to the extent that, those governors are re-appointed.

S. 16 (6) and (7)
If S. 16 applies to a Voluntary Aided school other than one requiring special measures, then the body entitled to appoint foundation governors (which phrase here and throughout these notes includes the diocesan authority in the case of a school which is a Church of England school, a Church in Wales school or a Roman Catholic Church school) may appoint as many additional foundation governors as the local education authority appoints in exercise of its powers. Those additional foundation governors only serve while the additional local education authority governors serve.

(8) If-

    (a) at any time this section applies to a voluntary aided school falling within section 15(6), and

    (b) neither of paragraphs (a) and (b) of section 14(3) for the time being applies in connection with the same report falling within section 15(6)(a),

the appropriate appointing authority may (subject to subsection (9)) appoint such number of additional foundation governors as they think fit.

(9) The power conferred by subsection (8) is only exercisable if the following conditions are satisfied, namely-

    (a) the relevant document has been sent to the Secretary of State;

    (b) the appropriate appointing authority have received a notice in writing from the Secretary of State informing them that he has received that document; and

    (c) a period of not less than ten days has elapsed since the date of the notice.

S. 16 (8) and (9)
If S. 16 applies to a Voluntary Aided school requiring special measures and the Secretary of State has not exercised his power to appoint additional governors or direct closure, then the body entitled to appoint foundation governors may appoint as many additional foundation governors as it thinks fit. Before the power can be exercised the local education authority must first have submitted its "action plan" under Ss 17 or 18 of the School Inspection Act 1996, the Secretary of State must have acknowledged receipt and 10 days must have elapsed.

(10) In the case of any appointment made by virtue of subsection (6) or (8) to the governing body of a school, the instrument of government for the school shall have effect as if (despite paragraph 14 of Schedule 9) the instrument provided for the appropriate appointing authority to appoint such number of additional foundation governors as they are authorised to appoint under subsection (6) or (8) (as the case may be).

(11) Subject to subsection (12), references in this section to the appropriate appointing authority in relation to any voluntary aided school are references-

(a) to the appropriate diocesan authority, if it is a Church of England school, Church in Wales school or Roman Catholic Church school; or

(b) in any other case, to the person or persons by whom the foundation governors are appointed.

(12) Where, in the case of any voluntary aided school not falling within subsection (11)(a), there are different powers to appoint foundation governors, references in this section to the appropriate appointing authority are references-

(a) to all those persons who have any such power acting jointly, or

(b) if they are unable to agree, to such of them acting jointly, or such one of them, as the Secretary of State may, after consulting all those persons, determine.

(13) In this section "the relevant document" means a copy of a statement prepared-

(a) under section 18 of the School Inspections Act 1996, or

(b) under section 17 of that Act, if the school does not have a delegated budget within the meaning of Part II of this Act.

17.–(1) If at any time-

(a) this section applies to a maintained school in accordance with section 14(1), and

(b) the school has a delegated budget within the meaning of Part II of this Act,

then (subject to subsections (2) and (3)) the local education authority may, by giving the governing body of the school notice in writing of the suspension, suspend the governing body's right to a delegated budget with effect from the receipt of the notice by the governing body.

(2) Where this section so applies in the case of a school falling within section 15(1) (school subject to formal warning), the power conferred by subsection (1) above is only exercisable within the period of two months following the end of the compliance period.

(3) Where this section so applies in the case of a school falling within section 15(6) (school requiring special measures), the power conferred by subsection (1) above is only exercisable if the following conditions are satisfied, namely-

(a) a copy of a statement prepared under section 18 of the (1996 c. 57.)School Inspections Act 1996 has been sent to the Secretary of State;

(b) the authority have received a notice in writing from the Secretary of State in which he acknowledges receipt of that document; and

(c) a period of not less than ten days has elapsed since the date of the notice.

(4) The Secretary of State may in respect of any particular school determine that subsection (3)(c) shall have effect as if the reference to ten days were to such shorter period as he may determine.

(5) A copy of a notice given under subsection (1) shall be given to the head teacher of the school at the same time as the notice is given to the governing body.

(6) A suspension imposed under this section shall have effect for the purposes of Chapter IV of Part II of this Act as if made under paragraph 1 of Schedule 15 to this Act, but there shall be no right of appeal under paragraph 3 of that Schedule against such a suspension.

S. 17

This section gives the local education authority the right to suspend the delegated budget of a school to which the section applies by virtue of S. 14 (1). It must give notice in writing to the governing body and to the headteacher and the budget will be suspended immediately on receipt of the notice. There is no right of appeal. The circumstances in which the right can be exercised and the conditions that apply are the same as those applying to the right to appoint additional governors under S. 15.

Intervention by Secretary of State

18.–(1) If at any time section 15 applies to a maintained school by virtue of subsection (6) of that section (school requiring special measures), the Secretary of State may appoint such number of additional governors as he thinks fit; and he may nominate one of those governors to be the chairman of the governing body in place of any person who has been elected as chairman of that body.

(2) Before making any such appointment in relation to a voluntary aided school, the Secretary of State shall consult-

(a) in the case of a Church of England school, a Church in Wales school or a Roman Catholic Church school, the appropriate diocesan authority; or

(b) in any other case, the person who appoints the foundation governors.

(3) A governor appointed under this section-

(a) shall hold office as governor for such term, and

(b) if nominated as chairman of the governing body, shall be chairman of that body for such period,

as the Secretary of State may determine.

(4) The Secretary of State may pay to any governor appointed under this section such remuneration and allowances as the Secretary of State may determine.

> **S. 18 (1) to (4)**
> *Where a school requires special measures the Secretary of State may appoint as many additional governors as he thinks fit and nominate one of them to act as Chair of the governing body for such period as he may specify. If the school is a Voluntary Aided school he must first consult with whoever has the power to appoint foundation governors. A governor so appointed may receive such remuneration and allowances as the Secretary of State may decide and will serve for such period as the Secretary of State may determine.*

(5) In relation to any appointment made by the Secretary of State by virtue of subsection (1) to the governing body of a school, the instrument of government for the school shall have effect as if (despite anything in Part II of Schedule 9) it provided for the Secretary of State to appoint such number of additional governors as he thinks fit.

(6) Where the Secretary of State has exercised his power under this section in relation to a school, then-

  (a) in any such case-
    (i) the local education authority may not exercise their power under paragraph 1 of Schedule 15 to suspend the governing body's right to a delegated budget, and
    (ii) if they have already exercised that power or their power under section 17(1), the Secretary of State shall, if requested to do so by the governing body, revoke the suspension; and
  (b) in the case of a voluntary aided school, nothing in paragraph 14 of Schedule 9 shall be read as authorising the appointment of foundation governors for the purpose of outnumbering the other governors as augmented by those appointed by the Secretary of State under this section.

> **S. 18 (6)**
> *If the Secretary of State exercises his powers under this section, the local education authority may not suspend the delegated budget. If it has done so already, it must revoke the suspension. The normal rule for Voluntary Aided schools (under para 14 of Schedule 9) enabling the body with power to appoint foundation governors to appoint as many foundation governors as are needed to outnumber the other governors does not apply in relation to governors appointed by the Secretary of State under this section.*

(7) The revocation of a suspension under subsection (6)(a) shall-

(a) be notified to the local education authority in writing; and
(b) take effect from such date as is specified in that notification.

19.–(1) If at any time section 15 applies to a maintained school by virtue of subsection (6) of that section (school requiring special measures), the Secretary of State may give a direction to the local education authority requiring the school to be discontinued on a date specified in the direction.

(2) Before giving a direction under subsection (1), the Secretary of State shall consult-

(a) the local education authority and the governing body of the school;
(b) in the case of a foundation or voluntary school which is a Church of England school, a Church in Wales school or a Roman Catholic Church school, the appropriate diocesan authority;
(c) in the case of any other foundation or voluntary school, the person who appoints the foundation governors; and
(d) such other persons as the Secretary of State considers appropriate.

(3) On giving a direction under subsection (1) the Secretary of State shall give notice in writing of the direction to the governing body of the school and its head teacher.

(4) Where the local education authority are given a direction under subsection (1), they shall discontinue the school in question on the date specified in the direction; and nothing in sections 29 to 33 shall apply to their discontinuance of the school under this section.

(5) In this section any reference to the discontinuance of a maintained school is to the local education authority ceasing to maintain it.

S. 19

The Secretary of State may direct closure of a school requiring special measures. He must first consult the local education authority, the governing body of the school, the body with the power to appoint foundation governors and others who he considers appropriate. He must give notice of the direction to the governing body and to the headteacher and the local education authority must discontinue the school on the specified date.

PART II NEW FRAMEWORK FOR MAINTAINED SCHOOLS

CHAPTER I INTRODUCTORY

The new categories of schools

20.–(1) Schools maintained by local education authorities on or after the appointed day shall be divided into the following categories-

(a) community schools;

(b) foundation schools;

(c) voluntary schools, comprising-

    (i) voluntary aided schools, and

    (ii) voluntary controlled schools;

(d) community special schools; and

(e) foundation special schools.

S. 20 (1)

As from 1st September 1999 there are five categories of schools as listed in the section. Community schools equate to former County schools, Voluntary Aided and Voluntary Controlled schools generally equate to schools previously in that category together with former special agreement schools and grant maintained schools that acquire voluntary status under Schedule 2. Foundation schools generally equate to those grant maintained schools that do not acquire voluntary status. Community Special schools are former maintained special schools and Foundation Special schools are former grant maintained special schools.

---

(2) A school maintained by a local education authority is a school falling within one of the categories set out in subsection (1) if-

    (a) it became a school of that category on the appointed day in accordance with Schedule 2 (and has not changed its category under Schedule 8); or

    (b) it was established as a school of that category under section 28 or 31 (and has not changed its category under Schedule 8); or

    (c) it has become a school of that category in accordance with Schedule 8.

S. 20 (2)

Existing schools are allocated to their new category in accordance with Schedule 2 unless they have changed their category as provided for in Schedule 8, New schools established under S. 28 (mainstream schools) or S. 31 (special schools) will also fall within one of the categories.

---

(3) Schedule 2 makes provision for, and in connection with, the allocation to the categories set out in subsection (1) of schools which immediately before the appointed day were (within the meaning of the Education Act 1996)-

    (a) county, voluntary or maintained special schools, or

    (b) grant-maintained or grant-maintained special schools.

(4) As from the appointed day a local education authority shall maintain (as a school falling within one of those categories)-

(a) any school within subsection (3)(a) which was maintained by the authority immediately before that day; and

(b) (subject to subsection (5)) any school within subsection (3)(b) which immediately before that day was situated within the authority's area.

> ## S. 20 (4)
> *Local education authorities are required to maintain any school previously (i.e. before 1st September 1999) maintained by it and any former grant maintained school within its area unless S. 20 (5) applies*

(5) Where a grant-maintained school within subsection (3)(b)-

(a) was, immediately before becoming such a school, maintained by a local education authority ("the former maintaining authority") other than the one within whose area it was then situated, and

(b) remains outside the area of the former maintaining authority immediately before the appointed day,

nevertheless, if an order made by the Secretary of State before that day so provides, as from that day the school shall be maintained (as a school falling within one of the categories set out in subsection (1)) by the former maintaining authority rather than the authority in whose area it is situated on that day.

> ## S. 20 (5)
> *If a former grant maintained school within an local education authority area was maintained by a different local education authority before it became grant maintained, the local education authority that originally maintained it will do so from 1st September 1999 if the Secretary of State made an order to that effect before that date.*

(6) In this section "school" means a primary, secondary or special school, including a nursery school which is a special school but excluding-

(a) a nursery school which is not a special school; and

(b) a pupil referral unit.

(7) In this Act-

"the appointed day" (except in Part I of Schedule 32) means such day as may be appointed for the purposes of this section by an order made by the Secretary of State;

"maintained school" means (unless the context otherwise requires) a community, foundation or voluntary school or a community or foundation special school.

(8) Any reference in this Act to the categories set out in subsection (1) or to any such category is to be read, in its application to voluntary.schools, as (or as including) a

reference to the sub-categories set out in subsection (1)(c)(i) and (ii) or to any such sub-category.

21.–(1) There may be three kinds of foundation school-

(a) those having a foundation established otherwise than under this Act;

(b) those belonging to a group of schools for which a foundation body acts under this section; and

(c) those not falling within either of paragraphs (a) and (b).

(2) There may be three kinds of voluntary controlled or voluntary aided school-

(a) those having a foundation established otherwise than under this Act;

(b) those belonging to a group of schools for which a foundation body acts under this section; and

(c) those not falling within either of paragraphs (a) and (b) but having been either of the following immediately before the appointed day, namely-

(i) a voluntary school, or

(ii) a grant-maintained school that was a voluntary school immediately before becoming grant-maintained,

within the meaning of the Education Act 1996.

S. 21 (1) and (2)

There are three types of foundation and voluntary schools, those with existing foundations, those with foundations set up under this Act and those with no foundation but which were previously voluntary schools under the old framework.

---

(3) For the purposes of this Act-

(a) "foundation", in relation to a foundation or voluntary school, means-

(i) any body of persons (whether incorporated or not but excluding the governing body) which holds land on trust for the purposes of the school, or

(ii) a foundation body;

(b) a school "has" a foundation if-

(i) such a body of persons exists for holding land on trust for the purposes of the school, or

(ii) the school belongs to a group of schools for which a foundation body acts under this section; and

(c) references to land or other property held on trust, or by trustees, for the purposes of a school include references to land or other property which-

(i) is held on trust for purposes which (whether the trust deed expressly so provides or not) include the purposes of the school, and

(ii) is used for the purposes of the school.

> **S. 21 (3)**
> *A school has a "foundation" if there is either a body that holds land on trust for the school or a foundation body as defined in S. 21 (4).*

(4) For the purposes of this Act-

    (a) "foundation body" means a body corporate established under this section to perform, in relation to three or more schools each of which is either a foundation or a voluntary school, the following functions, namely-

        (i) to hold property of those schools for the purposes of the schools, and

        (ii) to appoint foundation governors for those schools; and

    (b) "the group", in relation to a foundation body, means the group of three or more schools for which the body performs those functions.

(5) The Secretary of State may by regulations make provision for and in connection with-

    (a) the establishment, membership, functions and winding up of a foundation body, and

    (b) the steps to be taken in connection with schools joining or leaving the group.

(6) Regulations under subsection (5) may, in particular, make provision-

    (a) with respect to the transfer of property, rights and liabilities to and from a foundation body when schools join or leave the group but do not change category in accordance with Schedule 8;

    (b) with respect to the revision or replacement of the instruments of government of schools joining or leaving the group in such circumstances and the reconstitution of their governing bodies;

    (c) authorising a foundation body to appoint foundation governors to every school in the group;

    (d) prescribing a model instrument of government for adoption by a foundation body subject to variations approved by the Secretary of State;

    (e) for conferring functions with respect to the resolution of disputes-

        (i) between schools in the group, or

        (ii) between one or more such schools and a foundation body,

    on such person or body as may be specified in the regulations;

    (f) in connection with a school leaving the group-

        (i) for requiring the publication of proposals under paragraph 2 of Schedule 8 (procedure for changing category of school);

        (ii) for enabling the Secretary of State to require the publication under that paragraph of proposals for the school to become a school of a category specified by him;

        (iii) for preventing a voluntary school from becoming one falling within subsection (2)(a) unless any conditions specified in pursuance of paragraph 4(2)(b) of that Schedule are satisfied in relation to the school;

(g) for the dissolution of a foundation body by order of the Secretary of State;

(h) for enabling the Secretary of State, in the case of any land held by a foundation body immediately before its dissolution which by virtue of this Act could not be disposed of without his consent, to determine how that land is to be dealt with on its dissolution;

(i) for conferring functions on school organisation committees and adjudicators including any functions which might otherwise be conferred on the Secretary of State.

S. 21 (4), (5) and (6)

A foundation body established under this Act is a body corporate which is set up to hold property (not necessarily land) for a group of three or more schools and to appoint foundation governors for those schools. Regulations deal with how the foundation body is established, financed and run and how schools may join or leave the group.

(7) Regulations made in pursuance of subsection (6)(b) may, in connection with the making or variation of instruments of government in preparation for schools joining or leaving the group, modify paragraph 1 of Schedule 12 in its operation in relation to such instruments of government.

(8) The Secretary of State may, after consulting a foundation body, make an order modifying the instrument of government adopted by that body.

(9) Regulations may make provision for applying to foundation special schools, with or without modifications-

(a) any of the provisions of subsections (3) to (8); or

(b) any provision of Schedule 21 to this Act (transfers of land on appointed day).

22.–(1) A local education authority are under a duty to maintain the following schools-

(a) any maintained schools which they are required to maintain by virtue of section 20(4) or (5);

(b) any maintained schools established by them under section 28 or 31;

(c) any maintained schools established in their area under section 28 otherwise than by them or any other local education authority; and

(d) any maintained nursery school established by them.

S. 22 (1)

The local education authority has the duty to maintain all schools within its area that fall within s. 20 and any new schools established under Ss 28 and 31 and any maintained nursery schools that they establish.

(2) Subsection (1) has effect subject to the transfer under this Part of a maintained school from the area of one local education authority to that of another, and to the provisions of this Part relating to the discontinuance of schools.

S. 22 (3)
The local education authority meets all costs of and provides premises for community, community special and maintained nursery schools.

(3) In the case of a community school, a community special school or a maintained nursery school, the local education authority's duty to maintain the school includes-

(a) the duty of defraying all the expenses of maintaining it, and

(b) the duty of making premises available to be used for the purposes of the school.

(4) In the case of a foundation, voluntary controlled or foundation special school, the local education authority's duty to maintain the school includes-

(a) the duty of defraying all the expenses of maintaining it, and

(b) the duty, under paragraph 2 of Schedule 3 or paragraph 13 or 15 of Schedule 6, of providing new premises for the school under and in accordance with paragraph 2 of Schedule 3 or (as the case may be) paragraph 16 of Schedule 6.

S. 22 (4)
The local education authority meets all costs of foundation, foundation special and voluntary controlled schools and the cost of providing new premises where appropriate.

(5) In the case of a voluntary aided school, the local education authority's duty to maintain the school includes-

(a) the duty of defraying all the expenses of maintaining it, except any expenses that by virtue of paragraph 3 of Schedule 3 are payable by the governing body, and

(b) the duty, under paragraph 4 of Schedule 3 or paragraph 14 of Schedule 6, of providing new premises for the school under and in accordance with that paragraph.

S. 22 (5)
The local education authority meets all costs of voluntary aided schools except costs that are governor liability under Schedule 3, broadly the cost of providing and improving the school premises and repair costs other than internal repair which is the liability of the local education authority. The local education authority also meets the cost of providing new premises where appropriate but this is effectively restricted to the provision of a site, with or without existing buildings.

(6) For the purposes of this Act the expenses of maintaining a foundation, voluntary or foundation special school include the payment of rates.

(7) Schedule 3 (which makes provision as to the functions of governing bodies, local education authorities and the Secretary of State as to the funding of foundation, voluntary and foundation special schools) shall have effect.

(8) In this Act-

(a) in relation to a school maintained (or proposed to be maintained) by a local education authority, "the local education authority" means that authority; and

(b) in relation to schools falling within subsections (3) to (6), "maintain" shall be read in accordance with those subsections.

(9) In this Act "maintained nursery school" means a nursery school which is maintained by a local education authority and is not a special school.

23.–(1) The following shall be charities which are exempt charities for the purposes of the (1993 c. 10.) Charities Act 1993-

(a) the governing body of any foundation, voluntary or foundation special school; and

(b) any foundation body established under section 21;

but no governing body of a community or community special school shall be a charity.

(2) So far as it is a charity, any institution which-

(a) is administered by or on behalf of any body to which subsection (1)(a) or (b) applies, and

(b) is established for the general purposes of, or for any special purpose of or in connection with, that body or any school or schools falling within subsection (1)(a),

shall also be an exempt charity for the purposes of the (1993 c. 10.) Charities Act 1993.

S. 23 (1) and (2)
The governing bodies of foundation and voluntary schools, and foundation bodies set up under the Act, are exempt charities as are any institutions set up for the purposes of the school or foundation body and administered by it. Exempt charities do not have to register with the Charity Commission or file accounts.

(3) Any foundation established otherwise than under this Act which has no property other than the premises of any school or schools falling within subsection (1)(a) shall be a charity which (subject to section 3(5B) of the (1993 c. 10.) Charities Act 1993) is not required to be registered for the purposes of that Act (but is not an exempt charity for the purposes of that Act).

(4) In this section-

(a) "charity" and "institution" have the same meaning as in the (1993 c. 10.)

     Charities Act 1993;

    (b) "premises" includes a teacher's dwelling-house.

New arrangements for organisation of schools

24.–(1) Each local education authority in England shall establish a school organisation committee for their area.

(2) A school organisation committee shall be constituted in accordance with regulations made by the Secretary of State.

(3) Those regulations must be so framed as to secure that every school organisation committee includes at least one person within each of the following categories-

    (a) a member of the local education authority;

    (b) a person nominated by the Diocesan Board of Education for any diocese of the Church of England any part of which is comprised in the authority's area; and

    (c) a person nominated by the bishop of any Roman Catholic Church diocese any part of which is comprised in the authority's area.

(4) In this Act any reference to "the school organisation committee" in relation to-

    (a) a local education authority in England,

    (b) a school maintained or proposed to be maintained by such a local education authority, or

    (c) any proposals relating to such a school,

is a reference to the school organisation committee established for the local education authority's area.

(5) Schedule 4 has effect in relation to school organisation committees.

25.–(1) The Secretary of State shall appoint for England such number of persons to act as adjudicators for the purposes of this Act as he considers appropriate.

(2) Any matter which by virtue of this Act is required to be referred to "the adjudicator" shall be referred to such person appointed under this section as may be determined in accordance with regulations under Schedule 5.

(3) Accordingly in this Act "the adjudicator", in relation to any such matter, means the person mentioned in subsection (2).

(4) Schedule 5 has effect in relation to adjudicators.

S. 25

The Secretary of State is to appoint adjudicators who have functions in relation to school organisation plans and admissions policies. The detailed provisions regarding the appointment are in Schedule 5 and regulations deal with the mechanics of referral. The section applies only to England.

26.–(1) Every local education authority shall prepare a school organisation plan for their area, and shall prepare further such plans at such times as may be prescribed.

(2) A school organisation plan is a statement which sets out-

(a) how the authority propose to exercise their functions during the prescribed period with a view to securing the provision of primary and secondary education that will meet the needs of the population of their area during that period; and

(b) any facilities which the authority expect to be available outside their area for providing such education.

(3) A school organisation plan must deal with such matters, and take such form, as may be prescribed.

(4) The matters prescribed for the purposes of subsection (3) shall include the provision which the authority propose to make during the period in question for children with special educational needs.

S. 26 (1) (2) (3) and (4)

Every local education authority, in England and in Wales, must produce a school organisation plan, in accordance with regulations, setting out how they propose to provide primary and secondary education in their area taking account of facilities available outside their area and including provision for children with special educational needs.

(5) A school organisation plan prepared by a local education authority in England requires the approval of the school organisation committee or the adjudicator; and regulations may make provision with regard to the procedure to be followed in connection with the preparation and approval of such plans.

(6) Regulations under subsection (5) may, in particular, make provision-

(a) requiring a local education authority in England to publish a draft school organisation plan prepared by them, and enabling objections to be made to it;

(b) requiring-

    (i) the draft plan (whether as published by the authority or as revised by them in the light of any such objections), and

    (ii) all such objections,

  to be submitted to the school organisation committee;

(c) authorising the matters so submitted to be also submitted, in any prescribed circumstances, to the adjudicator;

(d) for the functions of the school organisation committee in relation to the matters submitted to them by the authority, or in relation to any proposals made by the adjudicator, including power for the committee-

    (i) to approve a draft plan with or without modifications, or

    (ii) to prepare a school organisation plan for publication by the authority as their approved plan;

(e) for the functions of the adjudicator in relation to any matters submitted to him by virtue of paragraph (c), or referred to him by the committee in the exercise of any function conferred by virtue of paragraph (d), including power for the adjudicator-

    (i) to approve a draft plan either with modifications proposed by the committee or without modifications, or

    (ii) to make proposals to the committee for modifications to be made to the draft plan;

(f) requiring the publication of the plan as approved;

(g) requiring anything falling to be done under the regulations to be done within such period as may be specified in or determined in accordance with the regulations.

> **S. 26 (5) and (6)**
>
> *A school organisation plan produced by an local education authority in England must be approved by the school organisation committee or by the adjudicator. Regulations deal with the mechanics of producing a draft, publishing it, seeking approval, referring a failure to agree to the adjudicator and eventual publication.*

(7) A school organisation plan prepared by a local education authority in Wales requires adoption by the authority; and regulations may make provision with regard to the procedure to be followed in connection with the preparation and adoption of such plans.

(8) Regulations under subsection (7) may, in particular, make provision-

(a) requiring a local education authority in Wales to publish a draft school organisation plan prepared by them, and to consult such bodies or persons in connection with the draft plan as may be prescribed;

(b) requiring the authority, in the light of such consultation, either-

    (i) to adopt the draft plan with or without modifications, or

    (ii) to prepare a further draft school organisation plan for publication and consultation in accordance with any provision made by virtue of paragraph (a);

(c) requiring the publication of the plan as adopted by the authority;

(d) requiring anything falling to be done under the regulations to be done within such period as may be specified in or determined in accordance with the regulations.

> **S. 26 (7) and (8)**
>
> *A school organisation plan produced by an local education authority in Wales must be approved by the authority and again regulations lay down the process.*

27.–(1) Regulations may make provision-

    (a) for the establishment by local education authorities in Wales of school organisation committees; and

    (b) for the appointment by the Secretary of State of adjudicators, or panels of adjudicators, for Wales;

and the regulations may provide for any of the provisions of sections 24 and 25 and Schedules 4 and 5 to apply for the purposes of the regulations with or without modifications.

(2) In connection with any provision made by virtue of subsection (1), regulations may make provision-

    (a) for applying in relation to Wales any provision of section 26, Chapter II of this Part or Chapter I of Part III which would otherwise apply in relation to England only;

    (b) for disapplying in relation to Wales any such provision which would otherwise apply in relation to Wales only;

    (c) for any statutory provision to have effect with such modifications as appear to the Secretary of State to be appropriate.

> **S. 27**
>
> *This section enables regulations to be made to establish school organisation committees, adjudicators and school organisation plans in Wales. The provisions need not be the same as in England.*

CHAPTER II

ESTABLISHMENT, ALTERATION OR DISCONTINUANCE OF SCHOOLS

Mainstream schools maintained by LEAs

28.–(1) Where a local education authority propose-

   (a) to establish a new community or foundation school, or
   (b) to make any prescribed alteration to a community school, or
   (c) to make any prescribed alteration to a foundation school consisting of an enlargement of the premises of the school,

S. 28

This section deals with the publication of and consultation on proposals to establish maintained schools or to make alterations falling within prescribed categories to existing schools. The Secretary of State has power to prescribe the alterations (which can include alterations to the character of the school as well as physical alterations to buildings but cannot include alterations to the religious character of a school) which require proposals to be published. Alterations outside the scope of those prescribed can be made without publication of proposals or consultation under this section. Different bodies have different powers according to the type of school.

S. 28 (1)

The local education authority may publish proposals that relate to establishing new community or foundation schools, altering existing community schools and enlarging existing foundation schools.

the authority shall publish their proposals under this section.

(2) Where-

   (a) any persons (referred to in this Part as "promoters") propose to establish a new foundation or voluntary school, or
   (b) the governing body of a foundation or voluntary school propose to make any prescribed alteration to the school,

those persons or (as the case may be) the governing body shall publish their proposals under this section.

S. 28 (2)

Proposals for establishing a new foundation or voluntary school may be published by the promoters of such a school and the governing body of an existing foundation or voluntary school may propose alterations.

(3) Proposals under this section shall-

    (a) contain such information, and

    (b) be published in such manner,

as may be prescribed.

> **S. 28 (3)**
> *Regulations will specify what must be contained in the proposals and how they are to be published.*

(4) Proposals under this section may if the relevant body or promoters think fit-

    (a) specify an age below 10 years and six months and an age above 12 years, and

    (b) provide that the school to which the proposals relate is to be a school providing full-time education suitable to the requirements of pupils whose ages are between the ages so specified.

(5) Before publishing any proposals under this section, the relevant body or promoters shall consult such persons as appear to them to be appropriate; and in discharging their duty under this subsection the relevant body or promoters shall have regard to any guidance given from time to time by the Secretary of State.

(6) Where any proposals published under this section relate to a school or proposed school in England, the relevant body or promoters shall send-

    (a) a copy of the published proposals, and

    (b) such information in connection with those proposals as may be prescribed,

to the school organisation committee for the area of the local education authority who maintain the school or (in the case of a new school) who it is proposed should maintain the school.

(7) Where any proposals published under this section relate to a school or proposed school in Wales, the relevant body or promoters shall send-

    (a) a copy of the published proposals, and

    (b) such information in connection with those proposals as may be prescribed,

to the Secretary of State.

(8) Schedule 6 has effect (for both England and Wales) in relation to-

    (a) the procedure for dealing with proposals under this section and their implementation; and

    (b) the provision of premises or other assistance in connection with their implementation.

S. 28 (5) (6) (7) and (8)
There must be consultation before publication and those publishing proposals must have regard to any guidance published by the Secretary of State. In England proposals must be sent to the school organisation committee and in Wales they must be sent to the Secretary of State. Detailed provisions relating to the procedure for dealing with proposals and their eventual implementation are in Schedule 6

(9) Where any proposals published under this section-

   (a) are for the transfer of a school to a site in a different area, or

   (b) relate to a school which is, or (in the case of a new school) is proposed to be, situated in an area other than that of the local education authority who maintain, or (as the case may be) who it is proposed should maintain, the school,

the provisions of subsection (6) and Schedule 6 shall have effect in relation to the proposals with such modifications as may be prescribed.

(10) In this section "the relevant body or promoters" means the local education authority, governing body or promoters mentioned in subsection (1) or (2) (as the case may be).

(11) In this Part-

   (a) "alteration", in the context of a prescribed alteration to a maintained school, means an alteration of whatever nature, including the transfer of the school to a new site but excluding any change-

      (i) in the religious character of the school, or

      (ii) whereby the school would acquire or lose a religious character; and

   (b) "area" (without more) means a local education authority area.

(12) Any regulations made for the purposes of subsection (1)(b) or (2)(b) may be framed by reference to the opinion of the local education authority.

29.–(1) Where a local education authority propose to discontinue-

   (a) a community, foundation or voluntary school, or

   (b) a maintained nursery school,

the authority shall publish their proposals under this section.

(2) Where the governing body of a foundation or voluntary school propose to discontinue the school, the governing body shall publish their proposals under this section.

S. 29
This section parallels S. 28 and deals with the process for publication of and consultation on proposals to discontinue schools. However, it does not apply when a governing body gives notice to discontinue a foundation or voluntary school under S. 30

S. 29 (1) and (2)
The local education authority may publish proposals to discontinue community, foundation. voluntary or maintained nursery schools and the governing body of foundation and voluntary schools may publish proposals to discontinue their school. They must consult as appropriate and have regard to guidance from the Secretary of State. The proposals must contain prescribed information.

(3) Proposals under this section shall-

   (a) contain such information, and
   (b) be published in such manner,

as may be prescribed.

S. 29 (3)
Regulations will specify what must be contained in the proposals and how they are to be published.

(4) Before publishing any proposals under this section, the relevant body shall consult such persons as appear to them to be appropriate; and in discharging their duty under this subsection the relevant body shall have regard to any guidance given from time to time by the Secretary of State.

(5) Where any proposals published under this section relate to a school in England, the relevant body shall send-

   (a) a copy of the published proposals, and
   (b) such information in connection with those proposals as may be prescribed,

to the school organisation committee for the area of the local education authority who maintain the school.

(6) Where any proposals published under this section relate to a school in Wales, the relevant body shall send-

   (a) a copy of the published proposals, and
   (b) such information in connection with those proposals as may be prescribed,

to the Secretary of State.

(7) Schedule 6 has effect (for both England and Wales) in relation to the procedure for dealing with proposals under this section and their implementation.

(8) Where any proposals published under this section relate to a school which is situated in an area other than that of the local education authority who maintain it, the provisions of subsection (5) and Schedule 6 shall have effect in relation to the proposals with such modifications as may be prescribed.

(9) In this section "the relevant body" means the local education authority or governing body mentioned in subsection (1) or (2) (as the case may be).

(10)   In this Part any reference to a local education authority-

   (a) discontinuing a school, or

   (b) implementing proposals to discontinue a school (whether published by the authority or the governing body),

is to the authority ceasing to maintain the school.

30.–(1) Subject to the following provisions of this section, the governing body of a foundation or voluntary school may discontinue the school by serving on the Secretary of State and the local education authority at least two years' notice of their intention to do so.

(2) If expenditure has been incurred on the school premises (otherwise than in connection with repairs)-

   (a) by the Secretary of State,
   (b) by the Funding Agency for Schools,
   (c) by any local education authority, or
   (d) by an authority which was a local education authority within the meaning of any enactment repealed by the Education Act 1944 or an earlier Act,

no such notice may be served without the consent of the Secretary of State.

(3) If discontinuing the school would affect the facilities for full-time education suitable to the requirements of persons over compulsory school age who have not attained the age of 19, the governing body shall, before serving a notice under this section, consult the appropriate further education funding council.

> **S. 30 (3)**
> *The governing body must consult the further education funding council if the closure would affect 16 to 19 education.*

(4) If, while a notice under subsection (1) is in force in respect of a foundation or voluntary school, the governing body inform the local education authority that they are unable or unwilling to carry on the school until the notice expires, the authority-

   (a) may conduct the school for all or part of the unexpired period of the notice as if it were a community school, and
   (b) shall be entitled to use the school premises free of charge for that purpose.

(5) While the school is being so conducted-

   (a) the authority shall keep the school premises in good repair, and
   (b) any interest in the premises which is held for the purposes of the school shall be deemed, for all purposes relating to the condition, occupation or use of the premises, or the making of alterations to them, to be vested in the authority.

(6) Despite the provisions of subsection (5) the governing body may use the premises, or any part of them, when not required for the purposes of the school to the same extent as if they had continued to carry on the school during the unexpired period of the notice.

> **S. 30 (4) (5) and (6)**
> *If the governing body serves notice but cannot or are not willing to continue the school until it expires, the local education authority may take over the school and run it as though it were a community school. It must keep the premises in good repair but the governing body may continue to use the school premises when they are not required for school use.*

(7) A notice served under subsection (1) may not be withdrawn without the consent of the local education authority.

(8) If a foundation or voluntary school is discontinued under this section, the duty of the local education authority to maintain the school as a foundation or voluntary school shall cease.

(9) Nothing in section 29 or 33 applies to any such discontinuance of a foundation or voluntary school.

(10) Where-

  (a) land occupied by a foundation or voluntary school is held by any trustees for the purposes of the school, and

  (b) the termination of the school's occupation of that land would have the result that it was not reasonably practicable for the school to continue to be conducted at its existing site,

then if the trustees (being entitled to do so) give any notice to the governing body which purports to terminate the school's occupation of the land, any such notice shall not be effective to terminate its occupation of the land unless the requirements of subsection (11) are complied with in relation to the notice (without prejudice to any other statutory or other requirements falling to be so complied with).

(11) The requirements of this subsection are-

  (a) that the period of notice must-
    (i) be reasonable having regard to the length of time that would be required to discontinue the school (if the governing body chose to do so), and
    (ii) in any event must not be less than two years; and

  (b) that a copy of the notice must be given to the Secretary of State and the local education authority at the time when the notice is given to the governing body.

S. 30 (10) and (11)
Where a foundation or voluntary school occupies land held by trustees and the trustees wish to terminate the right of occupation so that the school could no longer carry on, the trustees must give as much notice (at least two years) as would be reasonable to enable the governing body to give notice of discontinuance under this section and must give that notice also to the Secretary of State and the local education authority.

(12) Where trustees give, at the same (or substantially the same) time, notices purporting to terminate a foundation or voluntary school's occupation of two or more pieces of land held by the trustees for the purposes of the school, then for the purpose of determining whether subsection (10)(b) applies in relation to any of those pieces of land, regard may be had to the combined effect of terminating the school's occupation of both or all of them.

(13) If a question arises as to whether the termination of a school's occupation of any land would have the result mentioned in subsection (10)(b) (including a question as to whether subsection (12) applies in any particular circumstances), it shall be determined by the Secretary of State.

S. 30 (12) and (13)
If different notices are given relating to different pieces of land, they have to be looked at together to decide whether the effect is that the school cannot carry on and if there is a dispute on the point the Secretary of State will decide it.

Special schools maintained by LEAs

31.–(1) Where a local education authority intend-

   (a) to establish a new community or foundation special school, or
   (b) to make any prescribed alteration to such a school, or
   (c) to discontinue such a school,

the authority shall publish their proposals under this section.

(2) Where the governing body of a foundation special school propose-

   (a) to make any prescribed alteration to the school, or
   (b) to discontinue the school,

the governing body shall publish their proposals under this section.

(3) Proposals under this section shall-

   (a) contain such information, and
   (b) be published in such manner,

as may be prescribed.

(4) Before publishing any proposals under this section, the relevant body shall consult such persons as appear to them to be appropriate; and in discharging their duty under this subsection the relevant body shall have regard to any guidance given from time to time by the Secretary of State.

(5) Where any proposals published under this section relate to a school or proposed school in England, the relevant body shall send-

   (a) a copy of the proposals, and
   (b) such information in connection with those proposals as may be prescribed,

to the school organisation committee for the area of the local education authority who maintain the school or (in the case of a new school) who it is proposed should maintain the school.

(6) Where any proposals published under this section relate to a school or proposed school in Wales, the relevant body shall send-

   (a) a copy of the proposals, and
   (b) such information in connection with those proposals as may be prescribed,

to the Secretary of State.

(7) The relevant body shall also send a copy of any proposals to which subsection (5) or (6) applies to such other bodies or persons as may be prescribed.

(8) Schedule 6 has effect (for both England and Wales) in relation to the procedure for dealing with proposals under this section and their implementation.

(9) In this section "the relevant body" means the local education authority or governing body mentioned in subsection (1) or (2) (as the case may be).

S. 31

This section contains provisions relating to the establishment, alteration and discontinuance of special schools imposing the same requirements as apply to mainstream schools under sections 28 and 29.

32.–(1) The Secretary of State may, if he considers it expedient to do so in the interests of the health, safety or welfare of pupils at a community or foundation special school, give a direction to the local education authority by whom the school is maintained requiring the school to be discontinued on a date specified in the direction.

(2) A direction under subsection (1) may require the local education authority to notify any persons or class of persons specified in the direction.

(3) Before giving a direction under subsection (1), the Secretary of State shall consult-

    (a) the local education authority;

    (b) any other local education authority who would in his opinion be affected by the discontinuance of the school;

    (c) in the case of a foundation special school which has a foundation, the person who appoints the foundation governors; and

    (d) such other persons as the Secretary of State considers appropriate.

(4) On giving a direction under subsection (1) the Secretary of State shall give notice in writing of the direction to the governing body of the school and its head teacher.

(5) Where a local education authority are given a direction under subsection (1), they shall discontinue the school in question on the date specified in the direction; and nothing in section 31 or 33 applies to any such discontinuance of the school under this section.

S. 32

This section empowers the Secretary of State to direct discontinuance of a special school if he considers it expedient in the interests of the health safety or welfare of the pupils. He must first consult with the local education authority and (if the school is a foundation special school) the body that appoints foundation governors. Notice of the direction must be given to the governing body and the headteacher and the local education authority must discontinue the school on the specified date.

Further provisions relating to establishment, alteration or discontinuance of schools

33.–(1) Except in pursuance of proposals falling to be implemented under paragraph 5 or 10 of Schedule 6-

(a) no maintained school shall be established or discontinued;
(b) no prescribed alteration shall be made to any such school; and
(c) no maintained nursery school shall be discontinued.

(2) No alteration falling within section 28(11)(a)(i) or (ii) shall be made to any maintained school.

(3) Subsection (1) has effect subject to sections 19(4), 30(9) and 32(5).

(4) Regulations may, in relation to proposals published under section 28, 29 or 31, require any of the following, namely-

(a) the body or promoters who published the proposals,
(b) the school organisation committee, and
(c) the adjudicator,

to provide such information relating to the proposals to such persons, and at such times, as may be prescribed.

S. 33

This section prohibits the establishment, alteration or discontinuance of schools except in accordance with the previous sections and regulations may require the provision of information.

Rationalisation of school places

34. Schedule 7 (which provides for the Secretary of State to give directions to local education authorities and governing bodies to bring forward proposals for the rationalisation of school places, and for such proposals to be made by him) shall have effect.

> **S. 34**
> *Schedule 7 contains detailed provisions relating to the Secretary of State's powers in relation to the rationalisation of school places.*

Change of category of school

35.–(1) Schedule 8 makes provision for and in connection with-

    (a) enabling a maintained school within one of the categories set out in section 20(1) to become a school within another of those categories, and

    (b) in certain circumstances, requiring proposals to be published for a voluntary aided school to become a school within another of those categories;

and a maintained school may not so change its category otherwise than in accordance with that Schedule.

(2) Except in relation to a change of category from voluntary aided to voluntary controlled school for which proposals are required to be published by virtue of paragraph 3 of Schedule 8, that Schedule does not apply at any time before the end of such period as may be prescribed.

> **S. 35**
> *Schedule 8 contains detailed provisions relating to the power for a school to change from one category to a different category.*

CHAPTER III GOVERNMENT OF MAINTAINED SCHOOLS

Governing bodies

36.–(1) Each maintained school shall have a governing body, which shall be a body corporate constituted in accordance with Schedule 9.

(2) Schedule 10 has effect in relation to the general powers of the governing body and other matters relating to it as a body corporate.

(3) Schedule 11 has effect in relation to the membership and proceedings of the governing body and other matters including the appointment of a clerk to, or to any committee of, the governing body.

> **S. 36**
> *Schedules 9, 10 and 11 contain detailed provisions for the structure, powers and proceedings of the governing body.*

Instruments of government

37.–(1) For every maintained school there shall be an instrument (known as the instrument of government) which determines the constitution of the governing body and other matters relating to the school.

(2) Schedule 12 has effect with respect to the contents and making of instruments of government and the review and variation of such instruments.

(3) The governing body of a maintained school shall not conduct the school under a name other than the one for the time being set out in the school's instrument of government.

S. 37

Every school must have an instrument of government which sets out the constitution of the governing body and other matters as specified in Schedule 12. A school may not change its name except by varying the instrument of government in accordance with the Schedule.

Functions of governing body

38.–(1) Subject to any other statutory provision, the conduct of a maintained school shall be under the direction of the school's governing body.

(2) The governing body shall conduct the school with a view to promoting high standards of educational achievement at the school.

S. 38 (1) and (2)

The governing body directs the conduct of the school and must do so with a view to promoting high standards of educational achievement. This is known as a "target" duty: failure to achieve it does not generally give rise to legal liability provided a proper attempt has been made.

(3) Regulations may-

(a) set out terms of reference for governing bodies of maintained schools;
(b) define the respective roles and responsibilities of governing bodies and head teachers of such schools, whether generally or with respect to particular matters, including the curriculum for such schools;
(c) confer functions on governing bodies and head teachers of such schools.

(4) The governing body of a maintained school shall, in discharging their functions, comply with-

(a) the instrument of government; and
(b) (subject to any other statutory provision) any trust deed relating to the school.

S. 38 (3) and (4)
Regulations will deal with the detailed way in which the governing body and headteachers are to deal with the running of the school. These replace the articles of government which applied under previous education legislation. The governing body must comply with the instrument of government and any trust deed.

39.–(1) The governing body of a maintained school shall in accordance with regulations-

    (a) establish procedures for dealing with all complaints relating to the school other than those falling to be dealt with in accordance with any procedures required to be established in relation to the school by virtue of any other statutory provision; and

    (b) publicise the procedures so established.

S. 39 (1)
Schools must establish and publicise general complaints procedures in accordance with regulations to deal with all complaints for which no other procedure applies, e.g. curriculum complaints which have their own laid-down procedures.

(2) The governing body of a maintained school may require pupils in attendance at the school to attend at any place outside the school premises for the purpose of receiving any instruction or training included in the secular curriculum for the school.

S. 39 (2)
Schools may require pupils to go to places other than the school for lessons or other curriculum purposes.

(3) The governing body and head teacher of-

    (a) a community or voluntary controlled school, or

    (b) a community special school,

shall comply with any direction given to them by the local education authority concerning the health or safety of persons on the school's premises or taking part in any school activities elsewhere.

> **S. 39 (3)**
> *Community, community special and voluntary controlled schools must comply with local education authority directions on health and safety. The local education authority has no such powers over foundation or voluntary aided schools.*

Control of school premises

40. Schedule 13 has effect in relation to the control by the governing body of a maintained school of the occupation and use of the school premises.

> **S. 40**
> *Schedule 13 has detailed provisions relating to the control of school premises by the governing body.*

Fixing of school holidays and times of sessions

41.–(1) In the case of a community, voluntary controlled or community special school-

(a) the local education authority shall determine the dates when the school terms and holidays are to begin and end; and

(b) the governing body shall determine the times of the school sessions.

(2) In the case of a foundation, voluntary aided or foundation special school the governing body shall determine-

(a) the dates and times when the school terms and holidays are to begin and end, and

(b) the times of the school sessions.

(3) Regulations may make provision-

(a) as to the procedure to be followed where the governing body of a school within subsection (1) propose to make any change in the times of the school sessions;

(b) as to the implementation of any such proposal;

(c) for enabling the local education authority to determine, for any purposes of the regulations, whether any person is to be treated as a parent of a registered pupil at the school;

(d) that for all or any prescribed purposes of the regulations references to parents are to be read as excluding those who are not individuals.

(4) In this section "the times of the school sessions" means the times at which each of the school sessions (or, if there is only one, the school session) is to begin and end on any day.

S. 41

The local education authority sets school term and holiday dates for community, community special and voluntary controlled schools. The governing body sets those dates for foundation and voluntary aided schools. The governing body of all schools decide the times of school sessions, i.e. the length of the school day. Regulations lay down the procedure.

Reports and parents' meetings

42.–(1) Once in every school year the governing body of a maintained school shall prepare a report (a "governors' report") dealing with such matters, and otherwise complying with such requirements, as may be specified in regulations.

(2) Such regulations may-

    (a) impose requirements on the governing body of a maintained school with respect to-

        (i) the giving of copies of a governors' report to such persons as may be prescribed, and

        (ii) making such copies available for inspection at the school;

    (b) make provision for-

        (i) enabling the governing body to determine the language or languages in which a governors' report is to be produced and the form or forms in which it is to be produced;

        (ii) requiring them to comply with any direction given by the local education authority with respect to any additional language to be used or with respect to any additional form in which the report is to be produced.

S. 42 (1) and (2)

Each year the governing body of each school must produce a report. Regulations specify what the report must cover and how it is to be published and distributed.

(3) The governing body of a maintained school shall provide the local education authority with such reports in connection with the discharge of their functions as the authority may require (either on a regular basis or from time to time) for the purposes of the exercise of any of their functions.

S. 42 (3)

The local education authority may require a governing body to provide it with reports, either generally or specifically.

(4) The head teacher of a maintained school shall provide the governing body or (as the case may be) the local education authority with such reports in connection with the discharge of his functions as the governing body or the authority may require (either on a regular basis or from time to time) for the purposes of the exercise of any of their functions.

(5) Where a requirement under subsection (4) is imposed on the head teacher by the authority-

(a) the authority shall notify the governing body of that requirement; and
(b) the head teacher shall give the governing body a copy of any report made by him in complying with it.

S. 42 (4) and (5)
The headteacher must provide the governing body and the local education authority with such reports as they may each require. If the local education authority requires reports it must also notify the governing body and the headteacher must supply the governing body with a copy of the report that is given.

43.–(1) Once in every school year the governing body of a maintained school shall hold a meeting (an "annual parents' meeting") which is open to-

(a) all parents of registered pupils at the school;
(b) the head teacher; and
(c) such other persons as the governing body may invite.

(2) The purpose of the meeting shall be to provide an opportunity for discussion of-

(a) the governors' report;
(b) the discharge by the governing body, the head teacher and the local education authority of their functions in relation to the school;
(c) the aims and values of the school;
(d) how the spiritual, moral, cultural, mental and physical development of pupils is to be promoted at the school;
(e) how pupils are to be prepared for the opportunities, responsibilities and experiences of adult life and citizenship;
(f) the standards of educational achievement of pupils; and
(g) how the governing body are to promote the good behaviour, discipline and well-being of pupils.

S. 43 (1) and (2)
This section provides for the holding each year of the annual parents' meeting and specifies what is to be open for discussion.

(3) A governing body may, however, refrain from holding an annual parents' meeting in a particular school year if-

(a) the school is a community or foundation special school which is established in a hospital and the governing body are of the opinion that it would be impracticable to hold such a meeting in that year; or

(b) the school is a maintained school other than one within paragraph (a), the governing body are of the opinion that it would be impracticable to hold such a meeting in that year, and at least 50 per cent. of the registered pupils at the school are boarders at the time when they form that opinion.

S. 43 (3)
There are limited exceptions to this general rule for hospital schools and schools where at least 50% of the pupils are boarders if the governing body think it impracticable to hold a meeting.

(4) Regulations may make provision-

(a) for the proceedings at an annual parents' meeting to be under the control of the governing body;

(b) as to the procedure to be followed at any such meeting, including provision restricting the right to vote on any question put to the meeting to parents of registered pupils at the school;

(c) imposing requirements on the governing body, the head teacher and the local education authority in relation to resolutions which have been passed at any such meeting, including requirements framed by reference to any opinion formed by the governing body;

(d) for enabling the governing body or (as the case may be) the local education authority to determine, for any purposes of the regulations, whether any person is to be treated as the parent of a registered pupil at the school.

S. 43 (4)
Regulations set out the detailed requirements regarding the proceedings at the meeting, voting, responding to resolutions passed at the meeting and for determining who are to be regarded as parents.

Government of new schools

44.-(1) Where proposals for the establishment of a maintained school fall to be implemented under paragraph 5 or 10 of Schedule 6, the local education authority shall make arrangements providing for the constitution of a temporary governing body for the school.

(2) Once constituted in accordance with arrangements made under subsection (1) the temporary governing body shall continue in existence until such time as the governing body are constituted for the school under an instrument of government.

(3) The local education authority shall secure that the governing body are so constituted-

(a) as soon as is reasonably practicable after the time when the requirement for there to be an instrument of government for the school takes effect in accordance with subsection (4), and

(b) in any event not later than the last day of the term in which the school first admits pupils.

(4) The requirement for there to be an instrument of government for a school (imposed by section 37) shall take effect in relation to a school falling within subsection (1) above as from the school opening date; and for the purposes of this Part proposals for the establishment of a maintained school shall be taken to be implemented on that date.

(5) Regulations may make provision with respect to-

(a) the making and termination of arrangements for the constitution of temporary governing bodies, including such arrangements made in anticipation of proposals falling to be implemented as mentioned in subsection (1);

(b) the constitution, meetings and proceedings of temporary governing bodies, the payment of allowances to temporary governors, and the appointment of clerks to such bodies;

(c) the transition from a temporary governing body to a governing body constituted under an instrument of government; and

(d) such other matters relating to temporary governing bodies as the Secretary of State considers appropriate.

(6) Regulations under subsection (5) may, in connection with any matters falling within that subsection-

(a) modify any provision made by or under any of Schedules 9 to 12;

(b) apply any such provision with or without modifications;

(c) make provision corresponding or similar to any such provision.

(7) Subject to subsection (8), the temporary governing body of a school shall be treated for the purposes of the Education Acts as if they were the governing body during the period-

(a) beginning with the school opening date, and

(b) ending with the time when the governing body are constituted for the school under an instrument of government;

and for the purposes of sections 495 to 498 of the Education Act 1996 (general default powers of the Secretary of State) the temporary governing body of a school shall also be so treated at any time falling before the school opening date.

(8) Despite subsection (7), nothing in any of the following provisions, namely-

(a) section 36,

(b) section 37(1) or (2), or

(c) (subject to any regulations made by virtue of subsection (5)) any of Schedules 9 to 12,

applies to any temporary governing body.

(9) In this Part "school opening date", in relation to a new maintained school, means the date when the school first admits pupils.

> **S. 44**
> *This section deals with the establishment of a temporary governing body of a new school to cover the period before the implementation of the proposals for the new school, i.e. until it opens, the making of the instrument of government and the transition to a permanent governing body. Regulations deal with the detail. A temporary governing body has the powers of the full governing body if the full governing body has not been set up by the time the school opens.*

CHAPTER IV FINANCING OF MAINTAINED SCHOOLS

Budgetary framework

45.–(1) For the purposes of the financing of maintained schools by local education authorities, every such school shall have, for each financial year, a budget share which is allocated to it by the authority which maintains it.

(2) Sections 46 and 47 have effect for determining the amount of a school's budget share for a financial year.

(3) In this Chapter-

(a) references to schools maintained by a local education authority do not include schools which are not maintained schools as defined by section 20(7);

(b) references, in a context referring to a local education authority, to a maintained school or to a school maintained by such an authority shall be read as including a new school-

(i) which on implementation of proposals under section 28 or 31 or paragraph 5 of Schedule 7 will be a community, foundation or voluntary school or a community or foundation special school maintained by the authority, and

(ii) which has a temporary governing body; and

(c) references to the governing body of a maintained school or of a school maintained by a local education authority shall accordingly be read as including the temporary governing body of a new school falling within paragraph (b).

(4) In this Chapter "new school" (without more) has the meaning given by section 72(3).

S. 45
This section provides for each maintained school, as defined by the Act and including schools which have been authorised and have a temporary governing body but which have not yet opened, to have a budget share allocated by the local education authority

46.–(1) For the purposes of this Part a local education authority's "local schools budget" for a financial year is the amount appropriated by the authority for meeting all expenditure by the authority in that year of a class or description prescribed for the purposes of this subsection (which may include expenditure incurred otherwise than in respect of schools).

(2) For the purposes of this Part a local education authority's "individual schools budget" for a financial year is the amount remaining after deducting from the authority's local schools budget for that year such planned expenditure by the authority in respect of the year as they may determine should be so deducted in accordance with regulations.

(3) Regulations under subsection (2) may-

(a) prescribe classes or descriptions of expenditure which are authorised or required to be deducted from an authority's local schools budget; and

(b) provide, in relation to any prescribed class or description of expenditure specified in the regulations, that such expenditure may only be so deducted subject to either or both of the following, namely-

(i) such limit or limits (however framed) as may be specified by the regulations; and

(ii) such other conditions as may be so specified.

S. 46
This section defines the local schools budget as the amount that the local education authority has each year for all school and other purposes as prescribed by regulations It then defines the individual schools budget as the amount left from the local schools budget after deducting any planned expenditure in accordance with regulations. The effect is that the local education authority may only hold back funds for its own direct spending if and to the extent that the regulations permit.

47.–(1) For the purposes of this Part a maintained school's budget share for a financial year is such amount as the local education authority may determine, in accordance with regulations, to allocate to the school out of the authority's individual schools budget for that year.

(2) Regulations under this section may, in particular, make provision-

(a) as to the time when schools' budget shares are to be initially determined by local education authorities;

(b) specifying-
   (i) factors or criteria which such authorities are to take into account, or
   (ii) requirements as to other matters with which such authorities are to comply,

in determining such shares, whether generally or in such cases as are specified in the regulations;

(c) requiring adjustments to be made to such shares by such authorities in respect of-
   (i) pupils permanently excluded from schools maintained by them, or
   (ii) pupils admitted to schools maintained by them who have been permanently excluded from other maintained schools;

(d) as to the treatment of new schools, including provision authorising the determination of nil amounts as the budget shares of such schools;

(e) authorising or requiring such authorities to take account of matters arising during the course of a financial year-
   (i) by redetermining budget shares for that year, or
   (ii) by making adjustments to such shares for the following year,
   in accordance with the regulations, and requiring them in that connection to disregard such matters as may be specified in the regulations;

(f) requiring consultation to be carried out by such authorities in relation to the factors or criteria which are to be taken into account in determining such shares and as to the time and manner of such consultation;

(g) enabling the Secretary of State, where it appears to him to be expedient to do so, to authorise such authorities to determine (or redetermine) budget shares, to such extent as he may specify, in accordance with arrangements approved by him (in place of those provided for by the regulations).

(3) Regulations made in pursuance of subsection (2)(c) may provide for the adjustments to be made on such basis as may be prescribed, which may involve the deduction from one school's budget share of an amount which is greater or less than that allocated to another school's budget share in respect of the excluded pupil.

S. 47
Having established the individual schools budget the local education authority determines each school's budget share. Again, this must be in accordance with regulations which will set out the criteria to apply, how the funding of permanently excluded pupils is to be dealt with, how new schools are to be treated, how changes may be made during the course of the year, what consultation will be required and what reserve powers the Secretary of State will have.

Local education authority schemes

48.–(1) Each local education authority shall prepare a scheme dealing with such matters connected with the financing of the schools maintained by the authority as are required to be dealt with in the scheme by or by virtue of–

(a) regulations made by the Secretary of State; or
(b) any provision of this Part.

(2) Regulations under subsection (1) may, in particular, require a scheme to deal with–

(a) the carrying forward from one financial year to another of surpluses and deficits arising in relation to schools' budget shares;
(b) amounts which may be charged against schools' budget shares;
(c) amounts received by schools which may be retained by their governing bodies and the purposes for which such amounts may be used;
(d) the imposition, by or under the scheme, of conditions which must be complied with by schools in relation to the management of their delegated budgets, including conditions prescribing financial controls and procedures;
(e) terms on which services and facilities are provided by the authority for schools maintained by them.

(3) Where there is any inconsistency between a scheme prepared by a local education authority under subsection (1) and any other rules or regulations made by the authority which relate to the funding or financial management of schools which they maintain, the terms of the scheme shall prevail.

(4) Schedule 14 (which provides for the approval or imposition of schemes by the Secretary of State and for the revision of schemes) shall have effect.

(5) In this Part any reference to "the scheme", in relation to a maintained school, is a reference to the scheme prepared (or by virtue of paragraph 1(6) of Schedule 14 treated as prepared) by the local education authority under this section, as from time to time revised under paragraph 2 of that Schedule.

S. 48
The local education authority must establish a scheme to cover financial issues which must comply with regulations. It must deal with carrying forward surpluses and deficits, what can be charged to individual schools, what schools can retain as reserves and how those reserves are to be dealt with, the conditions (including financial controls and procedures that are to apply) and the terms under which the local education authority can provide services to schools. The scheme takes precedence over any other local education authority rules or regulations. Schedule 14 deals with the mechanics of approval and modification of schemes. That Schedule requires that all schemes be approved by the Secretary of State.

Financial delegation

49.–(1) Every maintained school shall have a delegated budget.

(2) A new school shall have a delegated budget as from the school opening date, unless a different date applies by virtue of subsection (3).

(3) Such a school shall have a delegated budget-

    (a) as from a date earlier than the school opening date if the local education authority so determine; or

    (b) as from a later date if the authority so determine with the written approval of the Secretary of State; or

    (c) as from such date as the Secretary of State may determine, if the authority have determined that the school should have a delegated budget as from a later date but that date is not approved by him.

(4) Subject to-

    (a) section 50 (right of governing body to spend budget share where school has a delegated budget),

    (b) paragraph 4 of Schedule 15 (power of governing body to spend amounts out of budget share where delegation of budget suspended),

    (c) section 489(2) of the Education Act 1996 (education standards grants), and

    (d) any provisions of the scheme,

a local education authority may not delegate to the governing body of any maintained school the power to spend any part of the authority's local schools budget.

> **S. 49 (1) to (4)**
> *All schools must have a delegated budget. New schools may have a delegated budget before the school opens if the local education authority or the Secretary of State so determines. The local education authority cannot delegate the power to spend the local schools budget beyond the individual school's budget share except in very limited circumstances, the main one being in relation to Standards Fund grants.*

(5) Any amount made available by a local education authority to the governing body of a maintained school (whether under section 50 or otherwise)-

    (a) shall remain the property of the authority until spent by the governing body or the head teacher; and

    (b) when spent by the governing body or the head teacher, shall be taken to be spent by them or him as the authority's agent.

(6) Subsection (5)(b) does not apply to any such amount where it is spent-

    (a) by way of repayment of the principal of, or interest on, a loan, or

    (b) (in the case of a voluntary aided school) to meet expenses payable by the governing body under paragraph 3(1) or (2) of Schedule 3 or paragraph 14(2) of Schedule 6.

> **S. 49 (5) and (6)**
> *The delegated money remains the property of the local education authority and the school spends the money as agent for the local education authority unless it relates to repayment of or interest on a loan or expenses that are the responsibility of the governing body of a voluntary aided school.*

(7) In this Part-

    (a) references to a school having a delegated budget are references to the governing body of the school being entitled to manage the school's budget share; and

    (b) where a school has a delegated budget the governing body are accordingly said to have a right to a delegated budget.

50.–(1) Where a maintained school has a delegated budget in respect of the whole or part of a financial year the local education authority shall secure that in respect of that year there is available to be spent by the governing body-

    (a) where the school has a delegated budget in respect of the whole of that year, a sum equal to the school's budget share for the year, or

    (b) where the school has a delegated budget in respect of only part of that year, a sum equal to that portion of the school's budget share for the year which has not been spent.

(2) The times at which, and the manner in which, any amounts are made available by the authority to the governing body in respect of any such sum shall be such as may be provided by or under the scheme.

(3) Subject to any provision made by or under the scheme, the governing body may spend any such amounts as they think fit-

    (a) for any purposes of the school; or

    (b) (subject also to any prescribed conditions) for such purposes as may be prescribed.

(4) In subsection (3) "purposes of the school" does not include purposes wholly referable to the provision of-

    (a) part-time education suitable to the requirements of persons of any age over compulsory school age, or

    (b) full-time education suitable to the requirements of persons who have attained the age of 19;

but any such purposes may be prescribed by regulations under paragraph (b) of that subsection.

(5) Nothing in subsection (3) shall be read as authorising the payment of allowances to governors otherwise than in accordance with regulations under paragraph 6 of

Schedule 11 (or, in the case of temporary governors of a new school, regulations under section 44(5)).

(6) The governing body may delegate to the head teacher, to such extent as may be permitted by or under the scheme, their powers under subsection (3) in relation to any amount such as is mentioned in that subsection.

> **S. 50 (1) to (6)**
> *This section deals with how the delegated budget is to be applied. The local education authority must make the appropriate amount available under the scheme, the governing body may spend it at its discretion for any school purpose (but subject to any conditions that regulations lay down) but not generally in relation to part-time post-16 education or full-time post-19 education. Regulations may, however, permit some spending for those purposes. The school may not pay allowances to governors beyond what regulations permit. The governing body may delegate spending to the headteacher to the extent that the scheme allows.*

(7) The governors of a school shall not incur any personal liability in respect of anything done in good faith in the exercise or purported exercise of their powers under subsection (3) or (6).

> **S. 50(7)**
> *Governors incur no personal liability in relation to how the delegated budget is spent so long as they act in good faith.*

Suspension of financial delegation

51. Schedule 15 (which provides for the suspension by a local education authority of a governing body's right to a delegated budget in the case of failure to comply with requirements as to delegation or of financial mismanagement, etc.) shall have effect.

> **S. 51**
> *The delegated budget may be suspended by the local education authority if the governing body fails to comply with the scheme or if there is financial mismanagement. Schedule 15 sets out the process and the rights of appeal.*

Information

52.–(1) Before the beginning of each financial year a local education authority shall prepare a statement containing such information relating to their planned expenditure in that year as may be prescribed.

(2) After the end of each financial year a local education authority shall prepare a statement containing such information with respect to the following matters as may be prescribed-

  (a) the planned expenditure in that year specified in the statement prepared by the authority under subsection (1),

  (b) expenditure actually incurred, or treated by the authority as having been incurred, by them in the year, and

  (c) any other resources allocated by the authority in the year to schools maintained by them during any part of the year.

(3) A statement under this section shall-

  (a) be prepared in such form, and

  (b) be published in such manner and at such times,

as may be prescribed.

(4) The authority shall furnish the governing body and head teacher of each school maintained by them with a copy of each statement prepared by the authority under this section or, if regulations so provide, with a copy of such part or parts of it as may be prescribed.

(5) A governing body provided with such a copy under subsection (4) shall secure that a copy of it is available for inspection (at all reasonable times and free of charge) at the school.

(6) Subsection (5) does not apply to a temporary governing body of a new school at any time before the school opening date.

> **S. 52**
> *The local education authority must provide information about planned expenditure in the coming year, actual expenditure in the previous year and other resources allocated to schools. The information must be provided to schools and the governing must make it available for inspection free of charge at the school. The form and content of the information is laid down by regulations.*

53.–(1) A local education authority shall, if directed to do so by the Secretary of State, require the Audit Commission for Local Authorities and the National Health Service in England and Wales to make arrangements in accordance with section 28(1)(d) of the Audit Commission Act 1998 for certifying-

  (a) such statement or statements prepared by the authority under section 52 above, or

  (b) such part or parts of any such statement or statements,

as may be specified in the directions; and for the purposes of section 28(1)(d) of that Act any statement under section 52 above shall be treated as a return by the authority.

(2) The arrangements made by the Audit Commission in pursuance of subsection (1) shall include arrangements for sending to the Secretary of State-

(a) a copy of the statement or statements so certified, or

(b) a copy of the part or parts so certified,

as the case may be.

(3) Directions given under subsection (1) may relate to any local education authority or to local education authorities generally or to any class or description of such authorities.

> **S. 53**
> *This section gives the Secretary of State power to direct the local education authority to require the Audit Commission to certify the information provided under S. 52.*

CHAPTER V STAFFING AND CONDUCT OF SCHOOLS

Staffing of schools

54.–(1) Schedule 16 has effect in relation to the staffing of community, voluntary controlled and community special schools.

> **S. 54 (1)**
> *Detailed provisions relating to the staffing of community, voluntary controlled and community special schools are in Schedule 16 unless the school does not have a delegated budget.*

(2) If at any time a community, voluntary controlled or community special school does not have a delegated budget by virtue of any suspension under section 17 or Schedule 15-

(a) Schedule 16 shall not apply; and

(b) subsections (3) to (5) below shall apply instead.

(3) The number of teachers and non-teaching staff to be employed at the school shall be determined by the local education authority.

(4) The authority may appoint, suspend and dismiss teachers and other staff at the school as the authority think fit.

(5) The authority shall, in connection with the exercise of their functions under subsection (4), consult the governing body to such extent as the authority think fit.

> **S. 54 (2) to (5)**
> *For those schools without a delegated budget, the remainder of the section applies. The local education authority decides on the number of staff to be employed at the school. It also deals with appointment suspension and dismissal but must consult with the governing body to such extent as it thinks fit.*

(6) In relation to reserved teachers at a voluntary controlled school, Schedule 16 or (as the case may be) subsection (4) above has effect subject to section 58.

S. 54 (6)
There are limits on the local education authority's powers in respect of reserved teachers in a voluntary controlled school and this is dealt with below under S. 58.

55.–(1) Schedule 17 has effect in relation to the staffing of foundation, voluntary aided and foundation special schools.

S. 55 (1)
Detailed provisions relating to the staffing of foundation voluntary aided and foundation special schools are in Schedule 17 unless the school does not have a delegated budget.

(2) If at any time a foundation, voluntary aided or foundation special school does not have a delegated budget by virtue of any suspension under section 17 or Schedule 15, Schedule 17 shall apply to the school subject to subsections (3) to (7) below.

(3) The number of teachers and non-teaching staff to be employed at the school shall be determined by the local education authority.

(4) Except with the consent of the authority, the governing body shall not-

(a) appoint any teacher to be employed at the school or engage, or make arrangements for the engagement of, any person to provide his services as a teacher at the school, or

(b) dismiss any teacher at the school.

(5) The authority may give the governing body directions-

(a) as to the educational qualifications of the teachers to be employed for giving secular education; or

(b) requiring them to dismiss any teacher at the school;

but the authority shall not give any directions under paragraph (a) except after consulting the governing body.

(6) The authority may give directions to the governing body as to the number and conditions of service of persons employed at the school for the purposes of the care and maintenance of the school premises.

(7) Where the trust deed relating to the school provides for a person other than the governing body to be entitled to control the occupation and use of the school premises to any extent, then, if and to the extent that (disregarding any transfer of control agreement under Schedule 13) the use of those premises is or would be under the control of any such person, the reference in subsection (6) to the governing body shall be read as a reference to that person.

S. 55 (2) to (7)

For those schools without a delegated budget, the remainder off the section applies. The local education authority decides on the number of staff to be employed at the school. The governing body remains the employer even though it has no delegated budget but cannot engage someone to teach at the school or dismiss a teacher without local education authority consent. The local education authority can, after consulting the governing body, give directions regarding the qualifications of anyone employed to give secular education. It can also require the governing body to dismiss any teacher and give directions regarding the employment of premises maintenance staff. Those directions are given to the governing body unless the school's trust deed provides for a different body (e.g. the trustees) to have control of the premises.

(8) Schedule 17 or (as the case may be) subsections (4) and (5) above have effect subject to section 58.

S. 55 (8)

S. 58 overrides anything in S. 55 or Schedule 17 in relation to teachers employed to provide religious education.

56.–(1) This section applies to a maintained school if-

(a) activities other than school activities ("non-school activities") are carried on on the school premises, and

(b) all non-school activities which are so carried on are carried on under the management or control of the school's governing body.

(2) The relevant staffing provisions shall, to such extent as the local education authority may determine, apply in relation to persons employed to work-

(a) partly for the purposes of school activities and partly for the purposes of non-school activities carried on on the school premises, or

(b) solely for the purposes of non-school activities so carried on,

as if all activities so carried on were school activities.

(3) The local education authority shall give the governing body notice in writing of any determination by the authority under subsection (2).

(4) In subsection (2) "the relevant staffing provisions" means-

(a) in relation to a community, voluntary controlled or community special school, the provisions of Schedule 16 and section 57; and

(b) in relation to a foundation, voluntary aided or foundation special school, the provisions of Schedule 17 and section 57.

(5) Nothing in this section applies to a school within subsection (1) at any time when the school does not have a delegated budget by virtue of any suspension under section 17 or Schedule 15.

> **S. 56**
> *This section relates only to schools with a delegated budget. It applies if a school carries on activities under the control of the governing body which are not school activities and allows the local education authority to apply the staffing provisions in Schedules 16 or 17 (depending on the category of school) to employees who are employed for those non-school purposes.*

57.–(1) It shall be for the governing body of a maintained school to determine-

(a) whether any payment should be made by the local education authority in respect of the dismissal, or for the purpose of securing the resignation, of any member of the staff of the school, and
(b) the amount of any such payment.

(2) Subsection (1) does not, however, apply in relation to a payment which the local education authority are required to make-

(a) by virtue of any contract other than one made in contemplation of the impending dismissal or resignation of the member of staff concerned, or
(b) under any statutory provision.

(3) The local education authority-

(a) shall take such steps as may be required for giving effect to any determination of the governing body under subsection (1), and
(b) shall not make, or agree to make, a payment in relation to which that subsection applies except in accordance with such a determination.

(4) Costs incurred by the local education authority in respect of any premature retirement of a member of the staff of a maintained school shall be met from the school's budget share for one or more financial years except in so far as the authority agree with the governing body in writing (whether before or after the retirement occurs) that they shall not be so met.

(5) Costs incurred by the local education authority in respect of the dismissal, or for the purpose of securing the resignation, of any member of the staff of a maintained school shall not be met from the school's budget share for any financial year except in so far as the authority have good reason for deducting those costs, or any part of those costs, from that share.

(6) The fact that the authority have a policy precluding dismissal of their employees by reason of redundancy is not to be regarded as a good reason for the purposes of subsection (5); and in this subsection the reference to dismissal by reason of

redundancy shall be read in accordance with section 139 of the Employment Rights Act 1996.

(7) Nothing in this section applies to a maintained school at any time when the school does not have a delegated budget by virtue of any suspension under section 17 or Schedule 15.

> **S. 57**
> *This section relates only to schools with a delegated budget. The governing body decides whether the local education authority should make any payment to a member of staff specifically in relation to dismissal or retirement and how much should be paid. The cost of premature retirement is charged to the school's delegated budget unless there is a prior written agreement with the local education authority that it will meet some or all of the cost. Other dismissal costs can only be charged to the delegated budget if the local education authority has good reason to do so. An local education authority policy against redundancy is not in itself good reason to charge redundancy cost back to the school.*

Appointment and dismissal of teachers of religious education

58.–(1) In this section-

   (a) subsections (2) to (6) apply to a foundation or voluntary controlled school which has a religious character; and
   (b) subsection (7) applies (subject to subsection (8)) to a voluntary aided school which has a religious character;

and references in this Chapter to a school which has (or does not have) a religious character shall be construed in accordance with section 69(3).

(2) Where the number of the teaching staff of a school to which this subsection applies is more than two, the teaching staff shall include persons who-

   (a) are selected for their fitness and competence to give such religious education as is required in accordance with arrangements under paragraph 3(3) of Schedule 19 (arrangements for religious education in accordance with the school's trust deed or with the tenets of the school's specified religion or religious denomination), and
   (b) are specifically appointed to do so.

(3) The number of reserved teachers in such a school shall not exceed one-fifth of the number of the teaching staff, including the head teacher (and for this purpose, where the number of the teaching staff is not a multiple of five, it shall be treated as if it were the next higher multiple of five).

(4) The head teacher of such a school shall not, while holding the post of head teacher of the school, be a reserved teacher.

(5) Where the appropriate body propose to appoint a person to be a reserved teacher in such a school, that body-

    (a) shall consult the foundation governors, and

    (b) shall not so appoint that person unless the foundation governors are satisfied as to his fitness and competence to give such religious education as is mentioned in subsection (2)(a).

(6) If the foundation governors of such a school consider that a reserved teacher has failed to give such religious education efficiently and suitably, they may require the appropriate body to dismiss him from employment as a reserved teacher in the school.

(7) If a teacher appointed to give religious education in a school to which this subsection applies fails to give such education efficiently and suitably, he may be dismissed on that ground by the governing body without the consent of the local education authority.

(8) Subsection (7) does not apply-

    (a) where the school has a delegated budget, or

    (b) to religious education in accordance with an agreed syllabus.

(9) In this section-

    "the appropriate body" means-

        (a) in relation to a foundation school, the governing body, and

        (b) in relation to a voluntary controlled school, the local education authority;

    "reserved teacher", in relation to a foundation or voluntary controlled school, means a person employed at the school in pursuance of subsection (2).

S. 58

Special rules apply to the appointment of staff in schools that have a religious character and who are appointed (and are competent) to teach religious education.

In a voluntary aided school without a delegated budget, unless the religious education to be taught is in accordance with an agreed syllabus, the governing body may dismiss such a teacher on competency grounds without local education authority consent.

In a foundation or voluntary controlled school (with or without a delegated budget) that has more than two teachers, the school must have a number (not more than one-fifth of the total teaching staff rounded up) of teachers appointed to teach religious education in accordance with the provisions for religious education set up under Schedule 19. Such teachers are known as "reserved teachers". The headteacher may not be a reserved teacher. Whoever is responsible for the appointment of teachers must consult the school's foundation governors before appointing a reserved teacher and must not make the appointment unless the foundation governors are satisfied that the proposed teacher is competent to give religious education.

Religious opinions etc. of staff

59.–(1) This section applies to-

    (a) a community school or a community or foundation special school, or

    (b) a foundation or voluntary school which does not have a religious character.

(2) No person shall be disqualified by reason of his religious opinions, or of his attending or omitting to attend religious worship-

    (a) from being a teacher at the school, or

    (b) from being employed for the purposes of the school otherwise than as a teacher.

(3) No teacher at the school shall be required to give religious education.

(4) No teacher at the school shall receive any less remuneration or be deprived of, or disqualified for, any promotion or other advantage-

    (a) by reason of the fact that he does or does not give religious education, or

    (b) by reason of his religious opinions or of his attending or omitting to attend religious worship.

> **S. 59**
>
> *This section preserves the right for teachers in schools that do not have a religious character not to be discriminated against because of religious opinions and not to be required to give religious education. This extends to initial employment, pay, promotion or other advantages that may apply. Non-teaching staff may not be disqualified from employment because of their religious opinions.*

60.–(1) This section applies to a foundation or voluntary school which has a religious character.

(2) If the school is a foundation or voluntary controlled school, then (subject to subsections (3) and (4) below) section 59(2) to (4) shall apply to the school as they apply to a foundation or voluntary controlled school which does not have a religious character.

(3) Section 59(2) to (4) shall not so apply in relation to a reserved teacher at the school; and instead subsection (5) below shall apply in relation to such a teacher as it applies in relation to a teacher at a voluntary aided school.

(4) In connection with the appointment of a person to be head teacher of the school (whether foundation or voluntary controlled) regard may be had to that person's ability and fitness to preserve and develop the religious character of the school.

(5) If the school is a voluntary aided school-

    (a) preference may be given, in connection with the appointment, remuneration or promotion of teachers at the school, to persons-

(i) whose religious opinions are in accordance with the tenets of the religion or religious denomination specified in relation to the school under section 69(4), or

(ii) who attend religious worship in accordance with those tenets, or

(iii) who give, or are willing to give, religious education at the school in accordance with those tenets; and

(b) regard may be had, in connection with the termination of the employment of any teacher at the school, to any conduct on his part which is incompatible with the precepts, or with the upholding of the tenets, of the religion or religious denomination so specified.

(6) If the school is a voluntary aided school, no person shall be disqualified by reason of his religious opinions, or of his attending or omitting to attend religious worship, from being employed for the purposes of the school otherwise than as a teacher.

(7) Where immediately before the appointed day a teacher at a school which on that day becomes a school to which this section applies enjoyed, by virtue of section 304 or 305 of the Education Act 1996 (religious opinions of staff etc.), any rights not conferred on him by this section as a teacher at a school to which it applies, he shall continue to enjoy those rights (in addition to those conferred by this section) until he ceases to be employed as a teacher at the school.

(8) In this section "reserved teacher", in relation to a foundation or voluntary controlled school, means a person employed at the school in pursuance of section 58(2).

S. 60

This section applies to schools that have a religious character. It applies to all staff except that if staff already employed had greater rights as a result of earlier legislation such staff keep those greater rights.

S. 59 is applied to all staff in foundation or voluntary controlled schools except reserved teachers (see S. 58). However, in appointing the headteacher regard may be had to whether the proposed appointee is able to preserve and develop the religious character of the school. Reserved teachers are to be treated in the same way as all teachers in voluntary aided schools.

In voluntary aided schools preference in appointment, pay and promotion may be given to those whose religious beliefs conform to the tenets of the school, or who attend religious worship in accordance with those tenets or who are willing to give religious instruction. Conduct incompatible with the school's tenets may be relevant in connection with termination of employment of teachers. However, non-teaching staff may not be disqualified from employment because of their religious opinions.

Discipline: general

Ss 61 to 68
These provisions relating to discipline relate to all maintained schools irrespective of their category.

61.–(1) The governing body of a maintained school shall ensure that policies designed to promote good behaviour and discipline on the part of its pupils are pursued at the school.

(2) In particular, the governing body-

(a) shall make, and from time to time review, a written statement of general principles to which the head teacher is to have regard in determining any measures under subsection (4); and

(b) where they consider it desirable that any particular measures should be so determined by the head teacher or that he should have regard to any particular matters-

(i) shall notify him of those measures or matters, and

(ii) may give him such guidance as they consider appropriate;

and in exercising their functions under this subsection the governing body shall have regard to any guidance given from time to time by the Secretary of State.

(3) Before making or revising the statement required by subsection (2)(a) the governing body shall consult (in such manner as appears to them to be appropriate)-

(a) the head teacher; and

(b) parents of registered pupils at the school.

S. 61 (1) to(3)
It is the responsibility of the governing body to ensure that policies designed to promote good behaviour and discipline are followed in the school (although it is the responsibility of the headteacher to implement them). It has to make and periodically review a written statement setting out the general principles that the headteacher has to follow. If it considers that there are particular measures that the headteacher should implement or consider it must so advise the headteacher and give any guidance it thinks appropriate. In doing this, the governing body must have regard to any guidance issued by the Secretary of State. The governing body must consult with the headteacher and parents before making or revising the statement of general principles. How it does this is left to the governing body to decide.

(4) The head teacher shall determine measures (which may include the making of rules and provision for enforcing them) to be taken with a view to-

(a) promoting, among pupils, self-discipline and proper regard for authority;

(b) encouraging good behaviour and respect for others on the part of pupils and, in particular, preventing all forms of bullying among pupils;

(c) securing that the standard of behaviour of pupils is acceptable; and

(d) otherwise regulating the conduct of pupils.

(5) The head teacher shall in determining such measures-

(a) act in accordance with the current statement made by the governing body under subsection (2)(a); and

(b) have regard to any notification or guidance given to him under subsection (2)(b).

(6) The standard of behaviour which is to be regarded as acceptable at the school shall be determined by the head teacher, so far as it is not determined by the governing body.

(7) The measures determined by the head teacher under subsection (4) shall be publicised by him in the form of a written document as follows-

(a) he shall make the measures generally known within the school and to parents of registered pupils at the school; and

(b) he shall in particular, at least once in every school year, take steps to bring them to the attention of all such pupils and parents and all persons employed, or otherwise engaged to provide their services, at the school.

S. 61 (4) to (7)

It is the responsibility of the headteacher to determine measures (which can include rules and ways of enforcing those rules) to promote self-discipline and proper regard for authority, encourage good behaviour and respect for others, prevent bullying, secure an acceptable standard of behaviour and otherwise regulate the conduct of the pupils. In doing this, the headteacher must act in accordance with the governors' general statement and have regard to their guidance (if any). If, and to the extent that, the governors have not determined what is to be regarded as an acceptable standard of behaviour, the headteacher must do so. The measures that the headteacher determines must be in writing, must be made known generally in the school and to parents and, once every year, must be brought to the attention of all pupils, parents, staff and others who provide services to the school.

62.–(1) The local education authority may, in the circumstances mentioned in subsection (2) or where subsection (3) applies, take such steps in relation to a maintained school as they consider are required to prevent the breakdown, or continuing breakdown, of discipline at the school.

(2) The circumstances are that-

    (a) in the opinion of the authority-

        (i) the behaviour of registered pupils at the school, or

        (ii) any action taken by such pupils or their parents,

is such that the education of any registered pupils at the school is (or is likely in the immediate future to become) severely prejudiced; and

    (b) the governing body have been informed in writing of the authority's opinion.

(3) This subsection applies where-

    (a) a warning notice has been given in accordance with section 15(2) referring to the safety of pupils or staff at the school being threatened by a breakdown of discipline at the school,

    (b) the governing body have failed to comply, or secure compliance, with the notice to the authority's satisfaction within the compliance period, and

    (c) the authority have given reasonable notice in writing to the governing body that they propose to exercise their powers under subsection (1) of this section (whether or not in conjunction with exercising their powers under either or both of sections 16 and 17);

and a notice under paragraph (c) of this subsection may be combined with a notice under section 15(1)(c).

(4) Steps taken by a local education authority under subsection (1) may include the giving of any direction to the governing body or head teacher.

> **S. 62**
> *The local education authority have powers to take whatever steps it thinks fit to prevent a breakdown or continuing breakdown of discipline in a school where it believes that behaviour of pupils or action taken by pupils or parents threaten to severely prejudice the education of any pupil in the school. The local education authority must first inform the governing body of its opinion that it needs to take action. It can also exercise those powers if it has served a warning notice under S. 15 which has not been complied with to the local education authority's satisfaction. The steps available to the local education authority include power to give directions to the governing body and/or the headteacher.*

School attendance targets

63.–(1) Regulations may make provision for and in connection with-

    (a) requiring, or

    (b) enabling the Secretary of State to require,

governing bodies of maintained schools to secure that annual targets are set for reducing the level of unauthorised absences on the part of relevant day pupils at their schools.

(2) Regulations under this section may, in particular, make provision-

   (a) for the Secretary of State to impose such a requirement on the governing body of a maintained school where-

   (i) the specified condition is for the time being satisfied in relation to the school, and

   (ii) he considers it appropriate to impose the requirement;

   (b) for such a requirement to be imposed by the Secretary of State in such manner, and for such period, as may be specified in or determined in accordance with the regulations;

   (c) for the Secretary of State, where he considers it appropriate to do so, to exempt the governing body of a maintained school, in relation to any school year, from a requirement imposed by virtue of subsection (1)(a) or (b).

(3) For the purposes of subsection (2)(a)(i) the specified condition is for the time being satisfied in relation to a maintained school if in the previous school year the level of unauthorised absences on the part of relevant day pupils at the school (as determined in accordance with the regulations) exceeded such level as may for that year be specified in or determined in accordance with the regulations.

(4) In this section-

"relevant day pupil" means a pupil registered at a maintained school who is of compulsory school age and is not a boarder;

"unauthorised absence", in relation to such a pupil, means any occasion on which the pupil is recorded as absent without authority pursuant to regulations under section 434 of the Education Act 1996 (registration of pupils).

S. 63
Governing bodies may be required by the Secretary of State to set annual targets for reducing unauthorised absences. Regulations will contain the detailed provisions and can include the power for the Secretary of State to provide that the requirement will only take effect in certain circumstances which could include unauthorised absence exceeding a prescribed level. The regulations may also allow the Secretary of State to exempt particular schools.

Exclusion of pupils

64.–(1) The head teacher of a maintained school may exclude a pupil from the school for a fixed period or permanently.

(2) The head teacher may not exercise the power to exclude a pupil from the school for one or more fixed periods such that the pupil is so excluded for more than 45 school days in any one school year.

(3) A pupil may not be excluded from a maintained school (whether by suspension, expulsion or otherwise) except by the head teacher in accordance with this section.

(4) In this Act "exclude", in relation to the exclusion of a child from a school, means exclude on disciplinary grounds (and "exclusion" shall be construed accordingly).

S. 64
The power to exclude pupils from school may only be exercised on disciplinary grounds, by the headteacher and either permanently or for a fixed period or periods not exceeding 45 school days in any school year. No other form of exclusion is lawful.

65.–(1) Where the head teacher of a maintained school excludes any pupil, the head teacher shall (without delay) take reasonable steps to inform the relevant person of the following matters-

(a) the period of the exclusion (or, if the pupil is being permanently excluded, that he is being so excluded);
(b) the reasons for the exclusion;
(c) that he may make representations about the exclusion to the governing body, and
(d) the means by which such representations may be made.

(2) Where the head teacher decides that any exclusion of a pupil for a fixed period should be made permanent, he shall (without delay) take reasonable steps to inform the relevant person of-

(a) his decision, and
(b) the matters specified in paragraphs (b) to (d) of subsection (1).

(3) Subsection (4) applies where the head teacher-

(a) excludes any pupil in circumstances where the pupil would, as a result of the exclusion-
  (i) be excluded from the school for a total of more than five school days in any one term, or
  (ii) lose an opportunity to take any public examination,
(b) excludes a pupil permanently, or
(c) decides that any exclusion of a pupil should be made permanent.

(4) Where this subsection applies, the head teacher shall (without delay) inform the local education authority and the governing body of the following matters-

(a) the period of the exclusion (or, if the pupil is being permanently excluded, that he is being so excluded), or
(b) his decision that any exclusion of a pupil for a fixed period should be made permanent,

and (in either case) of the reasons for it.

(5) In this section and in sections 66 and 67 "the relevant person" means-

(a) in relation to a pupil under the age of 18, a parent of his;

(b) in relation to a pupil who has attained that age, the pupil himself.

(6) Where regulations under paragraph 4 of Schedule 11 require the governing body of a maintained school to establish a discipline committee, references in this section and sections 66 to 68 to the governing body of such a school shall be construed as references to their discipline committee.

S. 65

When a pupil is excluded the headteacher must take reasonable steps to tell a parent if the pupil is under 18, or the pupil if 18 or over, of the period of the exclusion, the reasons for it, the right to make representations to the governing body and how to do this. The same applies if the headteacher decides to turn a fixed period exclusion into a permanent one. If the exclusion is a permanent one, or if it will lead to the pupil being excluded for more than five school days in the term or to miss a public examination the headteacher must also inform the local education authority and the governing body of the exclusion and the reasons for it.

66.–(1) Subsections (2) to (6) apply where the governing body of a maintained school are informed under section 65(4) of any exclusion or decision to which that provision applies.

(2) The governing body shall in any such case-

(a) consider the circumstances in which the pupil was excluded;

(b) consider any representations about the exclusion made to the governing body-
(i) by the relevant person in pursuance of section 65(1)(c) or (2)(b), or
(ii) by the local education authority;

(c) allow each of the following, namely-
(i) the relevant person, and
(ii) an officer of the local education authority nominated by the authority,
to attend a meeting of the governing body and to make oral representations about the exclusion; and

(d) consider any oral representations so made.

(3) In a case where it would be practical for the governing body to give a direction to the head teacher requiring the reinstatement of a pupil, they shall in addition consider whether he should be reinstated immediately, reinstated by a particular date or not reinstated.

(4) If the governing body decide that the pupil should be reinstated, they shall forthwith-

(a) give the appropriate direction to the head teacher, and

(b) inform the relevant person and the local education authority of their decision.

(5) The head teacher shall comply with any direction of the governing body for the reinstatement of a pupil who has been excluded from the school.

(6) If the governing body decide that the pupil should not be reinstated, they shall forthwith-

  (a) inform the relevant person, the head teacher and the local education authority of their decision, and

  (b) in addition, in the case of a pupil who is permanently excluded, give the relevant person notice in writing referring to that decision and stating the following matters-

  (i) the reasons for the decision,

  (ii) his right to appeal against the decision,

  (iii) the person to whom he should give any notice of appeal,

  (iv) that any notice of appeal must contain the grounds of appeal, and

  (v) the last date on which an appeal may be made.

S. 66 (1) to (6)
Where the governing body is informed of an exclusion it must consider the circumstances, consider any representations made by the parent (or pupil if 18 or over) and the local education authority, allow each to attend a meeting of the governing body to make oral representations and consider those representations. It must consider whether or not to reinstate the pupil where that is practicable and give appropriate directions to the headteacher who must comply with them. It must inform all concerned of the decision and. if a permanent exclusion is upheld, give reasons and inform the parent or pupil of the right to appeal, how to do so and by when.

(7) Where-

  (a) the head teacher of a maintained school excludes a pupil otherwise than as mentioned in section 65(3), and

  (b) the governing body receive any representations made in pursuance of section 65(1)(c) or (2)(b) by the relevant person about the exclusion,

they shall consider those representations.

S. 66 (7)
Even if it is not practicable to direct reinstatement the governing body must still consider any representations that are made.

(8) Regulations may provide that, where a governing body of a maintained school are required under this section to take any step, the duty must, subject to such exceptions as may be prescribed, be performed within the prescribed period; but such a provision shall not relieve the governing body of the duty to take any step which has not been taken within that period.

S. 66 (8)
Regulations may lay down time limits for taking steps under this section.

67.–(1) A local education authority shall make arrangements for enabling the relevant person to appeal against any decision of the governing body under section 66 not to reinstate a pupil who has been permanently excluded from a school maintained by the authority.

(2) Schedule 18 has effect in relation to the making and hearing of appeals pursuant to arrangements made under subsection (1); and in subsections (3) and (4) "appeal panel" means an appeal panel constituted in accordance with paragraph 2 of that Schedule.

(3) The decision of an appeal panel on an appeal pursuant to arrangements made under subsection (1) shall be binding on the relevant person, the governing body, the head teacher and the local education authority.

(4) Where on such an appeal the appeal panel determines that the pupil in question should be reinstated, the panel shall either-

(a) direct that he is to be reinstated immediately, or
(b) direct that he is to be reinstated by a date specified in the direction.

S. 67
The local education authority must make arrangements for appeals against permanent exclusion. Schedule 18 contains the detail. The appeal panel's decision is binding and includes the right to specify when the pupil should return to school if the appeal is allowed.

68.–(1) This section applies to any functions of-

(a) the head teacher or the governing body of a maintained school,
(b) a local education authority, or
(c) an appeal panel constituted in accordance with paragraph 2 of Schedule 18,

conferred by or under any of sections 64 to 67 and Schedule 18.

(2) In discharging any such function, such a person or body shall have regard to any guidance given from time to time by the Secretary of State.

S. 68
All concerned in dealing with exclusions must have regard to any guidance issued by the Secretary of State.

CHAPTER VI RELIGIOUS EDUCATION AND WORSHIP

Religious education

69.–(1) Subject to section 71, in relation to any community, foundation or voluntary school-

(a) the local education authority and the governing body shall exercise their functions with a view to securing, and

(b) the head teacher shall secure,

that religious education is given in accordance with the provision for such education included in the school's basic curriculum by virtue of section 352(1)(a) of the Education Act 1996.

(2) Schedule 19 has effect for determining the provision for religious education which is required by section 352(1)(a) of that Act to be included in the basic curriculum of schools within each of the following categories, namely-

(a) community schools and foundation and voluntary schools which do not have a religious character,

(b) foundation and voluntary controlled schools which have a religious character, and

(c) voluntary aided schools which have a religious character.

(3) For the purposes of this Part a foundation or voluntary school has a religious character if it is designated as a school having such a character by an order made by the Secretary of State.

(4) An order under subsection (3) shall state, in relation to each school designated by the order, the religion or religious denomination in accordance with whose tenets religious education is, or may be, required to be provided at the school in accordance with Schedule 19 (or, as the case may be, each such religion or religious denomination).

(5) The procedure to be followed in connection with-

(a) the designation of a school in an order under subsection (3), and

(b) the inclusion in such an order, in relation to a school, of the statement required by subsection (4),

shall be specified in regulations.

S. 69

Religious education in all maintained schools is the direct responsibility of the Headteacher. The local education authority and the governing body must exercise their functions so as to secure that this is done. Schedule 19 contains the detailed provisions which vary according to the type of school and whether or not it is one that is designated by the Secretary of State in accordance with regulations as having a religious character.

Religious worship

70.–(1) Subject to section 71, each pupil in attendance at a community, foundation or voluntary school shall on each school day take part in an act of collective worship.

(2) Subject to section 71, in relation to any community, foundation or voluntary school-

  (a) the local education authority and the governing body shall exercise their functions with a view to securing, and

  (b) the head teacher shall secure,

that subsection (1) is complied with.

(3) Schedule 20 makes further provision with respect to the collective worship required by this section, including provision relating to-

  (a) the arrangements which are to be made in connection with such worship, and

  (b) the nature of such worship.

S. 70
Subject to the right of parents to withdraw their children, every child in a maintained school must take part each school day in an act of collective worship. The term is not defined but Schedule 20 has detailed provisions as to its organisation.

Exceptions and special arrangements etc.

71.–(1) If the parent of a pupil at a community, foundation or voluntary school requests that he may be wholly or partly excused-

  (a) from receiving religious education given in the school in accordance with the school's basic curriculum,

  (b) from attendance at religious worship in the school, or

  (c) both from receiving such education and from such attendance,

the pupil shall be so excused until the request is withdrawn.

(2) In subsection (1)-

  (a) the reference to religious education given in accordance with the school's basic curriculum is to such education given in accordance with the provision included in the school's basic curriculum by virtue of section 352(1)(a) of the Education Act 1996, and

  (b) the reference to religious worship in the school includes religious worship which by virtue of paragraph 2(6) of Schedule 20 takes place otherwise than on the school premises.

S. 71 (1) and (2)
Parents have the right to withdraw their children from religious education and/or worship

(3) Where in accordance with subsection (1) a pupil has been wholly or partly excused from receiving religious education or from attendance at religious worship and the local education authority are satisfied-

(a) that the parent of the pupil desires him to receive religious education of a kind which is not provided in the school during the periods of time during which he is so excused,

(b) that the pupil cannot with reasonable convenience be sent to another community, foundation or voluntary school where religious education of the kind desired by the parent is provided, and

(c) that arrangements have been made for him to receive religious education of that kind during school hours elsewhere,

the pupil may be withdrawn from the school during such periods of time as are reasonably necessary for the purpose of enabling him to receive religious education in accordance with the arrangements.

(4) A pupil may not be withdrawn from school under subsection (3) unless the local education authority are satisfied that the arrangements there mentioned are such as will not interfere with the attendance of the pupil at school on any day except at the beginning or end of a school session (or, if there is only one, the school session) on that day.

S. 71 (3) and (4)
Parents who wish their children to receive religious education that is different from that provided by the school, and which is not provided at another school that the child can conveniently be sent to, may arrange for the child to receive religious education elsewhere. They may withdraw the child from school for that purpose provided that this is only at the beginning or the end of a school session.

(5) Where the parent of a pupil who is a boarder at a community, foundation or voluntary school requests that the pupil be permitted-

(a) to receive religious education in accordance with the tenets of a particular religion or religious denomination outside school hours, or

(b) to attend worship in accordance with such tenets on Sundays or other days exclusively set apart for religious observance by the religious body to which his parent belongs,

the governing body shall make arrangements for giving the pupil reasonable opportunities for doing so.

(6) Arrangements under subsection (5) may provide for making facilities for such education or worship available on the school premises, but any expenditure entailed by the arrangements shall not be met from the school's budget share or otherwise by the local education authority.

S. 71 (5) and (6)

The governing body of a maintained boarding school must, if requested by parents, give pupils reasonable opportunities for religious education and/or worship outside school hours or on Sundays or other days exclusively set aside for observance by the relevant religious body to which the parent belongs but the cost may not fall on the school's delegated budget or be met by the local education authority.

(7) Regulations shall make provision for securing that, so far as practicable, every pupil attending a community or foundation special school-

    (a) receives religious education and attends religious worship, or

    (b) is withdrawn from receiving such education or from attendance at such worship in accordance with the wishes of his parent.

CHAPTER VII MISCELLANEOUS AND SUPPLEMENTAL

Further provisions relating to new schools

72.–(1) Regulations may make provision for-

    (a) the staffing and conduct of a new school in advance of the school opening date;

    (b) the determination of matters in connection with a new school in advance of that date;

    (c) the taking of decisions by a temporary governing body, or (where power to do so is delegated to him) by the head teacher, as to expenditure in connection with a new school at a time when it does not have a delegated budget;

    (d) such other matters relating to new schools as the Secretary of State considers appropriate.

(2) Regulations under subsection (1) may, in connection with any matters falling within that subsection, apply any provision of the Education Acts with or without modification.

(3) In this section "new school" means a school or proposed school-

    (a) for which there is a temporary governing body constituted under section 44, or

    (b) for which there is no such body but for which such a body-

        (i) are required to be so constituted by virtue of subsection (1) of that section, or

        (ii) may be so constituted in accordance with such anticipatory arrangements as are mentioned in subsection (5)(a) of that section.

S. 72

Regulations will provide for the detail of the initial management, staffing etc of a new school.

Transfers of staff and land

73.–(1) Subsections (5) to (7) below ("the staff transfer provisions") apply where on the appointed day-

    (a) a special agreement school becomes a voluntary aided school, or

    (b) a grant-maintained school becomes a community or voluntary controlled school, or

    (c) a grant-maintained special school becomes a community special school,

in accordance with Schedule 2.

(2) Subject to subsection (3), the staff transfer provisions apply in the circumstances mentioned in subsection (1) to any person who immediately before the appointed day-

    (a) is employed by the local education authority to work solely at an existing school within subsection (1)(a), or

    (b) is employed by the local education authority to work at such an existing school and is designated for the purposes of this subsection by an order made by the Secretary of State, or

    (c) is employed by the governing body of an existing school within subsection (1)(b) or (c).

(3) The staff transfer provisions do not apply-

    (a) to any person employed as mentioned in subsection (2) whose contract of employment terminates on the day immediately preceding the appointed day; or

    (b) to any person employed as mentioned in subsection (2)(a) or (b) who before that day-

        (i) has been appointed or assigned by the local education authority to work solely at another school as from that day, or

        (ii) has been withdrawn from work at the school with effect from that day.

(4) A person who before the appointed day has been appointed or assigned by-

    (a) the local education authority, or

    (b) the governing body of an existing school within subsection (1)(b) or (c),

to work at a school, or (as the case may be) at the existing school, as from that day shall be treated for the purposes of this section as if he had been employed by the authority or governing body immediately before that day to do such work at the school as he would have been required to do on or after that day under his contract of employment with the authority or that body.

(5) The contract of employment between a person to whom the staff transfer provisions apply and his former employer shall have effect from the appointed day as if originally made between him and his new employer.

(6) Without prejudice to subsection (5)-

(a) all the former employer's rights, powers, duties and liabilities under or in connection with the contract of employment shall by virtue of this section be transferred to the new employer on the appointed day, and

(b) anything done before that date by or in relation to the former employer in respect of that contract or the employee shall be deemed from that day to have been done by or in relation to the new employer.

(7) Subsections (5) and (6) are without prejudice to any right of an employee to terminate his contract of employment if a substantial change is made to his detriment in his working conditions, but no such right shall arise by reason only of the change in employer effected by this section.

(8) In this section-

"existing school" means a school which becomes a school of a different category on the appointed day as mentioned in subsection (1), and "new school" means the school of a different category which an existing school then becomes;

"the former employer" and "the new employer"-

(a) where the staff transfer provisions apply by virtue of subsection (2)(a) or (b), means the local education authority and the governing body of the new school respectively, and

(b) where the staff transfer provisions apply by virtue of subsection (2)(c), means the governing body of the existing school and the local education authority respectively;

and references to a special agreement, grant-maintained or grant-maintained special school are references to such a school within the meaning of the Education Act 1996.

(9) A person employed by a local education authority in connection with the provision of meals shall not be regarded for the purposes of subsection (2)(a) as employed to work solely at a school unless the meals are provided solely for consumption by persons at the school.

(10) An order under this section may designate a person either individually or as a member of a class or description of employees.

S. 73

One effect of the change of categories of schools that arises under the Act is that employees may technically become employed by a new employer. This section preserves their employment rights while at the same time denying them the right to treat their employment as terminated which could give rise to claims for unfair dismissal. Thus, where a special agreement school becomes a voluntary aided school, anyone employed by the local education authority solely to work at the school will become an employee of the governing body. Where a grant maintained school becomes a community or voluntary controlled school, or a grant maintained special school becomes a community special school, anyone employed by the school will become an employee of the local education authority. In each case, the terms and conditions of employment are unchanged and the employee has continuity of employment for employment protection purposes. An employee whose working conditions are substantially and detrimentally changed following the change of category of school has the right to terminate his or her employment but cannot do so merely because of the change of category.
The section does not apply to anyone whose employment comes to an end on the day before the day on which the change of category takes place nor does it apply to an employee of the local education authority who is assigned by the local education authority to work elsewhere or is withdrawn from working at the school as from that day. It also does not apply to anyone employed to provide meals for the school unless the meals are provided only for that school.

74. Schedule 21 (which makes provision for transfers of land and certain rights and liabilities on the appointed day in respect of schools which become community, foundation, voluntary or community special schools on that day) shall have effect.

S. 74

Schedule 21 deals with the mechanics of land transfer arising from the change of category of schools when the Act comes into force.

75.–(1) Where a building is to be provided for a foundation or voluntary school and the building-

    (a) is to form part of the school premises, and

    (b) is to be constructed partly on land held by the governing body and partly on land held on trust for the purposes of the school by persons other than the governing body,

the governing body shall transfer to those persons the land held by the governing body on which the building is to be constructed.

(2) Paragraph 1 of Schedule 22 does not apply to any transfer required by subsection (1).

S. 75

If, in the case of a foundation or voluntary school, some land is owned by trustees for the school and other land is owned by the governing body and school premises are to be built partly on the one and partly on the other, the governing body must transfer the part that it owns (but only to the extent that it is built on) to the trustees.

Disposals of land and on discontinuance

76. Schedule 22 (which makes provision as to the disposal of land held for the purposes of foundation, voluntary or foundation special schools and as to the property of maintained schools on their discontinuance) shall have effect.

S. 76

Schedule 22 deals with what is to happen to land and property owned by maintained schools if they are closed.

77.–(1) Except with the consent of the Secretary of State, a body to whom this subsection applies shall not dispose of any playing fields-

(a) which are, immediately before the date of the disposal, used by a maintained school for the purposes of the school, or

(b) which are not then so used but have been so used at any time within the period of 10 years ending with that date.

(2) Subsection (1) applies-

(a) to a local authority; and

(b) in any case where the consent of the Secretary of State is not required to any such disposal by virtue of either of paragraphs 1 and 2 of Schedule 22-

(i) to the governing body of a maintained school, and

(ii) to a foundation body.

(3) Except with the consent of the Secretary of State, a local authority shall not take any action (other than the making of a disposal falling within subsection (1)) which is intended or likely to result in a change of use of any playing fields-

(a) which are, immediately before the date when the action is taken, used by a maintained school for the purposes of the school, or

(b) which are not then so used but have been so used at any time within the period of 10 years ending with that date,

whereby the playing fields will be used for purposes which do not consist of or include their use as playing fields by such a school for the purposes of the school.

(4) Subsection (3) does not, however, apply where the land in question will, on a change of use falling within that subsection, become used in connection with the provision by a local authority of educational facilities for a maintained school or any recreational facilities.

(5) For the purposes of this section the Secretary of State's consent may be given in relation to a particular disposal or change of use or generally in relation to disposals or changes of use of a particular description, and in either case may be given subject to conditions.

(6) This section has effect despite anything in section 123 or 127 of the Local Government Act 1972 (general power to dispose of land) or in any other enactment; and any consent which a local authority are required to obtain by virtue of this section shall be in addition to any consent required by virtue of either of those sections.

(7) In this section-

"local authority" includes a parish council;

"playing fields" means land in the open air which is provided for the purposes of physical education or recreation, other than any prescribed description of such land.

(8) For the purposes of this section any reference to a maintained school includes, in relation to any time falling before the appointed day, a reference to the school as-

(a) a county, voluntary or maintained special school, or
(b) a grant-maintained or grant-maintained special school,

within the meaning of the Education Act 1996.

(9) Nothing in this section applies in relation to Wales.

S. 77
Consent of the Secretary of State is needed for the disposal of any land in England (whether owned by the local education authority or by the governing body or by a foundation body of a foundation school) used as playing fields at any time in the 10 years prior to the disposal. Playing fields are defined as land in the open air provided for physical education or recreation. There is a similar prohibition on a local authority taking any action which may lead to a change of use of playing fields unless that change of use relates to the provision of educational facilities for maintained schools or any recreational facilities.

Rating

78. For the purposes of Part III of the Local Government Finance Act 1988 (non-domestic rating) the occupier of any hereditament so far as consisting of the premises of a maintained school shall be taken to be-

(a) the local education authority, where it is a community, voluntary controlled or community special school; or

(b) the governing body, where it is a foundation, voluntary aided or foundation special school.

S. 78

For rating purposes the local education authority is the occupier (i.e. the person liable to pay rates) of a community, community special or voluntary controlled school and the governing body is the occupier of all other types of school.

Stamp duty

79.–(1) Subject to subsection (2), stamp duty shall not be chargeable in respect of any transfer to a local authority under any of the following provisions, namely-

(a) paragraph 4 or 7 of Schedule 21 or any corresponding provision of regulations under paragraph 10 of Schedule 2,

(b) paragraph 4(2), 5(4), 6(2)(b), 7(2) or 8(2)(b) of Schedule 22, or

(c) any regulations under paragraph 5 of Schedule 8.

(2) No instrument (other than a statutory instrument) made or executed under or in pursuance of any of the provisions mentioned in subsection (1) shall be treated as duly stamped unless-

(a) it is stamped with the duty to which it would be liable but for that subsection, or

(b) it has, in accordance with section 12 of the (1891 c. 39.)Stamp Act 1891, been stamped with a particular stamp denoting that it is not chargeable with any duty or that it has been duly stamped.

(3) In subsection (1) any reference to a transfer under any provision or regulations mentioned in that subsection shall be read as a reference to a transfer under that provision or those regulations taken with section 198 of, and Schedule 10 to, the Education Reform Act 1988 if those provisions of that Act apply to the transfer by virtue of any provision of this Act or that Act.

S. 79

No stamp duty is payable on transfers of land to the local education authority carried out under various provisions of the Act. [N. B. although the Act does not deal with stamp duty on transfers of land to governing bodies of foundation, foundation special or voluntary aided schools these will not bear stamp duty because those bodies are charities by virtue of S. 23 and charities are exempt from stamp duty.]

Further education

80.–(1) The governing body of any maintained school shall be responsible for determining whether or not to provide-

(a) part-time education suitable to the requirements of persons of any age over compulsory school age; or

(b) full-time education suitable to the requirements of persons who have attained the age of 19;

but the governing body of a community or foundation special school shall not determine to provide, or to cease to provide, such education without the consent of the local education authority.

(2) It shall be the duty of the governing body of any such school which provides such education to secure that, except in such circumstances as may be prescribed, such education is not provided at any time in a room where pupils are at that time being taught.

(3) This section shall not apply to part-time education provided under a partnership arrangement to which section 60A of the Further and Higher Education Act 1992 (as inserted by section 125(4) of this Act) applies.

S. 80

Governing bodies have power to decide whether or not to provide part-time education to those over compulsory school age or full time education for those age 19 or more. A governing body of a community or foundation special school requires local education authority consent before deciding to make, or cease such provision. Except in circumstances prescribed by regulations this type of education must be kept physically separate from that being provided to full-time pupils. The section does not apply to part-time education in Wales provided under a partnership arrangement.

Modification of employment law

81.–(1) The Secretary of State may by order make such modifications in any enactment relating to employment, and in particular in any enactment-

(a) conferring powers or imposing duties on employers,

(b) conferring rights on employees, or

(c) otherwise regulating the relations between employers and employees,

as he considers necessary or expedient in consequence of the operation of sections 54 and 57(1) to (3), Schedule 16 and paragraph 27 of Schedule 17.

(2) Before making any order under this section the Secretary of State shall consult-

(a) such associations of local authorities,

(b) such bodies representing the interests of governors of foundation or voluntary schools, and

(c) such organisations representing staff in maintained schools,

as appear to him to be concerned.

S. 81

The Secretary of State is given a general power to modify employment legislation in relation to the employment of staff by local education authorities in community, community special and voluntary controlled schools after consultation with representatives of employers, governing bodies and staff.

Supplementary provisions

82.–(1) The Secretary of State may by order make such modifications of any trust deed or other instrument relating to-

(a) a school which is or is to become a foundation, voluntary or foundation special school, or

(b) property held on trust for the purposes of such a school,

as appear to him to be necessary or expedient in connection with the operation of any provision of this Act or anything done under or for the purposes of any such provision.

(2) Before making an order under this section the Secretary of State shall consult-

(a) the governing body of the school in question;

(b) any trustees holding property on trust for the purposes of the school;

(c) in the case of a Church of England, Church in Wales or Roman Catholic Church school, the appropriate diocesan authority; and

(d) such other persons as he considers appropriate.

(3) Any modification made by an order under this section may be made so as to have permanent effect or to have effect for such period as is specified in the order.

S. 82

The Secretary of State may modify the trust deed applicable to any foundation, foundation special or voluntary school or to any land held on trust for such a school ass he thinks fit in connection with the operation of any part of the Act. He must consult with the relevant interested parties. The modification may be permanent or temporary.

83.–(1) Where any provision of a trust deed or other instrument made before 1st July 1981 would, apart from this subsection, have the effect that the persons who are for the time being governors of a foundation or voluntary school were by virtue of their office trustees of any property held for the purposes of, or in connection with, the school, that provision shall instead have effect as if the only governors of the school were-

(a) the foundation governors,

(b) those appointed by the local education authority, and

(c) any co-opted governor nominated by a minor authority.

(2) Subsection (1) is without prejudice to any power to amend any such provision as is mentioned in that subsection.

> **S. 83**
> *If a trust deed made before 1st July 1981 relating to a foundation or voluntary school would have the effect of making the school governors trustees of any property held for the school, only the foundation governors, those appointed by the local education authority and any co-opted governor representing a minor authority shall be treated as trustees. "Minor authority" is defined in S. 141.*

PART III SCHOOL ADMISSIONS

CHAPTER I Admission arrangements

Code of practice

84.–(1) The Secretary of State shall issue, and may from time to time revise, a code of practice containing such practical guidance as he thinks appropriate in respect of the discharge by-

(a) local education authorities,

(b) the governing bodies of maintained schools,

(c) appeal panels, and

(d) adjudicators,

of their respective functions under this Chapter.

(2) The code may include guidelines setting out aims, objectives and other matters in relation to the discharge of their functions under this Chapter by local education authorities and such governing bodies.

(3) It shall be the duty of-

(a) each of the bodies and persons mentioned in subsection (1) when exercising functions under this Chapter, and

(b) any other person when exercising any function for the purposes of the discharge by a local education authority, or the governing body of a maintained school, of functions under this Chapter,

to have regard to any relevant provisions of the code.

(4) The Secretary of State shall publish the code as for the time being in force.

(5) The Secretary of State may under subsection (1)-

(a) make separate provision (by means of separate codes of practice) in relation to different functions under this Chapter of the bodies and persons mentioned in that subsection;

(b) make different provision for England and for Wales (whether or not by means of separate codes of practice);

and references in this section to "the code" or to functions under this Chapter shall have effect, in relation to any such separate code of practice, as references to that code or to functions under this Chapter to which it relates (as the case may be).

(6) In this Chapter-

"admission arrangements" and "the admission authority" have the meaning given by section 88;

"appeal panel" means a panel constituted under Schedule 24 or 25 for the purpose of hearing an appeal under this Chapter;

"child" (except in sections 96 and 97) includes a person who has not attained the age of 19;

"maintained school" means a community, foundation or voluntary school;

"the relevant standard number", in relation to a maintained school, a relevant age group and a school year, means the standard number applying under Schedule 23 to the school in relation to that age group and year.

S. 84

The Secretary of State may issue a Code of Practice (which may be in more than one part and apply differently in Wales to England) dealing with and giving practical guidance on all aspects of admission to maintained schools and appeals against refusal to admit. The Code may set out aims and objectives for those involved in admissions decisions. The Code of Practice will apply to local education authorities, governing bodies, appeal panels and adjudicators and all concerned must have regard to its provisions.

85.-(1) Where the Secretary of State proposes to issue or revise a code of practice under section 84, he shall prepare a draft of the code (or revised code).

(2) The Secretary of State shall consult such persons about the draft as he thinks fit and shall consider any representations made by them.

(3) If he determines to proceed with the draft (either in its original form or with such modifications as he thinks fit) he shall lay a copy of the draft before each House of Parliament.

(4) If, within the 40-day period, either House resolves not to approve the draft, the Secretary of State shall take no further steps in relation to the proposed code.

(5) If no such resolution is made within the 40-day period, the Secretary of State shall issue the code (or revised code) in the form of the draft, and it shall come into force on such date as the Secretary of State may by order appoint.

(6) Subsection (4) does not prevent a new draft of a proposed code from being laid before Parliament.

(7) In this section "40-day period", in relation to the draft of a proposed code, means-

(a) if the draft is laid before one House on a day later than the day on which it is laid before the other House, the period of 40 days beginning with the later of the two days, and

(b) in any other case, the period of 40 days beginning with the day on which the draft is laid before each House,

no account being taken of any period during which Parliament is dissolved or prorogued or during which both Houses are adjourned for more than four days.

(8) In this section references to a proposed code include a proposed revised code.

S. 85

Where the Secretary of State proposes to issue a Code of Practice or revise an existing one, he must consult as he thinks fit, consider representations and then lay a copy of the proposed Code before Parliament. It is then subject to negative resolution, i.e. if either House of Parliament resolves not to approve the draft the Secretary of State cannot issue it (although he can go through the process again with a fresh draft) but in the absence of such a resolution within 40 days (excluding recesses or periods when Parliament is dissolved) the Code is to be issued.

Parental preferences

86.–(1) A local education authority shall make arrangements for enabling the parent of a child in the area of the authority-

(a) to express a preference as to the school at which he wishes education to be provided for his child in the exercise of the authority's functions, and

(b) to give reasons for his preference.

S. 86 (1)

Arrangements must be made by the local education authority to enable parents to express their preference for the school they wish their child to go to and to give reasons for that preference. The preference may be expressed to the governing body where the governing body deals with admissions - see S. 86 (7).

(2) Subject to subsections (3) and (6) and section 87 (children excluded from two or more schools), a local education authority and the governing body of a

maintained school shall comply with any preference expressed in accordance with arrangements made under subsection (1).

(3) The duty imposed by subsection (2) does not apply-

(a) if compliance with the preference would prejudice the provision of efficient education or the efficient use of resources;

(b) if the preferred school is a foundation or voluntary aided school and compliance with the preference would be incompatible with any special arrangements under section 91 (admission arrangements to preserve the religious character of a foundation or voluntary aided school); or

(c) if the arrangements for admission to the preferred school-

(i) are wholly based on selection by reference to ability or aptitude, and

(ii) are so based with a view to admitting only pupils with high ability or with aptitude,

and compliance with the preference would be incompatible with selection under those arrangements.

S. 86 (2) and (3)

The preference must be complied with unless

- *compliance would prejudice the provision of efficient education or the efficient use of resources ("prejudice")*

- *the school is a foundation or voluntary aided school with a religious character that has special arrangements (see S. 91) to preserve that character and compliance would be incompatible with those arrangements*

- *the school is a selective school and compliance would be incompatible with the arrangements for selection. S. 86 (9) makes it clear that the fact that a school that only admits pupils of by reference to ability or aptitude is to be regarded as a selective school even though over-subscription criteria may not be related to ability or aptitude, for example where preference is given to siblings or those living nearest the school.*

- *the child has been excluded twice from a school and S. 87 applies*

The duty to comply with parental preference applies equally to applications from parents from a different local education authority and to applications by parents for a particular school to be named in a school attendance order - see S. 86 (8).

---

(4) For the purposes of subsection (3)(a) prejudice of the kind referred to in that provision may arise by reason of measures required to be taken in order to ensure compliance with the duty imposed by section 1(6) (duty of local education authority and governing body to comply with limit on infant class sizes).

(5) No prejudice shall, however, be taken to arise for the purposes of subsection (3)(a) from the admission to a maintained school in a school year of a number of pupils in a relevant age group which does not exceed-

    (a) the relevant standard number, or

    (b) the admission number fixed in accordance with section 93,

whichever is the greater.

> **S. 86 (4) and (5)**
> *Prejudice may be deemed to arise if complying with the preference would be contrary to arrangements designed to restrict infant class sizes. Apart from this, no prejudice is deemed to arise unless the school has admitted up to whichever is the higher of its standard number or its admission number.*

(6) Where-

    (a) the admission arrangements for two or more maintained schools provide for co-ordinated admissions on the part of those schools, and

    (b) they are approved by the Secretary of State for the purposes of this subsection,

they shall have effect in relation to each of those schools despite anything in subsection (2).

(7) Where the arrangements for the admission of pupils to a maintained school provide for applications for admission to be made to (or to a person acting on behalf of) the governing body of the school, a parent who makes such an application shall be regarded for the purposes of this section as having expressed a preference for that school in accordance with arrangements made under subsection (1).

(8) The duty imposed by subsection (2) in relation to a preference expressed in accordance with arrangements made under subsection (1) shall apply also in relation to-

    (a) any application for the admission to a maintained school of a child who is not in the area of the authority maintaining the school, and

    (b) any application made by a parent as mentioned in section 438(4) or 440(2) of the Education Act 1996 (application for a particular school to be named in a school attendance order);

and references in subsection (3) to a preference and a preferred school shall be construed accordingly.

(9) Where admission arrangements for a school provide for all pupils admitted to the school to be selected by reference to ability or aptitude, those arrangements shall be taken for the purposes of this section to be wholly based on selection by reference to ability or aptitude, whether or not they also provide for the use of additional criteria in circumstances where the number of children in a relevant age group who are assessed to be of the requisite ability or aptitude is greater than the number of pupils which it is intended to admit to the school in that age group.

87.–(1) The duty imposed by section 86(2) does not apply in the case of a child to whom subsection (2) below applies.

(2) Where a child has been permanently excluded from two or more schools, this subsection applies to him during the period of two years beginning with the date on which the latest of those exclusions took effect.

(3) Subsection (2) applies to a child whatever the length of the period or periods elapsing between those exclusions and regardless of whether it has applied to him on a previous occasion.

(4) However, a child shall not be regarded as permanently excluded from a school for the purposes of this section if-

(a) although so excluded he was reinstated as a pupil at the school following the giving of a direction to that effect to the head teacher of the school; or

(b) he was so excluded at a time when he had not attained compulsory school age.

(5) In this section "school" means-

(a) in relation to any time before or after the appointed day, a school maintained by a local education authority; or

(b) in relation to any time before the appointed day, a grant-maintained or grant-maintained special school within the meaning of the Education Act 1996.

(6) For the purposes of this section the permanent exclusion of a child from a school shall be regarded as having taken effect on the school day as from which the head teacher decided that he should be permanently excluded.

(7) Nothing in this section applies to a child unless at least one of the two or more exclusions mentioned in subsection (2) took effect on or after 1st September 1997.

S. 87

If a child has been permanently excluded from more than one school, and at least one was on or after 1st September 1997, then for two years after the later of the two exclusions the parental right to express a preference and have it complied with does not apply. Exclusions that took place before the child was of compulsory school age, and exclusions where the child was subsequently reinstated do not count. For the purposes of this section, a permanent exclusion takes effect on the school day when the headteacher decides to permanently exclude.

Admission arrangements

88.–(1) In this Chapter "the admission authority"-

(a) in relation to a community or voluntary controlled school, means-

(i) the local education authority, or

(ii) where with the governing body's agreement the authority have delegated to them responsibility for determining the admission arrangements for the school, the governing body; and

(b) in relation to a foundation or voluntary aided school, means the governing body.

(2) In this Chapter "admission arrangements", in relation to a maintained school, means the arrangements for the admission of pupils to the school, including the school's admission policy.

S. 88
This section defines admission authorities as the local education authority for community and voluntary controlled schools and the governing body of foundation and voluntary aided schools. Where the local education authority has delegated responsibility for admissions to the governing body of a community or voluntary controlled school then the governing body is the admission authority for that school.

89.–(1) The admission authority for a maintained school shall, before the beginning of each school year, determine in accordance with this section the admission arrangements which are to apply for that year.

(2) Before determining the admission arrangements which are to apply for a particular school year, the admission authority shall consult the following about the proposed arrangements, namely-

(a) the local education authority (where the governing body are the admission authority),

(b) the admission authorities for all other maintained schools in the relevant area or for such class of such schools as may be prescribed, and

(c) the admission authorities for maintained schools of any prescribed description.

(3) In subsection (2) "the relevant area" means-

(a) the area of the local education authority; or

(b) if regulations so provide, such other area (whether more or less extensive than the area of the local education authority) as may be determined by or in accordance with the regulations.

(4) Once the admission authority have carried out any such consultation, the authority shall-

(a) determine that their proposed arrangements (either in their original form or with such modifications as the authority think fit) shall be the admission arrangements for the school year in question; and

(b) (except in such cases as may be prescribed) notify the bodies whom they consulted under subsection (2) of those admission arrangements.

S. 89 (1) to (4)
Each admission authority must, before the beginning of each school year, determine the admission arrangements to apply in that year. Before doing so, it must consult with other admission authorities as prescribed by regulations within a prescribed area. After the consultation, the arrangements, either as proposed or with modifications, are to be finally determined and notified to the consultees.

(5) Where an admission authority-

    (a) have in accordance with subsection (4) determined the admission arrangements which are to apply for a particular school year, but

    (b) at any time before the end of that year consider that the arrangements should be varied in view of a major change in circumstances occurring since they were so determined,

the authority shall (except in a case where their proposed variations fall within any description of variations prescribed for the purposes of this subsection) refer the proposed variations to the adjudicator, and shall (in every case) notify the bodies whom they consulted under subsection (2) of the proposed variations.

(6) The adjudicator shall consider whether the arrangements should have effect with those variations until the end of that year; and if he determines that the arrangements should so have effect or that they should so have effect subject to such modification of those variations as he may determine-

    (a) the arrangements shall have effect accordingly as from the date of his determination; and

    (b) the admission authority shall (except in such cases as may be prescribed) notify the bodies whom they consulted under subsection (2) of the variations subject to which the arrangements are to have effect.

(7) In relation to a maintained school in Wales any reference to the adjudicator in subsection (5) or (6) shall be read as a reference to the Secretary of State.

S. 89 (5) to (7)
If an admission authority wishes to change admission arrangements during the year to which they relate because of a major change in circumstances, it must refer the proposed changes to the adjudicator (in Wales to the Secretary of State) who will decide the extent, if at all, that the change may be made. Again. the consultees must be notified.

(8) Regulations may make provision-

    (a) specifying matters to which any consultation required by subsection (2) is, or is not, to relate;

    (b) as to the manner in which, and the time by which, any such consultation is to be carried out;

    (c) as to the manner in which, and the time by which, any notification required by this section is to be given;

    (d) specifying matters which are, or are not, to constitute major changes in circumstances for the purposes of subsection (5)(b);

    (e) authorising an admission authority, where they have in accordance with subsection (4) determined the admission arrangements which are to apply for a particular school year, to vary those arrangements to such extent or in such circumstances as may be prescribed;

(f) for the application of any of the requirements of subsections (5) and (6) to variations proposed to be made by virtue of paragraph (e), or to any prescribed description of such variations, as if they were variations proposed to be made under subsection (5);

(g) as to such other matters connected with the procedure for determining or varying admission arrangements under this section as the Secretary of State considers appropriate.

> **S. 89 (8)**
> *Regulations deal with the detail relating to consultation, notification and other matters covered by this section.*

(9) Where the local education authority are the admission authority for a community or voluntary controlled school, they shall-

(a) when preparing for consultation under subsection (2) their proposed arrangements for any school year, consult the governing body about the admission arrangements which the authority may propose for the school; and

(b) in addition consult the governing body before making any reference under subsection (5).

> **S. 89 (9)**
> *The local education authority must consult with the governing body of each community and voluntary controlled school for which it is the admission authority regarding its proposed admission arrangements for that school.*

90.–(1) Where-

(a) admission arrangements have been determined by an admission authority under section 89(4), but

(b) a body consulted by the admission authority under section 89(2) wish to make an objection about those arrangements, and

(c) the objection does not fall within any description of objections prescribed for the purposes of this paragraph,

that body may refer the objection to the adjudicator.

(2) Where-

(a) admission arrangements have been determined by an admission authority under section 89(4), but

(b) any parent of a prescribed description wishes to make an objection about those arrangements, and

(c) the objection falls within any description of objections prescribed for the purposes of this paragraph,

that person may refer the objection to the adjudicator.

(3) On a reference under subsection (1) or (2) the adjudicator shall either-

    (a) decide whether, and (if so) to what extent, the objection should be upheld, or

    (b) in such cases as may be prescribed, refer the objection to the Secretary of State for that question to be decided by him.

(4) Where the objection is referred to the Secretary of State under subsection (3)(b), the adjudicator shall, if the Secretary of State so requests, give his advice on the question referred to in that provision.

(5) In relation to a maintained school in Wales-

    (a) the reference to the adjudicator in subsection (1) or (2) shall be read as a reference to the Secretary of State;

    (b) subsections (3) and (4) shall not apply; and

    (c) where any objection is referred to the Secretary of State by virtue of paragraph (a) above, he shall decide whether, and (if so) to what extent, the objection should be upheld.

(6) Where the adjudicator or the Secretary of State decides that an objection referred to him under this section should be upheld to any extent, his decision on the objection may specify the modifications that are to be made to the admission arrangements in question.

(7) In the case of any objection referred to him under this section, the adjudicator or the Secretary of State (as the case may be) shall publish his decision on the objection and the reasons for it.

(8) The decision of the adjudicator or the Secretary of State on the objection shall, in relation to the admission arrangements in question, be binding on the admission authority and on all persons by whom an objection about those arrangements may be made under subsection (1) or (2); and if that decision is to uphold the objection to any extent, those arrangements shall forthwith be revised by the admission authority in such a way as to give effect to the decision.

(9) Regulations may make provision-

    (a) as to any conditions which must be satisfied before-

        (i) an objection can be referred to the adjudicator or the Secretary of State under subsection (1) or (2), or

        (ii) the adjudicator or the Secretary of State is required to determine an objection referred to him under subsection (2);

    (b) prescribing the steps which may be taken by an admission authority where an objection has been referred to the adjudicator or the Secretary of State under subsection (1) or (2) but has not yet been determined;

    (c) as to the manner in which any matters required to be published under subsection (7) are to be published;

    (d) requiring such matters to be notified to such persons, and in such manner, as may be prescribed;

(e) prohibiting or restricting the reference under subsection (1) or (2), within such period following a decision by the adjudicator or the Secretary of State under this section as may be prescribed, of any objection raising the same (or substantially the same) issues in relation to the admission arrangements of the school in question;

(f) prescribing circumstances in which an admission authority may revise the admission arrangements for their school in the light of any decision by the adjudicator or the Secretary of State relating to the admission arrangements for another school, and the procedure to be followed in such a case.

(10) Regulations shall make provision for the cases to be referred to the Secretary of State under subsection (3)(b) to include cases where the objection is concerned with admissions criteria relating to a person's religion or religious denomination.

S. 90

Objections to proposed admission arrangements may be made by an admission authority, or by parents in limited circumstances, to the adjudicator in England or to the Secretary of State in Wales. The adjudicator may decide whether and to what extent the objection should be upheld and how, in consequence, an admission arrangement should be modified. The Secretary of State may prescribe that certain types of objections (which must include admissions criteria relating to religion or religious denomination) be dealt with by the Secretary of State and not by the adjudicator. The adjudicator also has the power to refer objections to the Secretary of State who in turn may seek the adjudicator's advice. Decisions of the adjudicator or Secretary of State are binding on the admission authority which then has to revise admission arrangements accordingly. The adjudicator, or the Secretary of State, must publish his decision on any objection and give reasons. Regulations deal with the detailed procedure.

91.–(1) This section makes provision for the inclusion in the admission arrangements for a foundation or voluntary aided school which has a religious character of arrangements in respect of the admission of pupils to the school for preserving the religious character of the school ("special arrangements").

(2) Where any special arrangements desired by the governing body of such a school are agreed to by the local education authority-

(a) the governing body may incorporate them in the proposed admission arrangements for a school year which are subject to consultation under section 89(2); and

(b) if the governing body do so, subsection (1) of section 90 shall apply to any objection about the special arrangements which-

(i) is made by any of the admission authorities consulted under section 89(2)(b) or (c), and

(ii) falls within that subsection,

as it applies to any other objection falling within that subsection.

(3) Where any special arrangements desired by the governing body of such a school are not agreed to by the local education authority-

    (a) the governing body may incorporate a draft of any such arrangements in the proposed admission arrangements for a school year which are subject to consultation under section 89(2); but

    (b) if the governing body do so-

        (i) they shall refer the draft arrangements to the adjudicator, and

        (ii) they shall not determine to adopt those arrangements for inclusion in the admission arrangements for the school unless (and to the extent that) the adjudicator or the Secretary of State decide under this section that they may do so, and

        (iii) any of the bodies consulted under section 89(2) may make an objection in the prescribed manner to the adjudicator about the draft arrangements.

(4) On such a reference the adjudicator shall either-

    (a) decide whether (having regard to any objections received by him under subsection (3)) the draft arrangements may be adopted by the governing body, whether with or without modification, or

    (b) in such cases as may be prescribed, refer the draft arrangements (and any objections so received) to the Secretary of State for that question to be decided by him.

(5) Where the draft arrangements are referred to the Secretary of State under subsection (4)(b), the adjudicator shall, if the Secretary of State so requests, give his advice on the question referred to in that provision.

(6) In relation to a maintained school in Wales-

    (a) any reference to the adjudicator in subsection (3)(b)(i) or (iii) shall be read as a reference to the Secretary of State;

    (b) subsections (4) and (5) shall not apply; and

    (c) where any draft arrangements are referred to the Secretary of State by virtue of paragraph (a) above, he shall decide whether (having regard to any objections received by him by virtue of that paragraph) the draft arrangements may be adopted by the governing body, whether with or without modification.

(7) In the case of any draft arrangements referred to him under this section, the adjudicator or the Secretary of State (as the case may be) shall publish his decision on the reference and the reasons for it.

(8) The decision of the adjudicator or the Secretary of State on any such reference shall, in relation to the draft arrangements in question, be binding on the governing body and on all the bodies whom they consulted under section 89(2).

(9) Regulations under section 90(3)(b) or (9) shall apply in relation to references and objections made under this section with such modifications as may be prescribed.

(10) Where a governing body have, in accordance with the preceding provisions of this section (and, so far as applicable, sections 89 and 90), determined that the admission arrangements for their school should include any special arrangements, those provisions shall apply, with any necessary modifications, on any subsequent occasion-

    (a) when the governing body desire to modify those special arrangements; or

    (b) where the local education authority agreed to any such arrangements, when the authority withdraw their agreement to those arrangements or any part of them, whether with a view to seeking any modification of them or otherwise.

> **S. 91**
>
> *Special arrangements may be agreed between the governing body of a foundation or voluntary aided school which has a religious character that are intended to preserve the religious character of the school. Those arrangements must be consulted on as part of the school's overall admission arrangements and objections may be taken to the adjudicator or Secretary of State. If the local education authority does not agree to what the school proposes then the school may include the draft proposals in its admission arrangements but must refer them to the adjudicator who may decide whether to approve them (with or without modifications) or refer them to the Secretary of State in prescribed cases. The process is essentially the same as under S. 90.*

92.–(1) A local education authority shall, for each school year, publish the prescribed information about-

    (a) the admission arrangements for each of the following, namely-

        (i) the maintained schools in their area, and

        (ii) if regulations so provide, such maintained schools outside their area as may be determined by or in accordance with the regulations;

    (b) the authority's arrangements for the provision of education at schools maintained by another local education authority or not maintained by a local education authority;

    (c) the arrangements made by the authority under sections 86(1) (parental preferences) and 94(1) (admission appeals); and

    (d) such other matters of interest to parents of pupils seeking admission to schools within paragraph (a) or (b) above as may be prescribed.

(2) The governing body of a foundation or voluntary aided school shall, for each school year, publish the prescribed information about-

    (a) the admission arrangements for the school;

    (b) the arrangements made by the governing body under section 94(2) (admission appeals); and

    (c) such other matters of interest to parents of pupils seeking admission to the school as may be prescribed.

(3) The governing body of a school maintained by a local education authority-

    (a) shall publish such information as respects that school as may be required by regulations; and

    (b) may publish such other information with respect to the school as they think fit.

(4) For the purposes of subsection (3) information about the continuing education of pupils leaving a school, or the employment or training taken up by such pupils on leaving, is to be treated as information about the school.

(5) A local education authority may, with the agreement of the governing body of any school maintained by the authority, publish on behalf of the governing body the information referred to in subsection (2) or (3).

(6) Regulations may make provision as to-

    (a) the procedure to be followed by a local education authority before publishing information under subsection (1); and

    (b) the time by which, and the manner in which, information required to be published under any provision of this section is to be published.

S. 92

This section requires the local education authority and schools to publish, in accordance with regulations, information about admission arrangements and about the school.

Admission numbers

93.–(1) The admission authority for a maintained school shall not fix as the admission number for any relevant age group and any school year a number which is less than the relevant standard number.

(2) Subject to section 1(6) (duty of local education authority and governing body to comply with limit on infant class sizes), the admission authority may fix as the admission number for any relevant age group and any school year a number which exceeds the relevant standard number.

(3) Schedule 23 (determination, variation and review of standard numbers) shall have effect.

S. 93 (1) to (3)

Every existing school has a "standard number" determined under previous legislation and every new school will have a specified standard number as part of the proposals to establish it. That standard number is the minimum number of pupils that the school must admit but an admission authority can set a higher "admission number". The higher of the two numbers is (subject to the requirement to limit infant class sizes) the number that the school will admit to the relevant year group. Schedule 23 deals with the setting varying and review of standard numbers.

(4) A proposal may be made to the admission authority in accordance with subsection (5) by whichever of the governing body and the local education authority are not the admission authority for fixing as the admission number for any relevant age group and any school year a number which exceeds both-

(a) the relevant standard number, and

(b) any admission number fixed, or proposed to be fixed, for that age group and year by the admission authority.

(5) Any such proposal-

(a) shall be made in writing,

(b) may relate to one or more relevant age groups, and

(c) may relate to a particular school year or to each school year falling within any period specified in the proposal.

(6) If the admission authority do not give the body making the proposal notice in writing rejecting the proposal within the period of two months beginning with the day after that on which the proposal was received by the admission authority, the admission authority shall give effect to the proposal.

(7) Where the admission authority give such notice within that period, the body making the proposal may, within 28 days of receiving the notice, make an application under paragraph 4(3) or 8(3) (as the case may be) of Schedule 23 for a decision increasing the relevant standard number.

> **S. 93 (4) to (7)**
> *A proposal to increase the admission number may be made by the governing body of a school where the local education authority is the admission authority and by the local education authority where the governing body is the admission authority. If the admission authority does not reject the proposal within two months then the admission number will be increased. If the proposal is rejected then the proposer may apply to the school organisation committee (in England) or the Secretary of State (in Wales) in accordance with Schedule 23 for a determination.*

(8) Regulations may provide for the operation of subsection (1) and section 86(5) to be suspended to such extent as the Secretary of State considers appropriate for the purpose of enabling-

(a) admission authorities to review under paragraph 11 of Schedule 23 any standard number applicable to admissions to an infant class at any maintained school, and

(b) any application to reduce any such number under paragraph 4(4) or 8(4) (as the case may be) of that Schedule to be decided in accordance with that Schedule,

following the coming into force of regulations under section 1 by virtue of which any limit on class sizes is to apply, or be varied, in relation to any such class.

(9) Regulations under subsection (8) may provide for any suspension to apply-

    (a) in relation to such age groups,

    (b) for such period, and

    (c) subject to such conditions,

as may be specified in the regulations; and in that subsection "infant class" has the meaning given by section 4.

> **S. 93 (8) and (9)**
> *Regulations may enable the Secretary of State to suspend the standard number provisions as he thinks appropriate to enable infant class size limits to be achieved.*

(10) In this section references, in relation to a school, to the "admission number" for any relevant age group and any school year are references to the number of pupils in that age group it is intended to admit to the school in that school year.

Admission appeals

94.–(1) A local education authority shall make arrangements for enabling the parent of a child to appeal against-

    (a) any decision made by or on behalf of the authority as to the school at which education is to be provided for the child in the exercise of the authority's functions, other than a decision leading to or embodied in a direction under section 96 (directions for admission), and

    (b) in the case of a community or voluntary controlled school maintained by the authority, any decision made by or on behalf of the governing body refusing the child admission to the school.

(2) The governing body of a foundation or voluntary aided school shall make arrangements for enabling the parent of a child to appeal against any decision made by or on behalf of the governing body refusing the child admission to the school.

(3) Joint arrangements may be made under subsection (2) by the governing bodies of two or more foundation or voluntary aided schools maintained by the same local education authority.

(4) A local education authority and the governing body or bodies of one or more foundation or voluntary aided schools maintained by the authority may make joint arrangements consisting of-

    (a) such of the arrangements made by the authority in pursuance of subsection (1) as the authority may determine; and

    (b) arrangements made by the governing body or bodies in pursuance of subsection (2).

(5) Schedule 24 has effect in relation to the making and hearing of appeals pursuant to arrangements made under this section.

(6) The decision of an appeal panel on an appeal under Schedule 24 shall be binding on-

(a) the local education authority or the governing body by whom or on whose behalf the decision under appeal was made, and

(b) in the case of a decision made by or on behalf of a local education authority, the governing body of a community or voluntary controlled school at which the appeal panel determines that a place should be offered to the child in question.

S. 94
Parents have a right of appeal against a refusal to admit a child to a school unless the child is a twice-excluded child to whom S. 87 applies. The arrangements for appeals must be made by the local education authority in relation to community and voluntary controlled schools and by the governing body in relation to foundation and voluntary aided schools. Joint arrangements are permitted. The detailed procedure is set out in Schedule 24 and appeal decisions bind the local education authority and the relevant school.

95.–(1) Nothing in section 94(1) or (2) requires any arrangements to be made for enabling the parent of a child to appeal against a decision-

(a) made by or on behalf of the admission authority for a maintained school, and
(b) refusing the child admission to the school,

in a case where, at the time when the decision is made, section 87(2) applies to the child.

(2) Where a local education authority are the admission authority for a community or voluntary controlled school, the authority shall make arrangements for enabling the governing body of the school to appeal against any decision made by or on behalf of the authority to admit to the school a child to whom, at the time when the decision is made, section 87(2) applies.

(3) Schedule 25 has effect in relation to the making and hearing of appeals pursuant to arrangements made under subsection (2).

(4) The decision of an appeal panel on an appeal made pursuant to arrangements under subsection (2) shall be binding on the local education authority and the governing body.

S. 95
Parents of a twice-excluded child to whom S. 87 applies have no right of appeal and the local education authority must make arrangements for a community or voluntary controlled school to appeal against any decision by the local education authority to admit such a child to that school. Schedule 25 applies to such appeals. Again, appeal decisions bind the local education authority and the relevant school.

Power to direct admission of child to school

96.–(1) The local education authority may give a direction under this section if, in the case of any child in their area, either (or both) of the following conditions is satisfied in relation to each school which is a reasonable distance from his home and provides suitable education, that is-

(a) he has been refused admission to the school, or

(b) he is permanently excluded from the school.

(2) A direction under this section shall specify a school-

(a) which is a reasonable distance from the child's home, and

(b) from which the child is not permanently excluded.

(3) A direction under this section shall, unless it is given on the determination of the Secretary of State under section 97(4), specify a school in the area referred to in subsection (1).

(4) A direction under this section to admit a child shall not specify a school if his admission would result in prejudice of the kind referred to in section 86(3)(a) by reason of measures required to be taken as mentioned in subsection (4) of that section.

(5) Where a school is specified in a direction under this section, the governing body shall admit the child to the school.

(6) Subsection (5) does not affect any power to exclude from a school a pupil who is already a registered pupil there.

(7) In this section "suitable education", in relation to a child, means efficient full-time education suitable to his age, ability and aptitude and to any special educational needs he may have.

(8) In this section and section 97 "school" means a maintained school.

S. 96

The local education authority has power to direct a child to a specified school n certain circumstances. The power only arises if the child has been refused admission to or has been permanently excluded from every suitable school within a reasonable distance from the home. The school must be one that is suitable to the age, ability and aptitude of the child (and any special educational needs) and must (unless the Secretary of State directs otherwise) be within the area of the local education authority. It must be within reasonable distance of the home and must be one from which the child has not been permanently excluded. The direction must not cause infant class limits to be exceeded.

97.–(1) Before deciding to give a direction under section 96, the local education authority shall consult-

(a) the parent of the child, and

(b) the governing body of the school they propose to specify in the direction.

(2) Where the local education authority decide to give such a direction specifying any school-

    (a) they shall, before doing so, serve a notice in writing of their decision on the governing body and head teacher of the school, and

    (b) they shall not give the direction until the period for referring the matter to the Secretary of State under subsection (3) has expired and, if it is so referred, the Secretary of State has made his determination.

(3) The governing body may, within the period of 15 days beginning with the day on which the notice was served, refer the matter to the Secretary of State and, if they do so, shall inform the local education authority.

(4) On a reference under subsection (3) the Secretary of State may determine which school is to be required to admit the child and, if he does so, that school shall be specified in the direction.

(5) The Secretary of State shall not make a determination under subsection (4) in relation to a school if the child's admission to the school would result in prejudice of the kind referred to in section 86(3)(a) by reason of measures required to be taken as mentioned in subsection (4) of that section.

(6) Where the local education authority give a direction specifying a school, they shall give notice in writing of that fact to the governing body and head teacher of the school.

> **S. 97**
> *Before making a direction under S. 96 the local education authority must consult the parent and the governing body of the school it proposes to name. It must then give the governing body and the headteacher written notice of its decision. The school has 15 days in which to refer the matter to the Secretary of State and the local education authority cannot implement it until that period has passed and (if relevant) the Secretary of State has ruled which school should admit the child.*

Nursery and special schools, etc: children with statements

98.–(1) Children admitted to a school for nursery education and subsequently transferred to a reception class at the school shall be regarded for the purposes of this Chapter as admitted to the school (otherwise than for nursery education) on being so transferred.

(2) The admission of children to a school for nursery education shall be disregarded for the purpose of-

    (a) applying in relation to a primary school any provision of section 93 or Schedule 23 which refers to the number of pupils admitted or intended to be admitted to a school in any school year, or

(b) determining for the purposes of any provision of section 93 or Schedule 23 what is a relevant age group in relation to a primary school.

(3) Subject to subsection (4), nothing in this Chapter applies in relation to-

(a) nursery schools, or

(b) children who will be under compulsory school age at the time of their proposed admission.

(4) Where the arrangements for the admission of pupils to a maintained school provide for the admission to the school of children who will be under compulsory school age at the time of their proposed admission, this Chapter shall apply in relation to the admission of such pupils to the school otherwise than for nursery education.

(5) Regulations may make provision in connection with the arrangements for the admission of pupils to community or foundation special schools, and for the allocation between the local education authority and the governing body of such a school of functions in connection with such arrangements.

(6) Apart from section 92(3) to (6) and subsection (5) above, nothing in this Chapter applies in relation to special schools.

(7) Subject to subsections (8) and (9), nothing in this Chapter applies in relation to children for whom statements of special educational needs are maintained under section 324 of the Education Act 1996.

(8) Any provision made by, or (as the case may be) by virtue of, section 84 or 92(3) to (6) or this section applies, or (as the case may be) may be made so as to apply, in relation to such children.

(9) Such children shall, in addition, be taken into account for the purposes of-

(a) the reference in section 86(5) or (9) to a number of pupils, and

(b) the fixing of admission numbers under section 93 and the determination, variation and review of standard numbers under Schedule 23.

(10) In subsection (8) the reference to any provision made by this section includes a reference to subsection (4) only so far as it has effect for the purposes mentioned in subsection (9).

S. 98

Nothing in the provisions relating to admission to schools applies to children admitted for nursery education (unless and until they are transferred to a reception class) or to special schools or to children with statements of special educational needs. However, such children are to be counted in relation to pupil numbers where relevant to the question of prejudice and in connection with standard numbers and admission numbers.

CHAPTER II SELECTION OF PUPILS

Partial selection

99.–(1) No admission arrangements for a maintained school may make provision for selection by ability unless-

(a) they make provision for a permitted form of such selection; or

(b) the school is a grammar school (as defined by section 104(7)).

(2) The following are permitted forms of selection by ability-

(a) any selection by ability authorised by section 100 (pre-existing arrangements);

(b) any selection by ability authorised by section 101 (pupil banding); and

(c) any selection by ability conducted in connection with the admission of pupils to the school for secondary education suitable to the requirements of pupils who are over compulsory school age.

(3) No admission arrangements for a maintained school may make provision for selection by aptitude unless they make provision for a permitted form of such selection.

(4) The following are permitted forms of selection by aptitude-

(a) any selection by aptitude authorised by section 100 (pre-existing arrangements); and

(b) any selection by aptitude authorised by section 102 (aptitude for particular subjects).

(5) For the purposes of this Chapter-

(a) a school's admission arrangements make provision for selection by ability or by aptitude if they make provision for all or any of the pupils who are to be admitted to the school in any relevant age group to be so admitted by reference to ability or to aptitude (as the case may be);

(b) "ability" means either general ability or ability in any particular subject or subjects;

(c) "admission arrangements" has the meaning given by section 88(2); and

(d) "maintained school" means a community, foundation or voluntary school.

S. 99

Admission arrangements that provide (wholly or in part) for selection by ability are permissible only for schools designated as grammar schools under S. 104 or if the form of selection is permitted either under S. 100 or S. 101 or relate to admission of pupils over compulsory school age, i.e. into Sixth Forms.

Similarly, admission arrangements that provide (wholly or in part) for selection by aptitude are permissible only if the form of selection is permitted under S. 100 or S. 102.

"Ability" is defined as being ability generally or ability in particular subjects.
"Aptitude" is not defined.

100.–(1) Where at the beginning of the 1997-98 school year the admission arrangements for a maintained school made provision for selection by ability or by aptitude (and they have at all times since that date continued to do so), the admission arrangements for the school may continue to make such provision so long as there is, as compared with the arrangements in force at the beginning of that year-

(a) no increase in the proportion of selective admissions in any relevant age group, and

(b) no significant change in the basis of selection.

(2) In relation to any time before the appointed day, the reference in subsection (1) to a maintained school is a reference to the school as a county, voluntary or grant-maintained school within the meaning of the Education Act 1996.

(3) In this section "the proportion of selective admissions", in relation to a relevant age group, means the proportion of the total number of pupils admitted to the school in that age group (determined in the prescribed manner) which is represented by the number of pupils so admitted by reference to ability or to aptitude (as the case may be).

(4) Nothing in this section applies to a school with selective admission arrangements (as defined by section 104(2)).

> **S. 100**
> *A school (other than a grammar school) that admitted pupils by reference to ability or aptitude at the beginning of the 1997/98 school year and has done so continuously since then may continue to do so but may not increase the proportion of pupils selected in that way or make a significant change to the basis of selection. Note, however, S. 103.*

101.–(1) Subject to subsections (2) to (4), the admission arrangements for a maintained school may make provision for selection by ability to the extent that the arrangements are designed to secure-

(a) that in any year the pupils admitted to the school in any relevant age group are representative of all levels of ability among applicants for admission to the school in that age group, and

(b) that no level of ability is substantially over-represented or substantially under-represented.

(2) Subsection (1) does not apply if the arrangements have the effect that, where an applicant for admission has been allocated to a particular range of ability by means of some process of selection by reference to ability, some further such process is required or authorised to be carried out in relation to him for the purpose of determining whether or not he is to be admitted to the school.

(3) The introduction for a maintained school of admission arrangements to which subsection (1) applies shall be one of the alterations to such a school which are prescribed for the purposes of section 28.

(4) Such arrangements are not authorised for any school by this section unless proposals for the school to have such arrangements have been published under section 28 and have fallen to be implemented under Schedule 6.

(5) Where the admission arrangements for a school make both such provision for selection by ability as is mentioned in subsection (1) above and such provision for selection by aptitude as is mentioned in section 102(1), nothing in this section shall be taken to prevent those arrangements-

(a) from authorising or requiring a process of selection to be carried out at any stage for the purpose of establishing that an applicant for admission has a relevant aptitude; or

(b) from having the effect of giving priority to such an applicant with a relevant aptitude irrespective of his level of ability.

S. 101
Selection of pupils by "banding", i.e. assessing the ability of each applicant in order to secure a balanced ability intake overall is permitted provided the arrangements are designed to secure that all levels of ability are represented and that no level is substantially over or under represented. This only applies if no other ability test is then carried out, i.e. it would not be permissible, having established which band the applicants fall into, then to give priority to the most able within the band. A school that does not have existing arrangements of this kind will have to publish proposals for change under S. 28 and secure approval before implementing them.

102.–(1) Subject to subsection (2), the admission arrangements for a maintained school may make provision for the selection of pupils for admission to the school by reference to their aptitude for one or more prescribed subjects where-

(a) the admission authority for the school are satisfied that the school has a specialism in the subject or subjects in question; and

(b) the proportion of selective admissions in any relevant age group does not exceed 10 per cent.

(2) Subsection (1) does not apply if the admission arrangements make provision for any test to be carried out in relation to an applicant for admission which is either a test of ability or one designed to elicit any aptitude of his other than for the subject or subjects in question.

(3) Where, however, the admission arrangements for a school make both such provision for selection by aptitude as is mentioned in subsection (1) and such provision for selection by ability as is mentioned in section 101(1), the reference in subsection (2) above to a test of ability does not include any such test for which provision may be made under that section.

(4) In this section "the proportion of selective admissions", in relation to a relevant age group, means the proportion of the total number of pupils admitted to the school in that age group (determined in the prescribed manner) which is represented by the number of pupils so admitted by reference to aptitude for the subject or subjects in question.

(5) In this section "test" includes assessment and examination.

> **S. 102**
> *A school that has a specialism in particular subjects may admit a maximum (in aggregate) of 10% of the intake by reference to aptitude for those subjects provided that no test is carried out to determine ability either in those subjects or in other subjects. other than a test to establish banding in accordance with S. 101. Again, there is no definition of aptitude nor is there any statutory indication of the distinction between determining aptitude and testing ability.*

103.–(1) In connection with the determination of a maintained school's admission arrangements for a particular school year, sections 89 and 90 shall, except to the specified extent, apply in relation to the making or abandonment by those arrangements of provision for any permitted form of selection by ability or aptitude as they apply in relation to the making or abandonment by those arrangements of provision for other matters.

(2) In subsection (1) "the specified extent" means the extent to which those admission arrangements would effect an alteration in the provision made by the school's admission arrangements as respects any such form of selection (whether by introducing, varying or abandoning any such form of selection) which constitutes a prescribed alteration for the purposes of section 28.

(3) Any admission arrangements to which section 101(1) applies (whether authorised by section 100 or section 101) may be varied if (and only if) the arrangements as varied are designed to secure the objectives mentioned in section 101(1)(a) and (b).

> **S. 103**
> *Any proposed change to arrangements for selection by ability or aptitude come within the scope of Ss 89 and 90 dealing with the annual process for consultation on and change to admission arrangements unless the proposed change is one that requires the publication of notices and approval under the procedure laid down in S. 28. The effect of this is that although a school may be entitled to continue selective arrangements under S. 100, those arrangements may be objected to each year by other admission authorities and be ruled on by the adjudicator and/or Secretary of State. Furthermore, the continuance of arrangements for partial selection is one that parents also can raise objections to.*

Grammar schools

104.–(1) Where the Secretary of State is satisfied that a maintained school had selective admission arrangements at the beginning of the 1997-98 school year, he may by order designate the school as a grammar school for the purposes of this Chapter.

(2) A school has selective admission arrangements for the purposes of this Chapter if its admission arrangements make provision for all (or substantially all) of its pupils to be selected by reference to general ability, with a view to admitting only pupils with high ability.

(3) For the purpose of deciding whether a school's admission arrangements fall within subsection (2), any such additional criteria as are mentioned in section 86(9) shall be disregarded.

(4) Where a maintained school is a grammar school-

(a) sections 105 to 109 have effect for prescribing procedures for altering the school's admission arrangements so that it no longer has selective admission arrangements; and

(b) its admission arrangements shall not be so altered except in accordance with those sections.

(5) Regulations may make provision-

(a) for enabling the Secretary of State to make an order designating as a grammar school for the purposes of this Chapter a maintained school established in substitution for one or more discontinued schools each of which either has been or could have been so designated under this section (whether by virtue of subsection (1) or by virtue of the regulations); and

(b) for any provisions of this Chapter, or any regulations made under it, to have effect in relation to any such school with such modifications as may be prescribed.

(6) In this section "maintained school" includes, in relation to any time before the appointed day-

(a) a county or voluntary school, or

(b) a grant-maintained school,

within the meaning of the Education Act 1996; and in the application of subsection (1) to a maintained school on or after the appointed day the reference to the school shall be read, in connection with determining the nature of its admission arrangements at the beginning of the 1997-98 school year, as a reference to it as a school within paragraph (a) or (b) above.

(7) In this Chapter "grammar school" means a school for the time being designated under this section.

S. 104

Schools that admitted pupils by reference to high ability at the beginning of the 1997/98 school year may be designated by the Secretary of State as grammar schools. Ss 105 to 109 will then apply in connection with changes to the school's admission arrangements rather than the other provisions of the Act.

105.–(1) The Secretary of State may by regulations make provision for ballots of parents to be held, at their request, for determining whether the grammar schools to which such ballots relate should retain selective admission arrangements.

(2) Ballot regulations may provide for a ballot under this section to relate-

(a) to all grammar schools within the area of a prescribed local education authority or within such other area as may be prescribed,

(b) to a prescribed group of grammar schools, or

(c) to any grammar school not falling within paragraph (a) or (b).

(3) Ballot regulations may make provision-

(a) requiring a request for a ballot under this section to be made by means of a petition signed by parents eligible to request the ballot;

(b) prescribing the form of any such petition and other requirements (whether as to the procedure to be followed or otherwise) which are to be complied with in relation to any such petition;

(c) prescribing the body ("the designated body") to which any such petition is to be sent and which, under arrangements made by the Secretary of State, is to-

(i) make the arrangements for the holding of ballots under this section, and

(ii) discharge such other functions with respect to such petitions and the holding of such ballots as may be prescribed (which may include the determination of any question arising as to the validity of any request for a ballot or as to a person's eligibility to request or vote in a ballot);

(d) requiring prescribed bodies or persons, or bodies or persons falling within any prescribed category-

(i) to provide the designated body or any other person with any prescribed information requested by that body or person, or

(ii) to publish prescribed information in such manner as may be prescribed;

(e) authorising any such bodies or persons to charge a fee (not exceeding the cost of supply) for documents supplied by them in pursuance of regulations made by virtue of paragraph (d)(i);

(f) prescribing the terms of the question on which a ballot under this section is to be held and the manner in which such a ballot is to be conducted;

(g) enabling the Secretary of State, in any prescribed circumstances, to declare a previous ballot under this section void and require the holding of a fresh ballot;

(h) requiring anything falling to be done under the regulations to be done within such period as may be specified in or determined in accordance with the regulations.

(4) Ballot regulations may provide-

(a) for parents of any prescribed description to register with the designated body, in such manner and at such time as may be prescribed, in order to be eligible to request or vote in a ballot;

(b) that for all or any prescribed purposes of the regulations references to parents are to be read as excluding those who are not individuals.

(5) Ballot regulations may provide for a request for a ballot under this section to be made, in any prescribed circumstances, by means of two or more petitions.

(6) The information required to be provided in pursuance of subsection (3)(d) may include the names and addresses of parents of any prescribed description.

(7) Ballot regulations may provide for sections 496 and 497 of the Education Act 1996 (default powers of Secretary of State) to apply to proprietors of independent schools in relation to a duty imposed by or under the regulations.

(8) Where-

(a) a ballot has been held under this section, and

(b) the result of the ballot was to the effect that the schools or school in question should retain selective admission arrangements,

no further ballot relating to the schools or school shall be held under this section within such period as is specified in ballot regulations.

(9) The Secretary of State may make (or arrange for the making of) payments in respect of any expenses incurred by-

(a) the governing body of a school maintained by a local education authority,

(b) the proprietor of an independent school, or

(c) a local education authority,

in complying with any obligations which may be imposed by regulations made under subsection (3)(d)(i) or (ii).

Payments under this subsection may be made on such terms as the Secretary of State may determine.

(10) For the purposes of this section and sections 106 and 107, in their application in relation to any time falling before the appointed day, a grant-maintained school or a grant-maintained special school within the meaning of the (1996 c. 56.)Education Act 1996 shall be taken-

(a) to be a school maintained by a local education authority, and

(b) to be maintained by the authority in whose area it is situated.

(11) In this section and section 106 "ballot regulations" means regulations made under this section.

S. 105

This section enables the Secretary of State to make regulations to enable parental ballots to be held to decide whether or not particular grammar schools should retain selective admission arrangements. The regulations, as well as specifying the detail of how the ballot is to be called and conducted may specify that all grammar schools in a particular local education authority or prescribed area be included in one ballot, or that a group of named grammar schools be included in one ballot or that a ballot shall relate to an individual named school. The significance of this is that a single ballot will determine the fate of each school included in it.

106.–(1) In relation to a ballot under section 105(2)(a), ballot regulations shall provide that, subject to such exceptions as may be prescribed, the parents eligible to request or vote in the ballot are-

(a) registered parents of registered pupils at the following schools, namely-
   (i) where the ballot relates to all grammar schools within the area of a prescribed local education authority, all schools maintained by that authority; or
   (ii) where the ballot relates to all grammar schools within a prescribed area, all schools maintained by a local education authority which are situated in such area as may be prescribed, together with (if the regulations so provide) all schools maintained by such local education authority as may be prescribed;

(b) registered parents of registered pupils at independent schools where-
   (i) such parents are resident, and
   (ii) the schools are situated,

within the area of the prescribed local education authority or (as the case may be) the prescribed area; and

(c) parents of children of a prescribed description where such parents-
   (i) are resident within the area of the prescribed local education authority or (as the case may be) the prescribed area, and
   (ii) have registered with the designated body in accordance with section 105(4)(a).

S. 106

This section deals with the eligibility of parents to vote in grammar school ballots and this depends on the type of ballot being held.

S. 106 (1)
Where a ballot is to be held in relation to all grammar schools within a single local education authority or a prescribed area the parents eligible to vote are parents of pupils in all maintained schools within the area, parents who live in the relevant area and who have a child at an independent school that is also in the relevant area and other parents with children falling within any particular category laid down by regulations who live in the relevant area and who have registered themselves as eligible to vote.

(2) In relation to a ballot under section 105(2)(b) or (c), ballot regulations shall provide that, subject to such exceptions as may be prescribed, the parents eligible to request or vote in the ballot are registered parents of registered pupils at any school from which a prescribed number of pupils have transferred to the grammar school or schools in question-

    (a) at such age or ages, and
    (b) during such period,

as may be determined in accordance with the regulations; and such regulations may provide that where, within that period, any such grammar school has been established in substitution for another school, the schools are to be treated as a single school for the purposes of determining eligibility.

S. 106 (2)
Where a ballot is to be held in relation to a group of named schools or in relation to a single school the parents eligible to vote are (subject to any exceptions that may be provided for in regulations) those with children at schools from which a specified number of children have transferred to the grammar school or schools in question over a prescribed period. The number and the period are to be specified in regulations.

(3) Ballot regulations shall provide-

    (a) in relation to a ballot under section 105(2)(a), that a request for such a ballot must be made by a number of eligible parents equal to at least 20 per cent. of all parents falling within subsection (1)(a) or (b) above; and
    (b) in relation to a ballot under section 105(2)(b) or (c), that a request for such a ballot must be made by at least 20 per cent. of all parents falling within subsection (2) above.

S. 106 (3)
A ballot is only triggered by a request from at least 20% of eligible parents here meaning parents other than those who qualify to vote in an area ballot because they have registered their qualification to vote.

(4) Ballot regulations may provide for a parent's eligibility for the purposes of-

    (a) making a request for a ballot,

    (b) voting in a ballot, or

    (c) determining the number of parents required to make a request by virtue of subsection (3),

to be determined by reference to such different times as may be determined in accordance with the regulations.

(5) Ballot regulations may make provision for determining whether parents are resident in an area for the purposes of subsection (1)(b) or (c).

107.–(1) An authority or body to whom this section applies shall not incur any expenditure for the purpose of-

    (a) publishing any material which, in whole or in part, appears designed to influence-

        (i) eligible parents in deciding whether or not to request a ballot under section 105, or

        (ii) the outcome of such a ballot; or

    (b) assisting any person to publish any such material; or

    (c) influencing, or assisting any person to influence, by any other means-

        (i) eligible parents in deciding whether or not to request such a ballot, or

        (ii) the outcome of such a ballot.

(2) This section applies to-

    (a) any local education authority, and

    (b) the governing body of any school maintained by a local education authority.

(3) Nothing in subsection (1) shall be taken to prevent an authority or body to whom this section applies from incurring expenditure on publishing or otherwise providing to any person (whether or not in pursuance of any duty to do so)-

    (a) any factual information so far as it is presented fairly; or

    (b) a fair and reasonable assessment by the authority or body of the likely consequences of the result of a ballot under section 105 being in favour of the schools or school in question ceasing to have selective admission arrangements; or

    (c) an accurate statement by the authority or body of their intentions or proposals in the event of such a result.

(4) In determining for the purposes of subsection (3) whether-

    (a) any information is presented fairly, or

    (b) an assessment is fair and reasonable,

regard shall be had to any guidance given from time to time by the Secretary of State.

(5) In this section any reference to expenditure-

    (a) in relation to the governing body of a school which has a delegated budget within the meaning of Part II of this Act (or, in relation to any time before the appointed day, Part II of the Education Act 1996), is a reference to expenditure out of the school's budget share; or

    (b) in relation to the governing body of a grant-maintained or grant-maintained special school within the meaning of that Act (where this section applies to such a school by virtue of section 105(10)), is a reference to expenditure out of maintenance grants paid under Chapter VI of Part III of that Act.

S. 107

Neither an local education authority nor a governing body of any maintained school may spend money on any material that, in effect, would influence whether or not there should be a ballot or what the outcome of the ballot should be. They may, however, spend money on providing factual information and a fair and reasonable assessment of the consequences of a vote to end selection. The Secretary of State may issue guidance on these issues and local education authorities and governing bodies must have regard to it. The restriction on a governing body spending money applies only to the delegated budget: by inference it can spend other money provided that other money is not held for other designated purposes and the governing body is satisfied that the expense is in the interests of the school.

108.–(1) Subsection (2) applies where the result of a ballot held under section 105 shows a simple majority of votes cast (by persons eligible to vote in the ballot) in favour of the grammar school or schools to which the ballot related ceasing to have selective admission arrangements.

(2) The admission authority for a grammar school to which the ballot related shall secure that their admission arrangements are revised (in accordance with sections 89 and 90) so that, as from the beginning of such school year as may be prescribed, the school no longer has selective admission arrangements.

(3) Where the Secretary of State is satisfied that, in pursuance of subsection (2), a grammar school no longer has selective admission arrangements, he shall revoke the order made by him with respect to the school under section 104.

S. 108

If a ballot results in a vote to end selective admissions the admission authority for the school or schools in question must propose revised arrangements in accordance with Ss 9 and 90 so that the selective arrangements will no longer apply. The timetable for the change will be governed by regulations and when they are implemented the Secretary of State will revoke the designation of the school as a grammar school.

109.–(1) This section has effect for enabling the admission arrangements of a grammar school to be revised (otherwise than in circumstances where section 108(2) applies) so that the school no longer has selective admission arrangements and its admission arrangements instead either-

(a) make no provision for selection by ability, or
(b) make provision for one or more of the following, namely-
  (i) any selection by ability authorised by section 101,
  (ii) any selection by aptitude authorised by section 102, and
  (iii) any selection by ability such as is mentioned in section 99(2)(c).

(2) Any such revision of the admission arrangements of a grammar school shall be one of the alterations to a maintained school which are prescribed for the purposes of section 28; but any proposals for any such revision of the admission arrangements of a grammar school which is a community school shall be published under that section by the governing body and not by the local education authority.

(3) Regulations may provide-

(a) that, in their application to any proposals for any such revision of the admission arrangements of a grammar school, any provision of section 28 or Schedule 6 shall have effect with such modifications as may be prescribed;
(b) that, in any prescribed circumstances following the making of a request for a ballot to be held under section 105, any such proposals under section 28 shall be of no effect.

(4) Regulations made under section 105 may make provision, in relation to cases where any such proposals under section 28 have fallen to be implemented under paragraph 5 or 10 of Schedule 6, for requiring the school to which the proposals relate to be disregarded for the purposes of any regulations made under section 105(2).

(5) Where the Secretary of State is satisfied that, by reason of the implementation of any such proposals, a grammar school no longer has selective admission arrangements, he shall revoke the order made by him with respect to the school under section 104.

S. 109
The governing body of a grammar school may, even if it is not its own admission authority, propose that selective admission arrangements be ended or be replaced by a selection process that is permitted for schools other than grammar schools. The procedure laid down by S. 28 must be followed. The local education authority cannot make such a proposal.

PART IV OTHER PROVISIONS ABOUT SCHOOL EDUCATION

Home-school agreements

110.–(1) The governing body of a school which is-

(a) a maintained school, or
(b) a city technology college or a city college for the technology of the arts,

shall adopt a home-school agreement for the school, together with a parental declaration to be used in connection with the agreement.

(2) For the purposes of this section and section 111 a "home-school agreement" is a statement specifying-

(a) the school's aims and values;
(b) the school's responsibilities, namely the responsibilities which the school intends to discharge in connection with the education of pupils at the school who are of compulsory school age;
(c) the parental responsibilities, namely the responsibilities which the parents of such pupils are expected to discharge in connection with the education of their children while they are registered pupils at the school; and
(d) the school's expectations of its pupils, namely the expectations of the school as regards the conduct of such pupils while they are registered pupils there;

and "parental declaration" means a document to be used by qualifying parents for recording that they take note of the school's aims and values and its responsibilities and that they acknowledge and accept the parental responsibilities and the school's expectations of its pupils.

(3) The governing body shall take reasonable steps to secure that the parental declaration is signed by every qualifying parent.

(4) Subsection (3) does not, however, require the governing body to seek the signature of a qualifying parent if, having regard to any special circumstances relating to the parent or the pupil in question, they consider that it would be inappropriate to do so.

(5) Where the governing body consider that a registered pupil at the school has a sufficient understanding of the home-school agreement as it relates to him, they may invite the pupil to sign the parental declaration as an indication that he acknowledges and accepts the school's expectations of its pupils.

(6) The governing body shall discharge their duty under subsection (3), and (where they decide to exercise it) shall exercise their power under subsection (5), as follows-

(a) in the case of a pupil attending the school on the relevant date, as soon after that date as is reasonably practicable; and

(b) in the case of a pupil admitted to the school after the relevant date, as soon after the date of his admission as is reasonably practicable.

S. 110 (1) to (6)

The governing body of every maintained school as well as technology and technology of the arts colleges must adopt a home-school agreement which will specify

- *the school's aims and values*

- *its responsibilities in connection with the education of pupils*

- *the responsibilities that parents are expected to discharge in connection with their children's education*

- *its expectations of pupil conduct*

The home-school agreement applies only to pupils of compulsory school age and their parents.

The governing body must also adopt a form of parental declaration recording that the parents take note of the school's aims, values and responsibilities and that they acknowledge and accept their responsibilities and what the school expects of its pupils. The governing body must take reasonable steps to secure that each parent signs the parental declaration unless there are special circumstances relating either to the parent or the child that make this inappropriate. The governing body may invite pupils who it considers to have sufficient understanding to sign the parental declaration in relation to the school's expectations of pupils.

The governing body must take steps to have the parental declaration signed by existing and new parents (and pupils where relevant) as soon as reasonably practicable.

---

(7) The governing body shall from time to time review the home-school agreement.

(8) Where the home-school agreement is revised by the governing body following such a review, subsections (3) to (6) shall, in the case of pupils admitted to the school after the revision takes effect, accordingly apply in relation to the revised agreement.

S. 110 (7) and (8)

The governing body must review the home-school agreement from time to time. It must seek fresh parental and pupil declarations if the agreement is revised.

---

(9) Before adopting the home-school agreement or parental declaration, or revising that agreement, the governing body shall consult-

(a) all qualifying parents, and

(b) such other persons as may be prescribed.

> **S. 110 (9)**
> *The governing body must consult all relevant parents and such other people as may be prescribed by regulations before making or revising the agreement. No particular consultation process is laid down.*

(10) In this section-

"qualifying parent" means a registered parent of a pupil at the school who is of compulsory school age;

"the relevant date" means such date as the Secretary of State may by order appoint or such later date as he may determine in the case of the school in question.

111.–(1) In discharging any function under section 110 the governing body of a school shall have regard to any guidance given from time to time by the Secretary of State.

(2) If the Secretary of State by order so provides, the governing body of a school to which subsection (1) of that section applies shall ensure that any form of words-

    (a) specified in the order, or
    (b) having such effect as is so specified,

is not used in a home-school agreement or (as the case may be) in a parental declaration.

(3) An order under subsection (2) may apply-

    (a) to any school specified in the order, or
    (b) to any description of school so specified.

> **S. 111 (1) to (3)**
> *Schools must have regard to any guidance issued by the Secretary of State in relation to home-school agreements. the Secretary of State may prescribe forms of words that are not to be used in a home-school agreement and that power may be applied to schools generally or to particular types of schools or to specifically named schools.*

(4) Neither the governing body of a school to which section 110(1) applies nor the local education authority where it is the admission authority for such a school shall-

    (a) invite any person to sign the parental declaration at a time when the child in question has not been admitted to the school;
    (b) make it a condition of a child being admitted to the school that the parental declaration is signed in respect of the child; or
    (c) make any decision as to whether or not to admit a child to the school by

reference to whether any such declaration is or is not likely to be signed in respect of the child;

and in this subsection "admission authority" has the meaning given by section 88(1).

> **S. 111 (4)**
>
> *A parent cannot be asked to sign the parental declaration before the child has joined the school. Places at schools may not be offered conditionally on a declaration being signed nor may a decision be made on an admission application based on whether or not a parent is likely to sign a declaration.*

(5) No person shall be excluded from such a school or suffer any other adverse consequences on account of any failure to comply with any invitation to sign the parental declaration.

> **S. 111 (5)**
>
> *No child may be excluded or be penalised in any other way because of a failure to sign a parental declaration.*

(6) A home-school agreement shall not be capable of creating any obligation in respect of whose breach any liability arises in contract or in tort.

> **S. 111 (6)**
>
> *No legal liabilities in either contract or tort can arise from a home-school agreement. In other words, neither school nor parent can sue the other for failure to comply with its terms.*

Extension of educational opportunities for Key Stage 4 pupils

112.–(1) Section 560 of the Education Act 1996 (work experience during compulsory schooling) shall be amended as follows.

(2) For subsections (1) and (2) there shall be substituted-

"(1) The enactments relating to the prohibition or regulation of the employment of children shall not apply to the employment of a child in his last two years of compulsory schooling if the employment is in pursuance of arrangements made-

    (a) by a local education authority, or
    (b) by the governing body of a school on behalf of such an authority,

with a view to providing him with work experience as a part of his education.

(2) For the purposes of subsection (1) a child shall be taken to be in his last two years

of compulsory schooling as from the beginning of the last two school years at his school during the whole or part of which he is of compulsory school age."

(3) In subsection (6) (disapplication of sections 495 and 496 of the Act), the words "or the governing body of a grant-maintained school" shall be omitted.

> ## S. 112
> *This section permits pupils in the last two years of compulsory schooling to take part in work experience even though employment law would otherwise prohibit or regulate it.*

113.–(1) In section 18(1) of the Further and Higher Education Act 1992 (principal powers of a further education corporation), after paragraph (a) there shall be inserted-
"(aa) in pursuance of arrangements made-
    (i) by a local education authority, or
    (ii) by the governing body of a school on behalf of such an authority,
provide secondary education to pupils in the fourth key stage, and".

(2) After section 52 of that Act there shall be inserted-

"52A.–(1) This section applies where secondary education is provided to pupils in the fourth key stage-

    (a) by a further education corporation in pursuance of arrangements falling within section 18(1)(aa) of this Act, or
    (b) by a designated institution in pursuance of arrangements made-
        (i) by a local education authority, or
        (ii) by the governing body of a school on behalf of such an authority.

(2) The governing body of the corporation or institution shall secure that, except in such circumstances as may be prescribed by regulations, no education is provided to a person who has attained the age of nineteen years in a room in which any such pupils are for the time being receiving secondary education."

> ## S. 113
> *Arrangements may be made for Key Stage 4 education to be provided in colleges of further education provided that, except in circumstances permitted by regulations, no person age 19 or over is to be taught in the same room as those Key Stage 4 pupils.*

School meals

114.–(1) Regulations may prescribe nutritional standards, or other nutritional requirements, which (subject to such exceptions as may be provided for by or under the regulations) are to be complied with in connection with the provision of school lunches for registered pupils at schools maintained by local education authorities.

(2) Where a local education authority or the governing body provide school lunches for registered pupils at such a school, they shall secure that any applicable provisions of regulations under this section are complied with.

(3) Subsection (2) applies-

(a) whether the lunches are provided on school premises or at any other place where education is being provided; and

(b) whether they are being provided in pursuance of any statutory requirement or otherwise.

(4) Regulations under this section may-

(a) make different provision for pupils of different ages;

(b) authorise the Secretary of State to determine the time as from which any provisions of the regulations are to apply to a particular local education authority or school.

(5) In this section "school lunch", in relation to a pupil, means food made available for consumption by the pupil as his midday meal on a school day, whether involving a set meal or the selection of items by him or otherwise.

S. 114

Regulations may prescribe nutritional standards for school lunches (including all food made available as a midday meal) and LEAs and governing bodies have a duty to comply with them. Different standards can be applied to different age pupils.

115.–(1) Section 512 of the Education Act 1996 (provision by LEAs of meals etc. at maintained schools) shall be amended as follows.

(2) After subsection (1) there shall be inserted-

"(1A) A local education authority shall, if requested to do so by or on behalf of any registered pupils at a school maintained by the authority, provide school lunches for those pupils; but the authority shall not be required to provide a school lunch-

(a) where in the circumstances it would be unreasonable for them to do so, or

(b) where the pupil in question has not attained compulsory school age and is being provided with part-time education.

(1B) Any school lunches provided by a local education authority under subsection (1A) may-

(a) be provided either on the school premises or at any place other than the school premises where education is being provided for the pupils in question; and

(b) take such form as the authority think fit."

(3) In subsection (2) (obligation to charge for meals etc.), after "subsection (1)" there shall be inserted "or (1A)".

(4) In subsection (3), for paragraphs (a) and (b) there shall be substituted-

"(a) shall so exercise their power under subsection (1) as to ensure that a school lunch is provided for him, which shall be provided free of charge, and
(b) if in the exercise of that power they provide him with milk, shall provide it free of charge."

(5) After subsection (5) there shall be added-

"(6) In this section "school lunch", in relation to a pupil, means food made available for consumption by the pupil as his midday meal on a school day, whether involving a set meal or the selection of items by him or otherwise."

S. 115
This section modifies provisions in Education Act 1996 relating to the provision of school lunches by an local education authority.

116. After section 512 of the Education Act 1996 there shall be inserted-

"512A.–(1) The Secretary of State may by order make provision for imposing on the governing body of any school to which the order applies a duty or duties corresponding to one or more of the duties of the local education authority which are mentioned in subsection (2).

(2) Those duties are-

(a) the duty to provide school lunches in accordance with section 512(1A) and (1B);
(b) the duty to provide school lunches free of charge in accordance with section 512(3)(a); and
(c) the duty to provide milk free of charge in accordance with section 512(3)(b).

(3) An order under this section may (subject to subsection (6)) apply to-

(a) all maintained schools; or
(b) any specified class of such schools; or
(c) all such schools, or any specified class of such schools, maintained by specified local education authorities.

(4) Where any duty falls to be performed by the governing body of a school by virtue of an order under this section-

(a) the corresponding duty mentioned in subsection (2) shall no longer fall to be performed by the local education authority in relation to the school; and
(b) if the duty corresponds to the one mentioned in subsection (2)(b) or (c), section 533(3) shall not apply to any school lunches or milk provided by the governing body in pursuance of the order.

(5) An order under this section may provide for section 513(2) not to apply-

    (a) to local education authorities generally, or

    (b) to any specified local education authority,

either in relation to all pupils for whom provision is made by the authority under section 513 or in relation to all such pupils who are of such ages as may be specified.

(6) An order under this section shall not operate to-

    (a) impose any duty on the governing body of a school, or

    (b) relieve a local education authority of any duty in relation to a school,

at any time when the school does not have a delegated budget; and such an order may provide for section 512(2)(b) above to have effect, in relation to any provision made at any such time by the local education authority for pupils at the school, with such modifications as may be specified.

(7) In this section-

"delegated budget" and "maintained school" have the same meaning as in the School Standards and Framework Act 1998;

"school lunch" has the same meaning as in section 512 above;

"specified" means specified in an order under this section."

S. 116

This section modifies provisions in Education Act 1996 relating to school lunches by enabling the Secretary of Sate to transfer the responsibility for their provision from the local education authority to governing bodies. The transfer may be in relation to all local education authorities or one or more and in relation to all schools, schools of particular descriptions or named schools, except that a school that does not have a delegated budget cannot be required to take on the responsibility.

PART V NURSERY EDUCATION

Nursery education

117. In this Part "nursery education" means full-time or part-time education suitable for children who have not attained compulsory school age (whether provided at schools or elsewhere).

S. 117

Sections 118 to 124 relate to nursery education which is defined as full-time or part-time education provided for children who have not reached compulsory school age.

General duty of local education authority

118.–(1) A local education authority shall secure that the provision (whether or not by them) of nursery education for children who-

(a) have not attained compulsory school age, but
(b) have attained such age as may be prescribed,

is sufficient for their area.

(2) In determining for the purposes of subsection (1) whether the provision of such education is sufficient for their area a local education authority-

(a) may have regard to any facilities which they expect to be available outside their area for providing such education; and
(b) shall have regard to any guidance given from time to time by the Secretary of State.

S.118
local education authorities have a general duty to provide sufficient nursery education for children in their area. They may take into account provision available outside their own area and they must have regard to guidance issued by the Secretary of State.

Early years development partnerships

119.–(1) Every local education authority shall establish for their area a body to be known as an early years development partnership ("the partnership").

(2) In establishing the partnership and determining its constitution the authority shall have regard to any guidance given from time to time by the Secretary of State.

(3) The authority may establish a sub-committee of the partnership for any part of their area.

(4) The authority shall make arrangements-

(a) for the meetings and proceedings of the partnership and any such sub-committee, and
(b) for the partnership (and any such sub-committee) to be provided with accommodation and with such services as the authority consider appropriate.

(5) The functions of the partnership shall be to work with the authority-

(a) in reviewing the sufficiency of the provision of nursery education for the authority's area for the purposes of section 118, and
(b) in preparing early years development plans under section 120.

(6) The Secretary of State may by order confer on early years development partnerships such additional functions as are specified in the order.

> **S. 119**
>
> *Each local education authority must set up an early years development partnership which has the task of reviewing the sufficiency of the local education authority nursery provision and of preparing an early years development plan. How the partnership is set up and how it operates is left to the local education authority but the local education authority must have regard to guidance from the Secretary of State who may also confer additional functions on such partnerships.*

Early years development plans

120.–(1) Every local education authority shall, in conjunction with the early years development partnership for their area-

(a) prepare an early years development plan for their area, and

(b) prepare further such plans at such intervals as may be determined by or in accordance with regulations.

(2) An early years development plan shall consist of-

(a) a statement of proposals, which sets out the authority's proposals for complying with their duty under section 118, and

(b) annexes to that statement.

(3) The statement of proposals must-
(a) deal with such matters, and relate to such period, as may be determined by or in accordance with regulations, and

(b) be approved by the Secretary of State under section 121.

(4) In relation to the form and content of the annexes to the statement the authority shall have regard to any guidance given from time to time by the Secretary of State.

121.–(1) Where an early years development plan has been prepared in accordance with section 120, the authority shall, by such date as may be determined by or in accordance with regulations, submit the plan to the Secretary of State for him to approve the authority's statement of proposals under this section.

(2) The Secretary of State may in the case of any statement submitted to him under this section-
(a) approve the statement in any of the following ways, namely wholly or in part, for a limited period of time, or subject to conditions;

(b) require the authority to make such modifications to the statement as he may specify; or

(c) reject the statement.

(3) If the Secretary of State approves the statement-
(a) he shall notify the authority of his decision; and

(b) the authority shall implement the proposals set out in the statement, so far as approved by the Secretary of State, as from such date as he may determine.

(4) If the Secretary of State requires the authority to make modifications or rejects the statement-

(a) he shall notify the authority of his decision and of his reasons for it; and

(b) the authority shall prepare a revised statement and submit it to the Secretary of State for his approval under this section by such date as he may determine.

(5) Once the Secretary of State has approved an authority's statement of proposals under subsection (2), he shall keep under review the authority's proposals, as approved by him, and their implementation by the authority, and-

(a) where he is of the opinion that the statement should be modified (or further modified), he may withdraw his approval and require the authority to make such modifications to the statement as he may specify; and

(b) where he is of the opinion that the authority's statement is not being properly implemented by them, he may withdraw his approval for such period as he thinks fit.

(6) If under subsection (5) the Secretary of State withdraws his approval of a statement of proposals-

(a) he shall notify the authority of his decision and of his reasons for it; and

(b) in a case falling within paragraph (a) of that subsection, the authority shall prepare a revised statement and submit it to him for his approval under this section by such date as he may determine.

(7) Section 120 shall apply to the preparation of a revised statement under subsection (4)(b) or (6)(b), with such modifications (if any) as the Secretary of State may determine.

(8) At any time after the Secretary of State has approved an authority's statement of proposals under subsection (2)-

(a) the authority may, with the agreement of the early years development partnership, submit modifications to the statement to the Secretary of State for his approval, and

(b) the Secretary of State may approve the modifications, whether in whole or in part, for a limited period of time, or subject to conditions, and

(c) if and to the extent that he approves those modifications, he shall notify the authority of his decision and-

(i) the statement shall have effect with the modifications, and

(ii) the authority shall implement their proposals as modified,

as from such date as he may determine.

(9) Once the Secretary of State has approved-

(a) an authority's statement of proposals under subsection (2), or

(b) the modification of an authority's statement of proposals under subsection (8),

the authority shall publish their early years development plan (or their plan as so modified) in such manner and by such date as may be prescribed, and shall provide such persons as may be prescribed with copies of that plan or of a summary of that plan.

> **Ss. 120 and 121**
> *Every local education authority must prepare early years development plans in accordance with regulations. Broadly the plan will set out how the local education authority proposes to meet its statutory obligations in relation to nursery education. It is to be prepared in conjunction with the early years development partnership having regard to guidance from the Secretary of State. The plan must be approved by the Secretary of State who has power t require amendments and who is required to keep the proposals under review. The Secretary of State has power to withdraw approval and require the local education authority to prepare a fresh plan.*

Inspection of nursery education

122.–(1) Schedule 26 (inspections, etc. of providers of nursery education) shall have effect.

(2) Schedule 1 to the Nursery Education and Grant-Maintained Schools Act 1996 (which is superseded by Schedule 26 to this Act) shall cease to have effect.

(3) Any register of nursery education inspectors established by the Chief Inspector under Schedule 1 to that Act shall be treated as established by him under Schedule 26 to this Act; and accordingly anything done under Schedule 1 to that Act in connection with the registration of (or any refusal to register) any person in that register shall, if effective immediately before the commencement of this section, continue to have effect as if done under Schedule 26 to this Act.

(4) In subsection (3) "the Chief Inspector" means Her Majesty's Chief Inspector of Schools in England or Her Majesty's Chief Inspector of Schools in Wales.

> **S. 122**
> *This section provides for the inspection of nursery education under the aegis of OFSTED. The detail is in Schedule 26.*

Further provisions relating to nursery education

123.–(1) It shall be the duty of-

(a) any local education authority or other person providing relevant nursery education, and

(b) any person employed by such an authority or other person, or otherwise engaged to provide his services, in the provision of such education,

(except where a duty is already imposed by subsection (2) of section 313 of the Education Act 1996) to have regard to the provisions of the code of practice issued under that section (practical guidance in respect of the discharge of functions under Part IV of that Act).

(2) That code of practice may include practical guidance in respect of the provision of relevant nursery education for children with special educational needs in circumstances where functions under Part IV of the Education Act 1996 do not fall to be discharged.

(3) But unless that code of practice includes provision made by virtue of subsection (2)-

(a) the Secretary of State shall publish a document explaining how the practical guidance contained in that code applies in circumstances where functions under Part IV of the (1996 c. 56.)Education Act 1996 do not fall to be discharged, and

(b) the duty imposed by subsection (1) includes a duty to have regard to the provisions of that document.

(4) In this section "relevant nursery education" means nursery education which is provided-

(a) by a local education authority, or

(b) by any other person who is in receipt of financial assistance given by such an authority and whose provision of nursery education is taken into account by the authority in formulating proposals for the purposes of section 120(2)(a).

S. 123

Those involved in the provision of nursery education must have regard to the Code of Practice relating to special educational needs and any additional guidance that the Secretary of State may issue.

124. After section 509 of the (1996 c. 56.)Education Act 1996 there shall be inserted-

"509A.–(1) A local education authority may provide a child with assistance under this section if they are satisfied that, without such assistance, he would be prevented from attending at any premises-

(a) which are not a school or part of a school, but

(b) at which relevant nursery education is provided,

for the purpose of receiving such education there.

(2) The assistance which may be provided for a child under this section consists of either-
  (a) making arrangements (whether for the provision of transport or otherwise) for the purpose of facilitating the child's attendance at the premises concerned, or
  (b) paying the whole or any part of his reasonable travel expenses.

(3) When considering whether to provide a child with assistance under this section in connection with his attendance at any premises, a local education authority may have regard (among other things) to whether it would be reasonable to expect alternative arrangements to be made for him to receive relevant nursery education at any other premises (whether nearer to his home or otherwise).

(4) Where the assistance to be provided for a child under this section consists of making arrangements for the provision of transport, the authority may, if they consider it appropriate to do so, determine that the assistance shall not be so provided unless-
  (a) the child's parent, or
  (b) the person providing the relevant nursery education concerned,

agrees to make to the authority such payments in respect of the provision of the transport (not exceeding the cost to the authority of its provision) as they may determine.

(5) In this section "relevant nursery education" means nursery education which is provided-
  (a) by a local education authority, or
  (b) by any other person-
    (i) who is in receipt of financial assistance given by such an authority and whose provision of nursery education is taken into account by the authority in formulating proposals for the purposes of section 120(2)(a) of the School Standards and Framework Act 1998, or
    (ii) who is in receipt of grants under section 1 of the Nursery Education and Grant-Maintained Schools Act 1996."

S. 124

This section expands the provisions in Education Act 1996 relating to assistance with travel to and from school by providing that the power for the local education authority to provide such assistance extends to nursery education that is not being provided in a school as such. All circumstances are to be taken into account, including the availability of nursery education elsewhere. The local education authority may require parents to meet all or part of the cost.

PART VI PARTNERSHIP ARRANGEMENTS IN WALES

125.–(1) The Further and Higher Education Act 1992 shall be amended as follows.

(2) In section 5 (administration of funds by further education funding councils), after subsection (5) there shall be inserted-

"(5A) The Further Education Funding Council for Wales may give financial support to a local education authority for an area in Wales for the purposes of any partnership arrangement made by the authority to which section 60A of this Act applies."

(3) In section 18 (principal powers of a further education corporation)-

(a) in subsection (1), the words "and those powers" to the end shall be omitted, and

(b) after subsection (3) there shall be added-

"(4) In addition to the powers conferred by subsection (1) above, a further education corporation which conducts one or more educational institutions situated in Wales may-

(a) secure the provision of full-time or part-time education suitable to the requirements of persons who are over compulsory school age but under the age of 19, but only if that provision is made under a partnership arrangement to which section 60A of this Act applies, and

(b) supply goods or services in connection with the securing of the provision of education under paragraph (a) above.

(5) Subsections (2) and (3) above shall apply for the purposes of subsection (4) above as they apply for the purposes of subsection (1), except that references in those subsections to the provision of education shall be construed as references to the securing of the provision of education.

(6) The powers conferred by subsection (1) above and the powers conferred by subsection (4) above are referred to in section 19 of this Act as the corporation's principal powers."

(4) After section 60 there shall be inserted-

"60A.–(1) An arrangement is a partnership arrangement to which this section applies if-

(a) it is made by-

(i) one or more local education authorities for areas in Wales, and

(ii) one or more governing bodies of Welsh further education institutions,

for the purpose of securing the provision of education within subsection (3),

(b) it provides for the facilities connected with the provision of education under the arrangement to be provided-

(i) in part, at one or more schools maintained by the local education authority which is a party to the arrangement (or where more than one local education authority is a party, by each of them), and

(ii) in part, at one or more Welsh further education institutions conducted by the governing body which is a party to the arrangement (or, where more than one governing body is a party, by each of them),

(c) it is made with the consent of-

(i) the Further Education Funding Council for Wales, and

(ii) the governing body of each school at which, in accordance with the arrangement, facilities are to be provided, and

(d) it is approved by the Secretary of State.

(2) For the purposes of subsection (1) above-

(a) "Welsh further education institution" means an institution which is within the further education sector and is situated in Wales, and

(b) a designated institution shall be treated as conducted by the governing body of the institution.

(3) Education is within this subsection if it is full-time or part-time education suitable to the requirements of persons who are over compulsory school age but under the age of 19.

(4) The following bodies shall exercise their functions with a view to securing that any education provided under a partnership arrangement to which this section applies is provided and funded in accordance with the arrangement-

(a) each local education authority which is a party to the arrangement;

(b) each governing body of an institution (or institutions) within the further education sector which is a party to the arrangement;

(c) the Further Education Funding Council for Wales;

(d) each governing body of a school which consented to the arrangement.

(5) Schedule 5A to this Act shall have effect in relation to partnership arrangements to which this section applies."

(5) After Schedule 5 there shall be inserted the Schedule set out in Schedule 27 to this Act.

126.–(1) The Education Act 1996 shall have effect in relation to education provided under relevant partnership arrangements subject to the following provisions of this section.

(2) For the purposes of that Act-

(a) full-time education suitable to the requirements of persons who are over compulsory school age but under the age of 19 which is provided at a school at which education within section 2(2)(a) of that Act is also provided shall not be regarded as secondary education, and

(b) a person for whom full-time or part-time education suitable to the requirements of such persons is being provided at a school shall not be regarded as a pupil,

if that education is being provided under a relevant partnership arrangement.

(3) Accordingly, education within subsection (2)(a) above which is provided under a relevant partnership arrangement shall, for the purposes of that Act, be regarded as further education.

(4) In this section "relevant partnership arrangement" means a partnership arrangement to which section 60A of the Further and Higher Education Act 1992 (as inserted by section 125(4)) applies.

Ss. 125 and 126
Schools and further education colleges in Wales may establish partnership arrangements to allow full-time or part-time education for pupils over compulsory school age but under 19 to be provided partly in maintained schools and partly in FE colleges. Consent of all relevant school governing bodies and of the Further Education Funding Council for Wales is required. Schedule 27 applies and education provided under such a partnership arrangement is to be regarded as further education rather than school education.

PART VII MISCELLANEOUS AND GENERAL

Code of practice for local education authorities and maintained schools

127.–(1) The Secretary of State shall issue, and may from time to time revise, a code of practice containing such practical guidance as he thinks appropriate with a view to securing effective relationships between local education authorities and the schools maintained by them-

(a) in relation to promoting high standards of education in such schools; and
(b) in relation to the discharge of relevant functions of such authorities in relation to such schools.

(2) In discharging their functions in relation to any maintained school, it shall be the duty of-

(a) the local education authority,
(b) the governing body, and
(c) the head teacher,

to have regard to any relevant provisions of the code.

(3) Section 85 shall apply in relation to the code as it applies in relation to a code of practice under section 84.

(4) The Secretary of State shall publish the code as for the time being in force.

(5) The Secretary of State may under subsection (1) make different provision for England and Wales (whether or not by means of separate codes of practice); and references in this section to "the code" accordingly apply to any such separate code of practice.

(6) For the purposes of this section the relevant functions of a local education authority are the functions exercisable by or on behalf of such an authority under-

(a) sections 6 and 7 (so far as they relate to schools maintained by the authority),
(b) section 15(2),
(c) section 16(1),
(d) section 17(1),
(e) section 42(3) and (4),
(f) sections 54 and 55,
(g) section 62(1),
(h) Schedules 9 and 11 (so far as they relate to the appointment and removal of LEA governors),
(i) Schedule 13,
(j) paragraphs 1 and 2 of Schedule 15,
(k) Schedules 16 and 17, and
(l) section 25 of the School Inspections Act 1996,

and such other functions exercisable by or on behalf of a local education authority as the Secretary of State may determine for the purposes of this subsection.

S. 127
The Secretary of State is given power to issue a code of practice dealing with all aspects of the relationships between local education authorities and the schools they maintain. The purpose of the code is to promote high standards of education in schools and to govern how local education authorities discharge their functions in relation to their schools. Section 85 applies to this code of practice which means that the same process for consultation and laying before Parliament apply as for the code of practice on admissions.

Financial assistance to non-maintained schools

128.–(1) For section 18 of the Education Act 1996 there shall be substituted-

"*Financial assistance to non-maintained schools.*

18.–(1) Subject to subsection (2), a local education authority may-

(a) assist any primary or secondary non-maintained school (whether inside or outside their area);
(b) make arrangements for pupils to be provided with primary or secondary education at such schools.

(2) Except in accordance with regulations, a local education authority may not under subsection (1) make any grant or other payment (whether to the proprietor of a school or otherwise) in respect of-

(a) fees or expenses (of whatever nature) which are payable in connection with the attendance of a pupil at a school, or

(b) such other matters as may be prescribed.

(3) Regulations made for the purposes of subsection (2)(a) may provide that, in such circumstances as may be specified in or determined in accordance with the regulations, a local education authority-

(a) shall exercise their power under subsection (1)(b) in relation to a pupil at a non-maintained school so as to pay the whole of-
   (i) the fees payable in respect of the education provided for the pupil, and
   (ii) if board and lodging are provided for him at the school, the fees payable in respect of the board and lodging, and
   (iii) any expenses of a prescribed description which are payable in connection with his attendance at the school; or
(b) may exercise that power in relation to such a pupil so as to pay the whole or part of any fees or expenses falling within all or any of sub-paragraphs (i) to (iii) of paragraph (a) above.

(4) In this section references to non-maintained schools are references to schools which are not maintained by any local education authority."

(2) In consequence of subsection (1), section 16(1)(c) of the (1996 c. 56.)Education Act 1996 (power of local education authority to assist primary or secondary school not maintained by the authority) shall cease to have effect.

S. 128
Local education authorities may, but only in conformity with regulations, give financial assistance to independent schools. Although the section is in general terms, in practice it gives an local education authority the power to pay the whole or part of the cost of a child at such a school including boarding costs.

129. For section 518 of the Education Act 1996 there shall be substituted-

"518.–(1) A local education authority, for the purpose of enabling persons to take advantage of any educational facilities available to them, may in such circumstances as may be specified in or determined in accordance with regulations-

(a) pay such expenses of children attending community, foundation, voluntary or special schools as may be necessary to enable them to take part in any school activities,

(b) grant scholarships, exhibitions, bursaries and other allowances in respect of persons over compulsory school age.

(2) Regulations may make provision-

(a) for requiring a local education authority to make, in relation to each financial year, a determination relating to the extent to which they propose to exercise their power under subsection (1)(b) in that year; and

(b) for authorising an authority to determine not to exercise that power in a financial year-

  (i) generally,

  (ii) in such cases as may be prescribed, or

  (iii) in such cases as may be determined by the authority."

S. 129
Local education authorities may make grants to enable children at maintained schools to take part in school activities and offer scholarships and the like to pupil over compulsory school age. Regulations may require local education authorities to determine each year how they will exercise this power.

130.–(1) In section 3(2) of the Education (Schools) Act 1997 (regulations for purposes of transitional arrangements), after paragraph (f) there shall be added-

"(g) provide for the Secretary of State, in a case where he is satisfied that it is reasonable to do so in view of any particular circumstances relating to a pupil who holds (or has at any time held) an assisted place provided by a school under section 2(1), to authorise another school which is either-

  (i) a former participating school, or

  (ii) a new school authorised to provide assisted places by virtue of paragraph (f) above,

to provide for the pupil under section 2(1) the assisted place which the first-mentioned school was authorised to provide."

(2) In section 75A(9A) of the Education (Scotland) Act 1980 (regulations in connection with assisted places)-

(a) the word "and" immediately preceding paragraph (b) shall be omitted; and

(b) after that paragraph there shall be inserted "; and

  (c) provide for the Secretary of State, in a case where he is satisfied that it is reasonable to do so in view of any particular circumstances relating to a pupil who holds (or has, at any time since the beginning of the first term of the 1997-98 school year, held) an assisted place at a school under a scheme operated by virtue of subsection (1) above, to authorise another school which is, or is treated as, a participating school to provide for the pupil under such a scheme the assisted place which the first-mentioned school was authorised to provide."

S. 130

This section enables the Secretary of State to transfer an assisted place from one school to another. This can only apply to assisted places held at the start of the 1997-98 school year.

Abolition of corporal punishment

131.–(1) For section 548 of the Education Act 1996 there shall be substituted-

"**548.**–(1) Corporal punishment given by, or on the authority of, a member of staff to a child-

(a) for whom education is provided at any school, or

(b) for whom education is provided, otherwise than at school, under any arrangements made by a local education authority, or

(c) for whom specified nursery education is provided otherwise than at school,

cannot be justified in any proceedings on the ground that it was given in pursuance of a right exercisable by the member of staff by virtue of his position as such.

(2) Subsection (1) applies to corporal punishment so given to a child at any time, whether at the school or other place at which education is provided for the child, or elsewhere.

(3) The following provisions have effect for the purposes of this section.

(4) Any reference to giving corporal punishment to a child is to doing anything for the purpose of punishing that child (whether or not there are other reasons for doing it) which, apart from any justification, would constitute battery.

(5) However, corporal punishment shall not be taken to be given to a child by virtue of anything done for reasons that include averting-

(a) an immediate danger of personal injury to, or

(b) an immediate danger to the property of,

any person (including the child himself).

(6) "Member of staff", in relation to the child concerned, means-

(a) any person who works as a teacher at the school or other place at which education is provided for the child, or

(b) any other person who (whether in connection with the provision of education for the child or otherwise)-

(i) works at that school or place, or

(ii) otherwise provides his services there (whether or not for payment),

and has lawful control or charge of the child.

(7) "Child" (except in subsection (8)) means a person under the age of 18.

(8) "Specified nursery education" means full-time or part-time education suitable for children who have not attained compulsory school age which is provided-

(a) by a local education authority; or

(b) by any other person-

   (i) who is (or is to be) in receipt of financial assistance given by such an authority and whose provision of nursery education is taken into account by the authority in formulating proposals for the purposes of section 120(2)(a) of the School Standards and Framework Act 1998, or

   (ii) who is (or is to be) in receipt of grants under section 1 of the Nursery Education and Grant-Maintained Schools Act 1996; or

(c) (otherwise than as mentioned in paragraph (a) or (b)) in any educational institution which would fall within section 4(1) above (definition of "school") but for the fact that it provides part-time, rather than full-time, primary education."

(2) The following provisions of the Education Act 1996, namely-

(a) section 549 (interpretation of section 548), and

(b) section 550 (no avoidance of section 548 by refusing admission to school etc.),

shall cease to have effect.

> **S. 131**
> *The existing law which has the effect of making corporal punishment unlawful is rewritten. It is now extended to all schools, including independent schools. Apart from this, the only change of substance is that it is made clear that action which is taken to avert immediate danger of personal injury to or damage to property of a child or other person is not to be treated as corporal punishment. The section covers all teachers and anyone else working in or providing services to a school (including independent nursery schools that receive public funding) who has lawful control of the child.*

The funding authorities

132.–(1) The Funding Agency for Schools shall be dissolved on such date as the Secretary of State may by order specify ("the dissolution date").

(2) Prior to their dissolution the Agency shall-

(a) prepare, and submit to the Secretary of State for his approval, a plan for the disposal of property of the Agency to persons other than the Secretary of State; and

(b) once the plan is approved by the Secretary of State, make arrangements for the disposal of the property in question in accordance with the plan.

(3) The Agency shall use their best endeavours to secure that any functions remaining to be discharged by them at any time after the commencement of this section are discharged by such date or dates falling before the dissolution date as the Secretary of State may determine.

(4) Section 24 of the (1996 c. 56.)Education Act 1996 (directions by Secretary of State) applies to functions of the Agency under this section; and paragraph 15 of Schedule 2 to that Act (accounts) shall have effect for the purposes of subsection (3) above subject to such modifications as the Secretary of State may determine.

(5) Any property, rights and liabilities to which the Agency are entitled or subject immediately before the dissolution date (whether or not capable of being transferred or assigned by the Agency) shall by virtue of this section become property, rights and liabilities of the Secretary of State on that date.

(6) Any legal proceedings to which the Agency are a party immediately before the dissolution date may be continued on or after that date by or in relation to the Secretary of State.

(7) Every agreement (whether written or not), and every instrument or other document, which relates to any property, right or liability of the Agency to which subsection (5) applies shall have effect, so far as may be required for continuing its effect on or after the dissolution date, as if-

(a) where the Agency is a party to it, the Secretary of State were substituted as that party,

(b) for any reference to the Agency there were substituted a reference to the Secretary of State,

(c) for any reference (however worded and whether express or implied) to the chairman, the chief officer or any member of the Agency there were substituted a reference to such officer or officers as the Secretary of State may appoint for the purpose, and

(d) for any reference to the office or place of business of the Agency there were substituted a reference to the principal office of the Secretary of State.

S. 132
The Funding Agency for Schools is abolished and is required to organise its own dissolution.

133. Section 21 of the Education Act 1996 (which confers on the Secretary of State a power, so far unexercised, to establish the Schools Funding Council for Wales) shall cease to have effect.

S. 133
The power (which had never been exercised) for the Secretary of State to set up a Funding Agency for Wales is abolished.

School and nursery inspections

134.–(1) After section 42 of the School Inspections Act 1996 there shall be inserted-

"*Publication of reports*

42A.–(1) The Chief Inspector may in the case of-

(a) any report by a member of the Inspectorate of an inspection carried out by him under any provision of this Act (whether the report is required by any such provision or is otherwise made in pursuance of his functions under that provision), or

(b) any report of an inspection under section 10 (other than one made by a member of the Inspectorate),

arrange for the report to be published in such manner as the Chief Inspector considers appropriate.

(2) Without prejudice to the generality of-

(a) section 2(7)(c) or 5(7)(c), or

(b) subsection (1) above,

the Chief Inspector may arrange for a report to which that provision applies to be published by electronic means.

(3) For the purposes of the law of defamation any report published by the Chief Inspector under any of those provisions shall be privileged unless the publication is shown to be made with malice.

(4) Nothing in subsection (3) shall be construed as limiting any privilege subsisting apart from that subsection."

(2) In Schedule 1 to the Nursery Education and Grant-Maintained Schools Act 1996 (inspections of nursery education), at the end of paragraph 13 (reports of inspections) there shall be added-

"(3) Section 42A(2) to (4) of the School Inspections Act 1996 shall apply in relation to the publication of any such report as they apply in relation to the publication of a report under any of the provisions mentioned in section 42A(2)."

(3) In section 39 of the Education Act 1997 (reports of inspections of local education authorities), at the end of subsection (4) (publication of such reports) there shall be added "; and section 42A(2) to (4) of the School Inspections Act 1996 shall apply in relation to the publication of any such report as they apply in relation to the publication of a report under any of the provisions mentioned in section 42A(2)."

S. 134
New provision is made for the publication of inspection reports by the Chief Inspector of Schools including power to publish by electronic means. This extends to inspection reports of all schools, nursery schools and local education authorities.

135. Schedule 28 (which contains amendments relating to inspections under the School Inspections Act 1996 and the Nursery Education and Grant-Maintained Schools Act 1996) shall have effect.

S. 135
Schedule 28 contains detailed changes in relation to inspections.

Education Assets Board

136.–(1) The Education Assets Board shall be known instead as the Education Transfer Council.

(2) For any reference to the Education Assets Board-

(a) in any statutory provision (other than this section), or
(b) in any instrument or document,

there shall be substituted, as respects any time after the commencement of this section, a reference to the Education Transfer Council.

(3) The Secretary of State may by order specify a different name by which the Council are to be known; and an order under this section may make such provision as appears to the Secretary of State to be necessary or expedient in consequence of the change of name effected by the order (including provision for amending statutory provisions).

137.–(1) Schedule 29 (which amends section 198 of, and Schedule 10 to, the Education Reform Act 1988, which relate to the functions of the Education Transfer Council) shall have effect.

(2) The Secretary of State may by order make such further amendments of those provisions of that Act as he considers expedient.

(3) Regulations may make provision-

(a) for the dissolution of the Education Transfer Council by order of the Secretary of State and for enabling him to determine how any property, rights and liabilities of the Council are to be dealt with in connection with their dissolution;
(b) for the subsequent establishment of a new body with such name as may be prescribed and constituted in the same manner as, or similarly to, the Council;
(c) for dealing with transfers of property, rights and liabilities under this Act or under the Education Reform Act 1988 at a time when the Council has been dissolved and either-
(i) a body has been subsequently established under paragraph (b), or
(ii) no such body has been so established.

(4) Regulations under subsection (3) may, in connection with any matters falling within paragraph (b) or (c) of that subsection-

(a) modify any of the provisions of section 197 or 198 of, or Schedule 8 or 10 to, the (1988 c. 40.)Education Reform Act 1988;

(b) apply any of those provisions with or without modifications;

(c) make provision corresponding or similar to any of those provisions.

Ss 136 and 137
The Education Assets Board is renamed the Education Transfer Council and Schedule 29 makes detailed changes to existing legislation which the Secretary of State can further modify. The Council may be wound up and replaced by a new body having similar functions.

Supplementary

Ss 138 to 140 and 142 to 144
These sections, together with Schedules 30 to 32, contain detailed provisions relating to the making of regulations, provision of money for the purposes of the Act, minor and consequential amendments to existing legislation, transitional provisions, interpretation of terms used in the Act that are not defined elsewhere and its commencement.

138.–(1) Subject to subsection (2), any power of the Secretary of State to make an order or regulations under this Act shall be exercised by statutory instrument.

(2) Subsection (1) does not apply to any order under-

(a) section 11(5), 20(5), 21(8), 73, 82, 111(3)(a) or 142(1); or

(b) paragraph 5 of Schedule 5, paragraph 2 or 3 of Schedule 7, paragraph 3(5) or 4 of Schedule 10, paragraph 1 of Schedule 14, paragraph 10 of Schedule 21, paragraph 4(2) or 7(3)(c) of Schedule 22 or paragraph 5(3) of Schedule 32.

(3) Subject to subsections (4) and (5), a statutory instrument containing any order or regulations under this Act shall be subject to annulment in pursuance of a resolution of either House of Parliament.

(4) Subsection (3) does not apply to any order under-

(a) section 20(7), 69(3), 85(5), 104, 110(10) or 145; or

(b) paragraph 4 or 8 of Schedule 23 or paragraph 1 of Schedule 32.

(5) Subsection (3) also does not apply to-

(a) any order under-
(i) section 1(5),
(ii) paragraph 18 of Schedule 18, or
(iii) paragraph 17 of Schedule 24 or paragraph 14 of Schedule 25; or

(b) the first regulations to be made under-
    (i) section 38(3) or 39(1),
    (ii) section 46, 47 or 48(1), or
    (iii) section 105 or 108(2);

and no such order or regulations shall be made (whether alone or with other provisions) unless a draft of the statutory instrument containing the order or regulations has been laid before, and approved by a resolution of, each House of Parliament.

(6) If a draft of the statutory instrument containing any such regulations under section 105 would, apart from this subsection, be treated for the purposes of the Standing Orders of either House of Parliament as a hybrid instrument, it shall proceed in that House as if it were not such an instrument.

(7) Any order or regulations under this Act may make different provision for different cases, circumstances or areas and may contain such incidental, supplemental, saving or transitional provisions as the Secretary of State thinks fit.

(8) Any order or regulations under this Act may make different provision in relation to England and Wales respectively.

(9) Nothing in this Act shall be read as affecting the generality of subsection (7).

139.–(1) There shall be paid out of money provided by Parliament-

(a) any sums required for the making by the Secretary of State of grants or loans under this Act;
(b) any other expenses of the Secretary of State under this Act; and
(c) any increase attributable to this Act in the sums so payable by virtue of any other Act.

(2) There shall be paid into the Consolidated Fund-

(a) any sums received by the Secretary of State under or by virtue of this Act; and
(b) any fees received by Her Majesty's Chief Inspector of Schools in England, or Her Majesty's Chief Inspector of Schools in Wales, under Schedule 26.

140.–(1) The minor and consequential amendments set out in Schedule 30 shall have effect.

(2) Unless the context otherwise requires, any reference in any enactment amended by this Act-

(a) to a maintained school, or
(b) to a community, foundation or voluntary school or a community or foundation special school,

is a reference to such a school within the meaning of this Act.

(3) The enactments specified in Schedule 31 (which include certain spent enactments) are repealed to the extent specified.

(4) Any articles of government of a school which are in force under the Education Act 1996 immediately before the appointed day shall cease to have effect on that day.

Construction

141.–(1) For the purposes of this Act a maintained school serves an area for which there are one or more minor authorities if the area served by the school is-

(a) a parish or community;

(b) an area in England which is not within a parish and is not situated in-

(i) a county for which there is no council, or

(ii) a county in which there are no district councils; or

(c) an area comprising two or more areas each of which falls within paragraph (a) or (b).

(2) Where the area served by the school is a parish-

(a) the parish council (if there is one), or

(b) the parish meeting (if there is no parish council),

is the minor authority in relation to the school.

(3) Where the area served by the school is a community, the community council is the minor authority in relation to the school.

(4) Where the area served by the school is an area falling within subsection (1)(b), any district council for the whole or part of the area is a minor authority in relation to the school.

(5) Where the area served by the school is an area falling within subsection (1)(c), each of the relevant authorities is a minor authority in relation to the school.

(6) In subsection (5) "the relevant authorities" means the bodies which, if the two or more constituent areas referred to in subsection (1)(c) were taken separately, would be minor authorities in relation to the school.

(7) References in this section to the area served by a school are references to the area appearing to the local education authority to be served by the school.

S. 141

This section defines the term "minor authority" which is relevant in relation to the composition of governing bodies. It applies only to primary schools that specifically serve a parish or community where there is a parish, community or district council. The relevant council is the minor authority and (if the school is a community or voluntary school) is entitled to nominate a governor to be co-opted to the governing body under paragraph 15 of Schedule 9.

142.–(1) In this Act, unless the context otherwise requires-

"the appropriate further education funding council" has the meaning given by section 1(6) of the Further and Higher Education Act 1992;

"Church in Wales school" means a school in the Province of Wales in relation to which the religion or religious denomination specified under section 69(4) is "Church in Wales" and "appropriate diocesan authority", in relation to such a school, means the Diocesan Board of Finance for the diocese of the Church in Wales in which the school is situated or such other person as the Secretary of State may by order designate in respect of that diocese;

"Church of England school" means a school in the Province of Canterbury or York in relation to which the religion or religious denomination specified under section 69(4) is "Church of England" and "appropriate diocesan authority", in relation to such a school, means the Diocesan Board of Education for the diocese of the Church of England in which the school is situated;

"community or foundation special school" means a community special school or a foundation special school;

"contract of employment", "employee" and "employer" have the same meaning as in the Employment Rights Act 1996;

"employment" (except in section 92(4)) means employment under a contract of employment, and "employed" shall be construed accordingly;

"maintained school" (except in Part III) has the meaning given by section 20(7);

"prescribed" means prescribed by regulations;

"reception class" means a class in which education is provided which is suitable to the requirements of pupils aged five and any pupils under or over that age whom it is expedient to educate with pupils of that age;

"regulations" means regulations made by the Secretary of State under this Act;

"relevant age group", in relation to a school, means an age group in which pupils are normally admitted (or, as the case may be, will normally be admitted) to the school;

"Roman Catholic Church school" means a school in relation to which the religion or religious denomination specified under section 69(4) is "Roman Catholic" and "appropriate diocesan authority", in relation to such a school, means the bishop of the Roman Catholic diocese in which the school is situated;

"school maintained by a local education authority", in relation to any time on or after the appointed day, means a community, foundation or voluntary school, a community or foundation special school, a maintained nursery school or a pupil referral unit;

"statutory provision" means a provision contained in an Act or in subordinate legislation within the meaning of the Interpretation Act 1978.

(2) Before making an order in respect of any diocese in Wales in exercise of the power conferred by the definition of "appropriate diocesan authority" the Secretary of State shall consult the bishop for the diocese.

(3) Any reference in this Act to the religion or religious denomination specified in relation to a school under section 69(4) shall be construed, in a case where more than one religion or religious denomination is so specified, as including a reference to any of those religions or religious denominations.

(4) As a result of subsection (3), subsection (1) has the effect that a school may, for example, be both a Church of England school and a Roman Catholic Church school and so have a different appropriate diocesan authority in each of those capacities; and, in the case of a school with two appropriate diocesan authorities, any reference in this Act to "the appropriate diocesan authority" is-

(a) in relation to anything required to be done by or in relation to that authority, a reference to both of the authorities concerned; or

(b) in relation to anything authorised to be done by or in relation to that authority, a reference to either or both of the authorities concerned (or, in the context of section 16(6) or (8), to both of them acting together).

(5) For the purposes of this Act children are to be regarded as admitted to a school for nursery education if they are or are to be placed on admission in a nursery class.

(6) For the purposes of this Act references to disposing of land include references to-

(a) granting or disposing of any interest in land;

(b) entering into a contract to dispose of land or to grant or dispose of any such interest; and

(c) granting an option to purchase any land or any such interest.

(7) For the purposes of this Act-

(a) a person employed by a local education authority is to be regarded as employed to work at a school if his employment with the authority for the time being involves work at that school; and

(b) a person employed by a local education authority is to be regarded as employed to work solely at a school if his only employment with the authority (disregarding any employment under a separate contract with the authority) is for the time being at that school.

(8) This Act shall be construed as one with the Education Act 1996; and (without prejudice to their generality) paragraphs 1 and 2 of Schedule 39 to that Act (construction of references etc.) apply to references in this Act to provisions of that Act.

(9) Where, however, an expression is given for the purposes of any provision of this Act a meaning different from that given to it for the purposes of that Act, the meaning given for the purposes of that provision shall apply instead of the one given for the purposes of that Act.

(10)   Subsection (1) of section 576 of that Act (meaning of "parent") shall, in its application for the purposes of-

(a) section 43 or 62(2) of this Act, or

(b) paragraph 4 of Schedule 2 or paragraph 4 or 14 of Schedule 9 to this Act,

be taken as referring only to persons within paragraph (a) or (b) of that subsection who are individuals.

143. The expressions listed in the left-hand column below are defined by, or (as the case may be) are to be interpreted in accordance with, the provisions of this Act listed in the right-hand column in relation to those expressions.

Expression	*Relevant provision*
ability (in Chapter II of Part III)	section 99(5)
adjudicator	section 25(3)
admission arrangements (in Part III in relation to a maintained school)	sections 88(2) and 99(5)
admission authority (in Chapter I of Part III in relation to a maintained school)	section 88(1)
admitted to a school for nursery education	section 142(5)
alteration (in Part II in the context of a prescribed alteration to a maintained school)	section 28(11)
appeal panel (in Chapter I of Part III)	section 84(6)
appointed day (except in Part I of Schedule 32)	section 20(7)
appropriate diocesan authority (in relation to a Church in Wales, Church of England or Roman Catholic Church school)	section 142(1) and (4)
appropriate further education funding council	section 142(1)
area (in Part II)	section 28(11)
budget share (in Part II)	section 47(1)
Chief Inspector (in Chapter IV of Part I)	section 14(4)
child (in Chapter I of Part III but not in sections 96 and 97)	section 84(6)
Church in Wales school	section 142(1)

Church of England school	section 142(1)
class (in Chapter I of Part I)	section 4
community or foundation special school	section 142(1)
"contract of employment" and other expressions relating to employment	section 142(1) and (7)
discontinuing, and implementing proposals to discontinue, a school (in Part II in relation to a local education authority)	section 29(10)
disposing of land	section 142(6)
education action zone (in Chapter III of Part I)	section 10(1)
exclude, exclusion (in relation to the exclusion of a child from a school)	section 64(4)
foundation (in relation to a foundation or voluntary school) (and having a foundation)	section 21(3)
foundation body	section 21(4)
foundation governor	paragraph 2 of Schedule 9
governing body (in Chapter III of Part I)	section 10(6)
(of a maintained school or of a school maintained by a local education authority) (in Chapter IV of Part II)	section 45(3)
grammar school (in Chapter II of Part III)	section 104(7)
group (in relation to a foundation body)	section 21(4)
individual schools budget (in Part II)	section 46(2)
infant class (in Chapter I of Part I)	section 4
land or other property held on trust, or by trustees, for the purposes of a school	section 21(3)(c)
local education authority (in relation to a school maintained, or proposed to be maintained, by such an authority)	section 22(8)
local schools budget (in Part II)	section 46(1)
maintain (in relation to a maintained school or a maintained nursery school)	section 22(8)

maintained school

   (generally)   section 20(7)

   (in Chapter IV of Part II in a context referring to a local education authority)   section 45(3)

   (in Chapter I of Part III)   section 84(6)

   (in Chapter II of Part III)   section 99(5)

maintained nursery school   section 22(9)

member of the Inspectorate (in Chapter IV of Part I)   section 14(4)

minor authority   section 141

new school (in Chapter IV of Part II)   section 45(4)

nursery education (in Part V)   section 117

ordinary teaching session (in Chapter I of Part I)   section 4

participating school (in Chapter III of Part I in relation to an education action zone)   section 10(6)

prescribed   section 142(1)

promoters (in Part II)   section 28(2)

qualified teacher (in Chapter I of Part I in relation to an infant class)   section 4

reception class   section 142(1)

regulations   section 142(1)

relevant age group   section 142(1)

relevant standard number (in Chapter I of Part III)   section 84(6)

right to a delegated budget (in Part II)   section 49(7)

Roman Catholic Church school   section 142(1)

scheme (in Part II in relation to a maintained school)   section 48(5)

school having a delegated budget (in Part II)   section 49(7)

school maintained by a local education authority

   (generally)   section 142(1)

   (in Chapter IV of Part II)   section 45(3)

school opening date   section 44(9)

school organisation committee   section 24(4)

school requiring special measures (in Chapter IV of Part I)	section 14(4)
school which has a religious character (in Part II in relation to a foundation or voluntary school)	section 69(3)
school which has selective admission arrangements (in Chapter II of Part III)	section 104(2)
specified religion or religious denomination	section 142(3)
statutory provision	section 142(1)

Final provisions

144.–(1) Regulations may at any time make such incidental, consequential, transitional or supplementary provision as appears to the Secretary of State to be necessary or expedient for the general purposes, or any particular purposes, of this Act or in consequence of any of its provisions or for giving full effect to it.

(2) Regulations under subsection (1) may, in particular, make provision-

(a) for enabling any authority or body by whom any functions will become exercisable on the appointed day by virtue of any provision made by or under this Act to take before that day any steps (such as the establishment of committees or the undertaking of consultation) which are necessary or expedient in preparation for the exercise of those functions;

(b) for requiring any body-
   (i) by whom any functions will cease to be exercisable at any time, or
   (ii) who are required to be reconstituted as from any time,
   by virtue of any provision made by or under this Act to take before that time any steps (such as the provision of information, the furnishing of other assistance or the taking of any decision) which are necessary or expedient in preparation for the exercise of functions conferred on any authority or other body, by virtue of any such provision, as from that time or (as the case may be) in preparation for their reconstitution;

(c) for the making before the appointed day of arrangements for securing the satisfactory operation from that day of any such provision and for defraying the cost of any such arrangements;

(d) for prohibiting or restricting the taking of steps before the appointed day which, by virtue of any such provision, will cease to be capable of being taken as from that day;

(e) for enabling the determination under the regulations of matters pending immediately before the appointed day;

(f) for any provision of this Act which comes into force before-
   (i) another such provision has come into force, or
   (ii) anything falling to be done under another such provision (such as the approval of a school organisation plan) has been done,

to have effect, until that other provision has come into force or (as the case may be) that thing has been done, with such modifications as are specified in the regulations;

(g) for amending, repealing or revoking (with or without savings) any statutory provision passed or made before the appointed day, for applying any such provision (with or without modification) and for making savings or additional savings from the effect of any amendment or repeal made by this Act.

(3) Without prejudice to the generality of subsection (1) or any provision of subsection (2), regulations under subsection (1) may provide-

(a) for any relevant provision to apply (with or without modification) to, or to any description of-
   (i) schools maintained by a local education authority within the meaning of the Education Act 1996, or
   (ii) grant-maintained or grant-maintained special schools within the meaning of that Act;
(b) for any provision so applied, or any provision of the regulations, to have effect in relation to schools despite anything in their articles or instruments of government;
(c) for any reference in this Act to the appointed day to have effect instead as a reference to such day as is specified in the regulations;

and accordingly references to the appointed day in subsection (2) include, in relation to any purposes for which any provision made by virtue of paragraph (c) above has effect, references to any such other day as is mentioned in that paragraph.

(4) In paragraph (a) of subsection (3) "relevant provision" means-

(a) (in relation to sub-paragraph (i) or (ii) of that paragraph) any provision of the Education Acts which is expressed to apply to, or to any description of, schools maintained by a local education authority within the meaning of this Act, or
(b) (in relation only to sub-paragraph (ii) of that paragraph) any provision of the Education Acts which is expressed to apply to, or to any description of, schools maintained by a local education authority within the meaning of the (1996 c. 56.)Education Act 1996;

and in that paragraph and this subsection "school" includes a proposed school.

(5) The amendments that may be made under subsection (2)(g) shall be in addition (and without prejudice) to those made by any other provision of this Act.

(6) Nothing in this Act shall be read as prejudicing the generality of subsection (1).

(7) The transitional provisions and savings in Schedule 32 shall have effect.

145.–(1) This Act may be cited as the School Standards and Framework Act 1998.

(2) This Act shall be included in the list of Education Acts set out in section 578 of the Education Act 1996.

(3) Subject to subsections (4) and (5), this Act shall come into force on such day as the Secretary of State may by order appoint; and different days may be appointed for different provisions and for different purposes.

(4) The following provisions come into force on the day on which this Act is passed-
sections 1 to 4;
sections 20 and 21;
section 36(3);
section 82;
sections 84 and 85;
section 130;
sections 138, 139, 141 to 144 and this section;
Schedule 2;
Parts I and III of Schedule 11;
paragraph 224 of Schedule 30 (and section 140(1) so far as relating thereto); and
Schedule 32.

(5) The following provisions come into force on the day on which this Act is passed, but for the purposes only of the preparation of instruments of government and the constitution of governing bodies and the exercise (in relation to those or any other matters) of any power to make regulations-
sections 36(1) and (2) and 37(1) and (2); and
Schedules 9, 10 and 12.

(6) Subject to subsections (7) and (8), this Act extends to England and Wales only.

(7) Section 130(2) extends to Scotland only; and this section extends also to Scotland.

(8) The amendment or (subject to subsection (9)) repeal by this Act of an enactment extending to Scotland or Northern Ireland extends also to Scotland or, as the case may be, Northern Ireland, and section 140 extends accordingly.

(9) The entry in Schedule 31 relating to the Education (Scotland) Act 1980 extends to Scotland only.

SCHEDULES

SCHEDULE 1

PROVISIONS RELATING TO AN EDUCATION ACTION FORUM

Powers

1.–(1) An Education Action Forum may, subject to sub-paragraph (2), do anything which is calculated to facilitate, or is incidental or conducive to, the carrying out of any of its functions.

(2) A Forum shall not have power to borrow money.

Chairman

2. The members of an Education Action Forum shall elect one of their number to be chairman of the Forum, who shall hold office for such period as is specified in the order by which the Forum is established under section 10(1).

Committees

3. An Education Action Forum may-

   (a) establish a committee for any purpose; and
   (b) authorise any such committee to exercise such of its functions as it may determine.

Proceedings

4. The Secretary of State may by regulations make provision as to the meetings and proceedings of an Education Action Forum.

5. The validity of the proceedings of an Education Action Forum shall not be affected by a vacancy among the members or any defect in the appointment of a member.

6. Subject to the preceding provisions of this Schedule, an Education Action Forum may regulate its own procedure and that of any of its committees.

Accounts

7.–(1) It shall be the duty of an Education Action Forum-

   (a) to keep proper accounts and proper records in relation to the accounts,
   (b) to prepare in respect of each financial year of the Forum a statement of accounts, and
   (c) to send copies of the statement to the Secretary of State and to the Comptroller and Auditor General before the end of the month of August next following the financial year to which the statement relates.

(2) The statement of accounts shall comply with any directions given by the Secretary of State as to-

(a) the information to be contained in it,

(b) the manner in which the information contained in it is to be presented, or

(c) the methods and principles according to which the statement is to be prepared.

(3) The Comptroller and Auditor General shall examine, certify and report on each statement received by him in pursuance of this paragraph and shall lay copies of each statement and of his report before each House of Parliament.

(4) In this paragraph "financial year" means the period beginning with the date on which the Forum is established and ending with the 31st March following that date, and each successive period of twelve months.

Application of seal and proof of instruments

8. The application of the seal of an Education Action Forum shall be authenticated by the signature-

(a) of the chairman or of some other person authorised either generally or specially by the Forum to act for that purpose, and

(b) of one other member.

9. Every document purporting to be an instrument made or issued by or on behalf of an Education Action Forum and to be duly executed under the seal of the Forum, or to be signed or executed by a person authorised by the Forum to act in that behalf, shall be received in evidence and be treated, without further proof, as being so made or issued unless the contrary is shown.

Charitable status

10. An Education Action Forum shall be a charity which is an exempt charity for the purposes of the Charities Act 1993.

Schedule 1
This Schedule contains the detailed provisions relating to the constitution of Education Action Forums, establishing them as having general powers (other than the power to borrow) and having exempt charity status.

SCHEDULE 2

Allocation of existing schools to new categories

Allocation of LEA-maintained schools

1. A school which immediately before the appointed day is (within the meaning of the Education Act 1996)-

    (a) a county school,
    (b) a controlled, aided or special agreement school, or
    (c) a maintained special school,

shall become on that day a school of the category to which it is allocated by the following table.

Existing school	*Allocated new category*
A county school	Community school.
A controlled school	Voluntary controlled school.
(1) An aided school	Voluntary aided school.
(2) A special agreement school	
A maintained special school	Community special school.

Allocation of grant-maintained and grant-maintained special schools

2. A school which immediately before the appointed day is (within the meaning of the Education Act 1996)-

    (a) a grant-fmaintained school, or
    (b) a grant-maintained special school,

shall become on that day a school of the category to which it is to be allocated in accordance with the following paragraphs of this Schedule.

Indicative allocation of schools within paragraph 2

3. For the purposes of this Schedule the indicative allocation of a school within paragraph 2 is shown in the following table.

Existing school	*Indicative new category*
(1) A grant-maintained school formerly a county or controlled school.	Foundation school
(2) A grant-maintained school established by the Funding Agency for Schools.	
(1) A grant-maintained school formerly an aided or special agreement school.	Voluntary aided school.

(2) A grant-maintained school established by promoters (within the meaning of Part III of the Education Act 1996)

A grant-maintained special school Foundation special school.

Any reference in the first column to a school of a particular description is a reference to a school of that description within the meaning of the Education Act 1996.

Preliminary decision by governing body as to new category

4.–(1) The governing body of a school within paragraph 2 shall in the first instance take a decision (their "preliminary decision") on the question whether-

(a) to accept the school's allocation to a particular category in accordance with its indicative allocation, or
(b) to opt for it to be allocated to a different category.

(2) Regulations may make provision as to the procedure to be followed in connection with the taking by governing bodies of their preliminary decisions under sub-paragraph (1).

(3) Regulations under sub-paragraph (2) may, in particular, make provision-

(a) as to the consultation to be carried out by governing bodies before taking their preliminary decisions;
(b) as to the time by which governing bodies are to take such decisions;
(c) as to the notification of such decisions to prescribed persons;
(d) as to the provision of prescribed information to prescribed persons;
(e) authorising governing bodies to charge a fee (not exceeding the cost of supply) for prescribed documents supplied by them in pursuance of regulations made by virtue of paragraph (d);
(f) requiring the holding of ballots of registered parents in prescribed cases;
(g) enabling the Secretary of State, in any prescribed circumstances, to declare a previous ballot void and require the holding of a fresh ballot;
(h) as to the conduct of ballots held under the regulations;
(i) specifying criteria for determining, for the purposes of the regulations and this Schedule, the result of any such ballot.

Final decision by governing body as to new category

5.–(1) Where-

(a) the governing body of a school within paragraph 2 have taken their preliminary decision under sub-paragraph (1) of paragraph 4, and
(b) the result of a ballot held by virtue of that paragraph does not accord with that decision,

the governing body shall reconsider the question set out in that sub-paragraph, having regard to the result of the ballot, and shall then take a further decision on that question.

(2) Where-

    (a) the governing body of a school within paragraph 2 have taken their preliminary decision under sub-paragraph (1) of paragraph 4, and

    (b) either-

        (i) a ballot was held by virtue of that paragraph whose result (if any) was not to disagree with that decision, or

        (ii) no such ballot was required to be held,

the governing body shall take a further decision confirming their preliminary decision.

(3) Regulations may make provision as to the procedure to be followed in connection with the taking by governing bodies of their final decisions (including, in particular, provision as to the time by which governing bodies are to take such decisions).

(4) In this Schedule any reference to a governing body's "final decision" is a reference to any such further decision as is required by sub-paragraph (1) or (2).

Notification of final decision

6.–(1) Once the governing body of a school within paragraph 2 have taken their final decision, they shall give written notification of that decision to the Secretary of State.

(2) Regulations may make provision-

    (a) requiring governing bodies-

        (i) when giving such notifications, to certify such matters as may be specified in the regulations, and

        (ii) to provide such information to such persons as may be so specified;

    (b) as to the time by which such notifications are to be given or such information is to be provided.

Final determination of new category

7.–(1) If-

    (a) the final decision of the governing body of a school within paragraph 2 accorded with the school's indicative allocation, and

    (b) either-

        (i) a ballot was held by virtue of paragraph 4 whose result (if any) was not to disagree with that allocation, or

        (ii) no such ballot was required to be held,

the school shall be allocated to the category provided for by its indicative allocation.

(2) If in the case of a school within paragraph 2-

    (a) the final decision of the governing body, or

    (b) the result of a ballot held by virtue of paragraph 4,

did not accord with the school's indicative allocation, the school shall be allocated to such category (whether or not that provided for by its indicative allocation) as the Secretary of State may determine in conformity with regulations under paragraph 8.

(3) The Secretary of State shall notify the governing body of each school within paragraph 2 of the category to which it is allocated in accordance with this paragraph.

Restrictions on decisions as to categories

8. Regulations may make provision for prohibiting a school of any description specified in the regulations-

(a) from being allocated under paragraph 7 to a category so specified; or
(b) from being so allocated unless such conditions are satisfied as are so specified.

Transitional arrangements: schools within paragraph 2

9.–(1) Where the category to which a school within paragraph 2 is to be allocated has not been finally determined, in accordance with the preceding paragraphs of this Schedule, by the appointed day, the school shall be taken to be allocated on that day to the category provided for by its indicative allocation.

(2) Sub-paragraph (1) does not prevent such a school from being subsequently allocated to a different category in accordance with paragraph 7.

(3) Where such a school is subsequently so allocated, section 20(2)(a) shall apply to it as if it had been allocated to the category in question on the appointed day.

Transitional arrangements: general

10.–(1) Regulations may make such provision as the Secretary of State considers appropriate in connection with the allocation to the new categories of maintained schools of schools-

(a) to which paragraph 9(1) applies; or
(b) whose school opening date falls on or after the date of the passing of this Act; or
(c) in relation to which a duty to implement proposals to discontinue the school has arisen, or a notice to discontinue the school has been given; or
(d) in relation to which a notice has been given under section 272 of the Education Act 1996 (school unsuitable to continue as grant-maintained school) which contains such a statement as is mentioned in subsection (3) or (5)(b) of that section.

(2) Regulations under sub-paragraph (1) may provide that any provision of the Education Acts shall apply to any such school with such modifications as are specified in the regulations.

Effect of allocation

11. The allocation of a school to a particular category under this Schedule shall not be taken as authorising or requiring any change as from the appointed day in the character of the school conducted by its governing body (including, in particular, any religious character of the school).

> **Schedule 2**
> *This Schedule sets out the new categories of schools and how they relate to the old ones. Broadly, schools that were county schools become community schools, those that were respectively controlled and aided schools become voluntary controlled and voluntary aided schools. Special agreement schools become voluntary aided schools.*
>
> *Former grant-maintained schools are given an indicative allocation depending on their status before becoming grant-maintained or (in the case of new grant-maintained schools) the basis on which they were incorporated. Governing bodies were required to consider and consult on whether the indicative category was acceptable and had the option, subject to parental ballot and Secretary of State approval, to seek an alternative category. The process was governed by regulations and was to have been completed by 1st September 1999. The indicative category for grant-maintained schools that were formerly county or controlled schools or which had been established by the Funding Agency for Schools was foundation status, that for former aided or special agreement schools or those established by promoters was voluntary aided status and grant-maintained special schools were to become foundation special schools.*

SCHEDULE 3

FUNDING OF FOUNDATION, VOLUNTARY AND FOUNDATION SPECIAL SCHOOLS

PART I FOUNDATION, VOLUNTARY CONTROLLED AND FOUNDATION SPECIAL SCHOOLS

Obligations of governing bodies

1.–(1) The governing body of a foundation, voluntary controlled or foundation special school are (in accordance with section 22(4)) not responsible for any of the expenses of maintaining the school.

(2) Sub-paragraph (1) does not apply to the repayment of the principal of, or interest on, a loan made to the governing body.

Obligations of LEAs as regards provision of sites and buildings (otherwise than in connection with statutory proposals)

2.–(1) In the case of a foundation, voluntary controlled or foundation special school, the local education authority shall provide-

(a) any new site which is to be provided in addition to, or instead of, the school's existing site (or part of its existing site), and

(b) any buildings which are to form part of the school premises.

(2) Sub-paragraph (1) does not-

(a) apply in relation to the provision of any site or buildings which the authority or promoters are required to provide by virtue of Part III of Schedule 6 (provision of premises in connection with statutory proposals); or

(b) require the local education authority to finance the acquisition by the governing body of any site or buildings provided otherwise than by the authority.

(3) Where a site is provided for a school under this paragraph, the local education authority shall transfer their interest in the site, and in any buildings on the site which are to form part of the school premises-

(a) to the trustees of the school, to be held by them on trust for the purposes of the school, or

(b) if the school has no trustees, to the school's foundation body or (in the absence of such a body) to the governing body, to be held by that body for the relevant purposes.

(4) If any doubt or dispute arises as to the persons to whom the authority are required to make the transfer, it shall be made to such persons as the Secretary of State thinks proper.

(5) The authority shall pay to the persons to whom the transfer is made their reasonable costs in connection with the transfer.

(6) Where-

(a) a transfer is made under this paragraph, and

(b) the transfer is made to persons who possess, or are or may become entitled to, any sum representing proceeds of the sale of other premises which have been used for the purposes of the school,

those persons shall notify the local education authority that paragraph (b) applies to them and they or their successors shall pay to the local education authority so much of that sum as, having regard to the value of the interest transferred, may be determined to be just, either by agreement between them and the authority or, in default of agreement, by the Secretary of State.

(7) In sub-paragraph (6)(b) the reference to proceeds of the sale of other premises includes a reference to-

(a) consideration for the creation or disposition of any kind of interest in other premises, including rent; and

(b) interest which has accrued in respect of any such consideration;

and for the purposes of any agreed determination under sub-paragraph (6) regard shall be had to any guidance given from time to time by the Secretary of State.

(8) Any sum paid under sub-paragraph (6) shall be treated for the purposes of section 14 of the Schools Sites Act 1841 (which relates to the sale or exchange of land held on trust for the purposes of a school) as a sum applied in the purchase of a site for the school.

(9) A determination may be made under sub-paragraph (6) in respect of any property subject to a trust which has arisen under section 1 of the Reverter of Sites Act 1987 (right of reverter replaced by trust for sale) if (and only if)-

(a) the determination is made by the Secretary of State, and

(b) he is satisfied that steps have been taken to protect the interests of the beneficiaries under the trust.

(10) Sub-paragraph (6) shall apply for the purpose of compensating the authority notified under that sub-paragraph only in relation to such part of the sum mentioned in sub-paragraph (6)(b) (if any) as remains after the application of paragraphs 1 to 3 of Schedule 22 to that sum.

(11) In this paragraph-

"the relevant purposes" means-
(a) in relation to a transfer to a school's foundation body, the purposes of the schools comprising the group for which that body acts, and
(b) in relation to a transfer to a school's governing body, the purposes of the school;

"site" does not include playing fields but otherwise includes any site which is to form part of the premises of the school in question.

PART II VOLUNTARY AIDED SCHOOLS

Obligations of governing bodies

3.–(1) In the case of a voluntary aided school, the expenses of discharging any liability incurred by or on behalf of-
(a) the governing body of the school,
(b) any former governors of the school, or
(c) any trustees of the school,

in connection with the provision of premises or specified equipment for the purposes of the school are payable by the governing body of the school.

In this sub-paragraph "specified equipment" means equipment of any description specified by the Secretary of State for the purposes of this sub-paragraph.

(2) In addition, any expenses incurred-

(a) in making to the school buildings of a voluntary aided school such alterations as may be required by the local education authority for the purpose of securing that the school premises conform to the standards prescribed under section 542 of the Education Act 1996, or

(b) in effecting repairs to the school buildings, other than repairs falling within sub-paragraph (3),

are payable by the governing body of the school.

(3) The governing body of a voluntary aided school are not responsible—

(a) for repairs to the interior of the school buildings, or

(b) for repairs to those buildings necessary in consequence of the use of the school premises, in pursuance of a direction or requirement of the local education authority, for purposes other than those of the school.

(4) Nothing in this paragraph imposes on the governing body of a voluntary aided school which was (either before or after the appointed day) a school of a different description any obligation in respect of a liability incurred at any time before the school became a voluntary aided school if at that time no obligation in respect of that liability was imposed on them, as the governing body of a school of that description, under this Act or the (1996 c. 56.)Education Act 1996, as the case may be.

Obligations of LEAs as regards provision of sites (otherwise than in connection with statutory proposals)

4.–(1) In the case of a voluntary aided school, the local education authority shall provide any new site which is to be provided in addition to, or instead of, the school's existing site (or part of its existing site).

(2) Sub-paragraph (1) does not-

(a) apply in relation to the provision of any site which persons other than the authority are required to provide by virtue of Part III of Schedule 6 (provision of premises in connection with statutory proposals); or

(b) require the local education authority to finance the acquisition by the governing body of any site or buildings provided otherwise than by the authority.

(3) Where a site is provided for a school under this paragraph, the local education authority shall transfer their interest in the site, and in any buildings on the site which are to form part of the school premises-

(a) to the trustees of the school, to be held by them on trust for the purposes of the school, or

(b) if the school has no trustees, to the school's foundation body to be held by that body for the relevant purposes.

(4) If any doubt or dispute arises as to the persons to whom the authority are required to make the transfer, it shall be made to such persons as the Secretary of State thinks proper.

(5) The authority shall pay to the persons to whom the transfer is made their reasonable costs in connection with the transfer.

(6) Where-

(a) a site is provided for a school under this paragraph, and

(b) work is required to be done to the site for the purpose of clearing it or making it suitable for building purposes,

the local education authority and the governing body of the school may make an agreement providing for the making of such payments, or of such other adjustments of their respective rights and liabilities, as will secure that the cost of the work is borne by the authority.

(7) Where-

(a) a site is provided for a school under this paragraph, and

(b) there are buildings on the site which are of value for the purposes of the school,

the local education authority and the governing body of the school may make an agreement providing for the making of such payments, or of such other adjustments of their respective rights and liabilities, as appear to be desirable having regard to the governing body's duties under paragraph 3 with respect to the school buildings.

(8) Where it appears to the Secretary of State that provision for any payment or other adjustment ought to have been made under sub-paragraph (6) or (7) but has not been made, he may give directions providing for the making of such payment or other adjustment as he thinks proper.

(9) In this paragraph-

"the relevant purposes" means, in relation to a transfer to a school's foundation body, the purposes of the schools comprising the group for which that body acts;

"site" does not include playing fields but otherwise includes any site which is to form part of the premises of the school in question.

Grants by Secretary of State in respect of expenditure on premises or equipment

5.–(1) The Secretary of State may make grants-

(a) to the governing body of a voluntary aided school in respect of qualifying expenditure incurred by them; or

(b) to a relevant body in the case of such a school, in respect of qualifying expenditure incurred by that body on behalf of the governing body.

(2) In sub-paragraph (1) "qualifying expenditure" means expenditure in respect of the provision, alteration or repair of premises or equipment for the school.

(3) The amount of any grant paid under this paragraph in respect of any such expenditure-

(a) shall not exceed 85 per cent. of the expenditure, and

(b) in the case of any prescribed class or description of such expenditure, shall be such as may be determined in accordance with regulations.

(4) The times at which, and the manner in which, payments are made in respect of a grant under this paragraph shall be such as may be determined from time to time by the Secretary of State.

(5) Without prejudice to any other duty of his, the Secretary of State shall, in performing functions relating to the exercise of the power under this paragraph to make grants in respect of expenditure on-

(a) such alterations to school buildings as are referred to in paragraph 3(2)(a), or

(b) the repair of school buildings,

give priority to paying grants in respect of expenditure which is necessary for the performance by governing bodies of their duties; and the amount of any grant paid in the exercise of that power in respect of such expenditure on the repair of school buildings shall be 85 per cent. of the expenditure.

(6) Any body to whom any payment is made in respect of a grant under this paragraph shall comply with such requirements determined by the Secretary of State as he may from time to time impose.

(7) Such requirements-

(a) may be imposed on, or at any time after, the making of any payment by reference to which they are imposed, and

(b) may at any time be waived, removed or varied by the Secretary of State;

but such requirements may be imposed after the making of any such payment only if the Secretary of State is satisfied that in all the circumstances it is reasonable for them to be so imposed.

(8) Such requirements may, in particular, if any conditions specified in the requirements are satisfied-

(a) require the application for purposes connected with the provision of education in appropriate schools of-

(i) any premises or equipment in respect of which the grant has been paid under this paragraph, or

(ii) an amount equal to so much of the value of any such premises or equipment as is determined in accordance with the requirements to be properly attributable to the payment of the grant; and

(b) in the event that that requirement is not complied with, require the payment to the Secretary of State of the whole or any part of the following amount.

(9) That amount is-

(a) the amount of the payments made in respect of the grant under this paragraph, or

(b) the amount mentioned in sub-paragraph (8)(a)(ii),

whichever the Secretary of State determines to be just.

(10) When deciding whether to make any grant to a body under this paragraph in circumstances where he considers that it would be appropriate to impose

requirements falling within sub-paragraph (8), the Secretary of State may have regard to whether, if such requirements were imposed, that body would have an enforceable right against some other person to be given by that person such financial assistance as would be necessary to enable them to pay to the Secretary of State the amount mentioned in sub-paragraph (9).

(11) No grant may be paid under this paragraph in respect of any expenses incurred in the provision of any premises which it is the duty of the local education authority to provide.

(12) In this paragraph-

"appropriate schools"-

(a) in relation to a voluntary aided school having a religious character, means schools which are either foundation or voluntary schools and whose specified religion or religious denomination under section 69(4) is the same as that school's, and

(b) in relation to any other voluntary aided school, means maintained schools;

"relevant body", in relation to a voluntary aided school, means the appropriate diocesan authority or the school's trustees;

"repair" does not include repair falling within paragraph 3(3).

Grants by Secretary of State in respect of preliminary expenditure

6.–(1) The Secretary of State may pay grants-

(a) to the governing body of a voluntary aided school in respect of preliminary expenditure incurred by them for the purposes of any scheme for the transfer of the school to a new site or the enlargement or alteration of the school premises, or

(b) to a relevant body in the case of such a school, in respect of any preliminary expenditure incurred by them, on behalf of the governing body, for the purposes of any such scheme.

(2) Where any persons propose or are considering whether to propose the establishment of a voluntary aided school, the Secretary of State may pay grants to them in respect of any preliminary expenditure incurred by them for the purposes of a scheme for the provision of a site for the school or of any buildings which would be school buildings.

(3) Grants under sub-paragraph (1) or (2) may be paid in respect of a scheme such as is mentioned in that sub-paragraph whether or not-

(a) the details of such a scheme had been formulated at the time when the expenditure was incurred,

(b) where such details were not formulated at that time, they are subsequently formulated,

(c) the governing body or persons in question had determined to proceed with such a scheme at that time, or

(d) where they had not determined to proceed with such a scheme at that time, they subsequently determine to proceed with such a scheme.

(4) Expenditure in respect of which such grants are payable includes, in particular, costs incurred in connection with-

(a) the preparation of plans and specifications for any proposed construction, enlargement or alteration of buildings which are or would be school buildings, and

(b) estimating the sums which would be expended if any such works were carried out,

but does not include any sums expended in carrying out any such works.

(5) A grant under sub-paragraph (1) or (2) shall not exceed 85 per cent. of the expenditure in respect of which it is paid.

(6) Where-

(a) a grant is paid under sub-paragraph (1) in the case of any voluntary aided school, or

(b) a grant is paid under sub-paragraph (2) in the case of any school which is established as a voluntary aided school,

the grant shall for the purposes of section 30(2) be treated as expenditure incurred by the Secretary of State (otherwise than in connection with repairs) in respect of the school premises.

(7) In this paragraph "relevant body", in relation to a voluntary aided school, means the appropriate diocesan authority or the school's trustees.

Loans by Secretary of State in respect of initial expenses

7.-(1) Where, on the application of the governing body of a voluntary aided school and after consulting persons representing the governing body, the Secretary of State-

(a) is satisfied that the governing body's share of any initial expenses required in connection with the school premises will involve capital expenditure, and

(b) having regard to all the circumstances of the case, considers that that expenditure ought properly to be met by borrowing,

he may make a loan to the governing body for the purpose of helping them meet that expenditure.

(2) The amount, rate of interest and other terms and conditions applicable to the loan shall be such as may be specified in an agreement made between the Secretary of State and the governing body with the consent of the Treasury.

(3) For the purposes of this paragraph "initial expenses" are expenses to be incurred in providing-

(a) a site or school buildings for a voluntary aided school in connection with-

      (i) the implementation of any proposals for a prescribed alteration to the school published under section 28, or

      (ii) the transfer of the school to a new site, or

    (b) a site or school buildings for a new voluntary aided school,

being expenses in respect of which grants may be paid under paragraph 5.

(4) For the purposes of this paragraph the governing body's share of any initial expenses shall be taken to be so much of the expenses as remains to be borne by the governing body after taking into account the amount of any grant under paragraph 5 that may be paid or payable in respect of them.

(5) The preceding provisions of this paragraph shall apply for the purpose of enabling loans to be made to a relevant body (within the meaning of paragraph 5) in respect of expenses incurred by that body on behalf of the governing body as it applies to expenses incurred by the governing body; and in those provisions, as they apply in relation to a new voluntary aided school, references to the governing body are to the promoters.

(6) Paragraph 3(3) of Schedule 10 (consent to borrowing) does not apply to any borrowing by a governing body under this paragraph.

Assistance by LEAs in respect of maintenance and other obligations of governing bodies

8. A local education authority may give to the governing body of a voluntary aided school such assistance as the authority think fit in relation to the carrying out by the governing body of any obligation under paragraph 3.

Duty to transfer interest in premises provided under paragraph 8

9.–(1) Where assistance under paragraph 8 consists of the provision of any premises for use for the purposes of a school, the local education authority shall transfer their interest in the premises-

    (a) to the trustees of the school, to be held by them on trust for the purposes of the school, or

    (b) if the school has no trustees, to the school's foundation body, to be held by that body for the relevant purposes.

(2) If any doubt or dispute arises as to the persons to whom the authority are required to make the transfer, it shall be made to such persons as the Secretary of State thinks proper.

(3) The authority shall pay to the persons to whom the transfer is made their reasonable costs in connection with the transfer.

(4) In this paragraph "the relevant purposes" means, in relation to a transfer to a school's foundation body, the purposes of the schools comprising the group for which that body acts.

PART III FOUNDATION, VOLUNTARY AND FOUNDATION SPECIAL SCHOOLS: COMMON PROVISIONS

Default powers of Secretary of State

10.–(1) Where it appears to the Secretary of State that a local education authority have defaulted in the discharge of their duties relating to the maintenance of a foundation, voluntary or foundation special school, he may-

(a) direct that any act done by or on behalf of the school's governing body for the purpose of securing the proper maintenance of the school shall be taken to have been done by or on behalf of the authority, and

(b) reimburse to the governing body any sums which in his opinion they have properly expended for that purpose.

(2) The amount of any sum reimbursed under sub-paragraph (1) shall be recoverable by the Secretary of State as a debt due to him from the authority; and without prejudice to any other method of recovery the whole or any part of any such sum may be deducted from any sums payable to the authority by the Secretary of State in pursuance of any regulations relating to the payment of grants.

Endowments

11. Where any sums accruing in respect of the income of an endowment are required by virtue of the provisions of a trust deed to be applied towards the maintenance of a foundation, voluntary or foundation special school, those sums shall not be payable to the local education authority but shall be applied by the governing body of the school-

(a) (in the case of a voluntary aided school) towards the discharge of their obligations under paragraph 3, or

(b) (in the case of any school) in such manner, if any, as may be determined by a scheme for the administration of the endowment made after 1st April 1945.

Disapplication of restriction on local authority disposals

12. Subsection (2) of section 123 of the Local Government Act 1972 (local authority prohibited from making disposal of land under that section below market value without consent of the Secretary of State) shall not apply in the case of a disposal-

(a) to the governing body of a foundation, voluntary or foundation special school, or

(b) to persons proposing to establish such a school.

Schedule 3

This Schedule deals with the basis on which foundation (including foundation special schools) and voluntary schools are funded and includes provisions relating to the school site (which in this context excludes playing fields).

Part 1 provides for all cost, both capital and revenue, relating to foundation and controlled schools to be met by the local education authority with the local education authority obliged to provide the school site except in those cases where site provision was the responsibility of the school's promoters under the school's incorporation proposals. Any site provided by the local education authority is to be transferred either to the school's trustees or its foundation body or, if it has neither, to the governing body but only for the purposes of the school.

Part 2 deals with voluntary aided schools. Site and equipment provision, the cost of building alterations and the repair of the premises other than internal repair are the responsibility of the governing body. The local education authority is responsible for the provision of any new site other than one which are the responsibility of the school's promoters under any statutory proposals. Any site provided by the local education authority is to be transferred either to the school's trustees or its foundation body but only for the purposes of the school. There are provisions for the sharing of cost of site provision where there are existing buildings of value and the Secretary of State may grant-aid any governing body expense up to 85% of the total. He also has power to grant-aid preliminary expenses in connection with site transfer or enlargement or alteration of the school premises, again up to 85% of the total He has the further power to make loans in relation to any capital expense that would involve work that would be eligible for grant. This power is exercisable in respect of the difference between the cost of the work and the amount of grant to be paid.

Part 3 gives enforcement powers to the Secretary of State if an local education authority is in default, provides that funds from any endowment are to be applied by the governing body towards the maintenance of the school rather than going to the local education authority and allows transfers of land to or for schools at less than market value.

SCHEDULE 4

SCHOOL ORGANISATION COMMITTEES

Interpretation

1. In this Schedule-

    "committee" means a school organisation committee;

    "the relevant authority", in the case of any such committee, means the local education authority by whom the committee are established.

Election of chairmen and appointment of members

2. Regulations may make provision with respect to-

    (a) the election by a committee of one of their number to be chairman, and one to be vice-chairman, of the committee;

    (b) the period for which the chairman and vice-chairman are to be elected; and

    (c) the appointment and tenure of office of, and the vacation of office by, members of a committee.

Allowances for members

3.–(1) For the purpose of the payment of financial loss allowance under section 173(4) of the Local Government Act 1972, that provision shall apply, with any necessary modifications, to any member of a committee as it applies to any member of a parish or community council; and a committee shall be included in the bodies to which section 174 of that Act (travelling and subsistence allowances) applies.

(2) In section 174(1) of that Act, in its application to a committee in accordance with sub-paragraph (1), the reference to payments at rates determined by the body in question shall be read as a reference to payments at rates determined by the relevant authority.

Financial and other assistance by LEA

4.–(1) The relevant authority in the case of a committee shall-

    (a) defray the expenses of the committee in accordance with sub-paragraphs (2) to (5); and

    (b) make arrangements for them to be provided with accommodation and with such services as the authority consider appropriate.

(2) Before the beginning of each financial year a committee shall submit to the relevant authority a statement of the estimated expenses of the committee in respect of that year (including estimates of any allowances payable to their members by virtue of paragraph 3).

(3) Where they have received such a statement the relevant authority shall approve it, either without modification or with such modifications as they may specify.

(4) Once they have approved the statement under sub-paragraph (3) the relevant authority shall (subject to sub-paragraphs (5) and (6)) defray the expenses of the committee, in respect of the financial year in question, up to the total amount of the expenses set out in the statement as so approved.

(5) The relevant authority are not required by sub-paragraph (4) to defray any expenses of the committee which do not relate to an activity of the committee mentioned in the statement.

(6) If they consider it appropriate to do so, the relevant authority may-

(a) defray the expenses of the committee in respect of a financial year up to an amount which exceeds the total amount referred to in sub-paragraph (4);

(b) defray any expenses of the committee to which sub-paragraph (5) applies.

Proceedings

5.–(1) Regulations may make provision as to the meetings and proceedings of a committee.

(2) Regulations under this paragraph may in particular-

(a) provide that, in any prescribed circumstances, the members within each category of members of a committee are to have collectively a single vote;

(b) require all decisions of a prescribed description which are taken by a committee (in accordance with regulations made by virtue of paragraph (a)) to be unanimous decisions of those voting.

(3) Regulations under this paragraph must, however, include provision-

(a) for the members within each category of members of a committee to have collectively a single vote in relation to any decision to which this sub-paragraph applies;

(b) requiring any such decision which is taken by a committee to be a unanimous decision of those voting.

(4) Sub-paragraph (3) applies to any decision of a committee as to whether or not-

(a) to give any approval under section 26(5) or to prepare such a plan as is mentioned in section 26(6)(d)(ii);

(b) to give any approval under paragraph 3 of Schedule 6 or to-
  (i) modify any proposals,
  (ii) specify any date, or
  (iii) make any determination,

under paragraph 5(2)(a) or (b) or (3) of that Schedule;

(c) to make, vary or revoke a transitional exemption order under paragraph 21 of that Schedule or paragraph 16 of Schedule 7;

(d) to give any approval under paragraph 8 of Schedule 7;

(e) to make any decision authorised by or by virtue of paragraph 6 of Schedule 23.

(5) Where regulations under paragraph 2(2) of Schedule 8 provide for either of the following provisions, namely paragraph 3 or 5(2)(a) of Schedule 6, to have effect in relation to proposals published under paragraph 2 or 3 of Schedule 8, the reference to that provision in sub-paragraph (4) above shall include a reference to it as it so has effect.

6. The validity of any proceedings of a committee shall not be affected by any vacancy among the members or by any defect in the appointment of a member.

7. Subject to any provision made by or under this Schedule, a committee may regulate their own procedure.

8. When taking any decision a committee shall have regard (so far as relevant) to the obligations which, by virtue of-

(a) Part III of the Sex Discrimination Act 1975, or

(b) Part III of the Race Relations Act 1976,

are owed by any local education authority or governing body which will be affected by the decision.

Indemnity

9. The relevant authority in the case of a committee shall indemnify the members of the committee against any reasonable legal costs and expenses reasonably incurred by those members in connection with any decision or action taken by them in good faith in pursuance of their functions as members of the committee.

Default powers of Secretary of State

10. Each of sections 496 and 497 of the Education Act 1996 (default powers of Secretary of State) shall apply in relation to a committee as it applies in relation to a body falling within subsection (2) of that section.

Schedule 4

This Schedule contains provisions relating to the formation powers and proceedings of school organisation committees. The detail regarding the committee's proceedings is to be governed by regulations.

SCHEDULE 5

ADJUDICATORS

Interpretation

1. In this Schedule "adjudicator" means a person appointed under section 25.

Tenure of office

2.–(1) Subject to sub-paragraphs (2) and (3), an adjudicator shall hold and vacate office in accordance with the terms of his appointment.

(2) An adjudicator-

(a) may at any time resign his office by notice in writing to the Secretary of State; and

(b) is eligible for re-appointment if he ceases to hold office.

(3) An adjudicator may be removed from office by the Secretary of State on the ground of incapacity or misbehaviour.

Remuneration and pensions

3.–(1) The Secretary of State may pay to an adjudicator such remuneration and allowances as the Secretary of State may determine.

(2) If the Secretary of State so determines in the case of any adjudicator, the Secretary of State may pay or make provision for the payment of such sums by way of pension, allowances and gratuities to or in respect of him as the Secretary of State may determine.

Staff and accommodation etc.

4. The Secretary of State may-

(a) provide an adjudicator with such administrative staff as the adjudicator may require; and

(b) provide, or defray the expenses of providing, an adjudicator with such accommodation and other facilities as the adjudicator may require.

Procedure

5.–(1) Regulations may make provision as to the procedure to be followed in connection with the reference, under this Part or Part III of this Act, of matters to adjudicators and their determination of matters so referred.

(2) The regulations may, in particular, make provision-

(a) as to the manner in which matters may be referred to adjudicators;

(b) for determining the adjudicators to which individual referrals are to be made;

(c) authorising adjudicators to hold local inquiries;

(d) as to the procedure to be followed where local inquiries are held by adjudicators (whether by virtue of paragraph (c) or otherwise);

(e) authorising adjudicators to appoint assessors to sit with them at such inquiries to advise them on matters arising;

(f) requiring anything falling to be done under the regulations to be done within such period as may be specified in or determined in accordance with the regulations.

(3) Subject to any provision made by the regulations, an adjudicator may regulate his own procedure.

(4) The Secretary of State may make orders-

(a) as to the costs of the parties at any local inquiry held by an adjudicator (whether by virtue of sub-paragraph (2)(c) or otherwise), and

(b) as to the parties by whom the costs are to be paid;

and any costs payable under any such order shall be subject to taxation in such manner as the Secretary of State may direct.

6. When taking any decision an adjudicator shall have regard (so far as relevant) to the obligations which, by virtue of-

(a) Part III of the Sex Discrimination Act 1975, or
(b) Part III of the Race Relations Act 1976,

are owed by any local education authority or governing body which will be affected by the decision.

Indemnity

7. The Secretary of State shall indemnify an adjudicator against any reasonable legal costs and expenses reasonably incurred by him in connection with any decision or action taken by him in good faith in pursuance of his functions as an adjudicator.

Parliamentary disqualification

8. In Part III of Schedule 1 to the House of Commons Disqualification Act 1975 (disqualifying offices), at the appropriate place there shall be inserted-

"Adjudicator appointed under section 25 of the School Standards and Framework Act 1998."

Parliamentary Commissioner

9. For the purposes of section 5 of the Parliamentary Commissioner Act 1967 (matters subject to investigation) administrative functions exercisable by any person provided by the Secretary of State under paragraph 4 above shall be taken to be administrative functions of the Department for Education and Employment.

Supervision of Council on Tribunals

10.–(1) In section 7 of the Tribunals and Inquiries Act 1992 (which restricts Ministers' powers to remove members of tribunals listed in Schedule 1 to that Act) in subsection (2) (tribunals to which that section does not apply) after "14," there shall be inserted "15(f),".

(2) In Schedule 1 to that Act (tribunals under the supervision of the Council on Tribunals) at the end of paragraph 15 (tribunals concerned with education) there shall be inserted-

"(f) an adjudicator appointed under section 25 of the School Standards and Framework Act 1998."

Schedule 5
This Schedule contains provisions relating to the powers and proceedings of adjudicators. The detail regarding proceedings is to be governed by regulations. The adjudicator is subject to the Parliamentary Ombudsman and to supervision by the Council on Tribunals.

SCHEDULE 6

STATUTORY PROPOSALS: PROCEDURE AND IMPLEMENTATION

PART I PROCEDURE FOR DEALING WITH STATUTORY PROPOSALS: ENGLAND

Application of Part I

1.–(1) This Part of this Schedule applies to proposals published under section 28, 29 or 31 which relate to a school or proposed school in England.

(2) In this Part of this Schedule "the relevant committee" means the school organisation committee for the area of the local education authority who maintain the school or (in the case of a new school) who it is proposed should maintain the school.

Objections

2.–(1) Any person may make objections to any proposals published under section 28, 29 or 31.

(2) Where the proposals were published by a local education authority-

   (a) any objections under this paragraph shall be sent to the authority within such period as may be prescribed ("the objection period"); and
   (b) within such period as may be prescribed the authority shall send to the relevant committee copies of all objections made (and not withdrawn in writing) within the objection period, together with the authority's observations on them.

(3) Where the proposals were published by a governing body or promoters, any objections under this paragraph shall be sent to the relevant committee within such period as may be prescribed.

Approval of proposals

3.–(1) Proposals published under section 28, 29 or 31 require approval under this paragraph if-

   (a) the proposals were published by a local education authority and either-
      (i) objections to the proposals have been made in accordance with paragraph 2 and any of them have not been withdrawn in writing within the objection period; or
      (ii) such approval is required by virtue of paragraph 4(5); or
   (b) the proposals were published by a governing body or promoters.

(2) Where any proposals require approval under this paragraph, they shall be considered in the first instance by the relevant committee, who may-

   (a) reject the proposals,
   (b) approve them without modification, or

(c) approve them with such modifications as the committee think desirable after consulting such persons or bodies as may be prescribed.

(3) Any approval given under this paragraph may be expressed to take effect only if an event specified in the approval occurs by a date so specified; and regulations may prescribe the events that may be so specified.

(4) When deciding whether or not to give any approval under this paragraph the committee shall have regard to-

(a) any guidance given from time to time by the Secretary of State, and

(b) the school organisation plan for the committee's area;

and the committee shall not give any such approval unless they are satisfied that adequate financial resources will be available to enable the proposals to be implemented.

(5) If-

(a) by the end of such period as may be specified in or determined in accordance with regulations, the committee have not voted on the question whether to give any approval under this paragraph, and

(b) the body or promoters by whom the proposals were published request the committee to refer the proposals to the adjudicator,

they shall refer the proposals to the adjudicator.

Regulations made for the purposes of this sub-paragraph (or any other corresponding provision of this Act) may be framed by reference to the opinion of the committee.

(6) If the committee-

(a) have voted on any matter which (in accordance with regulations under paragraph 5 of Schedule 4) falls to be decided by them under this paragraph by a unanimous decision, but

(b) have failed to reach such a decision on that matter,

they shall refer the proposals to the adjudicator.

(7) Where any proposals are referred to the adjudicator under sub-paragraph (5) or (6)-

(a) he shall consider the proposals afresh; and

(b) sub-paragraphs (2) to (4) shall apply to him in connection with his decision on the proposals as they apply to the committee.

(8) Sub-paragraph (1) does not prevent the body or promoters by whom any proposals have been published under section 28, 29 or 31 from withdrawing those proposals by notice in writing given to the relevant committee at any time before the proposals are determined under this paragraph.

Determination by LEA whether to implement proposals

4.–(1) Where any proposals have been published by a local education authority under section 28, 29 or 31 and either-

(a) no objections were made in accordance with paragraph 2, or
(b) all objections so made were withdrawn in writing within the objection period,

then (subject to the following provisions of this paragraph) the authority shall determine whether the proposals should be implemented.

(2) Any determination under sub-paragraph (1) must be made within the period of four months beginning with the date of publication of the proposals (as determined in accordance with regulations); and the authority shall notify the relevant committee of any determination made by them under sub-paragraph (1).

(3) The requirement to make a determination under sub-paragraph (1) in the case of any proposals only applies if, at the time when the authority's determination falls to be made under that sub-paragraph, they are satisfied that the proposals are not related to any of the following, namely-

(a) any undetermined proposals published under section 28(2) to establish a new foundation or voluntary school in the area of the authority;
(b) any undetermined proposals published under section 28(2), 29(2) or 31(2) by the governing body of a foundation, voluntary or foundation special school in the area of the authority;
(c) any undetermined proposals published by the authority which, by virtue of sub-paragraph (1)(a) of paragraph 3, require approval under that paragraph; or
(d) any order under paragraph 2(2) or 3(2) of Schedule 7.

(4) For the purposes of sub-paragraph (3) proposals are "undetermined" if they have not been withdrawn and-

(a) they have not been approved or rejected under paragraph 3 or under paragraph 8 or 9 of Schedule 7, or
(b) the authority have not determined under this paragraph whether to implement them,

as the case may be; and when deciding under sub-paragraph (3) whether any proposals are related to other proposals the authority shall have regard to any guidance given from time to time by the Secretary of State.

(5) Where, in the case of any proposals within sub-paragraph (1)-

(a) the authority fail to make a determination under that sub-paragraph within the period mentioned in sub-paragraph (2), or
(b) the requirement to make such a determination does not apply by virtue of sub-paragraph (3),

the proposals require approval under paragraph 3.

Requirement to implement proposals

5.–(1) Where-

(a) any proposals published under section 28, 29 or 31 have been approved under paragraph 3, or

(b) a local education authority have determined under paragraph 4 to implement any such proposals,

then (subject to the following provisions of this paragraph) the proposals shall be implemented, in the form in which they were so approved or determined, in accordance with Part III of this Schedule.

(2) At the request of any prescribed body or persons, the relevant committee-

(a) may modify the proposals after consulting such persons or bodies as may be prescribed; and

(b) where any approval under paragraph 3 was given in accordance with sub-paragraph (3) of that paragraph, may specify a later date by which the event in question must occur.

(3) If the relevant committee are satisfied-

(a) that implementation of the proposals would be unreasonably difficult, or

(b) that circumstances have so altered since approval was given under paragraph 3 that implementation of the proposals would be inappropriate,

the committee may determine that sub-paragraph (1) shall cease to apply to the proposals.

(4) The committee may only make a determination under sub-paragraph (3) where proposals that they should do so have been published, in accordance with regulations, by the body or promoters who published the proposals referred to in sub-paragraph (1)(a) or (b); and regulations so made may provide for any of the provisions of sections 28, 29 and 31 and this Part of this Schedule to have effect in relation to any such further proposals with or without modifications.

(5) If-

(a) by the end of such period as may be specified in or determined in accordance with regulations, the committee have not voted on any matter falling to be decided by them under this paragraph, and

(b) the body or promoters who published the proposals referred to in sub-paragraph (1)(a) or (b) request the committee to refer that matter to the adjudicator,

they shall refer that matter to the adjudicator.

(6) If the committee-

(a) have voted on any matter which (in accordance with regulations under paragraph 5 of Schedule 4) falls to be decided by them under this paragraph by a unanimous decision, but

(b) have failed to reach such a decision on that matter,

they shall refer that matter to the adjudicator.

(7) Where any matter is referred to the adjudicator under sub-paragraph (5) or (6)-

(a) he shall consider the matter afresh; and

(b) such of the provisions of sub-paragraphs (2) to (4) as are relevant shall apply to him in connection with his decision on that matter as they apply to the committee.

(8) Where-

(a) any approval under paragraph 3 was given in accordance with sub-paragraph (3) of that paragraph, and

(b) the event specified under that sub-paragraph does not occur by the date in question (whether as specified under that sub-paragraph or as specified under sub-paragraph (2)(b) above),

sub-paragraph (1) above shall cease to apply to the proposals.

(9) Where, by virtue of sub-paragraph (3) or (8), sub-paragraph (1) ceases to apply to any proposals, those proposals shall be treated for the purposes of this Schedule as if they had been rejected under paragraph 3.

PART II PROCEDURE FOR DEALING WITH STATUTORY PROPOSALS: WALES

Application of Part II

6. This Part of this Schedule applies to proposals published under section 28, 29 or 31 which relate to a school or proposed school in Wales.

Objections

7.–(1) Any person may make objections to any proposals published under section 28, 29 or 31.

(2) Where the proposals were published by a local education authority-

(a) any objections under this paragraph shall be sent to the authority within such period as may be prescribed ("the objection period"); and

(b) within such period as may be prescribed the authority shall send to the Secretary of State copies of all objections made (and not withdrawn in writing) within the objection period, together with the authority's observations on them.

(3) Where the proposals were published by a governing body or promoters, any objections under this paragraph shall be sent to the Secretary of State within such period as may be prescribed.

Approval of proposals

8.–(1) Proposals published under section 28, 29 or 31 require approval under this paragraph if-

(a) the Secretary of State, within two months after a copy of the published proposals is sent to him under that section, gives notice to the body or promoters by whom the proposals were published that they require such approval; or

(b) objections to the proposals have been made in accordance with paragraph 7 and any of them have not been withdrawn in writing within the objection period.

(2) Where any proposals require approval under this paragraph, the Secretary of State may-

(a) reject the proposals,

(b) approve them without modification, or

(c) approve them with such modifications as he thinks desirable after consulting such persons or bodies as may be prescribed.

(3) Any approval given under this paragraph may be expressed to take effect only if an event specified in the approval occurs by a date so specified.

(4) When deciding whether or not to give any approval under this paragraph the Secretary of State shall have regard to the school organisation plan for the area in which the school is, or (in the case of a new school) is proposed to be, situated.

(5) Sub-paragraph (1) does not prevent the body or promoters by whom any proposals have been published under section 28, 29 or 31 from withdrawing those proposals by notice in writing given to the Secretary of State at any time before the proposals are approved under this paragraph.

Determination whether to implement proposals

9.–(1) Where any proposals published under section 28, 29 or 31 do not require approval under paragraph 8, the body or promoters by whom the proposals were published shall determine whether the proposals should be implemented.

(2) Any determination under sub-paragraph (1) must be made within four months after a copy of the published proposals was sent to the Secretary of State under section 28, 29 or 31.

(3) The body or promoters in question shall notify the Secretary of State of any determination made by them under sub-paragraph (1).

Requirement to implement proposals

10.–(1) Where-

(a) any proposals published under section 28, 29 or 31 have been approved under paragraph 8, or

   (b) the body or promoters by whom such proposals were published have determined under paragraph 9 to implement the proposals,

then (subject to the following provisions of this paragraph) the proposals shall be implemented, in the form in which they were so approved or determined, in accordance with Part III of this Schedule.

(2) At the request of any prescribed body or persons, the Secretary of State-

   (a) may modify the proposals after consulting such persons or bodies as may be prescribed; and

   (b) where any approval under paragraph 8 was given in accordance with sub-paragraph (3) of that paragraph, may specify a later date by which the event in question must occur.

(3) If the Secretary of State is satisfied-

   (a) that implementation of the proposals would be unreasonably difficult, or

   (b) that circumstances have so altered since approval was given under paragraph 8 that implementation of the proposals would be inappropriate,

he may determine that sub-paragraph (1) shall cease to apply to the proposals.

(4) The Secretary of State may only make a determination under sub-paragraph (3) where proposals that he should do so have been published, in accordance with regulations, by the body or promoters who published the proposals referred to in that sub-paragraph; and regulations so made may provide for any of the provisions of sections 28, 29 and 31 and this Part of this Schedule to have effect in relation to any such further proposals with or without modifications.

(5) Where-

   (a) any approval under paragraph 8 was given in accordance with sub-paragraph (3) of that paragraph, and

   (b) the event specified under that sub-paragraph does not occur by the date in question (whether as specified under that sub-paragraph or as specified under sub-paragraph (2)(b) above),

sub-paragraph (1) above shall cease to apply to the proposals.

(6) Where, by virtue of sub-paragraph (3) or (5), sub-paragraph (1) ceases to apply to any proposals, those proposals shall be treated for the purposes of this Schedule as if they had been rejected under paragraph 8.

PART III MANNER OF IMPLEMENTATION OF STATUTORY PROPOSALS

Introductory

11. In this Part of this Schedule "proposals" means proposals falling to be implemented under paragraph 5 or 10.

Proposals relating to community or maintained nursery schools

12.–(1) This paragraph applies to proposals relating to a community or proposed community school or to a maintained nursery school.

(2) The proposals shall be implemented by the local education authority by whom they were published under section 28(1) or 29(1).

Proposals relating to foundation or voluntary controlled schools

13.–(1) This paragraph applies to proposals relating to a foundation or voluntary controlled school or a proposed such school.

(2) Where the proposals were published by a local education authority under section 28(1) or 29(1), they shall be implemented by the authority.

(3) Where the proposals were published under section 28(2)-

(a) by promoters, or
(b) by the governing body,

they shall be implemented by the local education authority and by the promoters or (as the case may be) the governing body, respectively, to such extent (if any) as the proposals provide for each of them to do so.

(4) Where the proposals were published by the governing body under section 29(2), they shall be implemented-

(a) by the governing body; and
(b) by the local education authority as well.

Proposals relating to voluntary aided schools

14.–(1) This paragraph applies to proposals relating to a voluntary aided school or a proposed such school.

(2) Where the proposals were published by the governing body under section 28(2) or 29(2), they shall be implemented-
(a) in the case of proposals published under section 28(2) so far as relating to the provision of any relevant premises for the school, by the local education authority;
(b) in the case of proposals published under section 29(2), by the governing body and the authority; and
(c) otherwise by the governing body.

(3) Where the proposals were published under section 28(2) by promoters, they shall be implemented-

(a) so far as relating to the provision of any relevant premises for the school (but subject to sub-paragraph (5)), by the local education authority; and
(b) otherwise by the promoters.

(4) In sub-paragraph (2) or (3) "relevant premises" means-

(a) playing fields, or

(b) buildings which are to form part of the school premises but are not to be school buildings.

(5) Nothing in sub-paragraph (3) requires a local education authority to provide any such premises where-

(a) the new voluntary aided school is to be established in place of one or more existing independent, foundation or voluntary schools falling to be discontinued on or before the date of implementation of the proposals; and

(b) those premises-

(i) were part of the premises of any of the existing schools (whether it was an independent school or a foundation or voluntary school); and

(ii) (if it was a foundation or voluntary school) were not provided by the authority.

(6) Where the proposals were published by a local education authority under section 29(1), they shall be implemented by the authority.

Proposals relating to community or foundation special schools

15.–(1) This paragraph applies to proposals relating to-

(a) a community or foundation special school; or

(b) a proposed such school.

(2) Where the proposals were published by a local education authority under section 31(1), they shall be implemented by the authority.

(3) Where the proposals were published by the governing body under section 31(2)(a), they shall be implemented by the local education authority and by the governing body, respectively, to such extent (if any) as the proposals provide for each of them to do so.

(4) Where the proposals were published by the governing body under section 31(2)(b), they shall be implemented-

(a) by the governing body; and

(b) by the local education authority as well.

PART IV PROVISION OF PREMISES AND OTHER ASSISTANCE

Provision of site and buildings for foundation, voluntary controlled or foundation special school

16.–(1) This paragraph applies where a local education authority are required-

(a) by virtue of paragraph 13(2) or (3) to provide a site for a foundation or voluntary controlled school or a proposed such school; or

(b) by virtue of paragraph 15(2) or (3) to provide a site for a foundation special school.

(2) The authority shall transfer their interest in the site and in any buildings on the site which are to form part of the school premises-

  (a) to the school's trustees, to be held by them on trust for the purposes of the school, or

  (b) if the school has no trustees, to the school's foundation body or (in the absence of such a body) to the governing body, to be held by that body for the relevant purposes.

(3) If any doubt or dispute arises as to the persons to whom the authority are required to make the transfer, it shall be made to such persons as the Secretary of State thinks proper.

(4) The authority shall pay to the persons to whom the transfer is made their reasonable costs in connection with the transfer.

(5) Where-

  (a) a transfer is made under this paragraph, and

  (b) the transfer is made to persons who possess, or are or may become entitled to, any sum representing proceeds of the sale of other premises which have been used for the purposes of the school,

those persons shall notify the local education authority that paragraph (b) applies to them and they or their successors shall pay to the local education authority so much of that sum as, having regard to the value of the interest transferred, may be determined to be just, either by agreement between them and the authority or, in default of agreement, by the Secretary of State.

(6) In sub-paragraph (5)(b) the reference to proceeds of the sale of other premises includes a reference to-

  (a) consideration for the creation or disposition of any kind of interest in other premises, including rent; and

  (b) interest which has accrued in respect of any such consideration;

and for the purposes of any agreed determination under sub-paragraph (5) regard shall be had to any guidance given from time to time by the Secretary of State.

(7) Any sum paid under sub-paragraph (5) shall be treated for the purposes of section 14 of the Schools Sites Act 1841 (which relates to the sale or exchange of land held on trust for the purposes of a school) as a sum applied in the purchase of a site for the school.

(8) A determination may be made under sub-paragraph (5) in respect of any property subject to a trust which has arisen under section 1 of the Reverter of Sites Act 1987 (right of reverter replaced by trust for sale) if (and only if)-

  (a) the determination is made by the Secretary of State, and

  (b) he is satisfied that steps have been taken to protect the interests of the beneficiaries under the trust.

(9) Sub-paragraph (5) shall apply for the purpose of compensating the authority notified under that sub-paragraph only in relation to such part of the sum mentioned in sub-paragraph (5)(b) (if any) as remains after the application of paragraphs 1 to 3 of Schedule 22 to that sum.

(10) In this paragraph-

"the relevant purposes" means-

(a) in relation to a transfer to a school's foundation body, the purposes of the schools comprising the group for which that body acts, or
(b) in relation to a transfer to a school's governing body, the purposes of the school;

"site" does not include playing fields but otherwise includes any site which is to form part of the premises of the school in question.

Grants in respect of certain expenditure relating to existing or proposed voluntary aided school

17.–(1) This paragraph applies where-

(a) the governing body of a voluntary aided school are required by virtue of paragraph 14(2) to implement proposals relating to a prescribed alteration to the school; or
(b) any promoters are required by virtue of paragraph 14(3) to implement proposals involving the establishment of a new voluntary aided school.

(2) Paragraph 5 of Schedule 3-

(a) shall apply in relation to the voluntary aided school mentioned in sub-paragraph (1)(a) above; and
(b) shall apply in relation to the new voluntary aided school mentioned in sub-paragraph (1)(b) above as it applies in relation to an existing voluntary aided school.

(3) In the application of that paragraph in relation to a new voluntary aided school-

(a) the references to the governing body, in relation to any time before the governing body are constituted, are to the promoters; and
(b) where requirements are imposed in relation to grant paid by virtue of this paragraph to the promoters, the requirements shall be complied with by the governing body, when they are constituted, as well as by the promoters.

Assistance in respect of maintenance and other obligations relating to voluntary aided school

18. A local education authority may give to the governing body of a voluntary aided school such assistance as the authority think fit in relation to the carrying out by the governing body of any obligation arising by virtue of paragraph 14(2) in relation to proposals published by them under section 28.

Assistance for promoters of new voluntary aided school

19. A local education authority may give to persons required by virtue of paragraph 14(3) to implement proposals involving the establishment of a voluntary aided school such assistance as the authority think fit in relation to the carrying out by those persons of any obligation arising by virtue of that provision.

Duty to transfer interest in premises provided under paragraph 18 or 19

20.–(1) Where assistance under paragraph 18 or 19 consists of the provision of any premises for use for the purposes of a school, the local education authority shall transfer their interest in the premises-

(a) to the trustees of the school to be held on trust for the purposes of the school; or

(b) if the school has no trustees, to the school's foundation body, to be held by that body for the relevant purposes.

(2) If any doubt or dispute arises as to the persons to whom the authority are required to make the transfer it shall be made to such persons as the Secretary of State thinks proper.

(3) The authority shall pay to the persons to whom the transfer is made their reasonable costs in connection with the transfer.

(4) In this paragraph "the relevant purposes" means, in relation to a transfer to a school's foundation body, the purposes of the schools comprising the group for which that body acts.

PART V TRANSITIONAL EXEMPTION ORDERS FOR PURPOSES OF SEX DISCRIMINATION ACT 1975

Single-sex schools: England

21.–(1) This paragraph applies to proposals for a school in England to cease to be an establishment which admits pupils of one sex only.

(2) Sub-paragraph (3) applies where-

(a) such proposals are made under section 28 and, in accordance with subsection (6) of that section, the relevant body send a copy of the published proposals to the school organisation committee; or

(b) such proposals are made under section 31 and, in accordance with subsection (5) of that section, the relevant body send a copy of the published proposals to the school organisation committee.

(3) The sending of the published proposals to the school organisation committee by the relevant body shall be treated as an application by the responsible body for the making by the school organisation committee of a transitional exemption order, and the committee may make such an order accordingly.

(4) Where-

(a) the school organisation committee have failed to reach a unanimous decision under sub-paragraph (3) above on whether to make a transitional exemption order, or

(b) the school organisation committee refer the proposals to the adjudicator under paragraph 3 or 5 of this Schedule,

they shall refer the question whether to make a transitional exemption order to the adjudicator.

(5) Where that question is referred to the adjudicator-

(a) he shall consider the matter afresh; and

(b) he may make a transitional exemption order accordingly.

(6) In this paragraph and in paragraph 22-

"the 1975 Act" means the Sex Discrimination Act 1975,

"make", in relation to a transitional exemption order, includes (so far as the context permits) vary or revoke,

"the responsible body" has the same meaning as in section 22 of the 1975 Act, and

"transitional exemption order" has the same meaning as in section 27 of the 1975 Act,

and references to proposals for a school to cease to be an establishment which admits pupils of one sex only are references to proposals which are or include proposals for such an alteration in a school's admissions arrangements as is mentioned in section 27(1) of the 1975 Act (single-sex establishments becoming co-educational).

Single-sex schools: Wales

22.–(1) This paragraph applies to proposals for a school in Wales to cease to be an establishment which admits pupils of one sex only.

(2) Sub-paragraph (3) applies where-

(a) such proposals are made under section 28 and, in accordance with subsection (7) of that section, the relevant body send a copy of the published proposals to the Secretary of State; or

(b) such proposals are made under section 31 and, in accordance with subsection (6) of that section, the relevant body send a copy of the published proposals to the Secretary of State.

(3) The sending of the published proposals to the Secretary of State shall be treated as an application by the responsible body for the making by the Secretary of State of a transitional exemption order, and he may make such an order accordingly.

Schedule 6

This Schedule deals with the process relating to the publication and approval of proposals that require this under ss 28, 29 or 31 of the Act.

Proposals in England published by an local education authority that have attracted objections or which the local education authority have not determined whether or not to implement, and all proposals from governing bodies or promoters require approval of the school organisation committee which must have regard to the relevant school organisation plan and to guidance from the Secretary of State. Proposals go on to the adjudicator if the school organisation committee fails to vote on them or do not reach a unanimous decision where unanimity is required or if the body promoting the proposals request the reference. Proposals that are approved must be implemented but there is power for the school organisation committee and/or the adjudicator to agree to modifications of the proposals.

In Wales proposals go to the Secretary of State who must have regard to the school organisation plan.

The Schedule contains further technical provisions relating to the implementation of approved proposals and to the transfer of land. These provisions are similar to those in Schedule 3 relating to the funding of maintained schools and include the power for an local education authority to give financial assistance to promoters of voluntary aided schools. There are also provisions enabling the school organisation committee or adjudicator (in England) or the Secretary of State (in Wales) to make a transitional exemption order for the purposes of the Sex Discrimination Act 1975 in relation to a proposal that a school ceases to be a single-sex school.

SCHEDULE 7

RATIONALISATION OF SCHOOL PLACES

PART I INTRODUCTORY

1. In this Schedule-

    (a) "powers to make proposals for the establishment, alteration or discontinuance of schools" means all or any of the powers of the local education authority to publish proposals under section 28, 29 or 31; and

    (b) "powers to make proposals for the alteration of their school", in relation to the governing body of a foundation, voluntary or foundation special school, means their powers to publish proposals under section 28(2)(b) or 31(2)(a).

PART II DIRECTIONS TO BRING FORWARD PROPOSALS

Directions to bring forward proposals to remedy excessive provision

2.–(1) This paragraph applies where the Secretary of State is of the opinion that the provision for primary or secondary education in maintained schools-
(a) in the area of any local education authority, or
(b) in any part of such an area,

is excessive.

(2) For the purpose of remedying the excess, the Secretary of State may-
  (a) by an order under this paragraph direct the local education authority to exercise their powers to make proposals for the establishment, alteration or discontinuance of schools, and
  (b) in the case of any foundation, voluntary or foundation special school maintained by the authority, by an order under this paragraph direct the governing body to exercise their powers to make proposals for the alteration of their school.

(3) An order under sub-paragraph (2) shall-
  (a) require the proposals to be published not later than such date as may be specified in the order, and
  (b) require the proposals to apply such principles in giving effect to the direction as may be specified in the order.

(4) An order under sub-paragraph (2)(a) may not require the proposals to relate to any named school.

(5) Where any proposals are published in pursuance of an order under sub-paragraph (2) which relates to an area in England, the body concerned shall (in addition to complying with section 28(6), 29(5) or 31(5), as the case may be) send-

  (a) a copy of the published proposals, and
  (b) such information in connection with those proposals as may be prescribed,

to the Secretary of State.

Directions to bring forward proposals to remedy insufficient provision

3.–(1) This paragraph applies where the Secretary of State is of the opinion that the provision for primary or secondary education in maintained schools-

  (a) in the area of any local education authority, or
  (b) in any part of such an area,

is, or is likely to become, insufficient.

(2) The Secretary of State may-

  (a) by an order under this paragraph direct the local education authority to exercise their powers to make proposals for the establishment, alteration or discontinuance of schools, and

(b) in the case of any foundation, voluntary or foundation special school maintained by the authority, by an order under this paragraph direct the governing body to exercise their powers to make proposals for the alteration of their school,

with a view (in each case) to securing that provision is made for such additional number of pupils in the area, or in any such part of the area, as may be specified in the order.

(3) An order under sub-paragraph (2) shall-

(a) require the proposals to be published not later than such date as may be specified in the order, and

(b) require the proposals to apply such principles in giving effect to the direction as may be specified in the order.

(4) An order under sub-paragraph (2)(a) may not require the proposals to relate to any named school.

(5) Where any proposals are published in pursuance of an order under sub-paragraph (2) which relates to an area in England, the body concerned shall (in addition to complying with section 28(6), 29(5) or 31(5), as the case may be) send-

(a) a copy of the published proposals, and

(b) such information in connection with those proposals as may be prescribed,

to the Secretary of State.

Supplementary provisions

4.–(1) Where the Secretary of State makes an order under paragraph 2(2) or 3(2) in relation to the area of any local education authority in England, he shall send a copy of the order-

(a) to the school organisation committee for the area, and

(b) to any adjudicator who appears to him to be likely to be considering proposals in relation to that area.

(2) Where the school organisation committee or any adjudicator receive a copy of the order under sub-paragraph (1), the committee or adjudicator shall send to the Secretary of State-

(a) a copy of all proposals relating to the area which have been received by them or him but have not been determined by the relevant time, and

(b) a copy of all proposals relating to the area, other than any made under paragraph 5, which they receive after the relevant time.

(3) Where sub-paragraph (2) applies, then unless the Secretary of State gives his consent-

(a) neither the school organisation committee nor the adjudicator shall make any determination, and

(b) the school organisation committee shall not make any reference to the adjudicator under paragraph 3 of Schedule 6 or paragraph 8 below,

in relation to any proposals within sub-paragraph (2) during the period beginning with the relevant time and ending with the time when the Secretary of State notifies the committee or the adjudicator, as the case may be, that they or he may make any such determination or reference in relation to those proposals without the Secretary of State's consent.

(4) The duty of the school organisation committee or any adjudicator to send copies of proposals to the Secretary of State under sub-paragraph (2) shall terminate at the end of the period mentioned in sub-paragraph (3).

(5) In sub-paragraphs (2) and (3)-

(a) references to the relevant time, in relation to the school organisation committee or to any adjudicator, are to the time when they or he receive the copy of the order under sub-paragraph (1);

(b) references to proposals are to proposals made under section 28, 29 or 31 or under paragraph 5; and

(c) references to the determination of any proposals are to-

(i) any determination whether or not to approve the proposals under paragraph 3 of Schedule 6 or paragraph 8 or 9 below, or

(ii) any determination whether or not to implement the proposals under paragraph 4 of Schedule 6.

(6) Where a local education authority publish any proposals in pursuance of an order under paragraph 2(2) or 3(2) which relates to an area in England, those proposals shall require approval under paragraph 3 of Schedule 6, despite anything in paragraph 3(1)(a) or 4 of that Schedule.

(7) Proposals made in pursuance of an order under paragraph 2(2) or 3(2) (whether relating to an area in England or in Wales) may not be withdrawn without the consent of the Secretary of State and such consent may be given on such conditions (if any) as the Secretary of State considers appropriate.

(8) Where the governing body of a foundation, voluntary or foundation special school make any proposals in pursuance of any such order under paragraph 2(2) or 3(2), the local education authority shall reimburse any expenditure reasonably incurred by the governing body in making the proposals.

(9) Where-

(a) proposals made by the governing body of a foundation, voluntary or foundation special school in pursuance of any such order under paragraph 2(2) or 3(2) are approved or, as the case may be, determined to be implemented, or

(b) proposals approved or adopted under paragraph 8, 9 or 14 have effect as mentioned in paragraph 10(b) or 15(b), as the case may be,

then, despite anything in Part III of Schedule 6, the local education authority shall defray the cost of implementing the proposals.

PART III PROPOSALS BY SECRETARY OF STATE

Publication of proposals

5.–(1) Where-

   (a) the Secretary of State has, in relation to the area of any local education authority or any part of such an area, made an order under paragraph 2(2) or 3(2) directing the local education authority or the governing body of a foundation, voluntary or foundation special school to make proposals for the establishment, alteration or discontinuance of schools or (as the case may be) for the alteration of their school, and

   (b) either-

     (i) any proposals have been published in pursuance of the order, or

     (ii) the time allowed under the order for the publication of the proposals has expired,

he may make any such proposals as might have been made in accordance with the order relating to that area or that part of that area by the body to whom the directions were given.

(2) Proposals under this paragraph shall-

   (a) contain such information, and

   (b) be published in such manner,

as may be prescribed.

(3) Where any proposals made under this paragraph relate to an area in England, the Secretary of State shall send a copy of the proposals to the school organisation committee for the area.

(4) Where any proposals made under this paragraph relate to an area in Wales, the Secretary of State shall send a copy of the proposals-

   (a) to the local education authority for the area, and

   (b) to the governing body of each school to which the proposals relate.

PART IV PROCEDURE FOR DEALING WITH PROPOSALS UNDER PARAGRAPH 5: ENGLAND

Application of Part IV

6. This Part of this Schedule applies to proposals published under paragraph 5 which relate to an area in England.

Objections

7.–(1) Any person may make objections to any proposals published under paragraph 5.

(2) Objections under this paragraph-

    (a) shall be sent to the school organisation committee for the area to which those proposals relate; and

    (b) shall be so sent within such period as may be prescribed.

Approval of proposals

8.–(1) Proposals published under paragraph 5 require the approval of the school organisation committee under this paragraph or of the adjudicator under paragraph 9.

(2) Where the school organisation committee receive a copy of the proposals published under paragraph 5, they must either-

    (a) approve them without modification, or

    (b) approve them with such modifications as the committee think desirable and to which the Secretary of State consents, or

    (c) refer them to the adjudicator under sub-paragraph (5) or (6).

(3) Any approval given under this paragraph may, with the consent of the Secretary of State, be expressed to take effect only if an event specified in the approval occurs by a date so specified; and regulations may prescribe the events that may be so specified.

(4) When deciding whether or not to give any approval under this paragraph the committee shall have regard to any guidance given from time to time by the Secretary of State.

(5) If-

    (a) by the end of such period as may be specified in or determined in accordance with regulations, the committee have not voted on the question whether to give any approval under this paragraph, and

    (b) the Secretary of State requests the committee to refer his proposals to the adjudicator,

they shall refer his proposals to the adjudicator.

(6) If the committee-

    (a) have voted on any matter which (in accordance with regulations under paragraph 5 of Schedule 4) falls to be decided by them under this paragraph by a unanimous decision but have failed to reach such a decision on that matter, or

    (b) have decided not to give any approval under this paragraph,

they shall refer the Secretary of State's proposals to the adjudicator.

(7) Where any proposals are referred to the adjudicator under sub-paragraph (5) or (6), the school organisation committee shall also refer to him-

    (a) any other proposals published under paragraph 5 in relation to the area of the local education authority (and not withdrawn),

(b) any proposals made by that authority in the exercise of their powers to make proposals for the establishment, alteration or discontinuance of schools (and not withdrawn), and

(c) any proposals made by the governing body of any foundation, voluntary or foundation special school in the area in the exercise of their powers to make proposals for the alteration of their school (and not withdrawn),

where those proposals are not determined before the adjudicator holds an inquiry under paragraph 9(1) and appear to the committee to be related to the proposals referred by them to the adjudicator under sub-paragraph (5) or (6).

(8) Sub-paragraph (7) applies to any proposals within that sub-paragraph whether or not the proposals have been previously referred to the adjudicator by the committee.

(9) Sub-paragraph (1) does not prevent the Secretary of State from withdrawing any proposals published under paragraph 5 by notice in writing given to the school organisation committee at any time before the proposals are determined under this paragraph or paragraph 9.

(10) References in this paragraph to the determination of any proposals are to-

(a) any determination whether or not to approve the proposals under paragraph 3 of Schedule 6, sub-paragraph (2)(a) or (2)(b) above or paragraph 9(3) below, or

(b) any determination whether or not to implement the proposals under paragraph 4 of Schedule 6.

Local inquiry into proposals

9.–(1) Where any proposals are referred to the adjudicator under paragraph 8(5) or (6), he shall hold a local inquiry to consider-

(a) those proposals,

(b) any additional proposals referred to him under paragraph 8(7),

(c) any objections made (under paragraph 2 of Schedule 6 or paragraph 7 above) to any proposals within paragraph (a) or (b) above unless such objections have been withdrawn, and

(d) any views expressed by the school organisation committee on any such proposals.

(2) It shall not be open to the inquiry to question the principles specified in the order under paragraph 2(2) or 3(2).

(3) After holding the inquiry, the adjudicator must, in the case of any proposals considered at the inquiry, either-

(a) approve them with or without modifications, or

(b) reject them.

(4) Any approval given under this paragraph may be expressed to take effect only if an event specified in the approval occurs by a date so specified; and regulations may prescribe the events that may be so specified.

(5) When deciding whether or not to give any approval under this paragraph, paragraph 8(4) shall apply to the adjudicator as it does to the committee.

Implementation of proposals

10. Proposals approved by the school organisation committee under paragraph 8 or by the adjudicator under paragraph 9 shall have effect as if they-

    (a) had been made by the local education authority under their powers to make proposals for the establishment, alteration or discontinuance of schools, or

    (b) in any case where the proposals are for the alteration of a foundation, voluntary or foundation special school, had been made by the governing body under their powers to make proposals for the alteration of their school,

and had been approved by the school organisation committee or the adjudicator, as the case may be, under paragraph 3 of Schedule 6.

PART V PROCEDURE FOR DEALING WITH PROPOSALS UNDER PARAGRAPH 5: WALES

APPLICATION OF PART V

11. This Part of this Schedule applies to proposals published under paragraph 5 which relate to an area in Wales.

Objections

12.–(1) Any person may make objections to any proposals published under paragraph 5.

(2) Objections under this paragraph-

    (a) shall be sent to the Secretary of State; and

    (b) shall be so sent within such period as may be prescribed.

Local inquiry into proposals

13.–(1) This paragraph applies where in relation to the area of any local education authority the Secretary of State has made proposals under paragraph 5 (otherwise than in pursuance of paragraph 14(1)) which he has not withdrawn.

(2) If objections have been made under paragraph 12(1) within the period prescribed in accordance with paragraph 12(2)(b), then, unless all objections so made have been withdrawn in writing within that period, the Secretary of State shall cause a local inquiry to be held to consider his proposals, any proposals he refers to the inquiry and any such objections.

(3) Any proposals referred to a local inquiry under this paragraph require the approval of the Secretary of State (if they would not require such approval apart from this sub-paragraph).

(4) Where the Secretary of State has a duty to cause a local inquiry to be held under this paragraph, he shall refer to the inquiry-

(a) any other proposals published under paragraph 5 in relation to the area of the local education authority (and not withdrawn),

(b) any proposals made by that authority in the exercise of their powers to make proposals for the establishment, alteration or discontinuance of schools (and not withdrawn), and

(c) any proposals made by the governing body of any foundation, voluntary or foundation special school in the area in the exercise of their powers to make proposals for the alteration of their school (and not withdrawn),

where those proposals are not determined before he causes the inquiry to be held and appear to him to be related to the proposals made under paragraph 5 in respect of which he is required under this paragraph to cause the inquiry to be held.

(5) If, before the Secretary of State causes the inquiry to be held, he forms the opinion that any proposals ought to be implemented, sub-paragraph (4) does not require him to refer those proposals to the inquiry unless-

(a) before the proceedings on the inquiry are concluded, or

(b) (if earlier) the proposals are determined,

he subsequently forms a different opinion.

(6) It shall not be open to the inquiry to question the principles specified in the order under paragraph 2(2) or 3(2).

(7) References in this paragraph to the determination of any proposals are to-

(a) any determination whether or not to approve or adopt the proposals under paragraph 8 of Schedule 6 or paragraph 14 below, or

(b) any determination whether or not to implement the proposals under paragraph 9 of Schedule 6.

Adoption of proposals

14.–(1) Where the Secretary of State has published proposals under paragraph 5 in respect of which he is required to cause a local inquiry to be held, he may when he has considered the report of the person appointed to hold the inquiry do one or more of the following-

(a) adopt, with or without modifications, or determine not to adopt the proposals or any other proposals made by him under that paragraph which he referred to the inquiry;

(b) approve, with or without modifications, or reject any other proposals which he referred to the inquiry; and

(c) make any such further proposals under paragraph 5 as might have been made in accordance with the order or orders relating to the area of the local education authority concerned by the body to whom the directions were given.

(2) Where the Secretary of State has published proposals under paragraph 5 in respect of which he is not required to cause a local inquiry to be held and which he is not required to refer to such an inquiry, he may, after considering any objections made under paragraph 12(1) (and not withdrawn) within the period prescribed in accordance with paragraph 12(2)(b)-

(a) adopt the proposals with or without modifications; or

(b) determine not to adopt the proposals.

(3) Any adoption of proposals under this paragraph may be expressed to take effect only if an event specified in the adoption occurs by a date so specified.

Implementation of proposals

15. Proposals adopted by the Secretary of State under paragraph 14 shall have effect as if they-

(a) had been made by the local education authority under their powers to make proposals for the establishment, alteration or discontinuance of schools, or

(b) in any case where the proposals are for the alteration of a foundation, voluntary or foundation special school, had been made by the governing body under their powers to make proposals for the alteration of their school,

and had been approved by the Secretary of State under paragraph 8 of Schedule 6.

PART VI TRANSITIONAL EXEMPTION ORDERS FOR PURPOSES OF SEX DISCRIMINATION ACT 1975

Single-sex schools: England

16.–(1) This paragraph applies to proposals for a school in England to cease to be an establishment which admits pupils of one sex only.

(2) Sub-paragraph (3) applies where such proposals are made under paragraph 5 of this Schedule and, in accordance with sub-paragraph (3) of that paragraph, the Secretary of State sends a copy of the published proposals to the school organisation committee.

(3) The sending of the published proposals to the school organisation committee by the Secretary of State shall be treated as an application by the responsible body for the making by the school organisation committee of a transitional exemption order, and the committee may make such an order accordingly.

(4) Where-

(a) the school organisation committee have failed to reach a unanimous decision under sub-paragraph (3) above on whether to make a transitional exemption order, or

(b) the school organisation committee refer the proposals to the adjudicator under paragraph 8 of this Schedule,

they shall refer the question whether to make a transitional exemption order to the adjudicator.

(5) Where that question is referred to the adjudicator-
    (a) he shall consider the matter afresh; and
    (b) he may make a transitional exemption order accordingly.

(6) In this paragraph and in paragraph 17-

"the 1975 Act" means the Sex Discrimination Act 1975,

"make", in relation to a transitional exemption order, includes (so far as the context permits) vary or revoke,

"the responsible body" has the same meaning as in section 22 of the 1975 Act, and

"transitional exemption order" has the same meaning as in section 27 of the 1975 Act,

and references to proposals for a school to cease to be an establishment which admits pupils of one sex only are references to proposals which are or include proposals for such an alteration in a school's admissions arrangements as is mentioned in section 27(1) of the 1975 Act (single-sex establishments becoming co-educational).

Single-sex schools: Wales

17.–(1) This paragraph applies to proposals for a school in Wales to cease to be an establishment which admits pupils of one sex only.

(2) Where such proposals are made under paragraph 5 of this Schedule, the responsible body shall be treated as having made an application to the Secretary of State for the making of a transitional exemption order, and the Secretary of State may make such an order accordingly.

Schedule 7
This Schedule gives the Secretary of State detailed powers to require an local education authority or the governing body of a foundation, voluntary or foundation special school to bring forward proposals for the reduction of excess school places or for the provision of additional places where these are needed. Although the Secretary of State may make orders in relation to specific foundation, voluntary or foundation special schools, he may not require the local education authority to make proposals in relation to specified schools - identifying where the reduction or increase is to be made within the authority is a matter for the local education authority.

Where the Secretary of State exercises these powers in England, the powers of the school organisation committee and adjudicator are restricted in relation to the local education authority in question. All current proposals relating to that area must be referred to the Secretary of State who then effectively takes control of them. The local education authority is responsible for all costs (including all implementation cost) incurred by any foundation, voluntary or foundation special school that is required to put forward proposals under this Schedule. This overrides the normal basis, set out in Schedule 6, on which the cost of implementation of proposals for change is met.

Once proposals have been made to the Secretary of State, he in turn may publish proposals for change. Those proposals may be objected to. Objections and approval in England go through the school organisation committee and adjudicator process. If a proposal is referred to the adjudicator he must hold a local enquiry. In Wales, objections go to the Secretary of State who must hold a local enquiry unless the objections are withdrawn. in each case, the local enquiry may not question the principles on which the Secretary of State's original requirement for change was made.

Proposals that are finally approved must be implemented and Schedule 6 applies. There are similar provisions to those in Schedule 6 relating to a transitional exemption order under the Sex Discrimination Act 1975.

SCHEDULE 8

CHANGES OF CATEGORY OF SCHOOL

Permitted changes of category

1.–(1) A community school may in accordance with this Schedule become a foundation school in pursuance of proposals published by the local education authority.

(2) A school within one of the following categories, namely-

    (a) a community school,
    (b) a foundation school,
    (c) a voluntary aided school, or
    (d) a voluntary controlled school,

may in accordance with this Schedule become a school within another of those categories in pursuance of proposals published by the governing body.

(3) A community special school may in accordance with this Schedule become a foundation special school in pursuance of proposals published by the local education authority.

(4) A community special school or a foundation special school may in accordance with this Schedule become a foundation special school or a community special school in pursuance of proposals published by the governing body.

Procedure for changing category of school

2.–(1) Where, in the case of any maintained school, the local education authority or the governing body propose that the school should become a school of another category as permitted by paragraph 1, they shall publish their proposals under this paragraph.

(2) Regulations may provide for any of the provisions of sections 28 and 31 and Part I or II of Schedule 6 to have effect in relation to any such proposals with or without modifications.

Mandatory publication of proposals for voluntary aided school to change category

3.–(1) If at any time the governing body of a voluntary aided school are unable or unwilling to carry out their obligations under Schedule 3, they shall publish proposals under this paragraph.

(2) If the proposals are published during the period mentioned in section 35(2), they shall be proposals for the school to become a voluntary controlled school.

(3) If the proposals are published after the end of that period, they shall be proposals for the school to become either a voluntary controlled school or a foundation school, as the governing body may determine.

(4) Sub-paragraph (2) of paragraph 2 shall apply in relation to proposals published under this paragraph as it applies in relation to proposals published under that paragraph.

Restrictions on changing category of school

4.–(1) Regulations may make provision for preventing a school of any description specified in the regulations from changing its category under this Schedule unless such conditions are satisfied as are so specified.

(2) The conditions which may be so specified include conditions requiring (according to the circumstances of the case) any of the following to be demonstrated to the satisfaction of any person so specified, namely-

(a) that the school will join a group of schools for which a foundation body acts or proposes to act;

(b) where a foundation is proposed to be established for the school otherwise than under this Act, that the foundation would meet such requirements as may be so specified;

(c) that the governing body will be able to carry out their obligations under Schedule 3;

(d) that the school's governing or foundation body or trustees have agreed to sell or otherwise transfer to the local education authority any land of a description so specified.

Implementation of proposals

5.–(1) Regulations may make such provision as the Secretary of State considers necessary or expedient in connection with the implementation of proposals published under paragraph 2 or 3, including provision with respect to-

(a) the revision or replacement of the school's instrument of government and the reconstitution of its governing body;

(b) the transfer of property, rights and liabilities (including such a transfer to or from a foundation body), and staff; and

(c) any transitional matters (whether relating to the implementation of proposals published under other provisions of this Act or otherwise).

(2) Regulations under sub-paragraph (1) may, in particular, make provision with respect to-

    (a) restricting the disposal of land by a local authority which is used or held for the purposes of a school in relation to which proposals to change category are, or may be, published under paragraph 2, as from-

        (i) the date of publication of such proposals; or

        (ii) such other time as may be prescribed;

    (b) restricting the taking of action by virtue of which any such land would cease to be so used or held to any extent;

    (c) the consequences of any contravention of any such restriction;

    (d) conferring on any prescribed body such functions as may be prescribed with respect to any such contravention.

(3) Regulations under sub-paragraph (1) may, in connection with any matters falling within that sub-paragraph-

    (a) modify any provision made by or under this Part of this Act;

    (b) apply any such provision with or without modifications;

    (c) make provision corresponding or similar to any such provision.

6. A school's change of category under this Schedule shall not be taken as authorising or requiring any change in the character of the school conducted by its governing body (including, in particular, any religious character of the school).

Schedule 8

This Schedule deals with the way in which a school may change from one category to another (other than in respect of grant-maintained schools changing from their initial indicative category which is dealt with in Schedule 2). The Schedule empowers community, foundation, voluntary controlled and voluntary aided schools to change to another of these categories under proposals to be published by the governing body or (in the case of a community school only) by the local education authority. The local education authority may propose that a community special school becomes a foundation special school and the governing body of either a community special school or a foundation special school changes to the other category.

The process will be governed by regulations which may prescribe conditions and limitations on the opportunity for change.

There is a requirement for the governing body of a voluntary aided school that cannot meet its financial obligations under Schedule 3 (i.e. its responsibility to maintain premises) to publish proposals to change either to a voluntary controlled or foundation school which has the effect of transferring the responsibility to the local education authority but with consequential effect on the composition of the governing body and other powers in relation, for example, to staff and the control of the school premises.

A change of category under this Schedule, however it comes about, will not affect or authorise any change to the character of the school so that, in particular, any religious character will be maintained.

SCHEDULE 9 CONSTITUTION OF GOVERNING BODIES

PART I CATEGORIES OF GOVERNOR

Co-opted governors

1. In this Schedule "co-opted governor" means a person who is appointed to be a member of the school's governing body by being co-opted by governors who have not themselves been so appointed.

Foundation governors

2. In this Act "foundation governor" means a person appointed to be a member of the school's governing body, otherwise than by a local education authority, who-

    (a) where the school has a particular religious character, is appointed for the purpose of securing that that character is preserved and developed, and
    (b) where the school has a trust deed, is appointed for the purpose of securing that the school is conducted in accordance with that deed,

    or, where the school has neither a religious character nor a trust deed, is appointed as a foundation governor of the school.

LEA governors

3. In this Schedule "LEA governor" means a governor appointed to the school's governing body by the local education authority.

Parent governors

4. In this Schedule "parent governor" means-

    (a) a person who is elected as a member of the school's governing body by parents of registered pupils at the school and is himself such a parent at the time when he is elected, or
    (b) a person who is appointed as a parent governor by the governing body in accordance with regulations.

Partnership governors

5. In this Schedule "partnership governor" means a person nominated as a partnership governor, and appointed as such, in accordance with regulations.

Staff governors

6. In this Schedule "staff governor" means a person-

    (a) who is elected as a member of the school's governing body by persons employed to work at the school otherwise than as teachers, and

(b) who is himself a person so employed at the time when he is elected;

and for this purpose "employed" means employed under a contract of employment or a contract for services.

Teacher governors

7. In this Schedule "teacher governor" means a person-

   (a) who is elected as a member of the school's governing body by teachers at the school, and
   (b) who is himself such a teacher at the time when he is elected;

and for this purpose "teacher" means a teacher employed under a contract of employment or a contract for services or otherwise engaged to provide his services as a teacher.

Head teacher

8. At any time when the head teacher is a governor, he shall be treated for all purposes as being an ex officio governor.

PART II CONSTITUTION OF GOVERNING BODIES

Community schools

9.–(1) The governing body of a community school shall consist of the following-

   (a) the head teacher, except at any time when he chooses not to be a governor,
   (b) governors of each of the categories specified in the first column of the following table, in the numbers specified in whichever of the other columns relates to the school, and
   (c) any additional governors required by virtue of paragraph 15.

(2) The option of having a smaller governing body constituted in accordance with the third or fifth column is available-

   (a) in the case of a secondary school, where the school has less than 600 registered pupils, and
   (b) in the case of a primary school, where the school has less than 100 registered pupils.

(3) As regards the alternatives specified in the fourth column of the table, the governing body of a primary school to which that column applies must be constituted in such a way as to reflect either all the first alternatives or all the second alternatives.

Category of governor	Secondary school- normal basis	Secondary school- option if less than 600 pupils	Primary school- normal basis	Primary school- option if less than 100 pupils
Parent governors	6.	5	4 *or* 5	3
LEA governors	5	4	3 *or* 4	2
Teacher governors	2	2	1 *or* 2	1
Staff governors	1	1	1	1 *or* 0
Co-opted governors	5	4	3 *or* 4	2

Community special schools

10.–(1) The governing body of a community special school shall consist of the following-

    (a) the head teacher, except at any time when he chooses not to be a governor,

    (b) governors of each of the categories specified in the first column of the table set out in paragraph 9, in the numbers specified in either the fourth or the fifth column, and

    (c) any additional governors required by virtue of paragraph 15.

(2) The option of having a smaller governing body constituted in accordance with the fifth column of the table is accordingly available whether or not the school has less than 100 registered pupils.

(3) As regards the alternatives specified in the fourth column of the table, the governing body of a community special school to which that column is applicable must be constituted in such a way as to reflect either all the first alternatives or all the second alternatives.

(4) Whichever set of numbers applies to the governing body of such a school under the fourth or fifth column-

    (a) the number of co-opted governors shall be reduced by one, and

    (b) in place of that governor there shall be a representative governor appointed under sub-paragraph (5) or (6),

except in a case where sub-paragraph (6) applies and no voluntary organisation is designated for the purposes of that sub-paragraph.

(5) Where the school is established in a hospital, a representative governor shall be appointed-

(a) (if the hospital is vested in the Secretary of State) by the Health Authority; or

(b) (if the hospital is vested in a National Health Service trust) by that trust.

(6) Where the school is not established in a hospital, then-

(a) if a voluntary organisation is designated by the local education authority, in relation to the school, as the appropriate voluntary organisation concerned with matters in respect of which the school is specially organised, a representative governor shall be appointed by that organisation; or

(b) if two or more voluntary organisations are so designated as appropriate voluntary organisations concerned with such matters, a representative governor shall be appointed by those organisations acting jointly.

Foundation schools

11.–(1) The governing body of a foundation school shall consist of the following-

(a) the head teacher, except at any time when he chooses not to be a governor,

(b) governors of each of the categories specified in the first column of the following table, in the numbers specified in whichever of the other columns relates to the school, and

(c) any additional governors required by virtue of paragraph 15.

Where the school does not have a foundation, the reference to foundation governors in the first column shall be read as a reference to partnership governors.

(2) The option of having a smaller governing body constituted in accordance with the third or fifth column is available-

(a) in the case of a secondary school, where the school has less than 600 registered pupils, and

(b) in the case of a primary school, where the school has less than 100 registered pupils.

(3) As regards the alternatives specified in the fourth column of the table, the governing body of a primary school to which that column applies must be constituted in such a way as to reflect either both of the first alternatives or both of the second alternatives.

Category of governor	Secondary school- normal basis	Secondary school- option if less than 600 pupils	Primary school- normal basis	Primary school- option if less than 100 pupils
Parent governors	7.	6	5 *or* 6	4
LEA governors	2	2	2	2
Teacher governors	2	2	1	1
Staff governors	1	1	1	1 *or* 0
Foundation governors	5	4	3 *or* 4	2
Co-opted governors	3	2	1	1

Foundation special schools

12.–(1) The governing body of a foundation special school shall consist of the following-

(a) the head teacher, except at any time when he chooses not to be a governor,
(b) governors of each of the categories specified in the first column of the table set out in paragraph 11, in the numbers specified in either the fourth or the fifth column, and
(c) any additional governors required by virtue of paragraph 15.

Where the school does not have a foundation, the reference to foundation governors in the first column shall be read as a reference to partnership governors.

(2) The option of having a smaller governing body constituted in accordance with the fifth column of the table is accordingly available whether or not the school has less than 100 registered pupils.

(3) As regards the alternatives specified in the fourth column of the table, the governing body of a foundation special school to which that column is applicable must be constituted in such a way as to reflect either both of the first alternatives or both of the second alternatives.

Voluntary controlled schools

13.–(1) The governing body of a voluntary controlled school shall consist of the following-

(a) the head teacher, except at any time when he chooses not to be a governor,

(b) governors of each of the categories specified in the first column of the following table, in the numbers specified in whichever of the other columns relates to the school, and

(c) any additional governors required by virtue of paragraph 15.

(2) The option of having a smaller governing body constituted in accordance with the third or fifth column is available-

(a) in the case of a secondary school, where the school has less than 600 registered pupils, and

(b) in the case of a primary school, where the school has less than 100 registered pupils.

(3) As regards the alternatives specified in the fourth column, the governing body of a primary school to which that column applies must be constituted in such a way as to reflect either both of the first alternatives or both of the second alternatives.

Category of governor	Secondary school- normal basis	Secondary school- option if less than 600 pupils	Primary school- normal basis	Primary school- option if less than 100 pupils
Parent governors	6.	5	4 *or* 5	3
LEA governors	4	3	3	2
Teacher governors	2	2	1	1
Staff governors	1	1	1	1 *or* 0
Foundation governors	5	4	3 or 4	2
Co-opted governors	2	2	1	1

Voluntary aided schools

14.–(1) The governing body of a voluntary aided school shall consist of the following-

(a) the head teacher, except at any time when he chooses not to be a governor,

(b) governors of each of the categories specified in the first column of the following table, in the numbers specified in whichever of the other columns relates to the school,

(c) any additional governors required by virtue of paragraph 15, and

(d) such number of foundation governors as will lead to their outnumbering the other governors mentioned in paragraphs (a) to (c)-

    (i) by three, in the case of a school to which the second column applies, or

    (ii) by two, in the case of any other school.

(2) The option of having a smaller governing body constituted in accordance with the third or fifth column is available-

    (a) in the case of a secondary school, where the school has less than 600 registered pupils, and

    (b) in the case of a primary school, where the school has less than 100 registered pupils.

(3) As regards the alternatives specified in the fourth column, the governing body of a primary school to which that column applies must be constituted in such a way as to reflect either both of the first alternatives or both of the second alternatives.

(4) The foundation governors required by sub-paragraph (1)(d) must include-

    (a) at least three governors who at the time of their appointment are parents of registered pupils at the school, in the case of a school to which the second column applies, or

    (b) at least two such governors in the case of any other school.

Category of governor	Secondary school- normal basis	Secondary school- option if less than 600 pupils	Primary school- normal basis	Primary school- option if less than 100 pupils
Parent governors	3.	2	1 *or* 2	1
LEA governors	2	1	1 *or* 2	1
Teacher governors	2	2	1	1
Staff governors	1	1	1	1 *or* 0

Additional governors

15.–(1) If the governing body of any maintained school so determine, or regulations so require, the instrument of government for the school shall provide for the governing body to include, in addition to the governors required by virtue of the preceding provisions of this Schedule, such number of co-opted governors as may be specified in or determined in accordance with regulations.

(2) Regulations shall specify-

(a) the circumstances in which provision for such appointments is authorised or required to be made under this paragraph; and

(b) the categories of person from whom or from amongst whose members nominations for such appointments are to be sought.

(3) The instrument of government for any community or voluntary school which-

(a) is a primary school, and

(b) serves an area for which there are one or more minor authorities,

shall provide for the governing body to include (in addition to the governors required by virtue of paragraph 9, 13 or 14, as the case may be, and any required by virtue of sub-paragraph (1)) one co-opted governor nominated by the minor authority or (as the case may be) one of the minor authorities in question.

(4) Where any such school serves an area for which there are two or more minor authorities, the relevant governors shall, for the purposes of the appointment of any such co-opted governor, seek nominations from such one or more of those authorities as the governors think fit.

(5) In sub-paragraph (4) "the relevant governors" means those members of the school's governing body who are not co-opted governors.

Substitutes for ex officio foundation governors

16. Regulations may make provision for, and in connection with, the appointment of foundation governors to act in the place of ex officio foundation governors in cases where-

(a) any person holding a foundation governorship ex officio is unable or unwilling to act as a foundation governor, or

(b) there is a vacancy in the office by virtue of which such a governorship exists.

Adjustment in number of governors

17.–(1) Where-

(a) a maintained school has more governors of a particular category than are provided for by the instrument of government for the school in accordance with this Part of this Schedule, and

(b) the excess is not eliminated by the required number of governors of that category resigning,

such number of governors of that category as is required to eliminate the excess shall cease to hold office.

(2) If the excess has arisen in relation to foundation governors, the excess shall be eliminated in accordance with such procedure as is set out in the instrument of government for the school.

(3) If the excess has arisen in relation to any other category of governor, the excess shall be eliminated in accordance with such procedure as may be prescribed.

(4) Where the governing body of a maintained school includes any additional governors appointed in pursuance of paragraph 15, this paragraph shall apply to the school as if such of those governors as are nominated by a particular category of person constituted a separate category of governor.

Schedule 9

This Schedule deals with the detailed constitution of governing bodies.

Part 1

The different categories of governors are defined. All schools will have at least one local education authority governor appointed by the local education authority that maintains the school and will have at least one parent, staff and teacher governor elected to that position or, in the case of parent governors where there are insufficient elected parent governors, appointed by the governing body. The Headteacher of every school is entitled to be a governor but need not be. Voluntary schools and those foundation schools that have a foundation body will have foundation governors. Those foundation schools that do not have a foundation body will have appointed partnership governors instead of foundation governors. Where governors (other than local education authority and foundation governors) have to be appointed, the appointment is carried out in accordance with regulations.

Part 2

The size and make-up of the governing body depends on three factors, the category of school, whether it is a primary or a secondary school and its size. The Schedule presents the composition of governing bodies in tabular form according to category. Further, schools may determine (in accordance with regulations) that the governing body should include additional co-opted governors under paragraph 15 of the Schedule. Community and voluntary primary schools serving an area where there is a minor authority as defined in S. 141 will also co-opt one governor nominated by that authority. If there is more than one minor authority the governing body will seek nominations from as many of them as it thinks fit but only one will be appointed. The Schedule also provides for the removal of excess governors which could arise in schools with foundation governors if the Headteacher decided to cease to be a governor or in any school if its size changed. Removal of foundation governors is dealt with in the Instrument of Government. Other removals are dealt with in regulations.

SCHEDULE 10

INCORPORATION AND POWERS OF GOVERNING BODIES

Introductory

1.–(1) In the following paragraphs of this Schedule "the governing body" means the governing body of a maintained school incorporated under section 36(1).

(2) Where an existing school (other than a grouped school) becomes a maintained school on the appointed day in accordance with Schedule 2, the governing body of the school-

(a) shall continue in existence as a body corporate; and
(b) shall so continue in existence as if incorporated under section 36(1);

but as from that day the governing body shall (subject to regulations under sub-paragraph (3) or (4)) conform with Part II of Schedule 9.

(3) For the purposes of sub-paragraph (2) the governing body of each such existing school shall (subject to regulations under sub-paragraph (4)) be reconstituted under the instrument of government required by paragraph 6 of Schedule 12 before the appointed day; and regulations may make such provision as the Secretary of State considers necessary or expedient in connection with the reconstitution of a governing body in pursuance of this sub-paragraph.

(4) Regulations may, in relation to cases where-

(a) the instrument of government required by paragraph 6 of Schedule 12 in the case of an existing school within sub-paragraph (2) above is not made before the appointed day, or
(b) the governing body of such a school are not reconstituted before that day,

make such provision as the Secretary of State considers necessary or expedient in connection with any of the following matters, namely-

(i) the making of such instruments of government on or after that day,
(ii) the reconstitution of governing bodies on or after that day, and
(iii) the existence of such bodies on and after that day pending their reconstitution at some later date.

(5) Regulations may, in relation to existing schools which are grouped schools, make such provision as the Secretary of State considers necessary or expedient in connection with the transition of such schools from being grouped under a single governing body to having their own governing bodies constituted under instruments of government made in accordance with Schedule 12.

(6) If the instrument of government required by paragraph 6 of Schedule 12 is not made before the appointed day in the case of an existing school, the following requirements, namely-

(a) the requirements of paragraph 2(1) below as to the name of the governing body, and
(b) the requirements of section 37(3) as to the name of the school,

shall not apply until such time as that instrument of government is made.

(7) In this paragraph "existing school" means (subject to sub-paragraph (8))-

(a) a county, controlled, aided or special agreement school or a maintained special school, or
(b) a grant-maintained or grant-maintained special school,

within the meaning of the Education Act 1996; and "grouped school" means a school grouped under section 89 or 280 of that Act.

(8) A school is not an existing school for the purposes of this paragraph if immediately before the appointed day-

(a) in the case of a school within paragraph (a) of sub-paragraph (7), it has a temporary governing body, or
(b) in the case of a school within paragraph (b) of that sub-paragraph, it has a governing body but it has not yet opened;

and for this purpose a school "opens" on the date when it first admits pupils.

(9) Regulations may make such provision as the Secretary of State considers necessary or expedient in connection with the transition of-

(a) any such school as is mentioned in sub-paragraph (8)(a) or (b), or
(b) any proposed school which would be a school within sub-paragraph (7)(a) and which has, or is required to have, a temporary governing body,

to a school with a governing body constituted under an instrument of government made in accordance with Schedule 12.

(10) Regulations under any provision of this paragraph may, in connection with any matters falling within that provision-

(a) modify any provision made by or under this Part of this Act;
(b) apply any such provision with or without modifications;
(c) make provision corresponding or similar to any such provision;
(d) provide for the continued application of any provision made by or under any of the Education Acts with or without modifications.

Name and seal of governing body

2.–(1) The governing body shall be known as "The governing body of . . ." with the addition of the name of the school as for the time being set out in the school's instrument of government.

(2) The application of the seal of the governing body must be authenticated by the signature-

(a) of the chairman of the governing body, or

(b) of some other member authorised either generally or specially by the governing body to act for that purpose,

together with the signature of any other member.

(3) Every document purporting to be an instrument made or issued by or on behalf of the governing body and-

(a) to be duly executed under the seal of the governing body, or

(b) to be signed or executed by a person authorised by the governing body to act in that behalf,

shall be received in evidence and be treated, without further proof, as being so made or issued unless the contrary is shown.

Powers of governing body

3.–(1) The governing body may do anything which appears to them to be necessary or expedient for the purposes of, or in connection with, the conduct of the school.

(2) The governing body may in particular-

(a) borrow such sums as the governing body think fit and, in connection with such borrowing, grant any mortgage, charge or other security over any land or other property of the governing body;

(b) acquire and dispose of land and other property;

(c) enter into contracts;

(d) invest any sums not immediately required for the purposes of carrying on any activities they have power to carry on;

(e) accept gifts of money, land or other property and apply it, or hold and administer it on trust, for any of those purposes; and

(f) do anything incidental to the conduct of the school.

(3) The power to borrow sums and grant security mentioned in sub-paragraph (2)(a) may only be exercised with the written consent-

(a) of the Secretary of State, or

(b) if an order under sub-paragraph (4) so provides, of the local education authority;

and any such consent may be given for particular borrowing or for borrowing of a particular class.

(4) The Secretary of State may by order make provision for his function of giving consent under sub-paragraph (3) to be instead exercisable-

(a) in the case of all maintained schools, or

(b) in the case of any class of such schools specified in the order,

by the local education authorities by whom those schools are maintained.

(5) In exercising that function those authorities shall comply with any directions contained in an order made by the Secretary of State.

(6) Where the school is a foundation, voluntary aided or foundation special school, the power to enter into contracts mentioned in sub-paragraph (2)(c) includes power to enter into contracts for the employment of teachers and other staff; but no such contracts may be entered into by the governing body of a community, voluntary controlled or community special school.

(7) Sub-paragraphs (1) and (2) have effect subject to-

(a) any provisions of the school's instrument of government; and
(b) any provisions of a scheme under section 48 which relates to the school.

Dissolution of governing body

4.–(1) If the school is discontinued, the governing body are dissolved by virtue of this paragraph-

(a) on the discontinuance date, or
(b) on such later date as the Secretary of State may specify by order made before the discontinuance date.

(2) In this paragraph "the discontinuance date" means-

(a) the date when proposals for discontinuing the school are implemented under Part III of Schedule 6,
(b) the date when the school is discontinued under section 30, or
(c) the date specified in a direction given under section 19(1) or 32(1),

as the case may be.

Schedule 10

This Schedule deals with the formal incorporation of governing bodies.

Existing schools, which are already corporate bodies under the Education Act 1996, continue so that there is no break in legal continuity – this means that existing contracts, rights, obligations and commitments continue despite the reorganisation – but must amend their constitution by adopting new Instruments of Government and must re-form their governing bodies to conform with Schedule 9. The process is to be carried out in accordance with regulations.

The Schedule re-enacts previous provisions dealing with the name of the schools, how formal documents are to be signed and specifying the powers of the governing body. This is necessary because an incorporated body (unlike an individual) has no inherent power or ability and can only work within a framework that is specified by the document or legislation that creates it. Paragraph 7 confers a general power to do anything that the governing body thinks necessary or expedient for the school. It then grants specific powers including the power to borrow money and give security but this power can only be exercised with the consent of the Secretary of State or (if the Secretary of State has devolved the power) by the local education authority. This is of greater importance than is often thought because technically hire-purchase or finance-lease transactions for, say, acquiring photo-copiers, computer equipment or vehicles often constitute borrowing.

Foundation, voluntary aided and foundation special schools have power to employ staff but community, voluntary controlled and community special schools do not have that power. All employees working at those schools are technically employed by the local education authority and the governing body exercises employment rights under delegated authority from the local education authority.

The powers of the governing body of all schools are constrained within the terms of the local education authority financial management scheme made under S. 48. The school does not have the power or right to go outside the terms of that scheme.

The significance of incorporation is that all liabilities, whether under contracts or otherwise (including any liability for negligence) are liabilities of the school itself and not of individual governors. Governors cannot have personal liability for anything that happens within a school if they have acted honestly and reasonably in dealing with their responsibilities.

SCHEDULE 11

MEMBERSHIP AND PROCEEDINGS ETC. OF GOVERNING BODIES

PART I MEMBERSHIP AND PROCEEDINGS

Regulations about governing bodies

1. Regulations may make in relation to governing bodies of maintained schools such provision as is authorised by the following provisions of this Part of this Schedule.

Election or appointment of governors

2.–(1) The regulations may make provision-

(a) as to the procedures to be followed in connection with the election or appointment of persons as governors of such schools or in connection with the nomination of persons to be so appointed;

(b) imposing requirements which must be complied with in relation to the appointment or nomination of persons as governors of any prescribed category;

(c) as to the circumstances in which persons are qualified or disqualified-

   (i) for being elected, appointed or nominated as governors of any such category, or

   (ii) for voting in an election of such governors.

(2) The regulations may make provision-

    (a) for enabling the local education authority or (as the case may be) the governing body to determine, for the purposes of any such election, whether any person is a person of such a description as is specified in the regulations;

    (b) for requiring appointments falling to be made by persons acting jointly to be made, in any prescribed circumstances, by or in accordance with a direction given by the Secretary of State.

Qualifications and tenure of office

3. The regulations may make provision as to-

    (a) the circumstances in which persons are qualified or disqualified for holding office as governors;

    (b) the term of office of governors (subject to any provision made by virtue of sub-paragraph (a));

    (c) the resignation or removal of governors from office.

Meetings and proceedings

4.–(1) The regulations may make provision as to the meetings and proceedings of governing bodies.

(2) The provision authorised by sub-paragraph (1) includes, in particular, provision-

    (a) for the election by the governors of a school of one of their number to be chairman, and one to be vice-chairman, of the governing body;

    (b) for the period for which the chairman and vice-chairman are to be elected and for the removal from office of either of those persons;

    (c) for the establishment by a governing body of committees (which may include persons who are not members of the governing body) and for the constitution, meetings and proceedings of committees so established;

    (d) for the delegation of functions of a governing body, in such circumstances as may be specified, to committees established by that body, to any member of that body or to the head teacher;

    (e) for the chairman, or such other member of a governing body as may be specified, to have power in specified circumstances to discharge any of the governing body's functions as a matter of urgency;

    (f) as to the quorum required in any specified circumstances;

    (g) for securing that proceedings of a governing body, or of any committee established by them, are not invalidated by any vacancy among the governors, or among the members of any such committee, or in any other specified circumstances;

    (h) requiring decisions taken by a governing body in any specified circumstances to be confirmed at a second meeting of that body held within such period as may be specified.

(3) In sub-paragraph (2) "specified" means specified in the regulations.

(4) The regulations may authorise or require governing bodies to make provision with respect to any matters relating to their meetings or proceedings (including any of the matters mentioned in sub-paragraph (2)).

(5) Subject to the regulations, a governing body may regulate their own procedure and that of any of their committees.

Information as to meetings and proceedings

5.–(1) The regulations may make provision requiring a governing body-

(a) to make minutes (including draft minutes) of their proceedings available for inspection by the local education authority;

(b) to make available-

(i) to such persons or classes of person as may be specified, and

(ii) in such form, and at such times, as may be specified,

such documents and information relating to their meetings and proceedings as may be specified.

(2) In sub-paragraph (1) "specified" means specified in the regulations.

PART II OTHER PROVISIONS ABOUT GOVERNORS

Governors' expenses

6.–(1) A governor shall be entitled to receive such allowances, payable at such rates, as the governing body may determine in accordance with regulations.

(2) Sub-paragraph (1) does not apply at any time when the school does not have a delegated budget, and the payment of allowances to a governor at any such time shall instead be in accordance with a scheme made by the local education authority for the purposes of section 519 of the Education Act 1996.

Training and support of governors

7. The local education authority shall-

(a) (to the extent that they are not otherwise required to secure the provision of such information) secure that every governor is provided, free of charge, with such information as they consider appropriate in connection with the discharge of his functions as a governor; and

(b) secure that there is made available to every governor, free of charge, such training as they consider necessary for the effective discharge of those functions.

PART III CLERK TO THE GOVERNING BODY

Appointment etc. of clerk

8. Regulations may make provision-

(a) requiring the appointment of a clerk to the governing body of a maintained school and authorising or requiring the appointment of clerks to committees of the governing body;

(b) prescribing the body by whom any such appointment is to be made and any restrictions or other requirements relating to any such appointment;

(c) as to the dismissal of any such clerk and the procedure to be followed in connection with his dismissal;

(d) authorising the governing body or a committee of the governing body, where the clerk fails to attend a meeting of theirs, to appoint one of their number to act as clerk for the purposes of that meeting.

Schedule 11

This Schedule deals with how governors are to be appointed and how governing bodies conduct themselves. The Schedule contains no detail. It merely provides that matters are to be covered by regulations but it does indicate areas that the regulations may deal with. Specifically the regulations may (which in practice means "will") cover:-

* *How governors are to be appointed, what qualifications governors in particular categories may need to have and who rules on whether or not a person has the required qualification*

* *Disqualification, term of office and resignation and retirement of governors*

* *How meetings are to be conducted*

* *How the chair and vice-chair is to be elected or removes*

* *The establishment of committees and how they will operate*

* *The delegation of functions including decision making*

* *The power to be given to the chair or vice-chair of governors to act in emergency*

* *Quorum for meetings*

* *Saving proceedings of governing bodies from being invalidated because of technical defects*

* *Requirement that certain decisions (in practice such as a decision to remove the chair of governors from office) to require ratification by a second governing body meeting*

* *Keeping minutes and making them and other documents available to the local education authority and others*

* *The appointment and removal of the clerk to the governing body*

The Schedule also deals with governor expenses and training (which is the responsibility of the local education authority for all categories of school).

SCHEDULE 12

Contents and form of instrument of government

1.–(1) The instrument of government for a maintained school shall set out–

  (a) the name of the school;

  (b) the category of school (within section 20(1)) to which the school belongs;

  (c) the name of the governing body of the school;

  (d) the manner in which the governing body are to be constituted, specifying–

   (i) the categories of governor and the number of governors in each category,

   (ii) the categories of person from whom or from amongst whose members nominations for the appointment of any additional governors required by virtue of paragraph 15 of Schedule 9 are to be sought,

   (iii) the number of such governors for whose appointment nominations are to be sought in the case of each such category of person,

   (iv) where the school is a community special school, whether it has a representative governor by virtue of paragraph 10 of Schedule 9, and

   (v) the total number of governors;

  (e) where the school has foundation governors–

   (i) the name of any foundation body or person who is entitled to appoint such governors and (if there is more than one such person) the basis on which such appointments are made,

   (ii) details of any foundation governorship to be held ex officio by the holder of a named office and the name of any person entitled to make any appointment by virtue of paragraph 16 of Schedule 9, and

   (iii) the procedure to be adopted for eliminating any excess in the number of foundation governors for the purposes of paragraph 17 of that Schedule;

  (f) where the school is a community special school, the names of any body or bodies by whom any representative governor is appointed under paragraph 10 of that Schedule;

  (g) where the school is a foundation or voluntary school which has a religious character, a description of the ethos of the school; and

  (h) the date when the instrument takes effect.

(2) The manner in which the governing body are to be constituted, as set out in the instrument in accordance with sub-paragraph (1)(d), must conform with the provisions of–

  (a) Part II of Schedule 9, and

  (b) any regulations made under paragraph 15 of that Schedule,

as they apply to a school of the category to which the school belongs.

(3) Where, for the purposes of any provision of that Part of that Schedule, it is material to determine the number of registered pupils at the school, that number shall be determined as at the date when the instrument is made.

(4) The instrument shall (subject to any other statutory provision) comply with any trust deed relating to the school.

(5) The instrument shall be made in such form as may be prescribed.

Making of instruments of government

2.–(1) Paragraph 3 shall apply in connection with the making of an instrument of government for a maintained school subject to any relevant modifications.

(2) In sub-paragraph (1) "relevant modifications" means-

 (a) where the instrument of government is to be made in pursuance of paragraph 6 for a school which is to become a maintained school on the appointed day in accordance with Schedule 2, modifications prescribed under that paragraph;

 (b) where the instrument of government is to be made in pursuance of regulations under section 44 for a new maintained school, modifications prescribed under that section; and

 (c) where the instrument of government is to be made in pursuance of regulations under paragraph 5 of Schedule 8 for a school changing its category in accordance with that Schedule, modifications prescribed by regulations under that paragraph.

Procedure for making instrument

3.–(1) The governing body shall prepare a draft of the instrument and submit it to the local education authority.

(2) Where the school has foundation governors, the governing body shall not submit the draft to the authority unless the following persons have agreed to the contents of the draft, namely-

 (a) the foundation governors;

 (b) any trustees under a trust deed relating to the school; and

 (c) in the case of a Church of England, Church in Wales or Roman Catholic Church school, the appropriate diocesan authority.

(3) On receiving the draft the authority shall consider whether it complies with all applicable statutory provisions, and if-

 (a) the authority are content with the draft, or

 (b) there is agreement between the authority, the governing body and (if the school has foundation governors) the persons mentioned in sub-paragraph (2) that the draft should be revised to any extent,

the instrument shall be made by order of the authority in the form of the draft or (as the case may be) in the form of the revised draft.

(4) If, in the case of a school which has foundation governors, there is at any time disagreement as to the contents of the draft among the bodies and persons mentioned in sub-paragraph (3)(b), any of those bodies or persons may refer the draft to the Secretary of State; and on such a reference the Secretary of State shall give such direction as he thinks fit having regard, in particular, to the category of school to which the school belongs.

(5) If neither of paragraphs (a) and (b) of sub-paragraph (3) applies in the case of a school which does not have foundation governors, the authority shall-

    (a) notify the governing body of the reasons why they are not content with the draft instrument, and

    (b) give the governing body a reasonable opportunity to reach agreement with the authority on revising the draft;

and the instrument shall be made by order of the authority either in the form of a revised draft agreed between the authority and the governing body or (in the absence of such agreement) in such form as the authority think fit having regard, in particular, to the category of school to which the school belongs.

(6) When taking any decision as to the name of the school the governing body, the authority and (if the school has foundation governors) the persons mentioned in sub-paragraph (2), shall have regard to any guidance given from time to time by the Secretary of State.

(7) Nothing in this paragraph requires the agreement of, or enables any objection to be made by, any body or person to any part of a draft instrument that reflects any decision taken by the governing body or any other person which the governing body or that person is required or authorised to take by virtue of any statutory provision.

Review of instruments of government

4.–(1) The governing body or the local education authority may review the instrument at any time after it is made.

(2) The governing body or the authority shall review the instrument on such occasions as may be prescribed; and regulations may require the instrument to be varied at the instance of the governing body in such circumstances as may be prescribed.

(3) Where-

    (a) on any review the governing body or the authority decide that the instrument should be varied, or

    (b) any regulations under sub-paragraph (2) require the instrument to be varied,

the governing body or (as the case may be) the authority shall notify the other of their proposed variation.

(4) Where the governing body have received a notification under sub-paragraph (3), they shall notify the authority as to whether or not they are content with it.

(5) Where the school has foundation governors, the governing body shall not give the authority-

(a) any notification under sub-paragraph (3), or

(b) any notification under sub-paragraph (4) to the effect that they are content with the authority's proposed variation,

unless the persons mentioned in paragraph 3(2) have agreed to the proposed variation.

(6) If-

(a) both the governing body and the authority are content with a proposed variation as notified under sub-paragraph (3), or

(b) there is agreement between the authority, the governing body and (if the school has foundation governors) the persons mentioned in paragraph 3(2) that some other variation should be made instead,

the instrument shall be varied accordingly by order of the authority.

(7) If, in the case of a school which has foundation governors, there is at any time disagreement as to the proposed variation among the bodies and persons mentioned in sub-paragraph (6)(b), any of those bodies or persons may refer the proposed variation to the Secretary of State; and on such a reference the Secretary of State shall give such direction as he thinks fit having regard, in particular, to the category of school to which the school belongs.

(8) If neither of paragraphs (a) and (b) of sub-paragraph (6) applies in the case of a school which does not have foundation governors, the authority shall-

(a) notify the governing body of the reasons-
(i) why they are not content with the governing body's proposed variation, or
(ii) why they wish to proceed with their own proposed variation,

as the case may be, and

(b) give the governing body a reasonable opportunity to reach agreement with the authority on revising the variation;

and the instrument shall be varied by order of the authority either in the manner agreed between the authority and the governing body or (in the absence of such agreement) in such manner as the authority think fit having regard, in particular, to the category of school to which the school belongs.

(9) Where there is no such agreement (and no variation is required by regulations under sub-paragraph (2)), sub-paragraph (8) does not require the authority to vary the instrument if they consider it appropriate not to do so.

(10) The following requirements under paragraph 3, namely-

(a) the requirement under sub-paragraph (3) for the authority to consider compliance with all applicable statutory provisions, and

(b) the requirement under sub-paragraph (6) to have regard, in connection with the name of the school, to guidance given by the Secretary of State,

shall apply in relation to a proposed variation of an instrument of government as they apply in relation to a draft of such an instrument.

(11) Where an instrument of government is varied under this paragraph-

(a) the instrument shall set out the date on which the variation takes effect, and

(b) paragraph 1(3) shall apply in relation to any variation relating to the manner in which the governing body are to be constituted as if it referred to the date when the variation is made rather than the date when the instrument is made.

(12) Nothing in this paragraph requires the agreement of, or enables any objection to be made by, any body or person to any proposed variation that reflects any decision taken by the governing body or any other person which the governing body or that person is required or authorised to take by virtue of any statutory provision.

Other requirements relating to instruments of government

5. Regulations may make provision imposing on local education authorities requirements with respect to the provision of-

(a) copies of instruments of government made or varied by them; or

(b) information relating to such instruments.

Duty to secure making of first instrument of government

6.–(1) A local education authority shall secure that, by the end of such period as may be prescribed, an instrument of government has been made in accordance with this Schedule for each school which is to be, or is, maintained by them as from the appointed day in accordance with section 20(4) or (5).

(2) Regulations may make such provision as the Secretary of State considers necessary or expedient in connection with the making of instruments of government in pursuance of sub-paragraph (1), including provision modifying any provision of this Schedule or Schedule 9.

Schedule 12

Every school must have an instrument of government. It is the responsibility of the local education authority to ensure that it is made and it must cover the following:-

- *The name of the school. All concerned are to have regard to guidance from the Secretary of State*

- *Its category*

- *The name of the governing body – normally "The governing body of [blank] school"*

- *How the governing body is to be constituted, which will follow the requirements of Schedule 9*

- *Provisions relating to foundation governors where applicable*

- *An ethos statement for foundation or voluntary schools with a religious character*

The form of the Instrument will be governed by regulations and, where applicable, must be consistent with the school's trust deed.

It is the governing body's responsibility to draft the Instrument. If the school has foundation governors the draft must be approved by the foundation governors and the body that appoints them. It is then submitted to the local education authority who will then formally make the Instrument if satisfied that the draft complies with the legislation. The Schedule provides for how disagreement is to be dealt with.

Instruments may be reviewed by the governing body and local education authority at any time and regulations may require review and variation in specified circumstances. The process for variation is essentially similar to that to be followed in making the Instrument initially.

SCHEDULE 13

CONTROL OF SCHOOL PREMISES BY GOVERNING BODIES

Community and community special schools: general

1.–(1) This paragraph applies to a community or community special school.

(2) The occupation and use of the premises of the school, both during and outside school hours, shall be under the control of the governing body, subject to-

   (a) any directions given by the local education authority under sub-paragraph (3);
   (b) any transfer of control agreement entered into by the governing body under paragraph 2; and
   (c) any requirements of an enactment other than this Act or regulations made under it.

(3) The local education authority may give such directions as to the occupation and use of the premises of a community or community special school as they think fit.

(4) In exercising control of the occupation and use of the premises of the school outside school hours the governing body shall have regard to the desirability of those premises being made available for community use.

Transfer of control agreement in case of community or community special school

2.–(1) Subject to sub-paragraph (2), the governing body of a community or community special school may enter into a transfer of control agreement with any body or person if their purpose, or one of their purposes, in doing so is to promote community use of the whole or any part of the school premises.

(2) The governing body shall not enter into any transfer of control agreement which makes or includes provision for the use of the whole or any part of the school premises during school hours unless they have first obtained the local education authority's consent to the agreement in so far as it makes such provision.

(3) A transfer of control agreement shall be taken to include the following terms, namely-

   (a) that the governing body shall notify the controlling body of any directions given to the governing body under paragraph 1(3);
   (b) that the controlling body, in exercising control of the use of any premises subject to the agreement-
      (i) shall do so in accordance with any directions from time to time notified to that body in pursuance of paragraph (a); and
      (ii) shall have regard to the desirability of the premises being made available for community use; and
   (c) that, if reasonable notice is given in writing by the governing body to the controlling body that such of the premises subject to the agreement as may be specified in the notice are reasonably required for use by or in connection with the school at such times as may be so specified, then-
      (i) the use of the specified premises at those times shall be under the control of the governing body, and
      (ii) accordingly, those premises may be used at those times by or in connection with the school for such purposes as may be specified in the notice,

even though their use at those times would, apart from this paragraph, be under the control of the controlling body.

(4) Sub-paragraph (5) applies where a transfer of control agreement makes express provision for the use of any school premises which are subject to the agreement to be occasionally under the control of the governing body, instead of the controlling body, in such circumstances, at such times or for such purposes as may be provided by or under the agreement.

(5) In such a case paragraph (c) of sub-paragraph (3) shall not have effect in relation to the transfer of control agreement if, at the time of entering into it, the governing body were of the opinion that the express provision would be more favourable to the interests of the school than the term that would otherwise be included by virtue of that paragraph.

(6) Where the governing body enter into a transfer of control agreement, they shall so far as reasonably practicable secure that the controlling body exercises control in accordance with any such directions as are notified to that body in pursuance of sub-paragraph (3)(a).

(7) In this paragraph-

"the controlling body" means the body or person (other than the governing body) which has control of the use of the whole or any part of the school premises under the transfer of control agreement in question;

"transfer of control agreement" means an agreement which (subject to sub-paragraph (3)) provides for the use of so much of the school premises as may be specified in the agreement to be under the control, at such times as may be so specified, of such body or person as may be so specified.

Foundation and foundation special schools: general

3.–(1) This paragraph applies to a foundation or foundation special school.

(2) The occupation and use of the premises of the school, both during and outside school hours, shall be under the control of the governing body, subject to-

  (a) any transfer of control agreement entered into by the governing body under paragraph 4; and
  (b) any requirements of an enactment other than this Act or regulations made under it.

(3) In exercising control of the occupation and use of the premises of the school outside school hours the governing body shall have regard to the desirability of those premises being made available for community use.

(4) Where the school has a trust deed which provides for any person other than the governing body to be entitled to control the occupation and use of the school premises to any extent, then, if and to the extent that (disregarding any transfer of control agreement made under paragraph 4) the use of those premises is or would be under the control of such a person-

  (a) this paragraph, and
  (b) paragraph 4,

shall have effect in relation to the school with the substitution of references to that person for references to the governing body.

Transfer of control agreement in case of foundation or foundation special school

4.–(1) Subject to sub-paragraph (2), the governing body of any foundation or foundation special school shall have power to enter into a transfer of control agreement with any body or person if their purpose, or one of their purposes, in doing so is to promote community use of the whole or any part of the school premises; and-

    (a) they may do so even though the school has a trust deed that would, apart from this sub-paragraph, expressly or impliedly preclude them from entering into such an agreement with that body or person or from conferring control on the controlling body in question; but

    (b) they shall not enter into a transfer of control agreement unless the use to which the premises may be put under the agreement is in all other respects in conformity with any such requirements, prohibitions or restrictions imposed by any such trust deed as would apply if control were being exercised by the governing body.

(2) The governing body shall not enter into any transfer of control agreement which makes or includes provision for the use of the whole or any part of the school premises during school hours unless they have first obtained the Secretary of State's consent to the agreement in so far as it makes such provision.

(3) A transfer of control agreement shall be taken to include the following terms, namely-

    (a) that the controlling body, in exercising control of the use of any premises subject to the agreement, shall have regard to the desirability of the premises being made available for community use; and

    (b) that, if reasonable notice is given in writing by the governing body to the controlling body that such of the premises subject to the agreement as may be specified in the notice are reasonably required for use by or in connection with the school at such times as may be so specified, then-

        (i) the use of the specified premises at those times shall be under the control of the governing body, and

        (ii) accordingly, those premises may be used at those times by or in connection with the school for such purposes as may be specified in the notice,

even though their use at those times would, apart from this paragraph, be under the control of the controlling body.

(4) Sub-paragraph (5) applies where a transfer of control agreement makes express provision for the use of any school premises which are subject to the agreement to be occasionally under the control of the governing body, instead of the controlling body, in such circumstances, at such times or for such purposes as may be provided by or under the agreement.

(5) In such a case paragraph (b) of sub-paragraph (3) shall not have effect in relation to the transfer of control agreement if, at the time of entering into it, the governing body were of the opinion that the express provision would be more favourable to the interests of the school than the term that would otherwise be included by virtue of that paragraph.

(6) In this paragraph—

"the controlling body" means the body or person (other than the governing body) which has control of the use of the whole or any part of the school premises under the transfer of control agreement in question;

"transfer of control agreement" means an agreement which (subject to sub-paragraph (3)) provides for the use of so much of the school premises as may be specified in the agreement to be under the control, at such times as may be so specified, of such body or person as may be so specified.

Voluntary schools: general

5.–(1) This paragraph applies to a voluntary school.

(2) The occupation and use of the premises of the school, both during and outside school hours, shall be under the control of the governing body, subject to—

    (a) any directions given by the local education authority—
        (i) (in the case of a voluntary controlled school) under sub-paragraph (3), or
        (ii) (in the case of a voluntary aided school) under paragraph 7(3);
    (b) any transfer of control agreement entered into by the governing body under paragraph 6; and
    (c) any requirements of an enactment other than this Act or regulations made under it.

(3) The local education authority may give such directions as to the occupation and use of the premises of a voluntary controlled school as they think fit (subject to paragraph 7(1) and (2)).

(4) Where the trust deed for a voluntary school provides for any person other than the governing body to be entitled to control the occupation and use of the school premises to any extent, then, if and to the extent that (disregarding any transfer of control agreement made under paragraph 6) the use of those premises is or would be under the control of such a person—

    (a) this paragraph, and
    (b) paragraphs 6 and 7,

shall have effect in relation to the school with the substitution of references to that person for references to the governing body.

Transfer of control agreement in case of voluntary school

6.–(1) Subject to sub-paragraph (2), the governing body of any voluntary school shall have power to enter into a transfer of control agreement with any body or person if their purpose, or one of their purposes, in doing so is to promote community use of the whole or any part of the school premises; and—

(a) they may do so even though the trust deed for the school would, apart from this sub-paragraph, expressly or impliedly preclude them from entering into such an agreement with that body or person or from conferring control on the controlling body in question; but

(b) they shall not enter into a transfer of control agreement unless the use to which the premises may be put under the agreement is in all other respects in conformity with any such requirements, prohibitions or restrictions imposed by the trust deed as would apply if control were being exercised by the governing body.

(2) The governing body shall not enter into any transfer of control agreement which makes or includes provision for the use of the whole or any part of the school premises during school hours unless they have first obtained the local education authority's consent to the agreement in so far as it makes such provision.

(3) A transfer of control agreement shall be taken to include the following terms, namely-

    (a) that the governing body shall notify the controlling body of-

        (i) any directions given to the governing body under paragraph 5(3) (in the case of a voluntary controlled school) or paragraph 7(3) (in the case of a voluntary aided school); and

        (ii) any determination made by the foundation governors under paragraph 7(2) (in the case of a voluntary controlled school);

    (b) that the controlling body, in exercising control of the use of any premises subject to the agreement-

        (i) shall do so in accordance with any directions or determinations from time to time notified to that body in pursuance of paragraph (a); and

        (ii) shall have regard to the desirability of the premises being made available for community use; and

    (c) that, if reasonable notice is given in writing by the governing body to the controlling body that such of the premises subject to the agreement as may be specified in the notice are reasonably required for use by or in connection with the school at such times as may be so specified, then-

        (i) the use of the specified premises at those times shall be under the control of the governing body, and

        (ii) accordingly, those premises may be used at those times by or in connection with the school for such purposes as may be specified in the notice,

even though their use at those times would, apart from this paragraph, be under the control of the controlling body.

(4) Sub-paragraph (5) applies where a transfer of control agreement makes express provision for the use of any school premises which are subject to the agreement to be occasionally under the control of the governing body, instead of the controlling body, in such circumstances, at such times or for such purposes as may be provided by or under the agreement.

(5) In such a case paragraph (c) of sub-paragraph (3) shall not have effect in relation to the transfer of control agreement if, at the time of entering into it, the governing body were of the opinion that the express provision would be more favourable to the interests of the school than the term that would otherwise be included by virtue of that paragraph.

(6) Where the governing body enter into a transfer of control agreement, they shall so far as reasonably practicable secure that the controlling body exercises control in accordance with any such directions or determinations as are notified to that body in pursuance of sub-paragraph (3)(a).

(7) In this paragraph-

"the controlling body" means the body or person (other than the governing body) which has control of the use of the whole or any part of the school premises under the transfer of control agreement in question;

"transfer of control agreement" means an agreement which (subject to sub-paragraph (3)) provides for the use of so much of the school premises as may be specified in the agreement to be under the control, at such times as may be so specified, of such body or person as may be so specified.

Control of use of premises of voluntary school outside school hours

7.–(1) The governing body may determine the use to which the premises of a voluntary controlled school (or any part of them) are put on Saturdays when not required-

(a) for the purposes of the school, or
(b) for any purpose connected with education or with the welfare of the young for which the local education authority desire to provide accommodation on the premises (or on the part in question).

(2) The foundation governors may determine the use to which the premises of a voluntary controlled school (or any part of them) are put on Sundays.

(3) If the local education authority-

(a) desire to provide accommodation for any purpose connected with education or with the welfare of the young, and
(b) are satisfied that there is no suitable alternative accommodation in their area for that purpose,

they may direct the governing body of a voluntary aided school to provide accommodation free of charge for that purpose on the school premises (or any part of them) on any weekday when not needed for the purposes of the school.

(4) The local education authority shall not exercise their power under sub-paragraph (3) so as to direct the governing body to provide accommodation on more than three days in any week.

(5) In exercising control of the occupation and use of the premises of a voluntary school outside school hours the governing body shall have regard to the desirability of those premises being made available for community use.

Saving

8. The power of the governing body of a maintained school to control the occupation and use of the premises of the school shall be subject to any arrangements made under or by virtue of-

   (a) an agreement made under paragraph 1 or 2 of Schedule 10 to the Education Reform Act 1988 or a determination made in accordance with paragraph 62 or 63 of Schedule 8 to the Further and Higher Education Act 1992; or

   (b) an agreement made under paragraph 1 or 2 of Schedule 5 to the (1992 c. 13.)Further and Higher Education Act 1992 or a determination made in accordance with paragraph 3 or 4 of that Schedule.

Interpretation

9. In this Schedule-

   "community use" means the use of school premises (when not required by or in connection with the school) by members of the local community;

   "school hours" means any time during a school session or during a break between sessions on the same day;

   "school session", in relation to any school, means a school session beginning and ending at such times as may from time to time be determined for that school in accordance with section 41.

Schedule 13

This Schedule deals with who controls school premises and with the transfer and sharing of responsibility. The position differs according to the category of the school.

Community and community special schools

Occupation and use of the premises are under the control of the governing body but the local education authority can give directions which must be complied with and the governing body must have regard to community use outside school hours.

The governing body may enter into a transfer of control agreement (which is an agreement which moves responsibility for the premises to an outside party) if it will promote community use of all or part of the premises. The governing body cannot transfer control during school hours without local education authority consent. Transfer of control agreements must provide for the controlling body to be informed of and comply with any local education authority directions, to have regard to the desirability of community use, and for the governing body to have the right (reasonably and on reasonable notice) to use the premises at reasonable times for school purposes even though this may be at times when the premises are under the control of the controlling body. This general right will not apply if the transfer of control agreement itself contains express provisions for the governing body to have the occasional use and control of the premises.

Foundation and foundation special schools

Similar provisions apply as for community and community special schools except that the local education authority has no power to give directions. If the school has a trust deed that provides for a body other than the governing body to have control of the premises that other body stands in the shoes of the governing body except that the governing body has the power (without consent from that other body) to enter into a transfer of control agreement provided that the intended community use is in all respects consistent with the terms of the school's trust deed. The governing body cannot transfer control during school hours without Secretary of State consent.

Voluntary schools

Occupation and use of the premises are under the control of the governing body. The local education authority may give such directions as it thinks fit to voluntary controlled schools although the governing body has the right to determine the use of the premises on Sundays and at any time on Saturdays when the school is not required for school purposes or for purposes connected with education or the welfare of the young that the local education authority wishes to provide. The local education authority may only give directions to a voluntary aided school if it wishes to provide accommodation for purposes connected with education or the welfare of the young that the local education authority wishes to provide and is satisfied that there is no suitable alternative accommodation in its area for that purpose. In those circumstances the local education authority may require the governing body to make the school available on any weekday when the school is not required for school purposes free of charge but not on more than 3 days in any one week.

The governing body may enter into a transfer of control agreement in the same way as a foundation or foundation special school except, logically, that the controlling body must comply with any directions that the local education authority has power to give.

The governing body of a voluntary controlled school must have regard to the desirability of the school being used for community use outside school hours. There is no such obligation on the governing body of a voluntary aided school.

SCHEDULE 14

LOCAL EDUCATION AUTHORITY SCHEMES: APPROVAL,IMPOSITION AND REVISION

Approval or imposition of schemes by Secretary of State

1.–(1) A scheme prepared by a local education authority under section 48(1) shall be submitted to the Secretary of State on or before such date as he may by order direct, whether-

(a) generally; or
(b) in relation to that authority or to any class or description of local education authorities to which that authority belongs.

(2) In preparing such a scheme a local education authority shall take into account any guidance given by the Secretary of State, whether-

(a) generally, or
(b) in relation to that authority or to any class or description of local education authorities to which that authority belongs,

as to the provisions he regards as appropriate for inclusion in the scheme.

(3) Before preparing such a scheme the local education authority shall consult-
(a) where this sub-paragraph applies in relation to any time before the appointed day-
(i) the governing body and the head teacher of every school maintained by the authority as a county, voluntary or maintained special school (within the meaning of the Education Act 1996), and
(ii) the governing body and the head teacher of every grant-maintained or grant-maintained special school (within the meaning of that Act) in the area of the authority; and
(b) where this sub-paragraph applies in relation to any time on or after the appointed day, the governing body and the head teacher of every school maintained by the authority (within the meaning of this Chapter);

and in paragraph (a)(i) "every school" includes any new school (within the meaning of Part II of the (1996 c. 56.) Education Act 1996).

(4) Such a scheme shall not come into force until it has been approved by the Secretary of State or until such date as he may, in giving his approval, specify; and the Secretary of State may approve such a scheme-

(a) either without modifications or with such modifications as he thinks fit after consulting the authority concerned; and
(b) subject to such conditions as he may specify in giving his approval.

(5) If in the case of any local education authority either-

- (a) the authority fail to submit a scheme as required by sub-paragraph (1), or
- (b) it appears to the Secretary of State that a scheme submitted by the authority as required by that sub-paragraph does not accord with any guidance given by him for the purposes of this paragraph and cannot be made to do so merely by modifying it,

he may, after consulting the authority and such other persons as he thinks fit, impose a scheme making such provision of a description required to be made by a scheme under section 48 as he considers appropriate.

(6) A scheme imposed by the Secretary of State by virtue of sub-paragraph (5)-

- (a) shall be treated as if made under section 48 by the local education authority concerned; and
- (b) shall come into force on such date as may be specified in the scheme.

(7) A scheme shall be published in such manner as may be prescribed-

- (a) on its coming into force, and
- (b) on such subsequent occasions as may be prescribed.

Revision of schemes

2.–(1) A local education authority may, in accordance with this paragraph, revise the whole or any part of the scheme prepared by them under section 48(1).

(2) Section 48(1) and paragraph 1(2) shall apply in relation to the preparation by the authority of any revision under this paragraph as they apply in relation to the preparation by the authority of a scheme.

(3) As regards any proposed variation of the scheme, the authority-

- (a) shall first consult every governing body and head teacher whom they are obliged to consult under paragraph 1(3), and
- (b) shall then submit a copy of their proposals to the Secretary of State for his approval.

(4) Where the proposals are so submitted, paragraph 1(4) shall apply to the scheme as revised as it applies to a scheme prepared under section 48.

(5) The Secretary of State may by a direction revise the whole or any part of any scheme as from such date as may be specified in the direction.

(6) Before giving such a direction the Secretary of State shall consult the local education authority and such other persons as he thinks fit.

Schedule 14
This Schedule deals with the approval of financial schemes relating to the financial management of schools prepared by local education authorities. It requires schemes to be submitted to the Secretary of State in accordance with a timetable that he may lay down and gives the Secretary of State power to issue guidance which the local education authority must have regard to. It requires that the local education authority consults with the governing body and the headteacher of every maintained school and specifies that the scheme will not come into force until the Secretary of State has approved it. The Secretary of State may modify a scheme but must first consult with the local education authority. He also has power to impose a scheme if the local education authority does not submit one. Again, he must first consult with the local education authority. The local education authority may revise its scheme but must follow a similar process.

SCHEDULE 15

SUSPENSION OF FINANCIAL DELEGATION

Suspension of financial delegation for mismanagement, etc.

1.–(1) This paragraph applies where it appears to the local education authority that the governing body of a school which has a delegated budget-

    (a) have been guilty of a substantial or persistent failure to comply with any delegation requirement or restriction, or

    (b) are not managing in a satisfactory manner the expenditure or appropriation of the sum referred to in section 50(1).

(2) The authority may suspend the governing body's right to a delegated budget by giving the governing body not less than one month's notice of the suspension, unless by reason of any gross incompetence or mismanagement on the part of the governing body or other emergency it appears to the authority to be necessary-

    (a) to give the governing body a shorter period of notice, or

    (b) to give the governing body a notice suspending their right to such a budget with immediate effect.

(3) The notice must specify the grounds for the suspension, giving particulars-

    (a) of any alleged failure on the part of the governing body to comply with any delegation requirement or restriction;

    (b) of any alleged mismanagement on their part; and

    (c) if applicable, of the basis upon which a period of notice of less than one month was given under sub-paragraph (2).

(4) The notice must also inform the governing body of their right to appeal against the suspension under paragraph 3 and of the time within which such an appeal may be brought.

(5) A copy of the notice must be given to the head teacher of the school at the same time as the notice is given to the governing body.

(6) The authority shall send a copy of the notice to the Secretary of State.

(7) In this paragraph "delegation requirement or restriction" means any requirement or restriction applicable, under or by virtue of the scheme or section 50(3), to the management by the governing body of the school's budget share.

(8) Any notice given under this paragraph must be in writing.

Review of suspension

2.–(1) The local education authority concerned-

    (a) shall review before the beginning of every financial year any suspension under paragraph 1 which is for the time being in force, unless the suspension took effect less than two months before the beginning of that year; and

    (b) may review at any time any suspension under paragraph 1 which is for the time being in force, if they consider it appropriate to do so.

(2) For the purposes of any review under sub-paragraph (1), the authority shall give the governing body and the head teacher of the school an opportunity of making representations with respect to the suspension.

(3) If on the review the authority consider it appropriate to do so, they shall revoke the suspension-

    (a) (in the case of a review under sub-paragraph (1)(a)) with effect from the beginning of the financial year next following the review; or

    (b) (in the case of a review under sub-paragraph (1)(b)) with effect from such time before the beginning of the financial year next following the review as they may determine.

(4) The authority shall give the governing body and the head teacher notice in writing of their decision on the review.

(5) If-

    (a) the review was conducted under sub-paragraph (1)(a), and

    (b) the authority's decision is to refuse to revoke the suspension,

the notice must inform the governing body of their right to appeal against the refusal under paragraph 3 and of the time within which such an appeal may be brought.

Appeal against suspension or refusal to revoke it

3.–(1) A governing body may appeal to the Secretary of State against-

    (a) the imposition of any suspension under paragraph 1 of their right to a delegated budget; or

    (b) any refusal of a local education authority to revoke any such suspension on a review under paragraph 2(1)(a).

(2) An appeal under this paragraph must be brought within the period of two months beginning with the date on which the governing body receive the authority's notice under paragraph 1(2) or 2(4), as the case may be.

(3) But if the authority's notice failed to comply with paragraph 1(4) or 2(5), such an appeal may be brought at any time before the end of the period of two months beginning with the date on which the governing body are informed by the authority in writing of their right of appeal under this paragraph.

(4) On an appeal under this paragraph, the Secretary of State-

    (a) may allow or reject the appeal; and

    (b) shall have regard, in making his determination, to the gravity of the default on the part of the governing body and the likelihood of its continuing or recurring.

(5) Where the Secretary of State allows an appeal under this paragraph, the suspension of the governing body's right to a delegated budget shall be revoked from a date determined by the Secretary of State.

Effect of suspension of right to delegated budget

4.–(1) During any period when a governing body's right to a delegated budget is suspended under paragraph 1-

    (a) the local education authority's duty under section 50(1) shall not apply in relation to the school; but

    (b) the authority may permit the governing body to take such decisions as to the spending of sums to be met from the school's budget share as the authority consider appropriate.

(2) Where in accordance with sub-paragraph (1)(b) the governing body have decided that a particular sum should be spent, they shall, in spending that sum, comply with such reasonable conditions as the authority think fit to impose.

(3) The governing body may, to such extent as they may specify, delegate their powers in relation to that sum to the head teacher.

Schedule 15

The local education authority may suspend a school's delegated budget where the school has seriously failed to comply with a specific requirement of the scheme or where it is not managing the finances of the school satisfactorily. It must give the governing body one month's notice of the suspension unless there has been gross incompetence or mismanagement in which case it may give a shorter or even no period of notice. The notice of suspension must give details of why delegation is to be suspended and why (if relevant) less than one month's notice is being given. It must advise the governing body of its right to appeal and a copy must go to the headteacher and to the Secretary of State. It must review the suspension each year before the beginning of the new financial year, except where the suspension takes place within two months before the beginning of that year and must similarly notify the governing body, headteacher and Secretary of State of the outcome of the review. The governing body has the right to appeal to the Secretary of State against a suspension of the budget or the refusal to reinstate the budget on review. The local education authority may, during a period of suspension, give the governing body the right to make some, specified, spending decisions and the governing body has the power to delegate that power to the headteacher.

Suspension has consequential effects on the powers of the school in relation to staffing and other issues. The local education authority also has the power to suspend the delegated budget as part of its intervention powers where a school is regarded as failing: in this case, there is no right of appeal.

SCHEDULE 16

STAFFING OF COMMUNITY, VOLUNTARY CONTROLLED AND COMMUNITY SPECIAL SCHOOLS

Introductory

1.–(1) In this Schedule "the school" means a community, voluntary controlled or community special school.

(2) References in this Schedule to a vacancy in any post include a prospective vacancy in the post, and references to a person's absence are to his absence, or prospective absence, from the school.

(3) References in this Schedule to staff qualification requirements are to any requirements with respect to-

    (a) qualifications,
    (b) registration,
    (c) health and physical capacity, or
    (d) fitness on educational grounds or in any other respect,

of teachers or other persons employed, or otherwise engaged to provide their services, in work that brings them regularly into contact with persons who have not attained the age of 19 which for the time being apply under regulations under section 218 of the Education Reform Act 1988 (regulations relating to employment of teachers etc.) or section 19 of the Teaching and Higher Education Act 1998 (induction training).

(4) References in this Schedule to the chief education officer of the local education authority include any officer of the authority nominated by the chief education officer.

Appointment of head teacher and deputy head teacher

2. Paragraphs 3 to 7 apply in relation to the filling of a vacancy in the post of head teacher or deputy head teacher of the school.

3. The governing body shall notify the local education authority of the vacancy in writing before taking any of the steps mentioned in paragraphs 4 to 7.

4.–(1) Where the vacancy is in the post of head teacher and either the post has not been filled, or it appears to the governing body that the post will not be filled, by an appointment made in accordance with paragraphs 5 to 7 before the date on which it falls vacant, the governing body shall either-

   (a) recommend a person for appointment as acting head teacher, or
   (b) exercise their power under sub-paragraph (5).

(2) Where the vacancy is in the post of deputy head teacher and either the post has not been filled, or it appears to the governing body that the post will not be filled, by an appointment made in accordance with paragraphs 5 to 7 before the date on which it falls vacant, the governing body may-

   (a) recommend a person for appointment as acting deputy head teacher, or
   (b) exercise their power under sub-paragraph (5).

(3) If the governing body recommend a person for appointment as acting head teacher or acting deputy head teacher, the local education authority shall appoint the person recommended unless he does not meet any staff qualification requirements which are applicable in relation to his appointment.

(4) If the authority decline to appoint a person recommended by the governing body for appointment as acting head teacher, the governing body shall recommend another person for appointment.

(5) Instead of making a recommendation under sub-paragraph (1) or (2) the governing body may for the purpose of filling the vacancy-

   (a) engage, or
   (b) make arrangements for the engagement of,

a person to provide his services as acting head teacher, or (as the case may be) acting deputy head teacher, otherwise than under a contract of employment with the local education authority.

(6) No person shall be engaged under sub-paragraph (5) unless he meets all the staff qualification requirements applicable in relation to the head teacher or (as the case may be) deputy head teacher at the school.

5. The governing body shall advertise the vacancy in such publications circulating throughout England and Wales as they consider appropriate.

6.–(1) The governing body shall appoint a selection panel consisting of at least three of their members to perform the functions conferred on them by this paragraph.

(2) The selection panel shall-

    (a) select for interview such applicants for the post as they think fit and, where the post is that of head teacher, notify the local education authority in writing of the names of the applicants so selected,

    (b) interview such of those applicants as attend for the purpose,

    (c) where they consider it appropriate to do so, recommend to the governing body for appointment one of the applicants interviewed by them, and

    (d) if their recommendation is approved by the governing body, recommend the applicant in question to the local education authority for appointment.

(3) Any decision of the selection panel shall be taken by a vote representing an absolute majority of all the members of the panel (whether or not taking part in the vote).

(4) If, within the period of 14 days beginning with the date when they receive a notification under sub-paragraph (2)(a), the authority make written representations to the selection panel that any of the applicants selected by the panel is not a suitable person for the appointment, the panel shall not recommend that person to the governing body for appointment unless the panel have-

    (a) considered those representations, and

    (b) notified the authority in writing of their response to the representations;

and when making such a recommendation the panel shall supply the governing body with a copy of those representations and of the panel's response to them.

(5) If the panel do not recommend a person to the governing body, or the governing body do not approve their recommendation, the governing body-

    (a) may, if they think fit, re-advertise the vacancy in the manner required by paragraph 5, and

    (b) whether or not they re-advertise the vacancy, may require the panel to repeat the steps mentioned in sub-paragraph (2).

(6) In determining whether a person is suitable for appointment as head teacher the authority shall have regard to any guidance given from time to time by the Secretary of State.

7.–(1) Where the governing body approve a recommendation of the selection panel, the local education authority shall appoint the person recommended by the panel unless he does not meet any staff qualification requirements which are applicable in relation to his appointment.

(2) If the authority decline to appoint the person recommended by the panel, the governing body-

  (a) may, if they think fit, re-advertise the vacancy in the manner required by paragraph 5, and

  (b) whether or not they re-advertise the vacancy, may require the panel to repeat the steps mentioned in paragraph 6(2).

8.–(1) The governing body may, in connection with any absence of the person for the time being holding the post of head teacher or deputy head teacher of the school, take either of the steps mentioned in paragraphs (a) and (b) of sub-paragraph (1) or (as the case may be) (2) of paragraph 4.

(2) For the purposes of this paragraph-

  (a) paragraph 4(3) shall apply in relation to any recommendation made by virtue of sub-paragraph (1) above as it applies in relation to any recommendation made by virtue of paragraph 4(1) or (2); and

  (b) paragraph 4(5) and (6) shall apply in connection with any such absence as is mentioned in sub-paragraph (1) above as they apply for the purpose of filling any such vacancy as is mentioned in paragraph 4(1) or (2).

Appointment of other teachers

9. Subject to paragraph 10, paragraphs 11 to 15 apply in relation to the filling of a vacancy in any teaching post (whether full-time or part-time) at the school, other than the post of head teacher or deputy head teacher.

10.–(1) Paragraphs 11 to 15 do not apply in relation to any temporary appointment or engagement to fill a vacancy in any such post as is mentioned in paragraph 9-

  (a) for a period not exceeding four months, or

  (b) where it appears to the governing body that the period for which the person appointed or engaged will act in the post in question will not exceed four months.

(2) Where it appears to the governing body in the case of any post that it would be appropriate for such an appointment as is mentioned in sub-paragraph (1) to be made-

  (a) they may recommend a person for appointment to the post on such terms as to the duration of the appointment as they may specify, and

  (b) the local education authority shall appoint the person recommended on the terms specified unless he does not meet any staff qualification requirements which are applicable in relation to his appointment.

(3) Where it appears to the governing body in the case of any post that it would be appropriate for such an engagement as is mentioned in sub-paragraph (1) to be made, the governing body may-

(a) engage, or
(b) make arrangements for the engagement of,

a person to provide his services as a teacher at the school otherwise than under a contract of employment with the local education authority.

(4) Any engagement under sub-paragraph (3) shall be on such terms as to the duration of the engagement as the governing body may specify; but no person shall be engaged under that sub-paragraph unless he meets all the staff qualification requirements applicable in relation to a teacher in the post in which he would be acting as a temporary teacher.

11. Before taking any of the steps mentioned below, the governing body shall-

(a) determine a specification for the post in consultation with the head teacher, and
(b) send a copy of the specification to the local education authority.

12.–(1) The local education authority may nominate for consideration for appointment to the post any person who appears to them to be qualified to fill it and who at the time of his nomination either-

(a) is an employee of theirs or has been appointed to take up employment with them at a future date, or
(b) is employed by the governing body of a foundation, voluntary aided or foundation special school maintained by them.

(2) No person who is employed at any school maintained by the authority shall be nominated by the authority under sub-paragraph (1) without the consent of the governing body of the school.

13.–(1) The governing body may advertise the vacancy at any time after they have sent a copy of the specification for the post to the local education authority in accordance with paragraph 11, and shall do so unless either-

(a) they accept for appointment to the post a person nominated by the local education authority under paragraph 12, or
(b) they decide to recommend to the authority for appointment to the post a person who is already employed to work at the school.

(2) Where the governing body advertise the vacancy, they shall do so in a manner likely in their opinion to bring it to the notice of persons (including employees of the authority) who are qualified to fill it.

14.–(1) Where the governing body advertise the vacancy, they shall-

(a) interview such applicants for the post and such of the persons (if any) nominated by the local education authority under paragraph 12 as they think fit, and

(b) where they consider it appropriate to do so, either recommend to the authority for appointment one of the applicants interviewed by them or notify the authority that they accept for appointment any person nominated by the authority under paragraph 12.

(2) If the governing body are unable to agree on a person to recommend or accept for appointment, they may repeat the steps mentioned in sub-paragraph (1)(a) and (b), with or without first re-advertising the vacancy in accordance with paragraph 13(2).

15.–(1) The local education authority shall appoint the person recommended or accepted for appointment by the governing body unless he does not meet any staff qualification requirements which are applicable in relation to his appointment.

(2) If the authority decline to appoint a person recommended by the governing body, the governing body shall repeat such of the steps mentioned in paragraph 14(1)(a) and (b) as they think fit, with or without first re-advertising the vacancy in accordance with paragraph 13(2).

16.–(1) The governing body may, in connection with any absence of the person for the time being holding any such post as is mentioned in paragraph 9-

(a) engage, or
(b) make arrangements for the engagement of,

a person to provide his services as a teacher at the school otherwise than under a contract of employment with the local education authority.

(2) No person shall be engaged under sub-paragraph (1) unless he meets all the staff qualification requirements applicable in relation to a teacher in the post in which he would be acting as a temporary teacher.

17. The governing body may, in relation to a particular vacancy or absence or a vacancy or absence of a kind specified by them, delegate any of their functions under paragraphs 10 to 16-

(a) to one or more governors,
(b) to the head teacher, or
(c) to one or more governors and the head teacher acting together.

Advice of chief education officer on appointments of teachers

18.–(1) The chief education officer of the local education authority shall be entitled to attend, for the purpose of giving advice-

(a) all proceedings (including interviews) of the governing body, and of any selection panel appointed under paragraph 6, relating to appointments or engagements to which any of the provisions of paragraphs 3 to 8 apply, and
(b) all proceedings (including interviews) of the governing body, and of any persons to whom any functions of the governing body under paragraphs 10 to 16 are delegated, relating to appointments or engagements to which any of the provisions of paragraphs 10 to 16 apply.

(2) The chief education officer shall offer such advice as he considers appropriate with respect to-

(a) the appointment of a head teacher or deputy head teacher or the appointment or engagement of an acting head teacher or acting deputy head teacher, or

(b) any matter arising in connection with any such appointment or engagement.

(3) If requested to do so by the governing body, the chief education officer shall give such advice as he considers appropriate in relation to any appointment or engagement to which any of the provisions of paragraphs 10 to 16 apply.

(4) Any advice given by the chief education officer to-

(a) the governing body,

(b) any selection panel appointed under paragraph 6, or

(c) any persons to whom any functions of the governing body under paragraphs 10 to 16 are delegated,

with respect to any matter which relates to an appointment or engagement and falls to be determined by them shall be considered by them before determining that matter, whether or not the advice was given at their request.

Advice of head teacher on appointments etc. of teachers

19. Except in relation to the appointment of a head teacher-

(a) paragraph 18(1) applies in relation to the head teacher (if not otherwise entitled to be present at the proceedings there mentioned) as it applies in relation to the chief education officer, and

(b) paragraph 18(4) applies in relation to advice given by the head teacher as it applies in relation to advice given by the chief education officer.

Appointment of non-teaching staff

20.–(1) Where the governing body desire the appointment of a person to work in a non-teaching post at the school, they may recommend a person to the local education authority for appointment to the post.

(2) A recommendation under this paragraph shall be in writing and shall specify-

(a) the duties to be performed by the person appointed (including, where the post is part-time, his hours of work) and such terms (if any) as to the duration of his appointment as are proposed by the governing body;

(b) the grade (on the scale of grades currently applicable in relation to employment with the authority) which the governing body consider appropriate for the post; and

(c) where the authority have a discretion with respect to the remuneration to be paid to a person appointed to the post, the determination of any matter to which that discretion applies and which the governing body consider appropriate in the case of the person recommended for appointment.

(3) Before selecting a person to recommend under this paragraph and determining in relation to such a recommendation any matters mentioned in sub-paragraph (2), the governing body shall consult-

(a) the head teacher (where he would not otherwise be involved in the decision), and
(b) the chief education officer of the authority.

(4) For the purposes of sub-paragraph (2)(c), the authority are to be regarded as having a discretion with respect to the remuneration to be paid to a person appointed to a post if any provisions regulating the rates of remuneration or allowances payable to persons in the authority's employment either-

(a) do not apply in relation to that appointment, or
(b) leave to the authority any degree of discretion as to rate of remuneration or allowances in the case of that appointment.

21.–(1) The local education authority shall appoint a person recommended to them under paragraph 20 unless he does not meet any staff qualification requirements which are applicable in relation to his appointment.

(2) Any such appointment shall be on such terms as to give effect, so far as they relate to any matter mentioned in paragraph 20(2), to the governing body's recommendation in respect of that matter.

Discipline

22.–(1) The regulation of conduct and discipline in relation to the staff of the school, and any procedures for giving members of the staff opportunities for seeking redress of any grievances relating to their employment, shall be under the control of the governing body.

(2) The governing body shall establish-

(a) disciplinary rules and procedures (including such rules and procedures for dealing with lack of capability on the part of members of the staff), and
(b) procedures such as are mentioned in sub-paragraph (1);

and shall take such steps as appear to the governing body to be appropriate for making them known to members of the staff.

(3) In determining the capability of members of the staff the governing body shall have regard to any guidance given from time to time by the Secretary of State.

(4) If the Secretary of State determines that any prescribed rules and procedures are to apply to the school or to any class or description of school to which the school belongs-

(a) the governing body shall act in accordance with those rules and procedures in determining the capability of members of the staff; and
(b) in the event of any inconsistency, those rules and procedures shall prevail over any rules and procedures established by the governing body under sub-paragraph (2)(a).

(5) Where the implementation of any determination made by the governing body in the exercise of their control over the conduct and discipline of the staff requires any action which-

(a) is not within the functions exercisable by the governing body by virtue of this Act, but

(b) is within the power of the local education authority,

the authority shall take that action at the request of the governing body.

LEA report on performance of head teacher

23.–(1) Where the authority have any serious concerns about the performance of the head teacher of the school-

(a) they shall make a written report of their concerns to the chairman of the governing body at the same time sending a copy to the head teacher; and

(b) the chairman of the governing body shall notify the authority in writing of the action which he proposes to take in the light of the report.

(2) In determining whether to make a report under this paragraph the authority shall have regard to any guidance given from time to time by the Secretary of State.

Suspension

24.–(1) Both the governing body and the head teacher shall have power to suspend any person employed to work at the school where, in the opinion of the governing body or (as the case may be) the head teacher, his exclusion from the school is required.

(2) The governing body or head teacher shall, when exercising that power, immediately inform the local education authority and the head teacher or (as the case may be) governing body.

(3) A suspension under this paragraph may only be ended by the governing body.

(4) The governing body shall, on ending such a suspension, immediately inform the authority and the head teacher.

(5) In this paragraph "suspend" means suspend without loss of emoluments.

Dismissal, etc.

25.–(1) Where the governing body determine that any person employed by the local education authority to work at the school should cease to work there, they shall notify the authority in writing of their determination and the reasons for it.

(2) If the person concerned is employed to work solely at the school (and he does not resign), the authority shall, before the end of the period of 14 days beginning with the date on which the notification under sub-paragraph (1) is given, either-

(a) give him such notice terminating his contract of employment with the authority as is required under that contract, or

(b) terminate that contract without notice if the circumstances are such that they are entitled to do so by reason of his conduct.

(3) If the person concerned is not employed to work solely at the school, the authority shall require him to cease to work at the school.

26.–(1) Where paragraph 25(3) applies, no part of the costs incurred by the local education authority in respect of the emoluments of the person concerned, so far as they relate to any period falling after the expiration of his contractual notice period, shall be met from the school's budget share.

(2) The reference in sub-paragraph (1) to the person's contractual notice period is to the period of notice that would have been required under his contract of employment with the authority for termination of that contract if such notice had been given on the date on which the notification under paragraph 25(1) was given.

27.–(1) The governing body shall-

(a) make arrangements for giving any person in respect of whom they propose to make a determination under paragraph 25(1) an opportunity of making representations as to the action they propose to take (including, if he so wishes, oral representations to such person or persons as the governing body may appoint for the purpose), and
(b) have regard to any representations made by him.

(2) The governing body shall also make arrangements for giving any person in respect of whom they have made a determination under paragraph 25(1) an opportunity of appealing against it before they notify the local education authority of the determination.

(3) Nothing in this paragraph shall, however, apply to a person who-

(a) is due to cease to work at the school by reason of the termination of his contract of employment by effluxion of time; and
(b) has not been continuously employed at the school for a period of two years or more (within the meaning of the (1996 c. 18.)Employment Rights Act 1996).

28.–(1) The head teacher (except where he is the person concerned) and the chief education officer of the local education authority shall be entitled to attend, for the purpose of giving advice, all proceedings of the governing body relating to a determination under paragraph 25(1).

(2) The governing body shall consider any advice given by a person who is entitled to attend such proceedings under this paragraph before making a determination under paragraph 25(1).

29.–(1) The local education authority shall not dismiss a person employed by them to work solely at the school except as provided by paragraph 25.

(2) Sub-paragraph (1) does not apply in a case where-

(a) the dismissal of the person in question is required by virtue of regulations under section 218 of the Education Reform Act 1988 or section 19 of the Teaching and Higher Education Act 1998, or

(b) the person in question is a teacher who is subject to a conditional registration, suspension or prohibition order made under Schedule 2 to the 1998 Act (disciplinary powers of General Teaching Council).

School meals staff

30. The Secretary of State may by regulations make provision as to the appointment, discipline, suspension and dismissal of persons employed or to be employed to work at a community, voluntary controlled or community special school solely in connection with the provision of meals.

Advisory rights for appropriate diocesan authorities

31.–(1) This paragraph applies to a voluntary controlled school which is a Church of England, Church in Wales or Roman Catholic Church school.

(2) The governing body may agree with the appropriate diocesan authority to accord to the appropriate diocesan officer-

(a) with respect to all teachers at the school, or

(b) with respect to any particular description of such teachers,

the same advisory rights in relation to their appointment, engagement or dismissal as are exercisable by the chief education officer in accordance with paragraphs 18 and 28.

(3) The agreement of the governing body for the purposes of sub-paragraph (2) must be given in writing and may only be withdrawn by notice in writing to the appropriate diocesan authority.

(4) In paragraphs 18 and 28, as they apply to a voluntary controlled school within sub-paragraph (1) above, references to the chief education officer accordingly include the appropriate diocesan officer, so far as necessary for giving effect to any advisory rights exercisable by him under this paragraph.

(5) In this paragraph "the appropriate diocesan officer" means such person as the appropriate diocesan authority may nominate.

Schedule 16
This Schedule deals with the appointment, discipline, suspension and dismissal of staff employed to work at community, voluntary controlled and community special schools. Although the whole appointment process is effectively in the hands of the governing body, the local education authority is the employer and therefore all appointments must be made by the local education authority on the recommendation of the governing body. In general, the local education authority must appoint the person recommended by the governing body unless that person is unsuitable, which is defined as being limited to

where the person to be appointed lacks qualification in terms of formal qualifications or registration, health or physical capacity or fitness for employment. Competence is not, unless it relates to fitness for employment, something that the local education authority can consider. The chief education officer of the local education authority is entitled to attend or be represented at all meetings, including interviews, that are held in relation to all staff appointments. He is required to offer advice on the appointment of headteachers and deputies and may be invited to give advice on any other teaching appointment. Where the chief education officer gives advice the governing body must consider it before making an appointment even if the advice was not requested. The headteacher has similar rights except in relation to the appointment of a new headteacher.

Appointment of Headteachers and Deputy Headteachers

The appointment is under the control of the governing body but it must comply with the prescribed procedure. It must notify the local education authority of the vacancy at the outset.

The governing body may, if it does not wish to make an immediate permanent appointment or cannot do so before the post becomes vacant, recommend the appointment of an acting head or deputy. If the local education authority declines to make the appointment the governing body can recommend another person. It can, as an alternative to employing someone, engage that person under a self-employed contract for services - a permanent appointment cannot be made on this basis – to act in this capacity. This contract may be made directly with the person concerned or indirectly, e.g. with an agency providing supply cover. Because a contract of this nature does not constitute employment, the governing body can enter into it directly and does not need to refer to the local education authority. It can act similarly to cover a long-term absence of the headteacher or a deputy.

A vacancy must be advertised nationally and the governing body must appoint a selection panel of at least three governors to deal with short-listing, interviewing and recommending a person for appointment to the governing body. The local education authority must be notified of those short-listed for appointment as headteacher but not in relation to the appointment of a deputy. Any decision of the selection panel must be of an absolute majority of members irrespective of the number at the meeting or actually voting.

If the governing body does not accept the recommendation of the selection panel, or if the panel makes no recommendation, the governing body may ask the selection panel to repeat the process, either in respect of the original applicants or following re-advertising the post.

If the local education authority considers that any short-listed candidate for appointment as headteacher is not suitable (within the limited definition mentioned above) it may make representations to the selection panel. Before deciding to short-list that person, the panel must consider those representations, respond to them to the local education authority in writing, and supply copies of both to the governing body.

Appointment of other teachers

The governing body again recommends appointments to the local education authority who must appoint unless the person concerned is unsuitable within the limited definition mentioned above. The governing body may cover temporary posts, i.e. for periods of up to four months or where it appears at the time that the appointment will not exceed four months, by engaging someone with the necessary qualifications under a self-employed contract as described above. The governing body may delegate the power to appoint to one or more governors, to the headteacher, or a combination of both. This delegation may be for a specific post or for specified types of appointment, so that a school may have different levels of delegated powers for different levels of staff appointment.

Before starting the appointment process, the governing body (which in what follows includes those to whom the responsibility has been delegated) must prepare a job specification in consultation with the headteacher and send a copy to the local education authority. The local education authority may nominate candidates for appointment who are either currently or prospectively employed by the authority or currently employed by any foundation, voluntary aided or foundation special school with the authority provided that the governing body of the school at which such person is employed consents.

The post must be advertised as the governing body thinks most likely to bring the post to the attention of people qualified to fill it (not necessarily nationally) unless the governing body decides to appoint an local education authority nominee or to appoint an internal candidate. If the post is advertised the governing body must interview such applicants and/or nominees as they think fit and then make a recommendation for appointment or accept one of the nominees. If there is no appointable candidate the governing body may repeat the process but does not have to re-advertise unless it wishes to do so.

Appointment of Non-teaching Staff

There are no prescribed formalities for the appointment of non-teaching staff. Again, the governing body makes a recommendation to the local education authority which must be implemented unless the person concerned is unsuitable within the limited definition mentioned above. The recommendation must specify the proposed terms of employment and the grade that the governing body considers appropriate. The governing body may specify how any discretion that the local education authority may have is to be exercised.

Staff Discipline

Discipline is in the hands of the governing body which must establish rules and procedures including ones to cover capability, having regard in this respect to guidance issued by the Secretary of State. If the Secretary of State makes rules applicable to the school (whether by name or by category) that conflict with those made by the governing body the rules made by the Secretary of State prevail. The local education authority must exercise its powers where necessary to implement proper decisions of the governing body.

Headteacher performance

The local education authority may report in writing to the chair of governors of any serious concerns about the performance of the headteacher and the chair of governors must notify the authority of the action that is proposed in the light of the report. The local education authority must have regard to guidance on this topic issued by the Secretary of State.

Suspension

The governing body and the headteacher have the power to suspend without loss of pay anyone employed to work at the school where this is thought necessary. Whoever exercises the power must inform the other and inform the local education authority. Only the governing body can lift a suspension and must inform the headteacher and the local education authority.

Dismissal

Only the governing body may recommend dismissal of a person employed to work at the school. This applies whatever the reason for the dismissal. The governing body must give an opportunity to make representations in writing and in person and to appeal unless the employment is being terminated because it was for a fixed term that has expired and the employee has not been continuously employed for two years (likely to be reduced to one year with the reduction in the minimum qualifying period for employment protection). Once the governing body has decided to dismiss, it must inform the local education authority which must then give appropriate notice of termination (or terminate without notice if the circumstances require this). If the decision relates to someone who is not employed to work only at the school, the local education authority must require the person to cease to work at the school and cannot charge the school for the cost of that person even if he or she continues to be employed by the local education authority.

The chief education officer and the headteacher (except where the headteacher is the person who the governing body is considering dismissing) are entitled to attend and advise at any meeting of the governing body that considers termination of employment and the governing body must have regard to such advice.

School Meals Staff

The Secretary of State may make regulations governing the employment of school meals staff.

Voluntary Controlled Schools

The governing body of a denominational voluntary controlled school may give the denominational body, i.e. the Church of England, Church in Wales or Roman Catholic Church, the same advisory rights as the local education authority chief education officer has. Rights given by the governing body can only be withdrawn by written notice.

SCHEDULE 17

Introductory

1.–(1) In this Schedule "the school" means a foundation or voluntary aided or foundation special school.

(2) References in this Schedule to a vacancy in any post include a prospective vacancy in the post, and references to a person's absence are to his absence, or prospective absence, from the school.

(3) References in this Schedule to staff qualification requirements are to any requirements with respect to-

(a) qualifications,

(b) registration,

(c) health and physical capacity, or

(d) fitness on educational grounds or in any other respect,

of teachers or other persons employed, or otherwise engaged to provide their services, in work that brings them regularly into contact with persons who have not attained the age of 19 which for the time being apply under regulations under section 218 of the Education Reform Act 1988 (regulations relating to employment of teachers etc.) or section 19 of the Teaching and Higher Education Act 1998 (induction training).

Advisory rights of chief education officer

2.–(1) This paragraph applies where-

(a) the governing body of the school have agreed with the local education authority to accord to the authority's chief education officer advisory rights in relation to the appointment, engagement or dismissal of teachers at the school, or

(b) in default of such agreement, the Secretary of State has determined that it would be appropriate that such advisory rights should be accorded to the chief education officer.

(2) Advisory rights accorded by an agreement or determination under sub-paragraph (1) shall be framed by reference to the rights conferred on the chief education officer by the following paragraphs of this Schedule and may relate to the appointment and engagement or dismissal, or both to the appointment and engagement and to the dismissal, either-

(a) of head teachers and deputy head teachers alone, or

(b) of all teachers at the school.

(3) During any period when an agreement or determination under sub-paragraph (1) is effective, the chief education officer shall be entitled to exercise such of the rights conferred on him under the following paragraphs of this Schedule as are accorded to him by virtue of the agreement or determination.

(4) The chief education officer shall not be entitled to exercise any of the rights so conferred except in accordance with sub-paragraph (3).

(5) The agreement of a governing body for the purposes of sub-paragraph (1)(a) must be given in writing and may only be withdrawn by notice in writing to the local education authority.

(6) A determination by the Secretary of State for the purposes of sub-paragraph (1)(b) may be withdrawn at any time (without prejudice to a further determination for those purposes).

(7) References in this Schedule to the chief education officer of the local education authority include any officer of the authority nominated by the chief education officer.

Appointment of head teacher and deputy head teacher

3. Paragraphs 4 to 8 apply in relation to the filling of a vacancy in the post of head teacher or deputy head teacher of the school (but paragraphs 6 to 8 so apply subject to paragraphs 29 and 30).

4. The governing body shall notify the local education authority of the vacancy in writing before taking any of the steps mentioned in paragraphs 5 to 8 (or, in a case where paragraph 29 or 30 applies, any of the steps falling to be taken under that paragraph).

5.-(1) Where the vacancy is in the post of head teacher and either the post has not been filled, or it appears to the governing body that the post will not be filled, by an appointment made in accordance with paragraphs 6 to 8 before the date on which it falls vacant, the governing body shall either-

(a) appoint a person as acting head teacher, or
(b) exercise their power under sub-paragraph (4).

(2) Where the vacancy is in the post of deputy head teacher and either the post has not been filled, or it appears to the governing body that the post will not be filled, by an appointment made in accordance with paragraphs 6 to 8 before the date on which it falls vacant, the governing body may-

(a) appoint a person as acting deputy head teacher, or
(b) exercise their power under sub-paragraph (4).

(3) A person shall not be appointed under sub-paragraph (1) or (2) unless he meets all the staff qualification requirements which are applicable in relation to his appointment.

(4) Instead of making an appointment under sub-paragraph (1) or (2) the governing body may for the purpose of filling the vacancy-

(a) engage, or
(b) make arrangements for the engagement of,

a person to provide his services as acting head teacher, or (as the case may be) acting deputy head teacher, otherwise than under a contract of employment.

(5) No person shall be engaged under sub-paragraph (4) unless he meets all the staff qualification requirements applicable in relation to the head teacher or (as the case may be) deputy head teacher at the school.

(6) In sub-paragraph (1) the reference to paragraphs 6 to 8 includes a reference to paragraph 29 or 30; and in sub-paragraph (2) the reference to paragraphs 6 to 8 includes a reference to paragraph 30.

6. The governing body shall advertise the vacancy in such publications circulating throughout England and Wales as they consider appropriate.

7.–(1) The governing body shall appoint a selection panel consisting of at least three of their members to perform the functions conferred on them by this paragraph.

(2) The selection panel shall-

  (a) select for interview such applicants for the post as they think fit and, where the post is that of head teacher, notify the local education authority in writing of the names of the applicants so selected,
  (b) interview such of those applicants as attend for the purpose, and
  (c) where they consider it appropriate to do so, recommend to the governing body for appointment one of the applicants interviewed by them.

(3) Any decision of the selection panel shall be taken by a vote representing an absolute majority of all the members of the panel (whether or not taking part in the vote).

(4) If, within the period of 14 days beginning with the date when they receive a notification under sub-paragraph (2)(a), the authority make written representations to the selection panel that any of the applicants selected by the panel is not a suitable person for the appointment, the panel shall not recommend that person to the governing body for appointment unless the panel have-

  (a) considered those representations, and
  (b) notified the authority in writing of their response to the representations;

and when making such a recommendation the panel shall supply the governing body with a copy of those representations and of the panel's response to them.

(5) If the panel do not recommend a person to the governing body, or the governing body do not approve their recommendation, the governing body-

  (a) may, if they think fit, re-advertise the vacancy in the manner required by paragraph 6, and
  (b) whether or not they re-advertise the vacancy, may require the panel to repeat the steps mentioned in sub-paragraph (2).

(6) Where the chief education officer has no advisory rights under paragraph 2 with respect to the appointment of head teachers and deputy head teachers, the selection panel's notification under sub-paragraph (2)(a) shall be accompanied by such information relating to each of the persons selected for interview as will enable the authority to determine his suitability for the appointment.

(7) In determining whether a person is suitable for appointment as head teacher the authority shall have regard to any guidance given from time to time by the Secretary of State.

8. Where the governing body approve a recommendation of the selection panel, the governing body shall appoint the person recommended by the panel unless he does not meet any staff qualification requirements which are applicable in relation to his appointment.

9.–(1) The governing body may, in connection with any absence of the person for the time being holding the post of head teacher or deputy head teacher of the school, take either of the steps mentioned in paragraphs (a) and (b) of sub-paragraph (1) or (as the case may be) (2) of paragraph 5.

(2) For the purposes of this paragraph-

   (a) paragraph 5(3) shall apply in relation to any appointment made by virtue of sub-paragraph (1) above as it applies in relation to any appointment made by virtue of paragraph 5(1) or (2); and
   (b) paragraph 5(4) and (5) shall apply in connection with any such absence as is mentioned in sub-paragraph (1) above as they apply for the purpose of filling any such vacancy as is mentioned in paragraph 5(1) or (2).

Appointment of other teachers

10. Subject to paragraph 11, paragraphs 12 to 15 apply in relation to the filling of a vacancy in any teaching post (whether full-time or part-time) at the school, other than the post of head teacher or deputy head teacher.

11.–(1) Paragraphs 12 to 15 do not apply in relation to any temporary appointment or engagement to fill a vacancy in any such post as is mentioned in paragraph 10-

   (a) for a period not exceeding four months, or
   (b) where it appears to the governing body that the period for which the person appointed or engaged will act in the post in question will not exceed four months.

(2) Where it appears to the governing body in the case of any post that it would be appropriate for such an appointment as is mentioned in sub-paragraph (1) to be made, they may appoint a person to the post on such terms as to the duration of the appointment as they think fit.

(3) A person shall not be appointed under sub-paragraph (2) unless he meets all the staff qualification requirements which are applicable in relation to his appointment.

(4) Where it appears to the governing body in the case of any post that it would be appropriate for such an engagement as is mentioned in sub-paragraph (1) to be made, the governing body may-

(a) engage, or

(b) make arrangements for the engagement of,

a person to provide his services as a teacher at the school otherwise than under a contract of employment.

(5) Any engagement under sub-paragraph (4) shall be on such terms as to the duration of the engagement as the governing body may specify; but no person shall be engaged under that sub-paragraph unless he meets all the staff qualification requirements applicable in relation to a teacher in the post in which he would be acting as a temporary teacher.

12. Before taking any of the steps mentioned below, the governing body shall-

(a) determine a specification for the post in consultation with the head teacher, and

(b) send a copy of the specification to the local education authority.

13.–(1) The local education authority may nominate for consideration for appointment to the post any person who appears to them to be qualified to fill it and who at the time of his nomination either-

(a) is an employee of theirs or has been appointed to take up employment with them at a future date, or

(b) is employed by the governing body of a foundation, voluntary aided or foundation special school maintained by them.

(2) No person who is employed at any school maintained by the authority shall be nominated by the authority under sub-paragraph (1) without the consent of the governing body of the school.

14.–(1) The governing body may advertise the vacancy at any time after they have sent a copy of the specification for the post to the local education authority in accordance with paragraph 12, and shall do so unless they appoint to the post either-

(a) a person nominated by the local education authority under paragraph 13, or

(b) a person who is already employed to work at the school.

(2) Where the governing body advertise the vacancy, they shall do so in a manner likely in their opinion to bring it to the notice of persons (including employees of the authority) who are qualified to fill it.

15.–(1) Where the governing body advertise the vacancy, they shall-

   (a) interview such applicants for the post and such of the persons (if any) nominated by the local education authority under paragraph 13 as they think fit, and

   (b) where they consider it appropriate to do so, appoint to the post either one of the applicants interviewed by them or a person so nominated by the authority;

and the person so appointed shall be employed by the governing body under a contract of employment.

(2) If the governing body are unable to agree on a person to appoint to the post, they may repeat the steps mentioned in sub-paragraph (1)(a) and (b), with or without first re-advertising the vacancy in accordance with paragraph 14(2).

(3) A person shall not be appointed under this paragraph unless he meets all the staff qualification requirements which are applicable in relation to his appointment.

16.–(1) The governing body may, in connection with any absence of the person for the time being holding any such post as is mentioned in paragraph 10-

   (a) engage, or

   (b) make arrangements for the engagement of,

a person to provide his services as a teacher at the school otherwise than under a contract of employment.

(2) No person shall be engaged under sub-paragraph (1) unless he meets all the staff qualification requirements applicable in relation to a teacher in the post in which he would be acting as a temporary teacher.

17. The governing body may, in relation to a particular vacancy or absence or a vacancy or absence of a kind specified by them, delegate any of their functions under paragraphs 11 to 16-

   (a) to one or more governors,

   (b) to the head teacher, or

   (c) to one or more governors and the head teacher acting together.

Advice of chief education officer on appointments of teachers

18.–(1) The chief education officer shall be entitled to attend, for the purpose of giving advice-

   (a) all proceedings (including interviews) of the governing body, and of any selection panel appointed under paragraph 7, relating to appointments or engagements to which any of the provisions of paragraphs 4 to 9 or 29 and 30 apply, and

   (b) all proceedings (including interviews) of the governing body, and of any persons to whom any functions of the governing body under paragraphs 11 to 16 are delegated, relating to appointments or engagements to which any of the provisions of paragraphs 11 to 16 apply.

(2) The chief education officer shall be entitled to offer such advice as he considers appropriate with respect to-

(a) the appointment of a head teacher or deputy head teacher or the appointment or engagement of an acting head teacher or an acting deputy head teacher, or

(b) any matter arising in connection with any such appointment or engagement.

(3) Any advice given by the chief education officer to-

(a) the governing body,

(b) any selection panel appointed under paragraph 7, or

(c) any persons to whom any functions of the governing body under paragraphs 11 to 16 are delegated,

with respect to any matter which relates to an appointment or engagement and falls to be determined by them shall be considered by them before determining that matter, whether or not the advice was given at their request.

(4) This paragraph has effect subject to paragraph 2(3) and (4).

Advice of head teacher on appointments etc. of teachers

19.–(1) Except in relation to the appointment of a head teacher-

(a) paragraph 18(1) applies in relation to the head teacher (if not otherwise entitled to be present at the proceedings there mentioned) as it applies in relation to the chief education officer, and

(b) paragraph 18(3) applies in relation to advice given by the head teacher as it applies in relation to advice given by the chief education officer.

(2) Paragraph 18 shall have effect for the purposes of sub-paragraph (1) above as if sub-paragraph (4) of that paragraph were omitted.

Appointment of non-teaching staff

20.–(1) Except in a case where the governing body and the authority agree that the appointment of a person to work in a non-teaching post at the school should be made by the authority-

(a) any such appointment shall be made by the governing body; and

(b) the person appointed shall be employed by the governing body under a contract of employment on such terms as they think fit.

(2) Before making an appointment under this paragraph the governing body shall consult the head teacher (where he would not otherwise be involved in the decision to make the appointment).

(3) No person shall be appointed to work in a non-teaching post at the school, whether-

(a) by the governing body, or

(b) by the authority,

unless he meets all the staff qualification requirements which are applicable in relation to his appointment.

Conduct and discipline of staff

21.–(1) The regulation of conduct and discipline in relation to the staff of the school, and any procedures for giving members of the staff opportunities for seeking redress of any grievances relating to their employment, shall be under the control of the governing body.

(2) The governing body shall establish-

    (a) disciplinary rules and procedures (including such rules and procedures for dealing with lack of capability on the part of members of the staff), and

    (b) procedures such as are mentioned in sub-paragraph (1);

and shall take such steps as appear to the governing body to be appropriate for making them known to members of the staff.

(3) In determining the capability of members of the staff the governing body shall have regard to any guidance given from time to time by the Secretary of State.

(4) If the Secretary of State determines that any prescribed rules and procedures are to apply to the school or to any class or description of school to which the school belongs-

    (a) the governing body shall act in accordance with those rules and procedures in determining the capability of members of the staff; and

    (b) in the event of any inconsistency, those rules and procedures shall prevail over any rules and procedures established by the governing body under sub-paragraph (2)(a).

LEA report on performance of head teacher

22.–(1) Where the authority have any serious concerns about the performance of the head teacher of the school-

    (a) they shall make a written report of their concerns to the chairman of the governing body at the same time sending a copy to the head teacher; and

    (b) the chairman of the governing body shall notify the authority in writing of the action which he proposes to take in the light of the report.

(2) In determining whether to make a report under this paragraph the authority shall have regard to any guidance given from time to time by the Secretary of State.

Suspension

23.–(1) Both the governing body and the head teacher shall have power to suspend any person employed to work at the school (whether or not he is employed by the governing body) where, in the opinion of the governing body or (as the case may be) the head teacher, his exclusion from the school is required.

(2) The governing body or head teacher shall, when exercising that power, immediately inform the head teacher or (as the case may be) governing body.

(3) A suspension under this paragraph may only be ended by the governing body.

(4) The governing body shall, on ending such a suspension, immediately inform the head teacher.

(5) In this paragraph "suspend" means suspend without loss of emoluments.

Dismissal

24.–(1) Before making a decision that a person employed to work at the school should have his contract of employment with the governing body terminated or should not have that contract renewed, the governing body shall-

(a) make arrangements for giving that person an opportunity of making representations as to the action they propose to take (including, if he so wishes, oral representations to such person or persons as the governing body may appoint for the purpose), and

(b) have regard to any representations made by him.

(2) The governing body shall also make arrangements for giving any person in respect of whom they have made such a decision an opportunity of appealing against the decision before they give effect to it.

(3) Where their decision is that a person should have his contract of employment terminated, then, subject to any such appeal, the governing body shall give effect to their decision by-

(a) giving the person in question such notice terminating his contract of employment as is required under that contract;

(b) terminating that contract without notice if the circumstances are such that they are entitled to do so by reason of his conduct.

(4) Nothing in this paragraph shall be read as referring to a person who-

(a) is due to cease to work at the school by reason of the termination of his contract of employment by effluxion of time; and

(b) has not been continuously employed at the school for a period of two years or more (within the meaning of the Employment Rights Act 1996).

25.–(1) The head teacher (except where he is the person concerned) and the chief education officer of the local education authority shall be entitled to attend, for the purpose of giving advice, all proceedings of the governing body relating to such a decision as is mentioned in paragraph 24(1).

(2) The governing body shall consider any advice given by a person who is entitled to attend such proceedings under this paragraph before making any such decision.

(3) Sub-paragraph (1), so far as relating to the chief education officer, has effect subject to paragraph 2(3) and (4).

26. The governing body are not required to comply with paragraph 24 in relation to the making of such a decision as is mentioned in sub-paragraph (1) of that paragraph in a case where-

(a) the termination or non-renewal of the contract of employment of the person in question is required by virtue of regulations under section 218 of the Education Reform Act 1988 or section 19 of the Teaching and Higher Education Act 1998, or

(b) the person in question is a teacher who is subject to a conditional registration, suspension or prohibition order made under Schedule 2 to the 1998 Act (disciplinary powers of General Teaching Council).

Staff employed by LEA

27.–(1) Nothing in paragraph 24 applies in relation to a person employed by the authority to work at the school.

(2) Paragraphs 25 to 29 of Schedule 16 apply in relation to the dismissal or withdrawal from the school of any member of the staff who is employed by the authority as they apply in relation to the dismissal or withdrawal from a school to which that Schedule applies of a person who is employed to work at the school.

(3) Any regulations in force under paragraph 30 of that Schedule shall apply to any person who is, or is to be, employed by the authority to work at the school solely in connection with the provision of meals as if it were a school to which that Schedule applies.

Advisory rights for appropriate diocesan authorities

28.–(1) This paragraph applies to a voluntary aided or foundation school which is a Church of England, Church in Wales or Roman Catholic Church school.

(2) If the school is a voluntary aided school, the appropriate diocesan officer shall have the same advisory rights in relation to the appointment, engagement or dismissal of teachers at the school as are for the time being exercisable by the chief education officer in accordance with paragraph 2(3).

(3) If the school is a foundation school, the governing body may agree with the appropriate diocesan authority to accord to the appropriate diocesan officer-

(a) with respect to all teachers at the school, or
(b) with respect to any particular description of such teachers,

the same advisory rights in relation to their appointment, engagement or dismissal as are exercisable by the chief education officer in accordance with paragraph 2(3).

(4) The agreement of the governing body for the purposes of sub-paragraph (3) must be given in writing and may only be withdrawn by notice in writing to the appropriate diocesan authority.

(5) In paragraphs 18 and 25, as they apply to a school within sub-paragraph (2) or (3) above, references to the chief education officer accordingly include the appropriate diocesan officer, so far as necessary for giving effect to any advisory rights exercisable by him under this paragraph.

(6) In this paragraph "the appropriate diocesan officer" means such person as the appropriate diocesan authority may nominate.

Appointment of head teachers for schools of Roman Catholic religious orders

29.–(1) This paragraph applies to a voluntary aided school if the trustees under a trust deed relating to the school are also the trustees of a Roman Catholic religious order.

(2) Subject to sub-paragraph (6), sub-paragraphs (3) to (5) shall have effect in relation to the filling of a vacancy in the post of head teacher of the school, in place of paragraphs 6 to 8.

(3) The governing body shall notify the Major Superior of the vacancy in writing.

(4) The governing body shall-

(a) interview such persons who are members of the order as are proposed as candidates for appointment to the post by the Major Superior; and

(b) appoint to the post one of the persons so interviewed by them unless, by virtue of sub-paragraph (5) or otherwise, they have good reason for not making any such appointment.

(5) No person shall be appointed under sub-paragraph (4)(b) if he does not meet any staff qualification requirements which are applicable in relation to his appointment.

(6) If no appointment is made by the governing body under sub-paragraph (4)(b), paragraphs 6 to 8 shall have effect in relation to the filling of the vacancy.

(7) In this paragraph-

"the Major Superior" means the Major Superior of the order;

"the order" means the order mentioned in sub-paragraph (1);

"Roman Catholic religious order" means a Roman Catholic religious institute or society of apostolic life.

Selection procedures involving whole governing body

30.–(1) If the governing body of a voluntary aided school so determine (and paragraph 29 does not apply), sub-paragraphs (2) to (6) below shall apply in relation to the filling of a vacancy in the post of head teacher or deputy head teacher of the school, in place of paragraphs 7 and 8.

(2) No selection panel need be appointed by the governing body under paragraph 7(1), but the following provisions, namely-

(a) paragraph 7(2)(a) and (b),

(b) paragraph 7(3), and

(c) paragraph 7(6),

shall apply to the governing body or (as the case may be) to any decision of that body taken by virtue of this paragraph as it applies to a selection panel or (as the case may be) to any decision of such a panel taken under paragraph 7.

(3) If, within the period of 14 days beginning with the date when they receive a notification under paragraph 7(2)(a) (as it applies in accordance with sub-paragraph (2) above) the local education authority make written representations to the governing body that any of the applicants selected by them is not a suitable person for appointment to the post of head teacher, the governing body shall not appoint that person unless they have-

(a) considered those representations, and

(b) notified the authority of their response to the representations.

(4) The governing body shall not appoint any person if he does not meet any staff qualification requirements which are applicable in relation to his appointment.

(5) If the governing body do not appoint any person interviewed by them, the governing body-

(a) may, if they think fit, re-advertise the vacancy in the manner required by paragraph 6, and

(b) whether or not they re-advertise the vacancy, may repeat the steps mentioned in paragraph 7(2)(a) and (b) (as they apply in accordance with sub-paragraph (2) above).

(6) Paragraph 7(7) shall apply for the purposes of this paragraph.

Schedule 17

This Schedule deals with the appointment, discipline, suspension and dismissal of staff employed to work at foundation, voluntary aided and foundation special schools. Essentially, the process is the same as for the appointment, discipline, suspension and dismissal of staff in community, voluntary controlled and community special schools dealt with in Schedule 16 with the following differences:-.

• *Because the governing body is the direct employer of all staff, the governing body (including those to whom the responsibility of appointment has been delegated) makes the actual appointment and effects any dismissal. The governing body may not appoint a person who is unsuitable, within the limited definition mentioned in relation to Schedule 16.*

- *The chief education officer does not have automatic advisory rights. The governing body may agree with the local education authority to give such advisory rights ether generally or in relation to specified categories of appointment and/or dismissal. In default of agreement, the Secretary of State may determine what rights should be given to the chief education officer. If the chief education officer is given advisory rights these are exercised in the same way as under Schedule 16. Rights given by the governing body can only be withdrawn by written notice.*

- *Where the chief education officer has no advisory rights in relation to the appointment of the headteacher or deputy headteacher the selection panel must, when notifying the local education authority of those who have been short-listed for appointment, also supply such information as the local education authority may need to be able to determine suitability.*

- *In appointing teachers other than heads and deputies, the governing body must determine the job specification in consultation with the headteacher and send a copy to the local education authority*

- *There is no requirement to report suspension to the local education authority*

- *The provisions of Schedule 16 apply to any local education authority employees, including school meals staff, who work at the school*

- *Denominational foundation schools may confer advisory rights on the denominational body in the same way as under Schedule 16 for voluntary controlled schools. Rights given to a denominational body can only be withdrawn by written notice. The denominational body of voluntary aided schools will automatically acquire the same rights as may be conferred on the chief education officer from time to time by the governing body or the Secretary of State. These cannot be withdrawn but will cease if the chief education officer's rights come to an end.*

- *The normal process for appointment of a headteacher of a voluntary aided Roman Catholic school where the trustees of a trust deed of the school are also trustees of a Roman Catholic religious order does not apply. Instead, the governing body must notify the Major Superior of the order of the vacancy and must appoint (if at all) from such embers of the order as may be proposed by the Major Superior. The usual rule about suitability does, however, apply.*

- *The governing body of a voluntary aided school may decide that the appointment of a headteacher or deputy headteacher should be dealt with by the whole governing body rather than by a selection panel. The governing body must, however, follow the same process for short-listing and notification to the local education authority.*

SCHEDULE 18

Time limits and notices waiving right to appeal

1.–(1) No appeal under section 67(1) against a decision not to reinstate a pupil may be made after the 15th school day after the day on which the relevant person is given notice in writing under section 66(6)(b).

(2) Any notice in writing given by the relevant person to the local education authority which states that he does not intend to appeal against a decision not to reinstate the pupil shall be final.

Constitution of appeal panels

2.–(1) An appeal pursuant to arrangements made by a local education authority under section 67(1) shall be to an appeal panel constituted in accordance with this paragraph.

(2) An appeal panel shall consist of three or five members appointed by the authority from-

    (a) persons who are eligible to be lay members; and
    (b) persons who have experience in education, are acquainted with educational conditions in the area of the authority or are parents of registered pupils at a school.

(3) Of the members of an appeal panel-

    (a) at least one must be a person who is eligible to be a lay member and is appointed as such; and
    (b) at least one must be a person falling within sub-paragraph (2)(b).

(4) For the purposes of this paragraph a person is eligible to be a lay member if he is a person without personal experience in the management of any school or the provision of education in any school (disregarding any such experience as a governor or in any other voluntary capacity).

(5) Sufficient persons may be appointed by the authority under this paragraph to enable two or more appeal panels to sit at the same time.

(6) No person shall be a member of an appeal panel if he is disqualified by virtue of sub-paragraph (7).

(7) The following persons are disqualified for membership of an appeal panel-

    (a) any member of the authority or of the governing body of the school in question;
    (b) any person employed by the authority or the governing body, other than a person employed as a teacher;

(c) any person who has, or at any time has had, any connection with-
    (i) the authority or the school, or with any person within paragraph (b), or
    (ii) the pupil in question or the incident leading to his exclusion,

of a kind which might reasonably be taken to raise doubts about his ability to act impartially in relation to the authority, the school or the pupil in question.

(8) A person employed by the authority as a teacher shall not be taken, by reason only of that employment, to have such a connection with the authority as is mentioned in sub-paragraph (7)(c).

(9) Where, at any time after an appeal panel consisting of five members have begun to consider an appeal, any of the members-

(a) dies, or
(b) becomes unable through illness to continue as a member,

the panel may continue with their consideration and determination of the appeal so long as the number of the remaining members is not less than three and the requirements of sub-paragraph (3) are satisfied.

Allowances for members

3.–(1) For the purpose of the payment of financial loss allowance under section 173(4) of the Local Government Act 1972, that provision shall apply, with any necessary modifications, to any member of an appeal panel constituted in accordance with paragraph 2 as it applies to any member of a parish or community council; and such an appeal panel shall be included in the bodies to which section 174 of that Act (travelling and subsistence allowances) applies.

(2) In section 174(1) of that Act, in its application to a panel in accordance with sub-paragraph (1), the reference to payments at rates determined by the body in question shall be read as a reference to payments at rates determined by the local education authority.

Duty to advertise for lay members

4. Regulations may require any local education authority who are required by section 67(1) to make arrangements under that provision-

(a) to advertise, in such manner and at such times as may be prescribed, for persons eligible to be lay members of any appeal panel required to be constituted for the purposes of such arrangements to apply to the authority for appointment as such members, and
(b) in appointing persons as such members, to consider any persons eligible to be so appointed who have applied to the authority in response to an advertisement placed in pursuance of sub-paragraph (a) above.

Indemnity

5. Any local education authority required to make arrangements under section 67(1) shall indemnify the members of any appeal panel required to be constituted for the purposes of those arrangements against any reasonable legal costs and expenses reasonably incurred by those members in connection with any decision or action taken by them in good faith in pursuance of their functions as members of that panel.

Procedure on an appeal

6. In the following provisions of this Schedule "appeal" means an appeal under section 67(1).

7. An appeal shall be by notice in writing setting out the grounds on which it is made.

8.–(1) The appeal panel shall meet to consider an appeal on such date as the local education authority may determine.

(2) Subject to sub-paragraph (3), the date so determined must not be later than the closing date for appeals, namely the 15th school day after the day on which the appeal is lodged.

(3) If the relevant person requests the local education authority to do so, they may in exceptional circumstances determine under sub-paragraph (1) a date later than the closing date for appeals.

9.–(1) For the purpose of fixing the time (in accordance with paragraph 8) at which the hearing of an appeal is to take place, the local education authority shall take reasonable steps to ascertain any times falling on or before the closing date for appeals when-

(a) the relevant person, or
(b) any other person who wishes, and would be entitled, to appear and make oral representations in accordance with paragraph 10,

would be unable to attend.

(2) Where in accordance with sub-paragraph (1) the authority have ascertained any such times in the case of any such person, they shall, when fixing the time at which the hearing is to take place, take those times into account with a view to ensuring, so far as it is reasonably practicable to do so, that that person is able to appear and make such representations at the hearing.

10.–(1) The appeal panel shall give the relevant person an opportunity of appearing and making oral representations, and shall allow him to be represented or to be accompanied by a friend.

(2) The panel shall also allow–

(a) the head teacher to make written representations and to appear and make oral representations,

(b) the local education authority and the governing body to make written representations,

(c) an officer of the authority nominated by the authority, and a governor nominated by the governing body, to appear and make oral representations, and

(d) the governing body to be represented.

11. Appeals shall be heard in private except when the local education authority direct otherwise; but–

(a) if the panel so direct, one member of the local education authority may attend, as an observer, any hearing of an appeal by an appeal panel; and

(b) one member of the Council on Tribunals may attend, as an observer, any meeting of an appeal panel at which an appeal is considered.

12. Two or more appeals may be combined and dealt with in the same proceedings if the appeal panel consider that it is expedient to do so because the issues raised by the appeals are the same or connected.

13. In the event of a disagreement between the members of an appeal panel, the appeal under consideration shall be decided by a simple majority of the votes cast and, in the case of an equality of votes, the chairman of the panel shall have a second or casting vote.

14. The decision of an appeal panel and the grounds on which it is made shall–

(a) be communicated by the panel in writing to the relevant person, the local education authority, the governing body and the head teacher, and

(b) be so communicated by the end of the second school day after the conclusion of the hearing of the appeal.

15.–(1) Subject to paragraphs 7 to 14, all matters relating to the procedure on appeals shall be determined by the local education authority.

(2) The local education authority shall, in setting any time limits in connection with appeals, have regard to the desirability of securing that appeals are disposed of without delay.

Notices

16.–(1) Where in accordance with section 66(6)(b) notice in writing is required to be given to a person, the notice may be given either–

(a) by delivering it to the person's last-known address, or

(b) by properly addressing, pre-paying and sending by first class post to the person's last-known address a letter containing the notice.

(2) For the purposes of calculating the period referred to in paragraph 1(1), a notice shall be taken to have been given-

(a) where first class post is used, on the second school day after the date of posting, or

(b) where the notice is delivered, on the date of delivery,

unless (in either case) the contrary is shown.

Meaning of "the relevant person"

17. In this Schedule "the relevant person" means-

(a) in relation to a pupil under the age of 18, a parent of his;

(b) in relation to a pupil who has attained that age, the pupil himself.

Power of Secretary of State to make amendments

18. The Secretary of State may by order make such amendments of this Schedule as he considers expedient.

Schedule 18

This Schedule deals with the process for appeals against permanent exclusions.

The time limit for appealing is 15 school days after the parent (or pupil if 18 or over) is given notice of the confirmation of the exclusion by the governing body. If the parent or pupil notifies the local education authority that he does not intend to appeal, that notice is final and cannot be withdrawn.

The local education authority makes the appeal arrangements. The appeal panel has either three or five members who must either be lay members (a person without personal experience in the management of a school or provision of education except as a governor or in another voluntary capacity) or a person who is either experienced in education, acquainted with the educational conditions in the area or a parent of a registered pupil in a school – not necessarily in that authority. The panel must have one member at least from each category.

No-one who is:-

- *A member of the local education authority*
- *A governor of the school in question*
- *A person employed by the local education authority (except as a teacher) or the governing body of the school in question*
- *Any person who has or at any time has had any connection with the authority, the school in question, any employee of either or the pupil, or who has had any connection with the incident leading to the exclusion of a kind that might reasonably throw doubt on that person's impartiality*

may be a member of the appeal panel.

An appeal panel that starts with five members may continue even if one or two members are unable to continue. An appeal panel cannot function with less than three members.

Appeal panel members may be paid expenses and must be indemnified against all costs and expenses incurred by them as a result anything they do in good faith as panel members.

The local education authority must advertise for lay members.

The Schedule sets out the procedure for conducting appeals. The notice of appeal must specify the grounds of the appeal. The appeal must be heard within 15 school days after it is lodged although exceptionally this may be extended if the appellant requests. The local education authority must take reasonable steps to fix a time and place convenient to all. The headteacher, local education authority and governing body must be given the opportunity to make written representations and they and the appellant must be allowed to make oral representations. The local education authority and governing body will make their representations through an officer and nominated governor respectively but the governing body has an additional express right to be represented at the appeal.

Appeals are normally heard in private although the local education authority can decide to hold them in public. The panel may allow a member of the local education authority to attend as an observer and the Council on Tribunals has the right for a member to observe. Two or more appeals may be heard at the same time if they raise the same issues or are connected and the decision is by simple majority. The decision, and reasons, must be given in writing to all concerned not later than the end of the second school day after the hearing ends.

The local education authority decides any procedural aspects that are not covered by the Schedule.

The Secretary of State may amend these provisions.

SCHEDULE 19

REQUIRED PROVISION FOR RELIGIOUS EDUCATION

Introductory

1.–(1) In this Schedule "the required provision for religious education", in relation to a school, means the provision for pupils at the school which is required by section 352(1)(a) of the Education Act 1996 to be included in the school's basic curriculum.

(2) In this Schedule "agreed syllabus" has the meaning given by section 375(2) of that Act.

Community schools and foundation and voluntary schools without a religious character

2.–(1) This paragraph applies to-

    (a) any community school; and

    (b) any foundation or voluntary school which does not have a religious character.

(2) Subject to sub-paragraph (4), the required provision for religious education in the case of pupils at the school is provision for religious education in accordance with an agreed syllabus adopted for the school or for those pupils.

(3) If the school is a secondary school so situated that arrangements cannot conveniently be made for the withdrawal of pupils from it in accordance with section 71 to receive religious education elsewhere and the local education authority are satisfied-

    (a) that the parents of any pupils at the school desire them to receive religious education in the school in accordance with the tenets of a particular religion or religious denomination, and

    (b) that satisfactory arrangements have been made for the provision of such education to those pupils in the school, and for securing that the cost of providing such education to those pupils in the school will not fall to be met from the school's budget share or otherwise by the authority,

the authority shall (unless they are satisfied that because of any special circumstances it would be unreasonable to do so) provide facilities for the carrying out of those arrangements.

(4) If immediately before the appointed day the school was a grant-maintained school (within the meaning of the Education Act 1996), and in relation to the school or any pupils at the school the appropriate agreed syllabus as defined by section 382 of that Act was a syllabus falling within subsection (1)(c) of that section, then until-

    (a) the end of such period as the Secretary of State may by order prescribe, or

    (b) such earlier date as the governing body may determine,

the required provision for religious education in the case of the school or (as the case may be) those pupils is provision for religious education in accordance with that syllabus.

(5) No agreed syllabus shall provide for religious education to be given to pupils at a school to which this paragraph applies by means of any catechism or formulary which is distinctive of a particular religious denomination (but this is not to be taken as prohibiting provision in such a syllabus for the study of such catechisms or formularies).

Foundation and voluntary controlled schools with a religious character

3.–(1) This paragraph applies to any foundation or voluntary controlled school which has a religious character.

(2) Subject to sub-paragraph (4), the required provision for religious education in the case of pupils at the school is provision for religious education-

(a) in accordance with any arrangements made under sub-paragraph (3), or
(b) subject to any such arrangements, in accordance with an agreed syllabus adopted for the school or for those pupils.

(3) Where the parents of any pupils at the school request that they may receive religious education-

(a) in accordance with any provisions of the trust deed relating to the school, or
(b) where provision for that purpose is not made by such a deed, in accordance with the tenets of the religion or religious denomination specified in relation to the school under section 69(4),

the foundation governors shall (unless they are satisfied that because of any special circumstances it would be unreasonable to do so) make arrangements for securing that such religious education is given to those pupils in the school during not more than two periods in each week.

(4) If immediately before the appointed day the school was a grant-maintained school (within the meaning of the Education Act 1996), and in relation to the school or any pupils at the school the appropriate agreed syllabus as defined by section 382 of that Act was a syllabus falling within subsection (1)(c) of that section, then until-

(a) the end of such period as the Secretary of State may by order prescribe, or
(b) such earlier date as the governing body may determine,

that syllabus shall be treated for the purposes of sub-paragraph (2)(b) as an agreed syllabus adopted for the school or (as the case may be) those pupils.

Voluntary aided schools with a religious character

4.–(1) This paragraph applies to any voluntary aided school which has a religious character.

(2) The required provision for religious education in the case of pupils at the school is provision for religious education-

(a) in accordance with any provisions of the trust deed relating to the school, or
(b) where provision for that purpose is not made by such a deed, in accordance with the tenets of the religion or religious denomination specified in relation to the school under section 69(4), or
(c) in accordance with any arrangements made under sub-paragraph (3).

(3) Where the parents of any pupils at the school-

(a) desire them to receive religious education in accordance with any agreed syllabus adopted by the local education authority, and
(b) cannot with reasonable convenience cause those pupils to attend a school at which that syllabus is in use,

the governing body shall (unless they are satisfied that because of any special circumstances it would be unreasonable to do so) make arrangements for religious education in accordance with that syllabus to be given to those pupils in the school.

(4) Religious education under any such arrangements shall be given during the times set apart for the giving of religious education in the school in accordance with the provision for that purpose included in the school's basic curriculum by virtue of section 352(1)(a) of the (1996 c. 56.)Education Act 1996.

(5) Any arrangements under sub-paragraph (3) shall be made by the governing body, unless the local education authority are satisfied that the governing body are unwilling to make them, in which case they shall be made by the authority.

(6) Subject to sub-paragraph (3), the religious education given to pupils at the school shall be under the control of the governing body.

Schedule 19

This Schedule deals with the requirements for the provision of religious education within the basic curriculum which differs according to the category of the school and whether or not it is designated under the Act as having a religious character.

Schools with no religious character

These schools are required to provide non-denominational religious education in accordance with the syllabus agreed in accordance with the provisions of the Education Act 1996. There are provisions enabling the local education authority to make special arrangements for secondary school pupils whose parents want them to receive religious education in accordance with their particular tenets or denomination if convenient arrangements cannot be made for this to be provided elsewhere and the cost of meeting the parents' wishes will not fall on the school's delegated budget or other authority funds.

Foundation and voluntary controlled schools with a religious character

Religious education is to be in accordance with the syllabus agreed in accordance with the provisions of the Education Act 1996. However, where parents request religious education in accordance with the school's trust deed, or where there is no such deed or it makes no provision, then in accordance with the tenets of the religion or denomination specified in the determination by the Secretary of State of the religious character of the school, the governing body must make arrangements for up to two periods a week of such education unless special circumstances (not defined) make this unreasonable.

Voluntary aided schools with a religious character

Religious education is to be in accordance with the school's trust deed, or where there is no such deed or it makes no provision, then in accordance with the tenets of the religion or denomination specified in the determination by the Secretary of State of the religious character of the school. Where parents want their children to receive religious education in accordance with the syllabus agreed under the provisions of the Education Act 1996 for use in the local education authority area and they cannot "with reasonable convenience" send their children to a school that uses such a syllabus then the governing body must, unless special circumstances (again not defined) make this unreasonable, make arrangements for those children to receive such education during the time set aside for religious education. If the governing body is unwilling to do this then the local education authority may make such arrangements. Apart from this, the governing body controls the provision of religious education.

SCHEDULE 20

COLLECTIVE WORSHIP

Introductory

1. In this Schedule "the required collective worship", in relation to a school, means the collective worship in that school which is required by section 70.

General provisions as to collective worship

2.–(1) This paragraph applies to any community, foundation or voluntary school.

(2) The arrangements for the required collective worship may, in respect of each school day, provide for a single act of worship for all pupils or for separate acts of worship for pupils in different age groups or in different school groups.

(3) For the purposes of sub-paragraph (2) a "school group" is any group in which pupils are taught or take part in other school activities.

(4) Subject to sub-paragraph (6), the arrangements for the required collective worship shall be made-

(a) if the school is a community school or a foundation school which does not have a religious character, by the head teacher after consulting the governing body;

(b) if the school is a foundation school which has a religious character or a voluntary school, by the governing body after consulting the head teacher.

(5) Subject to sub-paragraph (6), the required collective worship shall take place on the school premises.

(6) If the governing body of a community, foundation or voluntary school are of the opinion that it is desirable that any act of collective worship in the school required by section 70 should, on a special occasion, take place elsewhere than on the school premises, they may, after consultation with the head teacher, make such arrangements for that purpose as they think appropriate.

(7) The powers of a governing body under sub-paragraph (6) shall not be exercised so as to derogate from the rule that the required collective worship must normally take place on the school premises.

Nature of collective worship in community schools and foundation schools without a religious character

3.–(1) This paragraph applies to-

(a) any community school; and
(b) any foundation school which does not have a religious character.

(2) Subject to paragraph 4, the required collective worship shall be wholly or mainly of a broadly Christian character.

(3) For the purposes of sub-paragraph (2), collective worship is of a broadly Christian character if it reflects the broad traditions of Christian belief without being distinctive of any particular Christian denomination.

(4) Not every act of collective worship in the school required by section 70 need comply with sub-paragraph (2) provided that, taking any school term as a whole, most such acts which take place in the school do comply with that sub-paragraph.

(5) Subject to sub-paragraphs (2) and (4)-

(a) the extent to which (if at all) any acts of collective worship required by section 70 which do not comply with sub-paragraph (2) take place in the school,
(b) the extent to which any act of collective worship in the school which complies with sub-paragraph (2) reflects the broad traditions of Christian belief, and
(c) the ways in which those traditions are reflected in any such act of collective worship,

shall be such as may be appropriate having regard to any relevant considerations relating to the pupils concerned which fall to be taken into account in accordance with sub-paragraph (6).

(6) Those considerations are-

(a) any circumstances relating to the family backgrounds of the pupils which are relevant for determining the character of the collective worship which is appropriate in their case, and
(b) their ages and aptitudes.

(7) In this paragraph references to acts of collective worship in the school include such acts which by virtue of paragraph 2(6) take place otherwise than on the school premises.

Disapplication of requirement under paragraph 3(2)

4.–(1) This paragraph applies where a standing advisory council on religious education have determined (under section 394 of the Education Act 1996) that it is not appropriate for the requirement imposed by paragraph 3(2) to apply in the case of any school to which paragraph 3 applies or in the case of any class or description of pupils at any such school.

(2) While the determination has effect-

    (a) paragraph 3 shall not apply in relation to the school or (as the case may be) the pupils in question, and

    (b) the collective worship required by section 70 in the case of the school or pupils shall not be distinctive of any particular Christian or other religious denomination;

but paragraph (b) shall not be taken as preventing that worship from being distinctive of any particular faith.

Nature of collective worship in foundation schools with a religious character and voluntary schools

5. In the case of a foundation school which has a religious character or a voluntary school, the required collective worship shall be-

    (a) in accordance with any provisions of the trust deed relating to the school, or

    (b) where-

        (i) provision for that purpose is not made by such a deed, and

        (ii) the school has a religious character,

in accordance with the tenets and practices of the religion or religious denomination specified in relation to the school under section 69(4).

Schedule 20
This Schedule deals with the statutory requirement for a daily act of collective worship in every school.

The collective worship may be a single, whole school, act or may be in separate groups provided that the groups are groups for some other school purpose. The arrangements are made by the headteacher in consultation with the governing body if the school is not one designated as having a religious character and vice versa if it is so designated. Except on special occasions, it must take place on the school premises.

The collective worship of schools that are not designated as having a religious character must be broadly Christian but there is considerable flexibility. Not all acts of collective worship need to be broadly Christian if, taken as a whole over a term, most are and family backgrounds and the age and aptitude of pupils can be taken into account. Individual schools may be exempted from the requirement that the act of worship be broadly Christian but the requirement to conduct a daily act of collective worship still applies.

The collective worship in a school designated as having a religious character must be in accordance with the school's trust deed, or where there is no such deed or it makes no provision, then in accordance with the tenets of the religion or denomination specified in the determination by the Secretary of State of the religious character of the school.

SCHEDULE 21

TRANSFERS OF LAND ON APPOINTED DAY

PART I GENERAL PROVISIONS

Introductory

1. In this Schedule any reference to a grant-maintained or grant-maintained special school is a reference to such a school within the meaning of the (1996 c. 56.) Education Act 1996.

Effect of transfers under this Schedule

2.–(1) Where any land is transferred to and vests in any body in accordance with this Schedule, any rights or liabilities-

(a) enjoyed or incurred by the transferor in connection with the land, and
(b) subsisting immediately before the appointed day,

shall also be transferred to, and by virtue of this Act vest in, that body.

(2) Any reference in this Schedule, in relation to a school, to land being transferred to, and vesting in, a foundation body is a reference to its being transferred to, and vesting in, that body for the purposes of the schools comprising the group for which that body acts.

(3) This Schedule is subject to section 198 of the Education Reform Act 1988 (which with Schedule 10 to that Act makes further provision in relation to transfers of property, rights and liabilities), and references in that Schedule as applied by virtue of this sub-paragraph to the transfer date are to the appointed day.

PART II RULES RELATING TO TRANSFERS

APPLICATION OF PART II

3.–(1) This Part of this Schedule applies to schools which, in accordance with Schedule 2, become community, foundation, voluntary or community special schools on the appointed day.

(2) This Part has effect subject to Part III of this Schedule.

Transfers for purposes of community schools

4.–(1) This paragraph applies where a grant-maintained school (an "existing school") becomes a community school.

(2) In such a case-

    (a) any publicly funded land shall on the appointed day be transferred to, and by virtue of this Act vest in, the local education authority;

    (b) any other land which, immediately before that day, is held by the governing body for the purposes of the existing school shall be transferred to, and vest in, the authority in accordance with a transfer agreement; and

    (c) any land which, immediately before that day, is held by any trustees for the purposes of the existing school shall be transferred to, and vest in, the authority in accordance with a transfer agreement.

(3) In this paragraph "publicly funded land" means land which-

    (a) immediately before the appointed day is held by the governing body for the purposes of the existing school, and

    (b) was acquired from a local authority under a transfer under section 201(1)(a) of the Education Act 1996 or from the Funding Agency for Schools or was acquired wholly by means of any maintenance, special purpose or capital grant (within the meaning of Chapter VI of Part III of that Act).

(4) In this paragraph "transfer agreement" means an agreement-

    (a) made for the purposes of sub-paragraph (2) between the local education authority and the governing body or (as the case may be) trustees mentioned in that sub-paragraph, and

    (b) providing for the land in question to be transferred to, and vest in, the authority on the appointed day, whether or not in consideration of the payment by the authority of such amount as may be agreed between the parties.

Transfers for purposes of foundation schools

5.–(1) This paragraph applies where-

    (a) a grant-maintained school (an "existing school") becomes a foundation school; and

    (b) as from the appointed day the school (as a foundation school) is a member of the group for which a foundation body acts.

(2) In such a case, any land which, immediately before the appointed day, was held by the governing body for the purposes of the existing school shall on that day be transferred to, and by virtue of this Act vest in, the foundation body.

Transfers for purposes of voluntary schools

6.–(1) This paragraph applies where-

  (a) a grant-maintained school (an "existing school") becomes a voluntary school;
      and
  (b) as from the appointed day the school (as a voluntary school) is a member of the
      group for which a foundation body acts.

(2) In such a case, any land which, immediately before the appointed day, was held by
    the governing body for the purposes of the existing school shall on that day be
    transferred to, and by virtue of this Act vest in, the foundation body.

Transfers for purposes of community special schools

7.–(1) This paragraph applies where a grant-maintained special school (an "existing
    school") becomes a community special school.

(2) In such a case-

  (a) any publicly funded land shall on the appointed day be transferred to, and by
      virtue of this Act vest in, the local education authority;
  (b) any other land which, immediately before that day, is held by the governing
      body for the purposes of the existing school shall be transferred to, and vest in,
      the authority in accordance with a transfer agreement; and
  (c) any land which, immediately before that day, is held by any trustees for the
      purposes of the existing school shall be transferred to, and vest in, the authority
      in accordance with a transfer agreement.

(3) In this paragraph "publicly funded land" means land which-

  (a) immediately before the appointed day is held by the governing body for the
      purposes of the existing school, and
  (b) was acquired from a local authority under a transfer under section 201(1)(a) of
      the Education Act 1996 or from the Funding Agency for Schools or was
      acquired wholly by means of any maintenance, special purpose or capital grant
      (within the meaning of Chapter VI of Part III of that Act).

(4) In this paragraph "transfer agreement" means an agreement-

  (a) made for the purposes of sub-paragraph (2) between the local education
      authority and the governing body or (as the case may be) the trustees
      mentioned in that sub-paragraph, and
  (b) providing for the land in question to be transferred to, and vest in, the authority
      on the appointed day, whether or not in consideration of the payment by the
      authority of such amount as may be agreed between the parties.

Outstanding transfers to existing school

8. Where immediately before the appointed day-

    (a) any land vested in a local authority is by virtue of any statutory provision required to be transferred to the governing body or any trustees of an existing school within the meaning of any of paragraphs 4 to 7, but
    (b) the land has not yet been so transferred,

that paragraph shall apply to the school as if it had been so transferred by that time.

Transfer of rights to use land

9.–(1) Where paragraph 4, 5, 6 or 7 applies to an existing school and any land held by a person or body other than the governing body of the school was, immediately before the appointed day, used for the purposes of the school, any rights or liabilities-

    (a) enjoyed or incurred by the governing body in connection with the use of the land, and
    (b) subsisting immediately before the appointed day,

shall on that day be transferred to, and by virtue of this Act vest in, the local education authority (in a case to which paragraph 4 or 7 applies) or the foundation body (in a case to which paragraph 5 or 6 applies).

(2) Where paragraph 4 or 7 applies to an existing school and any land held by a person or body other than any trustees who hold any land for the purposes of the school was, immediately before the appointed day, used for the purposes of the school, any rights or liabilities-

    (a) enjoyed or incurred by any such trustees in connection with the use of the land, and
    (b) subsisting immediately before the appointed day,

shall on that day be transferred to, and vest in, the local education authority in accordance with a transfer agreement.

(3) Nothing in this paragraph applies in relation to land to which paragraph 4, 5, 6 or 7 applies.

(4) In this paragraph-

    "existing school" has the meaning given by paragraph 4, 5, 6 or 7, as the case may be;

    "transfer agreement" means an agreement-

    (a) made for the purposes of sub-paragraph (2) between the local education authority and the trustees mentioned in that sub-paragraph, and
    (b) providing for the rights or liabilities in question to be transferred to, and vest in, the authority on the appointed day, whether or not in consideration of the payment by the authority of such amount as may be agreed between the parties.

PART III PROPERTY EXCLUDED FROM TRANSFERS

10.–(1) Nothing in Part II of this Schedule has the effect of transferring to, or vesting in, any body-

(a) any land, rights or liabilities excluded under sub-paragraph (2) or (3),

(b) any rights or liabilities under a contract of employment,

(c) any liability of a governing body in respect of the principal of, or any interest on, any loan,

(d) any liability in tort, or

(e) any rights or liabilities which are determined in accordance with regulations to be rights or liabilities falling within this paragraph.

(2) If before the appointed day-

(a) the prospective transferee and transferor have agreed in writing that any land should be excluded from the operation of Part II of this Schedule, and

(b) the Secretary of State has given his written approval of the agreement,

the land (and any rights or liabilities relating to it) shall be so excluded.

(3) If in default of agreement under sub-paragraph (2)-

(a) the prospective transferee or transferor have applied to the Secretary of State to exclude any land from the operation of Part II of this Schedule, and

(b) the Secretary of State has by order directed its exclusion,

the land (and any rights or liabilities relating to it) shall be so excluded.

(4) An agreement under sub-paragraph (2) may provide for the land to be used or held for the purposes of the school (as a school of a new category) on such terms as may be specified in or determined in accordance with the agreement; and directions under sub-paragraph (3)-

(a) may confer any rights or impose any liabilities that could have been conferred or imposed by such an agreement, and

(b) shall have effect as if contained in such an agreement.

(5) In this paragraph-

"new category" means one of the categories set out in section 20(1);

"the prospective transferee", in relation to any land, means the body to whom, apart from sub-paragraph (2) or (3), the land would fall to be transferred under Part II of this Schedule; and

"the prospective transferor" shall be construed accordingly.

Schedule 21

This Schedule deals with the technical aspects of land transfer consequent on grant maintained schools becoming foundation, voluntary or community schools under the new framework. It applies only to land that was owned by the governing body. Land that was previously owned by trustees or by a foundation body is not affected.

In essence, school land of community schools is transferred to the local education authority, that of foundation schools that have a foundation established under the Act is transferred to that foundation body, that of voluntary schools that have a foundation body is transferred to that foundation body and (by default) that of foundation schools that have no foundation body remains in the ownership of the governing body.

SCHEDULE 22

DISPOSALS OF LAND IN CASE OF CERTAIN SCHOOLS AND DISPOSALS ON DISCONTINUANCE

PART I FOUNDATION, VOLUNTARY AND FOUNDATION SPECIAL SCHOOLS:
DISPOSALS OF LAND

Disposal of land by governing body of foundation, voluntary or foundation special school

1.–(1) This paragraph applies to any disposal by the governing body of a foundation, voluntary or foundation special school of-

(a) any land acquired under a transfer under section 201(1)(a) of the Education Act 1996, or acquired under paragraph 2 of Schedule 3 or paragraph 16 of Schedule 6 or paragraph 5(4)(c) of this Schedule or under any regulations made under paragraph 5 of Schedule 8;

(b) any land acquired from a foundation body;

(c) any land acquired from the Funding Agency for Schools;

(d) any land acquired, or enhanced in value, wholly or partly by means of any maintenance, special purpose or capital grant (within the meaning of Chapter VI of Part III of the (1996 c. 56.)Education Act 1996);

(e) any land acquired, or enhanced in value, wholly or partly by means of expenditure incurred for the purposes of the school and treated by the local education authority as expenditure of a capital nature; or

(f) any land acquired, or enhanced in value, wholly or partly with the proceeds of disposal of any land acquired or enhanced in value as mentioned in any of paragraphs (a) to (e).

(2) The governing body shall not make any such disposal without the written consent of the Secretary of State.

(3) Where the governing body apply to the Secretary of State for his consent to any such disposal, he may do one or more of the following, namely-

    (a) require the land or any part of the land to be transferred to such local authority as he may specify, subject to the payment by that authority of such sum by way of consideration (if any) as he determines to be appropriate; and

    (b) give the governing body, when the land or any part of the land is disposed of-

        (i) a direction to pay, either to him or to such local authority as he may specify, the whole or any part of the proceeds of disposal; and

        (ii) a direction as to the use to which the whole or any part of the proceeds of disposal should be put.

(4) More than one direction may be given under sub-paragraph (3)(b)(i) in relation to a disposal of land within sub-paragraph (1) where it is just to do so, in particular where the disposal involves the creation of a lease.

(5) Sub-paragraph (1)(e) shall not apply in the case of any expenditure incurred on or after the appointed day unless the authority-

    (a) prepared a statement in writing-

        (i) containing details of the amount of the expenditure, the acquisition or works funded (or to be funded) by such expenditure, and the total cost (or estimated total cost) of that acquisition or those works, and

        (ii) indicating that the expenditure was being treated by them as expenditure of a capital nature; and

    (b) sent a copy of the statement to the governing body either before, or no later than 12 months after, the expenditure was incurred.

Disposal of land by foundation body

2.–(1) This paragraph applies to any disposal by a foundation body of-

    (a) any land acquired under paragraph 2, 4 or 9 of Schedule 3, paragraph 16 or 20 of Schedule 6 or paragraph 5 or 6 of Schedule 21 or under any regulations made under paragraph 5 of Schedule 8;

    (b) any land acquired from the governing body of a maintained school;

    (c) any land acquired from another foundation body;

    (d) any land acquired, or enhanced in value, wholly or partly by means of any grant provided by the Secretary of State on or after the appointed day;

    (e) any land acquired, or enhanced in value, wholly or partly by means of expenditure incurred for the purposes of any of the schools comprising the group for which the body acts and treated by the local education authority as expenditure of a capital nature; or

    (f) any land acquired, or enhanced in value, wholly or partly with the proceeds of disposal of any land acquired or enhanced in value as mentioned in any of paragraphs (a) to (e).

(2) The foundation body shall not make any such disposal without the written consent of the Secretary of State.

(3) Where the foundation body apply to the Secretary of State for his consent to any such disposal, he may do either or both of the following, namely-

(a) make any such requirement as is mentioned in paragraph 1(3)(a); and

(b) give any such direction to the foundation body as he could give to a governing body under paragraph 1(3)(b).

(4) More than one direction may be given under sub-paragraph (3)(b) to make a payment in relation to the proceeds of disposal of land within sub-paragraph (1) where it is just to do so, in particular where the disposal involves the creation of a lease.

(5) Sub-paragraph (1)(e) shall not apply in the case of any expenditure incurred on or after the appointed day unless the authority-

(a) prepared a statement in writing-

(i) containing details of the amount of the expenditure, the acquisition or works funded (or to be funded) by such expenditure, and the total cost (or estimated total cost) of that acquisition or those works, and

(ii) indicating that the expenditure was being treated by them as expenditure of a capital nature; and

(b) sent a copy of the statement to the foundation body either before, or no later than 12 months after, the expenditure was incurred.

Disposal of land by trustees of foundation, voluntary or foundation special school

3.–(1) This paragraph applies to any disposal by the trustees of a foundation, voluntary or foundation special school of-

(a) any land acquired under section 60, 61 or 70 of the Education Act 1996, under paragraph 2, 4 or 9 of Schedule 3 or paragraph 16 or 20 of Schedule 6 or under any regulations made under paragraph 5 of Schedule 8;

(b) any land acquired, or enhanced in value, wholly or partly by means of expenditure incurred on or after the appointed day for the purposes of the school and treated by the local education authority as expenditure of a capital nature;

(c) any land acquired by the governing body of the school-

(i) under a transfer under section 201(1)(a) of the Education Act 1996, or

(ii) wholly or partly with the proceeds of disposal of any land so acquired,

and transferred by the governing body to be held on trust by the trustees;

(d) any land acquired from the Funding Agency for Schools;

(e) any land acquired, or enhanced in value, wholly or partly by means of-

(i) any maintenance, special purpose or capital grant (within the meaning of Chapter VI of Part III of the (1996 c. 56.)Education Act 1996), or

(ii) any grant paid under section 216(2) of that Act;

(f) any land acquired wholly or partly with the proceeds of disposal of any land acquired or enhanced in value as mentioned in paragraph (d) or (e); or

(g) any land acquired, or enhanced in value, wholly or partly by means of any grant made in pursuance of a special agreement (as defined by section 32(5) of the (1996 c. 56.)Education Act 1996).

(2) If a voluntary aided school was, immediately before the appointed day, a controlled school within the meaning of the (1996 c. 56.)Education Act 1996, this paragraph also applies to any disposal by the trustees of the school of any land acquired, or enhanced in value, wholly or partly by means of expenditure incurred under section 63 or 64 of that Act.

(3) Where paragraph (a), (b) or (c) of sub-paragraph (1) or sub-paragraph (2) applies, the trustees shall notify the local education authority that that provision applies to them and they or their successors shall pay to the authority so much of the proceeds of disposal as may be determined to be just, either by agreement between them and the authority or, in default of agreement, by the Secretary of State.

(4) In making any determination under sub-paragraph (3), the trustees and the authority, or the Secretary of State, as the case may be, shall have regard in particular to-

(a) the value, as at the date of the determination, of the land acquired from the authority;
(b) any enhancement in value of the land attributable to expenditure by the local education authority, the trustees or the governing body of the school on school buildings on the land; and
(c) any payments already made by the trustees to the authority-
  (i) in respect of the current school site; or
  (ii) under section 60(4) of the (1996 c. 56.)Education Act 1996 or under paragraph 2(6) of Schedule 3 or paragraph 16(5) of Schedule 6 to this Act.

(5) More than one determination may be made under sub-paragraph (3) in relation to a disposal of land within sub-paragraph (1) or (2) where it is just to do so, in particular where the disposal involves the creation of a lease.

(6) Sub-paragraph (1)(b) shall not apply in the case of any expenditure unless the authority-

(a) prepared a statement in writing-
  (i) containing details of the amount of the expenditure, the acquisition or works funded (or to be funded) by such expenditure, and the total cost (or estimated total cost) of that acquisition or those works, and
  (ii) indicating that the expenditure was being treated by them as expenditure of a capital nature; and
(b) sent a copy of the statement to the trustees either before, or no later than 12 months after, the expenditure was incurred.

(7) Sub-paragraph (3) does not apply in the case of land acquired under section 60 or 61 of the Education Act 1996 or under paragraph 2 or 4 of Schedule 3 to this Act by the trustees of an institution which is, or has at any time been, within the further education sector (as defined by section 4(3) of the (1996 c. 56.)Education Act 1996).

(8) Where paragraph (d), (e) or (f) of sub-paragraph (1) applies, the trustees shall notify the local education authority that that paragraph applies to them and they and their successors shall (subject to sub-paragraph (9)) undertake to the authority to use the proceeds of disposal-

(a) for the purposes of the school, or
(b) for the purposes-
    (i) of any other existing foundation, voluntary or foundation special school, or
    (ii) of any other proposed foundation, voluntary or foundation special school, whether or not proposals have yet been published under section 28 or 31 in respect of that proposed school.

(9) Where it appears to the Secretary of State that the trustees have not given a suitable undertaking under sub-paragraph (8), the Secretary of State may direct the trustees to pay to the authority either the whole or any part of the proceeds of disposal as he determines to be just.

(10) More than one direction may be given under sub-paragraph (9) in relation to a disposal of land within sub-paragraph (1) where it is just to do so, in particular where the disposal involves the creation of a lease.

(11) Where paragraph (g) of sub-paragraph (1) applies, the governing body of the school shall repay the grant referred to in that paragraph to the local education authority by whom the school is maintained, unless the governing body and the authority otherwise agree.

(12) Where the trustees of a foundation, voluntary or foundation special school wish, in the case of any land held by them for the purposes of the school, to use the land for purposes not connected with the provision of education in maintained schools-

(a) the preceding provisions of this paragraph shall apply as if any such change of use of the land were a disposal of the land; and
(b) the value of the land as at the date of any determination under sub-paragraph (3) or of any direction under sub-paragraph (9) shall be treated as proceeds of the disposal of the land.

Land required by local education authority for new school

4.-(1) This paragraph applies where, on an application made by a local education authority, the Secretary of State is satisfied-

    (a) that any relevant land-

        (i) held, or held on trust, for the purposes of a foundation, voluntary or foundation special school by the governing body or the trustees of the school, or

        (ii) held by a foundation body for the purposes of the group of schools for which it acts, is not required for the purposes of the school or (as the case may be) those schools; and

    (b) that that land is required by the authority as the site for a new maintained school or as the site to which a maintained school is to be transferred.

(2) In such a case the Secretary of State may by order require the relevant land to be transferred to the authority by the body or trustees holding the land, subject to the payment by the authority of such sum by way of consideration (if any) as he determines to be appropriate.

(3) In this paragraph "relevant land" means land which was acquired by the governing body of the school, or (as the case may be) one of the schools, mentioned in sub-paragraph (1)(a) under a transfer under section 201(1)(a) of the Education Act 1996.

PART II MAINTAINED SCHOOLS: DISPOSALS ON DISCONTINUANCE

Discontinuance of foundation, voluntary and foundation special schools: land

5.–(1) This paragraph applies where-

    (a) proposals to discontinue a foundation, voluntary or foundation special school under section 29(1) or (2), section 31(1) or (2) or paragraph 5 of Schedule 7-

        (i) have been approved or adopted under paragraph 3 or 8 of Schedule 6 or paragraph 8, 9 or 14 of Schedule 7, or

        (ii) have been determined to be implemented under paragraph 4 or 9 of Schedule 6, or

    (b) the Secretary of State has given a direction-

        (i) under section 19(1) requiring a maintained school to be discontinued, or

        (ii) under section 32(1) requiring a foundation special school to be discontinued.

(2) The governing body of the school shall apply to the Secretary of State for him to exercise his powers under sub-paragraph (4) below in relation to any land falling within paragraphs (a) to (f) of paragraph 1(1) which is held by them for the purposes of the school.

(3) Where the school is a member of the group for which a foundation body acts, the body shall apply to the Secretary of State for him to exercise his powers under sub-paragraph (4) below in relation to any land falling within paragraphs (a) to (f) of paragraph 2(1) which is held by it for the purposes of the schools comprising the group.

(4) On an application under sub-paragraph (2) or (3), the Secretary of State may do one or more of the following, namely-

(a) make any such requirement as is mentioned in paragraph 1(3)(a);

(b) direct the governing body or the foundation body, as the case may be, to pay, either to him or to such local authority as he may specify, the whole or any part of the value, as at the date of the direction, of the whole or any part of the land referred to in sub-paragraph (2) or (3), as the case may be; and

(c) in a case where the discontinuance of the school is connected with proposals under section 28 or 31 or paragraph 5 of Schedule 7 to establish, or to make a prescribed alteration to, any other school or schools, require the land or any part of the land to be transferred to the governing body of such maintained school or the temporary governing body of such new school as he may specify.

(5) Where the governing body or foundation body fail to make an application as required by sub-paragraph (2) or (3), as the case may be, the Secretary of State may nevertheless make any such requirement or give any such direction as is mentioned in sub-paragraph (4).

(6) Where the trustees of the school-

(a) dispose of any land falling within paragraph 3(1) or (2), or

(b) wish to use any such land for purposes not connected with the provision of education in maintained schools,paragraph 3 shall apply to them.

Discontinuance of foundation or voluntary school by notice given by its governing body: land and premises

6.–(1) This paragraph applies where the governing body of a foundation or voluntary school apply for the Secretary of State's consent to serve a notice under section 30(1).

(2) If the Secretary of State gives such consent, he may impose any requirements in relation to the governing body or, where the school is a member of the group for which a foundation body acts, the foundation body that he thinks just-

(a) in respect of the repayment of all or part of any expenditure incurred by him as mentioned in section 30(2);

(b) in respect of the transfer to the local education authority of any premises used for the purposes of the school which he is satisfied the authority will need for any purpose connected with education;

(c) (where any premises are to be so transferred) in respect of the payment by the authority of so much of the value of those premises as is just having regard to the extent to which the premises were provided otherwise than at public expense;

(d) (where any premises used for the purposes of the school are not to be so transferred) in respect of the payment by the governing body or the foundation body, as the case may be, to the authority of so much of the value of those premises as is just having regard to the extent to which they were provided at public expense.

(3) In sub-paragraph (2) "at public expense" means at the expense of-
  (a) the Funding Agency for Schools, or
  (b) any local education authority or an authority within section 30(2)(d).

(4) Where the trustees of the school-
  (a) dispose of any land falling within paragraph 3(1) or (2), or
  (b) wish to use any such land for purposes not connected with the provision of education in maintained schools,
paragraph 3 shall apply to them.

Disposal of property held by governing body of maintained school on their dissolution

7.–(1) This paragraph applies in connection with the dissolution of the governing body of a maintained school by virtue of paragraph 4 of Schedule 10.

(2) Where a governing body are so dissolved-
  (a) all land or other property of the governing body which is used or held for the purposes of the school, and
  (b) all rights and liabilities (including rights and liabilities in relation to staff) of the governing body subsisting immediately before the date of dissolution which were acquired or incurred for the purposes of the school,
shall on the date of dissolution be transferred to, and by virtue of this Act vest in-
  (i) the local education authority, or
  (ii) one or more of the following, namely the governing body of a maintained school and the temporary governing body of a new school, if the Secretary of State so directs before the date of dissolution.

(3) Sub-paragraph (2) does not apply to-
  (a) any land or other property for which provision has been made for transfer or payment under paragraph 5(4) or 6(2),
  (b) any property of whatever nature which is held by the governing body on trust for the purposes of the school, or
  (c) unless the Secretary of State otherwise directs by order made before the date of dissolution, any liabilities of the governing body in respect of any loan made to the governing body.

(4) Subject to sub-paragraph (5), a governing body who are to be dissolved as mentioned in sub-paragraph (1) may transfer any land or other property which is held by them on trust for the purposes of the school to any person to hold such land or other property on trust for purposes connected with the provision of education in maintained schools.

(5) Sub-paragraph (4) does not apply to any land or other property so held by the governing body of a foundation, voluntary or foundation special school where any other persons also hold any property on trust for the purposes of the school; and any such land or other property shall on the date of dissolution be transferred to, and by virtue of this Act vest in, those persons.

(6) If any doubt or dispute arises as to the persons to whom any land or other property within sub-paragraph (5) falls to be transferred under that sub-paragraph, it shall be treated as falling to be so transferred to such persons as the Secretary of State thinks proper.

Notice by trustees terminating foundation or voluntary school's occupation of existing site

8.–(1) This paragraph applies where trustees have given a notice falling within section 30(10) which is effective to terminate a foundation or voluntary school's occupation of any land ("the relevant premises").

(2) If any expenditure has been incurred on the relevant premises as mentioned in section 30(2)(a) to (d), the Secretary of State may impose any requirements that he thinks just-

(a) in respect of the repayment by the trustees of all or part of any such expenditure which was incurred by him;

(b) in respect of the transfer by the trustees to the local education authority of the whole or part of the relevant premises where he is satisfied the authority will need them for any purpose connected with education;

(c) (to the extent that the relevant premises are to be so transferred) in respect of the payment by the authority to the trustees of so much of the value of those premises as is just having regard to the extent to which the premises were provided otherwise than at public expense;

(d) (to the extent that the relevant premises are not to be so transferred) in respect of the payment by the trustees to the authority of so much of the value of those premises as is just having regard to the extent to which they were provided at public expense.

(3) In sub-paragraph (2) "at public expense" means at the expense of-

(a) the Funding Agency for Schools, or

(b) any local education authority or an authority within section 30(2)(d).

PART III GENERAL

9.–(1) Where a transfer under paragraph 1(3)(a), 2(3)(a), 4(2), 5(4)(a) or (c), 6(2)(b) or 8(2)(b) of this Schedule relates to registered land, it shall be the duty of the transferor-

(a) to execute any such instrument under the Land Registration Acts 1925 to 1986,

(b) to deliver any such certificate under those Acts, and

(c) to do such other things under those Acts,

as he would be required to execute, deliver or do in the case of a transfer by agreement between the transferor and the transferee.

(2) Paragraphs 6 to 8 of Schedule 10 to the Education Reform Act 1988 (construction of agreements) shall apply in relation to transfers under paragraph 7 of this Schedule as they apply in relation to transfers to which that Schedule applies.

10.–(1) In this Schedule-

(a) "the trustees", in relation to a school, means any person (other than the governing body) holding property on trust for the purposes of the school;

(b) "disposal" includes-

    (i) a compulsory disposal; and

    (ii) in the case of any premises held under a tenancy to which Part II of the Landlord and Tenant Act 1954 ("the 1954 Act") applies, the termination of that tenancy under that Part of that Act;

(c) references to "proceeds of disposal", in relation to a disposal of land, are references to-

    (i) any consideration for the disposal, including rent;

    (ii) any compensation for the disposal, including any compensation paid by the landlord on the quitting of any premises within paragraph (b)(ii) by the governing body, foundation body or trustees (whether or not the compensation is required to be paid by section 37 of the 1954 Act (compensation where order for new tenancy precluded on certain grounds)); and

    (iii) interest which has accrued in respect of any such consideration or compensation;

(d) "new school" has the meaning given by section 72(3).

(2) In paragraphs (b)(ii) and (c)(ii) of sub-paragraph (1) expressions to which a meaning is given for the purposes of the 1954 Act have the same meaning as in that Act.

(3) In paragraphs 1(1), 3(1) and 4(3) references, in relation to the governing body or trustees of a foundation, voluntary or foundation special school and in relation to a time before the appointed day-

(a) to any land being acquired in a particular way, or

(b) to any grant being provided in a particular way,

are references to the land being acquired in that way by, or (as the case may be) to the grant being provided in that way to, the governing body or trustees of that school at a time when it was a voluntary, grant-maintained or grant-maintained special school within the meaning of the Education Act 1996.

(4) In paragraphs 1(1) and 3(1) references, in relation to the governing body or trustees of a foundation, voluntary or foundation special school and in relation to a time before the appointed day, to any expenditure being incurred for the purposes of the school are references to such expenditure being incurred for the purposes of that school at a time when it was a voluntary, grant-maintained or grant-maintained special school within the meaning of the (1996 c. 56.)Education Act 1996.

(5) In paragraph 1(1) references, in relation to the governing body of a foundation, voluntary or foundation special school, to any land being acquired in a particular way include references to the land being acquired in that way by the temporary governing body for the school.

Schedule 22

This Schedule deals with the application of the proceeds of a disposal of school land that, in broad terms, was acquired under the provisions of the education legislation or where public money (from the local education authority or DfEE or the Funding Agency for Schools) has been used for the acquisition or has increased the value of the land, for example by the provision of new buildings.. It's primary objective is to ensure that where land or buildings were provided with public money the value is returned to the public sector.

Three distinct circumstances can arise. The first is where a foundation, voluntary or foundation special school disposes of land, possibly on relocation or because the land is surplus to school requirements, but the school continues in existence, the second is where land is disposed of on closure of a school of any description and the third is where school land is held by trustees or a foundation body that has given a valid notice to the school terminating its right of occupation.

The principles are the same in each case. Land held by a governing body or a foundation body established under the Act may only be disposed of with consent of the Secretary of State. The Secretary of State may give directions as to how the proceeds of sale are to be disposed of.

Where land within the categories covered by the Schedule, i.e. land on which public money as mentioned above has been spent, is being disposed of by trustees, the trustees must notify the local education authority of the disposal and the Secretary of State may direct payment to the authority. The trustees must undertake to apply the proceeds for the purpose of the school or for another foundation, voluntary or foundation special school. If that undertaking is not given the Secretary of State may direct what is to be paid to the authority. A change of use of land by trustees for purposes other than provision of education in maintained schools, for example if the trustees decided to open an independent school on the site, is treated as a sale and the value of the land is treated as the sale proceeds.

If land held by trustees or a foundation body or a governing body is surplus to school requirements and is required by the local education authority for school purposes, the Secretary of State may direct a transfer of that land to the authority for such payment as he thinks fit.

If a foundation, voluntary or foundation special school closes, the Secretary of State will give directions as to the disposal of land held by the governing body which may include directions regarding payments to the Secretary of State (n respect of capital grants made to the school) and the local education authority or the transfer of the land to another school. Similar provisions apply to any proposed disposal of land by trustees or any proposal to use the land for purposes not connected with the provision of education n maintained school. Other property held by a school governing body and existing rights and liabilities (including staff rights and liabilities) will, on dissolution of the school pass either to the local education authority or to another school as the Secretary of State may direct. This does not apply to property held by the governing body on a specific trust for the school, which the governing body may transfer to others on trust for purposes connected with the provision of education in maintained schools, or to loans made to the governing body unless the Secretary of State directs otherwise.

Where trustees validly terminate a school's right to occupy premises the Secretary of State may, if public funds have been spent on the land, require repayment of grant money and/or payment to the local education authority. He may also require the trustees to transfer the land, or part of it, to the local education authority if it is needed for education purposes.

SCHEDULE 23

DETERMINATION, VARIATION AND REVIEW OF STANDARD NUMBERS

PART I DETERMINATION OF STANDARD NUMBERS

Standard numbers for admission to maintained schools

1.–(1) This paragraph applies to any maintained school which immediately before the appointed day was a county, voluntary or grant-maintained school (within the meaning of the (1996 c. 56.)Education Act 1996).

(2) Subject to paragraph 2(1), the standard number applying to a school for any relevant age group in any school year beginning on or after the appointed day shall be-

  (a) in the case of a school which immediately before that day was a county or voluntary school, the standard number applying to the school under sections 417 to 420 of the (1996 c. 56.)Education Act 1996 for that age group in the last school year beginning before that day, or

  (b) in the case of a school which immediately before that day was a grant-maintained school, the approved admission number applying to the school under sections 426 to 428 of that Act for that age group in the school year mentioned in paragraph (a).

Standard numbers on establishment or alteration of school

2.–(1) If proposals under section 28 or paragraph 5 of Schedule 7 have fallen to be implemented in relation to a maintained school-

(a) any number stated in the proposals as the number of pupils which it is intended to admit to the school in any relevant age group shall constitute the standard number applying to the school for that age group in any school year in relation to which the proposals have been implemented; and

(b) in the case of any such proposals which provide for their implementation in stages, any number stated in the proposals as the number of pupils which it is intended to admit to the school in any relevant age group at any particular stage of implementation of the proposals shall constitute the standard number applying to the school for that age group in any school year in relation to which that stage of the proposals has been implemented.

(2) Any standard number applying under sub-paragraph (1) is without prejudice to the application under that sub-paragraph of a new standard number if further proposals under section 28 or paragraph 5 of Schedule 7 fall to be implemented.

(3) References in this paragraph to proposals under section 28 or paragraph 5 of Schedule 7 are to the proposals with any modifications made-

(a) where the school is in England, by the school organisation committee or the adjudicator under paragraph 3 or 5 of Schedule 6 or paragraph 8 or 9 of Schedule 7, or

(b) where the school is in Wales, by the Secretary of State under paragraph 8 or 10 of Schedule 6 or paragraph 14 of Schedule 7.

PART II VARIATION OF STANDARD NUMBERS: ENGLAND

APPLICATION OF PART II

3. This Part of this Schedule applies to schools in England.

Variation of standard numbers

4.–(1) The Secretary of State may by order applying to maintained schools of any class or description vary any standard number that would otherwise apply by virtue of paragraph 1 or 2.

(2) Subject to sub-paragraphs (3) to (5), the school organisation committee or the adjudicator may make a decision varying any standard number that would otherwise apply to an individual school by virtue of paragraph 1 or 2 or by virtue of any order made under sub-paragraph (1).

(3) A decision under sub-paragraph (2) increasing a standard number may be made on the application of the admission authority for the school or on an application made by the governing body or local education authority in accordance with section 93(7).

(4) A decision under sub-paragraph (2) reducing a standard number may only be made on the application of the admission authority for the school.

(5) A decision under sub-paragraph (2) is subject to the procedure provided for in paragraphs 5 and 6.

Procedure for application to vary standard number

5.–(1) Where the local education authority or the governing body intend to apply for a variation under paragraph 4(2) of any standard number applying to a school under paragraph 1, 2 or 4 for any age group in any year-

(a) they shall publish their proposals relating to the variation in such manner, and containing such information, as may be prescribed, and

(b) they shall send-
    (i) their application,
    (ii) a copy of the published proposals, and
    (iii) such information in connection with those proposals as may be prescribed,
    to the school organisation committee.

(2) Before making such an application, the local education authority or the governing body shall consult the governing body or the local education authority, as the case may be.

(3) Sub-paragraph (2) shall not apply in relation to any application made by the local education authority or the governing body in accordance with section 93(7).

(4) Any person may make objections to any proposals published under sub-paragraph (1)

(5) Objections under sub-paragraph (4) shall be sent to the school organisation committee within such period as may be prescribed.

(6) Where any proposals published under this paragraph relate to a school which is situated in an area other than that of the local education authority who maintain the school, the provisions of this paragraph and paragraph 6 shall have effect in relation to the proposals with such modifications as may be prescribed.

Decision on application to vary standard number

6.–(1) Subject to the following provisions of this paragraph, on an application for a decision under paragraph 4(2), the school organisation committee may-

(a) make a decision under that provision varying the standard number to the number proposed;

(b) where the application is for an increase in the standard number, make a decision under that provision increasing the standard number to such number (less than the number proposed) as they think desirable;

(c) where the application is for a reduction of the standard number, make a decision under that provision reducing the standard number to such number (greater than the number proposed) as they think desirable; or

(d) decide not to vary the standard number.

(2) Before making any decision in accordance with paragraph (b) or (c) of sub-paragraph (1), the committee shall consult the local education authority and the governing body of the school.

(3) When making any decision in accordance with sub-paragraph (1), the committee shall have regard to-

   (a) any guidance given from time to time by the Secretary of State,

   (b) the school organisation plan for the area in which the school is situated, and

   (c) where the application is for the reduction of a standard number at a primary school, any limit imposed under section 1 which applies to that school and to any other school which is likely to be affected if any reduction of that number were to be made.

(4) Subject to sub-paragraph (5), the committee shall not make a decision reducing a standard number unless they are satisfied that the reduction is necessary, having regard to the school's capacity to accommodate pupils.

(5) Where-

   (a) an application is for a reduction of any standard number applicable to admissions to an infant class (as defined by section 4); and

   (b) the committee are satisfied that the admission to the school in any school year of a number of children in any relevant age group equal to the relevant standard number would cause prejudice of the kind referred to in section 86(3)(a) by reason of measures required to be taken as mentioned in subsection (4) of that section,

the committee shall make a decision under paragraph 4(2) reducing the standard number by the smallest number which they consider sufficient to avoid such prejudice arising.

(6) Where the school organisation committee make a decision in accordance with paragraph (a), (b) or (c) of sub-paragraph (1), then subject to sub-paragraph (2) the committee may decide that the standard number shall be varied with effect from a date other than that specified in the application.

(7) If-

   (a) by the end of such period as may be specified in or determined in accordance with regulations, the committee have not voted on the question whether to vary the standard number under sub-paragraph (1), and

   (b) the body by whom the application was made request the committee to refer the application to the adjudicator, they shall refer the application to the adjudicator.

(8) If the committee-

   (a) have voted on any matter which (in accordance with regulations under paragraph 5 of Schedule 4) falls to be decided by them under sub-paragraph (1) by a unanimous decision, but

   (b) have failed to reach such a decision on that matter,

they shall refer the application to the adjudicator.

(9) Where any application is referred to the adjudicator under sub-paragraph (7) or (8)-

(a) he shall consider the application afresh; and

(b) sub-paragraphs (1) to (6) shall apply to him in connection with his decision on the application as they apply to the committee.

(10) Regulations may make provision for enabling the school organisation committee or the adjudicator-

(a) to review any decision of theirs made in accordance with sub-paragraph (1), and

(b) (if appropriate) to revoke or vary any such decision,

in such circumstances as may be prescribed.

(11) For the purposes of sub-paragraph (4) a school's capacity to accommodate pupils shall be calculated having regard to any guidance given from time to time by the Secretary of State.

PART III VARIATION OF STANDARD NUMBERS: WALES

APPLICATION OF PART III

7. This Part of this Schedule applies to schools in Wales.

Variation of standard numbers

8.–(1) The Secretary of State may by order applying to maintained schools of any class or description vary any standard number that would otherwise apply by virtue of paragraph 1 or 2.

(2) Subject to sub-paragraphs (3) to (5), the Secretary of State may make a decision varying any standard number that would otherwise apply to an individual school by virtue of paragraph 1 or 2 or by virtue of any order made under sub-paragraph (1).

(3) A decision under sub-paragraph (2) increasing a standard number may be made on the application of the admission authority for the school or on an application made by the governing body or local education authority in accordance with section 93(7).

(4) A decision under sub-paragraph (2) reducing a standard number may only be made on the application of the admission authority for the school.

(5) A decision under sub-paragraph (2) is subject to the procedure provided for in paragraphs 9 and 10.

Procedure for application to vary standard number

9.–(1) Where the local education authority or the governing body intend to apply for a variation under paragraph 8(2) of any standard number applying to a school under paragraph 1, 2 or 8 for any age group in any year-

(a) they shall publish their proposals relating to the variation in such manner, and containing such information, as may be prescribed, and

(b) they shall send-
    (i) their application,
    (ii) a copy of the published proposals, and
    (iii) such information in connection with those proposals as may be prescribed,
to the Secretary of State.

(2) Before making such an application, the local education authority or the governing body shall consult the governing body or the local education authority, as the case may be.

(3) In making such an application, the local education authority or the governing body shall have regard to any guidance given from time to time by the Secretary of State (including any such guidance as to the manner in which a school's capacity to accommodate pupils should be calculated).

(4) Sub-paragraph (2) shall not apply in relation to any application made by the local education authority or the governing body in accordance with section 93(7).

(5) Any person may make objections to any proposals published under sub-paragraph (1)

(6) Objections under sub-paragraph (5) shall be sent to the Secretary of State within such period as may be prescribed.

(7) Where any proposals published under this paragraph relate to a school which is situated in an area other than that of the local education authority who maintain the school, the provisions of this paragraph and paragraph 10 shall have effect in relation to the proposals with such modifications as may be prescribed.

Decision on application to vary standard number

10.–(1) Subject to the following provisions of this paragraph, on an application for a decision under paragraph 8(2), the Secretary of State may-

  (a) make a decision under that provision varying the standard number to the number proposed;
  (b) where the application is for an increase in the standard number, make a decision under that provision increasing the standard number to such number (less than the number proposed) as he thinks desirable;
  (c) where the application is for a reduction of the standard number, make a decision under that provision reducing the standard number to such number (greater than the number proposed) as he thinks desirable; or
  (d) decide not to vary the standard number.

(2) Before making any decision in accordance with paragraph (b) or (c) of sub-paragraph (1), the Secretary of State shall consult the local education authority and the governing body of the school.

(3) When making any decision in accordance with sub-paragraph (1), the Secretary of State shall have regard to-

  (a) the school organisation plan for the area in which the school is situated, and

(b) where the application is for the reduction of a standard number at a primary school, any limit imposed under section 1 which applies to that school and to any other school which is likely to be affected if any reduction of that number were to be made.

(4) Subject to sub-paragraph (5), the Secretary of State shall not make a decision reducing a standard number unless he is satisfied that the reduction is necessary, having regard to the school's capacity to accommodate pupils.

(5) Where-

(a) an application is for a reduction of any standard number applicable to admissions to an infant class (as defined by section 4); and

(b) the Secretary of State is satisfied that the admission to the school in any school year of a number of children in any relevant age group equal to the relevant standard number would cause prejudice of the kind referred to in section 86(3)(a) by reason of measures required to be taken as mentioned in subsection (4) of that section,

the Secretary of State shall make a decision under paragraph 8(2) reducing the standard number by the smallest number which he considers sufficient to avoid such prejudice arising.

(6) Where the Secretary of State makes a decision in accordance with paragraph (a), (b) or (c) of sub-paragraph (1), then subject to sub-paragraph (2) he may decide that the standard number shall be varied with effect from a date other than that specified in the application.

(7) Regulations may make provision for enabling the Secretary of State-

(a) to review any decision of his made in accordance with sub-paragraph (1), and

(b) (if appropriate) to revoke or vary any such decision,

in such circumstances as may be prescribed.

PART IV REVIEW OF STANDARD NUMBERS

11.–(1) The admission authority for a maintained school shall keep under review any standard numbers applying to the school under paragraph 1, 2, 4 or 8, as the case may be, having regard to-

(a) the school's capacity to accommodate pupils, and

(b) in the case of any standard number applicable to admissions to an infant class (as defined by section 4), the need to secure that the admission to the school in any school year of a number of children in any relevant age group equal to the relevant standard number would not cause prejudice of the kind referred to in section 86(3)(a) by reason of measures required to be taken as mentioned in subsection (4) of that section.

(2) The admission authority for a maintained school containing any infant class (as defined by section 4) shall in particular carry out a review under sub-paragraph (1) as soon as reasonably practicable following the coming into force of regulations under section 1 by virtue of which any limit on class sizes is to apply, or be varied, in relation to any such class at the school.

(3) Where, as a result of a review under sub-paragraph (1), the authority consider that any standard number at the school should be varied in order to enable the objective referred to in sub-paragraph (1)(b) to be achieved, they shall make an application for a decision under paragraph 4(2) or 8(2) (as the case may be) varying the standard number.

(4) For the purposes of sub-paragraph (1) a school's capacity to accommodate pupils shall be calculated having regard to any guidance given from time to time by the Secretary of State.

Schedule 23

This Schedule deals with standard numbers for school admission purposes.

Existing schools carry forward their previous standard number. New schools, or schools that implement alterations approved under the Act, will have a standard number as shown in the relevant proposals.

Standard numbers for schools in England can be varied by the Secretary of State, the school organisation committee and the adjudicator. A proposal to increase the standard number can come from the local education authority or governing body. A proposal to reduce it can only come from the school's admission authority. If the proposal comes from the local education authority it must first consult with the governing body and vice versa unless the proposal is made under S. 93 (7) in which case consultation would be pointless since the application follows a proposal which has already been notified. The proposal must then be published. Anyone can object to the school organisation committee which then has to consider the proposal. The school organisation committee has power to approve the proposal as it stands or in modified form but only after consultation with the local education authority and the governing body. It must have regard to Secretary of State guidance, the school organisation plan and, if the school is a primary school and the proposal is to reduce its standard number, any limit on infant class sizes applying to the school and any other school likely to be affected by the change. A reduction can only be authorised if it is necessary in the light of the school's capacity to accommodate pupils (as to which the school organisation committee must have regard to Secretary of State guidance) and where the reduction is necessary in connection with infant class size limits it must be the smallest reduction that can be made to comply. If the school organisation committee does not deal with the application within time limits the applicant may ask for it to go to the adjudicator. If the committee votes but is not unanimous then it is automatically referred to the adjudicator.

In Wales a broadly similar process applies but decisions are made the Secretary of State who has to act under the same principles.

Standard numbers have to be kept under review by the admission authority for the school. It must have regard to the school's capacity to accommodate pupils, and the obligation to comply with infant class size limits.

SCHEDULE 24

ADMISSION APPEALS

PART I CONSTITUTION OF APPEAL PANELS

Appeal arrangements made by local education authorities

1.–(1) An appeal pursuant to arrangements made by a local education authority under section 94(1) shall be to an appeal panel constituted in accordance with this paragraph.

(2) An appeal panel shall consist of three or five members appointed by the authority from-

(a) persons who are eligible to be lay members; and

(b) persons who have experience in education, are acquainted with educational conditions in the area of the authority or are parents of registered pupils at a school.

(3) Of the members of an appeal panel-

(a) at least one must be a person who is eligible to be a lay member and is appointed as such; and

(b) at least one must be a person falling within sub-paragraph (2)(b).

(4) For the purposes of this paragraph a person is eligible to be a lay member if he is a person without personal experience in the management of any school or the provision of education in any school (disregarding any such experience as a governor or in any other voluntary capacity).

(5) Sufficient persons may be appointed by the authority under this paragraph to enable two or more appeal panels to sit at the same time.

(6) No person shall be a member of an appeal panel if he is disqualified by virtue of sub-paragraph (7).

(7) The following persons are disqualified for membership of an appeal panel-

(a) any member of the authority or of the governing body of the school in question;

(b) any person employed by the authority or the governing body, other than a person employed as a teacher;

(c) any person who has, or at any time has had, any connection with the authority or the school, or with any person within paragraph (b), of a kind which might reasonably be taken to raise doubts about his ability to act impartially in relation to the authority or the school.

(8) A person employed as a teacher by the authority shall not be taken, by reason only of that employment, to have such a connection with the authority as is mentioned in sub-paragraph (7)(c).

(9) A person shall not be a member of an appeal panel for the consideration of an appeal against a decision if he was among those who made the decision or took part in discussions as to whether the decision should be made.

(10) A person who is a teacher at a school shall not be a member of an appeal panel for the consideration of an appeal involving a question whether a child is to be admitted to that school.

(11) Where, at any time after an appeal panel consisting of five members have begun to consider an appeal, any of the members-

(a) dies, or
(b) becomes unable through illness to continue as a member,

the panel may continue with their consideration and determination of the appeal so long as the number of the remaining members is not less than three and the requirements of sub-paragraph (3) are satisfied.

Appeal arrangements made by governing bodies

2.–(1) An appeal pursuant to arrangements made by the governing body of a foundation or voluntary aided school under section 94(2) shall be to an appeal panel constituted in accordance with this paragraph.

(2) An appeal panel shall consist of three or five members appointed by the governing body from-

(a) persons who are eligible to be lay members; and
(b) persons who have experience in education, are acquainted with educational conditions in the area of the school or are parents of registered pupils at a school.

(3) Of the members of an appeal panel-

(a) at least one must be a person who is eligible to be a lay member and is appointed as such; and
(b) at least one must be a person falling within sub-paragraph (2)(b).

(4) For the purposes of this paragraph a person is eligible to be a lay member if he is a person without personal experience in the management of any school or the provision of education in any school (disregarding any such experience as a governor or in any other voluntary capacity).

(5) Sufficient persons may be appointed by the governing body under this paragraph to enable two or more appeal panels to sit at the same time.

(6) No person shall be a member of an appeal panel if he is disqualified by virtue of sub-paragraph (7).

(7) The following persons are disqualified for membership of an appeal panel-

(a) any member of the local education authority by whom the school is maintained or of the governing body;

(b) any person employed by the authority or the governing body, other than a person employed as a teacher;

(c) any person who has, or at any time has had, any connection with the authority or the school, or with any person within paragraph (b), of a kind which might reasonably be taken to raise doubts about his ability to act impartially in relation to the authority or the school.

(8) A person employed as a teacher by the authority shall not be taken, by reason only of that employment, to have such a connection with the authority as is mentioned in sub-paragraph (7)(c).

(9) A person who is a teacher at a school shall not be a member of an appeal panel for the consideration of an appeal involving a question whether a child is to be admitted to that school.

(10) Where, at any time after an appeal panel consisting of five members have begun to consider an appeal, any of the members-

(a) dies, or

(b) becomes unable through illness to continue as a member,

the panel may continue with their consideration and determination of the appeal so long as the number of the remaining members is not less than three and the requirements of sub-paragraph (3) are satisfied.

3.–(1) Where (by virtue of section 94(3)) joint arrangements are made under section 94(2) by the governing bodies of two or more schools, paragraph 2 shall apply as if-

(a) (except in sub-paragraph (7)) any reference to the governing body were a reference to the governing bodies of both or all the schools; and

(b) in sub-paragraph (7), any reference to the governing body of the school in question or to that school were a reference to any of those governing bodies or to any of those schools (as the case may be).

(2) An appeal pursuant to such joint arrangements shall be to an appeal panel constituted in accordance with paragraph 2 as it so applies.

Joint arrangements by local education authorities and governing bodies

4.–(1) Where (by virtue of section 94(4)) joint arrangements are made by a local education authority and the governing body or bodies of one or more schools, paragraph 1 shall apply in relation to those arrangements as it applies in relation to arrangements made by a local education authority under section 94(1), but as if in sub-paragraph (7) any reference to the governing body of the school in question or to that school were a reference to the governing body of any school to which the arrangements relate or to any such school (as the case may be).

(2) An appeal pursuant to such joint arrangements shall be to an appeal panel constituted in accordance with paragraph 1 as it so applies.

Allowances for members

5.–(1) For the purpose of the payment of financial loss allowance under section 173(4) of the Local Government Act 1972, that provision shall apply, with any necessary modifications, to any member of an appeal panel constituted in accordance with paragraph 1 or 2 (or in accordance with either of those paragraphs as it applies by virtue of paragraph 3 or 4) as it applies to any member of a parish or community council; and such an appeal panel shall be included in the bodies to which section 174 of that Act (travelling and subsistence allowances) applies.

(2) In section 174(1) of that Act, in its application to a panel in accordance with sub-paragraph (1), the reference to payments at rates determined by the body in question shall be read as a reference to payments at rates determined-

(a) by the authority, if the panel is constituted in accordance with paragraph 1 (or in accordance with that paragraph as it applies by virtue of paragraph 4); and
(b) otherwise by the governing body or bodies of the school or schools in question.

Duty to advertise for lay members

6. The Secretary of State may by regulations require any local education authority or governing body who are required by section 94(1) or (2) to make arrangements under that provision-

(a) to advertise, in such manner and at such times as may be prescribed, for persons eligible to be lay members of any appeal panel required to be constituted for the purposes of such arrangements to apply to the authority or body for appointment as such members, and
(b) in appointing persons as such members, to consider any persons eligible to be so appointed who have applied to the authority or body in response to an advertisement placed in pursuance of sub-paragraph (a) above.

Indemnity

7.–(1) Any local education authority or governing body required to make arrangements under section 94(1) or (2) shall indemnify the members of any appeal panel required to be constituted for the purposes of those arrangements against any reasonable legal costs and expenses reasonably incurred by those members in connection with any decision or action taken by them in good faith in pursuance of their functions as members of that panel.

(2) Where any such panel is constituted in accordance with-

(a) paragraph 1 as it applies by virtue of paragraph 4, or
(b) paragraph 2 as it applies by virtue of paragraph 3,

any liability arising under sub-paragraph (1) above shall be a joint and several liability of the bodies by whom the joint arrangements are made unless otherwise previously agreed in writing between those bodies.

PART II PROCEDURE

8. In this Part of this Schedule "appeal" means an appeal pursuant to any arrangements made under section 94.

9. An appeal shall be by notice in writing setting out the grounds on which it is made.

10. An appeal panel shall give the appellant an opportunity of appearing and making oral representations, and may allow him to be accompanied by a friend or to be represented.

11. The matters to be taken into account by an appeal panel in considering an appeal shall include-

    (a) any preference expressed by the appellant in respect of the child as mentioned in section 86, and
    (b) the arrangements for the admission of pupils published by the local education authority or the governing body under section 92.

12. Where the decision under appeal was made on the ground that prejudice of the kind referred to in section 86(3)(a) would arise as mentioned in subsection (4) of that section, an appeal panel shall determine that a place is to be offered to the child only if they are satisfied-

    (a) that the decision was not one which a reasonable admission authority would make in the circumstances of the case; or
    (b) that the child would have been offered a place if the admission arrangements (as published under section 92) had been properly implemented.

13.–(1) Appeals shall be heard in private except when the body or bodies by whom the arrangements under section 94 are made direct otherwise; but-

    (a) if the panel so direct, one member of the local education authority may attend, as an observer, any hearing of an appeal by an appeal panel constituted in accordance with paragraph 1;
    (b) if the panel so direct, one member of the governing body of the school in question may attend, as an observer, any hearing of an appeal by an appeal panel constituted in accordance with paragraph 1 or 2 (or in accordance with paragraph 2 as it applies by virtue of paragraph 3); and
    (c) one member of the Council on Tribunals may attend, as an observer, any meeting of any appeal panel at which an appeal is considered.

(2) For the purposes of sub-paragraph (1), an appeal to an appeal panel constituted in accordance with paragraph 1 as it applies by virtue of paragraph 4 shall be treated-

    (a) as an appeal to an appeal panel constituted in accordance with paragraph 1 if it relates to a community or voluntary controlled school; and
    (b) as an appeal to an appeal panel constituted in accordance with paragraph 2 if it relates to a foundation or voluntary aided school.

14. In the event of a disagreement between the members of an appeal panel, the appeal under consideration shall be decided by a simple majority of the votes cast and, in the case of an equality of votes, the chairman of the panel shall have a second or casting vote.

15.–(1) The decision of an appeal panel and the grounds on which it is made shall be communicated by the panel in writing to-

    (a) the appellant and the local education authority, and

    (b) in the case of an appeal to an appeal panel constituted in accordance with paragraph 2 (or in accordance with that paragraph as it applies by virtue of paragraph 3), to the governing body by whom or on whose behalf the decision appealed against was made.

(2) For the purposes of sub-paragraph (1), an appeal to an appeal panel constituted in accordance with paragraph 1 as it applies by virtue of paragraph 4 shall be treated as an appeal to an appeal panel constituted in accordance with paragraph 2, if it relates to a foundation or voluntary aided school.

16. Subject to paragraphs 9 to 15, all matters relating to the procedure on appeals, including the time within which they are to be brought, shall be determined by the body or bodies by whom the arrangements under section 94 are made.

Power of Secretary of State to make amendments

17. The Secretary of State may by order make such amendments of this Schedule as he considers expedient.

Schedule 24

This Schedule deals with the process for appeals against a refusal to comply with parental preference for admission to a school.

The appeal panel, whether set up by the local education authority for appeals in relation to community or voluntary controlled schools or by the governing body for appeals in relation to foundation or voluntary aided schools, has either three or five members who must either be lay members (a person without personal experience in the management of a school or provision of education except as a governor or in another voluntary capacity) or a person who is either experienced in education, acquainted with the educational conditions in the area or a parent of a registered pupil in a school – not necessarily in that authority. The panel must have one member at least from each category.

No-one who is:-

- *A member of the local education authority*

- *A governor of or teacher at the school in question*

- *A person employed by the local education authority (except as a teacher) or the governing body of the school in question*

- *Any person who has or at any time has had any connection with the authority, the school in question, or any employee of either of a kind that might reasonably throw doubt on that person's impartiality*

- *Any person who was involved in the decision not to admit the pupil*

may be a member of the appeal panel.

An appeal panel that starts with five members may continue even if one or two members are unable to continue. An appeal panel cannot function with less than three members.

Appeal panel members may be paid expenses and must be indemnified against all costs and expenses incurred by them as a result anything they do in good faith as panel members.

The local education authority must advertise for lay members.

The appeal must be in writing and specify the grounds on which it is made. The appellant must have an opportunity to appear and be heard and to be accompanied by a friend or be represented. The appeal panel must take into account the reasons for the parent's preference and the published admission arrangements. If the appeal relates to an application for a place where infant class size limits would be breached if allowed then the panel can only allow the appeal if satisfied either that the decision was not one that a reasonable admission authority would make or that the place would have been offered if the published admission arrangements had been properly implemented.

Appeals are normally heard in private although the body making the appeal arrangements can decide to hold them in public. The panel may allow a member of the admission authority (i.e. the local education authority or the governing body) to attend as an observer and the Council on Tribunals has the right for a member to observe. The decision is by simple majority. The decision, and reasons, must be given in writing to all concerned.

The body setting up the appeal decides any procedural aspects that are not covered by the Schedule.

The Secretary of State may amend these provisions.

SCHEDULE 25

Duty to notify governing body of decision to admit child

1. Where any such decision as is mentioned in section 95(2) is made by or on behalf of a local education authority, the authority shall give the governing body of the school notice in writing-

   (a) of that decision; and

   (b) of the governing body's right to appeal against the decision in accordance with paragraph 2.

Time limit on appealing

2. An appeal by the governing body against any such decision must be made not later than the 15th school day after the day on which they are given the notice under paragraph 1.

Appeal panels

3.–(1) Subject to sub-paragraphs (2) and (3) below, paragraphs 1, 5, 6 and 7 of Schedule 24 (school admission appeals) shall have effect in relation to appeals under section 95(2) as they have effect in relation to appeals under section 94(1).

(2) A person shall not be a member of an appeal panel for the consideration of an appeal under section 95(2) if he has to any extent been involved in any previous consideration of the question whether the child in question should or should not be reinstated at any school from which he has at any time been permanently excluded, or in any previous appeal relating to the child under section 95(2).

(3) In this paragraph "appeal panel" means an appeal panel constituted in accordance with Part I of Schedule 24, as it applies in accordance with this paragraph.

Procedure on an appeal

4. In the following provisions of this Schedule-

   "appeal" means an appeal under section 95(2); and

   "appeal panel" means such an appeal panel as is mentioned in paragraph 3(3) above.

5. An appeal shall be by notice in writing setting out the grounds on which it is made.

6.–(1) The appeal panel shall meet to consider an appeal on such date as the local education authority may determine.

(2) The date so determined must not be later than the 15th school day after the day on which the appeal is lodged.

7. On an appeal the panel shall allow-

   (a) the local education authority and the governing body to make written representations;
   (b) an officer of the authority nominated by the authority, and a governor nominated by the governing body, to appear and make oral representations; and
   (c) the governing body to be represented.

8. In considering an appeal the appeal panel shall have regard to-

   (a) the reasons for the local education authority's decision that the child in question should be admitted; and
   (b) any reasons put forward by the governing body as to why the child's admission would be inappropriate.

9. Appeals shall be heard in private except when the local education authority direct otherwise; but-

   (a) if the panel so direct, one member of the local education authority may attend, as an observer, any hearing of an appeal by an appeal panel; and
   (b) one member of the Council on Tribunals may attend, as an observer, any meeting of an appeal panel at which an appeal is considered.

10. Two or more appeals may be combined and dealt with in the same proceedings if the appeal panel consider that it is expedient to do so because the issues raised by the appeals are the same or connected.

11. In the event of a disagreement between the members of an appeal panel, the appeal under consideration shall be decided by a simple majority of the votes cast and, in the case of an equality of votes, the chairman of the panel shall have a second or casting vote.

12. The decision of an appeal panel and the grounds on which it is made shall-

   (a) be communicated by the panel in writing to the local education authority and the governing body, and
   (b) be so communicated by the end of the second school day after the conclusion of the hearing of the appeal.

13. Subject to paragraphs 5 to 12, all matters relating to the procedure on appeals shall be determined by the local education authority.

Power of Secretary of State to make amendments

14. The Secretary of State may by order make such amendments of this Schedule as he considers expedient.

Schedule 25

This Schedule deals with the process whereby a governing body can appeal against a decision by the local education authority to admit a pupil who has been permanently excluded twice and to whom S. 87 applies, excluding the right for parental preference to be complied with. This will apply only to community and voluntary controlled schools that do not deal with their own admissions.

The appeal panel is constituted in the same way as for admission appeals under Schedule 24. The governing body must give notice of appeal in writing with grounds within 15 school days of notification of the decision to admit. The local education authority arranges the appeal which must be heard within 15 school days after the appeal is lodged. The local education authority and the governing body may make written representations and be heard at the hearing. The governing body may be represented and the panel must consider the reasons put forward by both sides. The parent has no right to attend or make representations.

Appeals are normally heard in private although the local education authority can decide to hold them in public. The panel may allow a member of the local education authority to attend as an observer and the Council on Tribunals has the right for a member to observe. Two or more appeals may be heard at the same time if they raise the same issues or are connected and the decision is by simple majority. The decision, and reasons, must be given in writing to all concerned not later than the end of the second school day after the hearing ends.

The local education authority decides any procedural aspects that are not covered by the Schedule.

The Secretary of State may amend these provisions.

SCHEDULE 26

INSPECTION OF NURSERY EDUCATION

Introductory

1.–(1) In this Schedule "relevant nursery education" means-

(a) nursery education which is provided by a local education authority;

(b) nursery education which is provided by any other person who is (or is to be) in receipt of financial assistance given by such an authority and whose provision of nursery education is taken into account by the authority in formulating proposals for the purposes of section 120(2)(a); or

(c) nursery education in respect of which grants are (or are to be) made under arrangements under section 1 of the Nursery Education and Grant-Maintained Schools Act 1996.

(2) In this Schedule "nursery education under consideration for funding" means nursery education provided by a person to whom a local education authority are considering giving financial assistance and whose provision of nursery education would fall to be taken into account by the authority in formulating proposals for the purposes of section 120(2)(a).

(3) Where-

(a) any education is for the time being provided at any premises for children who have not attained the age prescribed for the purposes of section 118(1)(b), and

(b) that education is provided by a person-

    (i) who proposes to provide nursery education at those premises, and

    (ii) to whom a local education authority are considering giving financial assistance in the event of his providing that nursery education, and

    (iii) whose provision of that nursery education would fall to be taken into account by the authority in formulating proposals for the purposes of section 120(2)(a),

this Schedule shall apply in relation to the education for the time being provided for the children mentioned in paragraph (a) above as it applies in relation to nursery education under consideration for funding.

2.–(1) In this Schedule "the Chief Inspector" means-

(a) as respects nursery education provided in England, Her Majesty's Chief Inspector of Schools in England, and

(b) as respects nursery education provided in Wales, Her Majesty's Chief Inspector of Schools in Wales.

(2) In this Schedule references to registered nursery education inspectors are to persons registered under paragraph 8.

(3) In this Schedule "members of the Inspectorate" means-

(a) the Chief Inspector,

(b) Her Majesty's Inspectors, and

(c) additional inspectors with whom the Chief Inspector has made arrangements to give him assistance under paragraph 2 of Schedule 1 to the School Inspections Act 1996.

(4) In sub-paragraph (3)(b) "Her Majesty's Inspectors" means-

(a) as respects nursery education provided in England, Her Majesty's Inspectors of Schools in England, and

(b) as respects nursery education provided in Wales, Her Majesty's Inspectors of Schools in Wales.

General functions of the Chief Inspector

3. The Chief Inspector has the general duty of keeping the Secretary of State informed about-

    (a) the quality and standards of relevant nursery education, and

    (b) the spiritual, moral, social and cultural development of children for whom relevant nursery education is provided.

4. When asked to do so by the Secretary of State, the Chief Inspector shall give advice to the Secretary of State on such matters relating to relevant nursery education as may be specified in the Secretary of State's request.

5. The Chief Inspector may at any time give advice to the Secretary of State on any matter connected with-

    (a) relevant nursery education generally, or

    (b) relevant nursery education, or nursery education under consideration for funding, provided at particular premises.

Inspections

6.–(1) The Chief Inspector-

    (a) shall secure that relevant nursery education provided at any premises is inspected by a registered nursery education inspector at such intervals as may be prescribed,

    (b) shall secure that relevant nursery education, or nursery education under consideration for funding, provided at any premises is inspected by a registered nursery education inspector at any time when the Secretary of State requires the Chief Inspector to secure its inspection, and

    (c) may secure that relevant nursery education, or nursery education under consideration for funding, provided at any premises is inspected by a registered nursery education inspector at any other time when the Chief Inspector considers that it would be appropriate for it to be inspected.

(2) Sub-paragraph (1)(a) does not apply to nursery education provided at a school to which section 10 of the School Inspections Act 1996 (inspections of certain schools by inspectors registered under that Act) applies.

(3) The Chief Inspector may comply with sub-paragraph (1) either by organising inspections or by making arrangements with others for them to organise inspections.

(4) Where an inspection under this paragraph is to be undertaken of nursery education provided at premises which are also liable to inspection under section 76 of the Children Act 1989 (inspection by person authorised by local authority of premises on which child minding is being carried on or day care is being provided for children), the person organising the inspection under this paragraph shall, before that inspection is undertaken, consult the local authority with power to authorise an inspection of the premises under that section.

(5) In prescribing the intervals mentioned in sub-paragraph (1)(a) the Secretary of State may make provision as to the period within which the first inspection of education provided at any premises is to take place under this Schedule.

(6) A requirement such as is mentioned in sub-paragraph (1)(b) may be imposed in relation to particular premises or a class of premises.

7. A person conducting an inspection under paragraph 6 shall report on the quality and standards of the nursery education provided and, so far as it is reasonably practicable to do so, on the spiritual, moral, social and cultural development of the children for whom the education is provided.

Registration of nursery education inspectors

8.–(1) Her Majesty's Chief Inspector of Schools in England shall establish and maintain a register of nursery education inspectors for England and Her Majesty's Chief Inspector of Schools in Wales shall establish and maintain a register of nursery education inspectors for Wales.

(2) The Chief Inspector-

(a) shall give guidance to registered nursery education inspectors and such other persons as he considers appropriate in connection with inspections under paragraph 6 and the making of reports of such inspections, and

(b) shall keep under review the system of inspections under paragraph 6 and, in particular, the standard of such inspections and of the reports made of them.

(3) The Chief Inspector shall not register a person under this paragraph unless, having regard to any conditions that he proposes to impose under sub-paragraph (5)(c), it appears to him that the person-

(a) is a fit and proper person for discharging the functions of a registered nursery education inspector, and

(b) will be capable of conducting inspections under paragraph 6 competently and effectively and no person shall be so registered if he falls within a category of persons prescribed for the purposes of this sub-paragraph.

(4) An application for registration under this paragraph-

(a) shall be made in such manner, and be accompanied by such particulars, as the Chief Inspector may direct, and

(b) shall be accompanied by such fee (if any) as may be prescribed.

(5) On an application duly made under this paragraph the Chief Inspector may-

(a) register the applicant,

(b) refuse to register him, or

(c) register him subject to such conditions as the Chief Inspector considers it appropriate to impose.

(6) Conditions imposed under sub-paragraph (5)(c) may be conditions applying generally in relation to all cases, or particular classes of case, or such conditions together with specific conditions applying in the particular case.

(7) Where a person is registered subject to conditions imposed under sub-paragraph (5)(c), he shall be taken to be authorised to act as a registered nursery education inspector only so far as those conditions permit.

(8) The period for which any registration is to have effect shall be determined by the Chief Inspector and shall be entered in the register kept by him.

(9) Nothing in sub-paragraph (8) is to be taken as preventing a registered nursery education inspector from applying for a fresh registration to take effect immediately on the expiry of his current registration.

9.–(1) If the Chief Inspector is satisfied that any of the conditions mentioned in sub-paragraph (2) is satisfied with respect to a nursery education inspector registered in his register, he may remove the name of that inspector from that register.

(2) The conditions are that-
  (a) he is no longer a fit and proper person for discharging the functions of a registered nursery education inspector under paragraph 6,
  (b) he is no longer capable of conducting inspections under that paragraph competently and effectively,
  (c) there has been a significant failure on his part to comply with any condition imposed under paragraph 8(5)(c) subject to which his registration has effect,
  (d) he has, without reasonable explanation, produced a report of an inspection under paragraph 6 which is, in whole or in part, seriously misleading.

(3) The Chief Inspector may vary any condition subject to which the registration of an inspector has effect, or vary the registration of an inspector by imposing a condition subject to which it will have effect, if he is satisfied-
  (a) that he is authorised by sub-paragraph (1) to remove the name of the inspector from his register, or
  (b) that it would otherwise be in the public interest for him to do so.

(4) References in this Schedule to a condition imposed under paragraph 8(5)(c) include a condition imposed under sub-paragraph (3).

(5) Either Chief Inspector may, in exercising his functions under this paragraph with respect to a registered nursery education inspector, have regard to any action taken by the other Chief Inspector with respect to that inspector.

10.–(1) Any person who is aggrieved by-
  (a) the refusal of the Chief Inspector to renew his registration under paragraph 8,
  (b) the imposition or variation of any condition subject to which he is registered under that paragraph, or
  (c) the removal of his name from the register under paragraph 9,
may appeal against the Chief Inspector's decision.

(2) An appeal under sub-paragraph (1) shall be made to a tribunal with the same constitution as a tribunal to hear an appeal under section 9 of the School Inspections Act 1996; and paragraph 2 (procedure) and paragraph 3 (staff) of Schedule 2 to that Act apply to tribunals to hear appeals under sub-paragraph (1) as they apply to tribunals to hear appeals under that section.

(3) No decision against which an appeal may be made under sub-paragraph (1) shall have effect until-

(a) any appeal against it which is duly made is disposed of, or
(b) the period within which an appeal may be made expires without an appeal being made.

(4) Sub-paragraph (3) shall not apply where the Chief Inspector-

(a) is satisfied that the circumstances of the case justify the decision in question taking effect immediately or earlier than would otherwise be the case, and
(b) notifies the person concerned to that effect.

(5) On determining any appeal under this paragraph, the tribunal may-

(a) confirm, reverse or vary the decision appealed against, or
(b) remit the case to the Chief Inspector with directions as to the action to be taken by him.

Training

11.–(1) A registered nursery education inspector shall not conduct an inspection under paragraph 6 unless he has, in the opinion of the Chief Inspector, satisfactorily completed a course of training provided by, or complying with arrangements approved by, the Chief Inspector.

(2) Sub-paragraph (1) shall not apply in such circumstances as may be specified, either generally or in relation to a particular case or class of case, by the Chief Inspector.

(3) Where the Chief Inspector provides such training he may charge such fees as are reasonable for the purpose of recovering the whole, or part, of the cost of providing it.

Impartiality

12. A person shall not undertake an inspection under paragraph 6 of nursery education provided by a person at any premises, or accompany a person undertaking such an inspection, if he has, or has at any time had, any connection with-

(a) the person by whom the education is provided (or, where it is provided by a body, any member of the body), or
(b) any person employed by that person (whether or not at the premises),

of a kind which might reasonably be taken to raise doubts about his ability to act impartially.

Reports of inspections

13.–(1) Where a person has conducted an inspection under paragraph 6 he shall make his report in writing to the Chief Inspector within such period as may be prescribed, subject to any extension not exceeding three months which the Chief Inspector may consider necessary.

(2) Once the report of an inspection has been made to the Chief Inspector under sub-paragraph (1) he shall without delay send a copy of it to such authorities and persons as may be prescribed.

(3) Section 42A(2) and (3) of the School Inspections Act 1996 shall apply in relation to the publication of any such report as they apply in relation to the publication of a report under any of the provisions mentioned in section 42A(2).

Annual reports of the Chief Inspector

14. The annual reports of the Chief Inspector required by subsection (7)(a) of sections 2 and 5 of the (1996 c. 57.)School Inspections Act 1996 to be made to the Secretary of State shall include an account of the exercise of the functions imposed or conferred on him by this Schedule; and the power conferred by subsection (7)(b) of those sections to make other reports to the Secretary of State includes a power to make reports with respect to matters which fall within the scope of his functions by virtue of this Schedule.

Reserve powers of the Chief Inspector

15. The Chief Inspector may, in any case where it appears to him to be appropriate to do so, secure that any inspection under paragraph 6 is conducted not by a registered nursery education inspector but by one or more members of the Inspectorate.

16. If the Chief Inspector elects in the case of an inspection within paragraph (b) or (c) of sub-paragraph (1) of paragraph 6 that the inspection shall be treated as if it were an inspection within paragraph (a) of that sub-paragraph, the inspection shall be so treated.

17. Where an inspection is being conducted by a registered nursery education inspector under paragraph 6, the Chief Inspector may arrange for the inspection to be monitored by one or more members of the Inspectorate.

Rights of entry

18.–(1) This paragraph applies to-
   (a) a registered nursery education inspector or member of the Inspectorate conducting an inspection under paragraph 6, or
   (b) a member of the Inspectorate monitoring such an inspection under paragraph 17.

(2) A person to whom this paragraph applies shall have at all reasonable times-
    (a) a right of entry to the premises at which the relevant nursery education concerned is provided; and
    (b) a right to inspect, and take copies of-
        (i) any records kept by the person providing that education, and
        (ii) any other documents containing information relating to the provision of that education,
    which he requires for the purposes of conducting or (as the case may be) monitoring the inspection.

(3) Section 42 of the School Inspections Act 1996 (inspection of computer records for purposes of Part I of that Act) shall apply for the purposes of this paragraph as it applies for the purposes of Part I of that Act.

(4) It shall be an offence wilfully to obstruct a member of the Inspectorate or a registered nursery education inspector in the exercise of his functions in relation to an inspection under paragraph 6.

(5) Any person guilty of an offence under sub-paragraph (4) shall be liable on summary conviction to a fine not exceeding level 4 on the standard scale.

(6) In this paragraph "documents" and "records" each include information recorded in any form.

Schedule 26

This Schedule effectively extends the provisions of the School Inspections Act 1996 to nursery education. It covers all nursery provision that is provided by the local education authority or is provided with the assistance of grants from the authority or under the Nursery Education and Grant-Maintained Schools Act 1996.

The inspection process is under the jurisdiction of the Chief Inspectors of Schools in England and Wales. It requires that the Chief Inspector arranges inspections and the registration and supervision of inspectors. There is to be a separate register of nursery inspectors but the provisions relating to the registration of inspectors and their removal from the register, as well as the provisions for the conduct of inspections and subsequent reporting and action very closely replicate the provisions in the School Inspections Act 1996 relating to mainstream school inspections. The Schedule clearly contemplates that a nursery inspection will be carried out by a single registered inspector: there is no provision for teams of inspectors under the auspices of a registered inspector as applies to mainstream schools. Reflecting this is a requirement that no registered nursery inspector shall conduct an inspection without first completing an approved training course.

SCHEDULE 27

FURTHER PROVISION ABOUT PARTNERSHIP ARRANGEMENTS IN WALES

"SCHEDULE 5A

FURTHER PROVISION ABOUT PARTNERSHIP ARRANGEMENTS IN WALES

Interpretation

1. In this Schedule-
    "the participating bodies", in relation to an arrangement, means-
    (i) the parties to the arrangement,
    (ii) the Further Education Funding Council for Wales, and
    (iii) each governing body of a school which has consented to the arrangement; and

    "the parties", in relation to an arrangement, means-
    (i) each local education authority, and
    (ii) each governing body of an institution (or institutions) within the further education sector,
    which is a party to the arrangement.

Approval by the Secretary of State

2.–(1) An application for approval of an arrangement by the Secretary of State for the purposes of section 60A of this Act ("an application") shall be made jointly by the parties to the arrangement.

(2) An application shall be in such form and contain such information as may be prescribed by regulations.

(3) In addition, the participating bodies shall provide the Secretary of State with such further information as he may require for the purpose of deciding whether or not to grant the approval.

Termination of arrangement etc

3.–(1) Subject to any provision of the arrangement to the contrary and to sub-paragraph (2) below, a partnership arrangement to which section 60A of this Act applies shall continue in force indefinitely.

(2) The Secretary of State may withdraw approval of a partnership arrangement to which section 60A of this Act applies.

(3) The Secretary of State shall exercise his powers under sub-paragraph (2) in accordance with the provisions of the arrangement.

Variation of arrangement

4.–(1) The parties to a partnership arrangement to which section 60A of this Act applies shall not make any change to the arrangement except-

   (a) with the consent of the other participating bodies, and
   (b) if the change amounts to a significant change to the arrangement, with the consent of the Secretary of State.

(2) If a question arises whether a change to an arrangement would be a significant change, that question shall be determined by the Secretary of State.

Interpretation of existing enactments

5.–(1) Regulations may provide-

   (a) for any reference in an enactment to secondary education to be construed as including further education provided under a partnership arrangement to which section 60A of this Act applies, and
   (b) for any enactment containing such a reference to apply in relation to such further education with such modifications (if any) as may be specified in the regulations.

(2) In sub-paragraph (1), enactment includes an enactment comprised in subordinate legislation (within the meaning of the Interpretation Act 1978)."

Schedule 27
This Schedule provides the machinery for the approval by the Secretary of State of partnership arrangements in Wales under S. 125.

SCHEDULE 28

AMENDMENTS RELATING TO SCHOOL AND NURSERY INSPECTIONS

PART I SCHOOL INSPECTIONS

Introductory

1. In this Part of this Schedule "the 1996 Act" means the School Inspections Act 1996.

Persons who may be registered inspectors

2. In section 7(3) of the 1996 Act (registration of inspectors), at the end there shall be added-

"and no person shall be so registered if he falls within a category of persons prescribed for the purposes of this subsection.

Decisions of Chief Inspector having immediate effect

3. In section 9(3)(a) of the 1996 Act (circumstances where Chief Inspector's decision to revoke registration may take immediate effect), the words "are exceptional and" shall be omitted.

Enrolment of persons to act as team members

4.–(1) For paragraph 3(1) of Schedule 3 to the 1996 Act (inspection teams) there shall be substituted-

"(1) Every inspection shall be conducted by a registered inspector with the assistance of a team (an "inspection team") consisting of persons who are enrolled in the list kept by the Chief Inspector under paragraph 3A."

(2) After paragraph 3 of that Schedule there shall be inserted-

"Enrolment of persons to act as team members

3A.–(1) The Chief Inspector shall keep a list of persons who may act as members of an inspection team ("the list"); and no person shall act as a member of an inspection team unless he is enrolled in the list.

(2) The Chief Inspector shall not enrol any person in the list unless, having regard to any conditions that he proposes to impose under section 7(5)(c) (as it applies in accordance with sub-paragraph (4) below), it appears to him that that person-

(a) is a fit and proper person for carrying out an inspection, and
(b) will be capable of assisting in an inspection competently and effectively.

(3) An application for enrolment in the list shall (except in such circumstances as may be prescribed) be accompanied by the prescribed fee.

(4) Subsections (5) to (9) of section 7 shall apply in relation to the enrolment of a person in the list and to acting as a member of an inspection team as they apply in relation to the registration of a person under subsection (1) or (2) of that section and to acting as a registered inspector.

(5) Sections 8 and 9 and Schedule 2 shall (with any necessary modifications) apply in relation to enrolment in the list and to a person so enrolled as they apply in relation to registration under section 7(1) or (2) and to a person so registered.

(6) In its application to an enrolled person in accordance with sub-paragraph (5) above, section 8 shall have effect as if the conditions mentioned in subsection (2) of that section were that-

(a) that person is no longer a fit and proper person to act as a member of an inspection team;
(b) he is no longer capable of assisting in an inspection competently and effectively;

(c) there has been a significant failure on his part to comply with any condition imposed under section 7(5)(c) (as it applies in accordance with sub-paragraph (4) above).

(7) Without prejudice to the generality of paragraph 2(1) of Schedule 2, regulations under that provision may provide that, where a person is appealing simultaneously-

(a) against a decision of the Chief Inspector relating to that person's registration, and
(b) against a decision of the Chief Inspector relating to that person's enrolment in the list,

both appeals are to be heard at the same time."

Replacement of inspectors

5. After paragraph 8 of Schedule 3 to the 1996 Act there shall be added-

"Replacement of inspector during course of inspection

9.–(1) This paragraph applies to an inspection where, at any time-

(a) after the meeting required by paragraph 6 is held, but
(b) before the making of the report of the inspection is completed,

the inspector conducting the inspection becomes (for any reason) unable to continue to discharge his functions as an inspector in relation to the inspection.

(2) If the conditions set out in sub-paragraph (3) are satisfied-

(a) the Chief Inspector may arrange for that person to be replaced as the inspector conducting the inspection by another registered inspector; and
(b) if he does so, anything done by or in relation to that person in connection with the inspection shall, so far as necessary for his effectual replacement by that other inspector, be regarded as done by or in relation to that other inspector.

(3) The conditions are-

(a) that the appropriate authority for the school concerned have given the Chief Inspector notice in writing of their agreement to the inspector mentioned in sub-paragraph (1) being replaced under this paragraph; and
(b) that the replacement inspector does not have, and has not at any time had, any connection of the kind mentioned in paragraph 3(5) with the school in question or with any other person mentioned there."

PART II NURSERY INSPECTIONS

Persons who may be registered nursery education inspectors

6. In paragraph 8(3) of Schedule 1 to the Nursery Education and Grant-Maintained Schools Act 1996 (registration of nursery education inspectors), at the end there shall be added-

    "and no person shall be so registered if he falls within a category of persons prescribed for the purposes of this sub-paragraph.

Decisions of Chief Inspector having immediate effect

7. In paragraph 10(4)(a) of Schedule 1 to the (1996 c. 50.)Nursery Education and Grant-Maintained Schools Act 1996 (circumstances where Chief Inspector's decision to revoke registration may take immediate effect), the words "are exceptional and" shall be omitted.

Powers of entry of registered nursery education inspectors

8. After paragraph 17 of Schedule 1 to the (1996 c. 50.)Nursery Education and Grant-Maintained Schools Act 1996 there shall be added-

    "Rights of entry

    18.–(1) This paragraph applies to-

    (a) a registered nursery education inspector or member of the Inspectorate conducting an inspection under paragraph 6, or
    (b) a member of the Inspectorate monitoring such an inspection under paragraph 17.

    (2) A person to whom this paragraph applies shall have at all reasonable times-

    (a) a right of entry to the premises at which the funded nursery education concerned is provided; and
    (b) a right to inspect, and take copies of-
        (i) any records kept by the person providing that education, and
        (ii) any other documents containing information relating to the provision of that education,
        which he requires for the purpose of conducting or (as the case may be) monitoring the inspection.

    (3) Section 42 of the School Inspections Act 1996 (inspection of computer records for purposes of Part I of that Act) shall apply for the purposes of this paragraph as it applies for the purposes of Part I of that Act.

    (4) It shall be an offence wilfully to obstruct a member of the Inspectorate or a registered nursery education inspector in the exercise of his functions in relation to an inspection under paragraph 6.

(5) Any person guilty of an offence under sub-paragraph (4) shall be liable on summary conviction to a fine not exceeding level 4 on the standard scale.

(6) In this paragraph "documents" and "records" each include information recorded in any form."

Schedule 28
This Schedule contains detailed amendments to the School Inspections Act 1996 and amendments to the Nursery and Grant-Maintained Schools Act 1996 so far as this Act relates to nursery education that are consequential amendments in the light of the new provisions for registration of nursery inspectors. The change of substance is the adding of a requirement that all members of an inspection team be enrolled on a list to be kept by the Chief Inspector of Schools who may not enrol someone unless satisfied that the person is a fit and proper person and capable of assisting in an inspection competently and effectively. The provisions relating to registration of inspectors and their removal and rights of appeal are applied to enrolment. There is also provision for the Chief Inspector to replace a registered inspector, if the inspector is unable to continue to discharge his or her functions and with the agreement of the school, and for the replacement inspector to continue with the inspection.

SCHEDULE 29

A<small>MENDMENTS RELATING TO FUNCTIONS OF</small> E<small>DUCATION</small> T<small>RANSFER</small> C<small>OUNCIL</small>

Introductory

1. In this Schedule "the 1988 Act" means the Education Reform Act 1988.

General provisions as to transfers

2.–(1) Section 198 of the 1988 Act (transfers under Parts I and II of that Act) shall be amended as follows.

(2) For subsections (1) to (4) substitute-

"(1) This section applies to any transfer under any of the following provisions, namely-

(a) section 126 or 130 of this Act,

(b) Schedule 21 to the School Standards and Framework Act 1998 ("the 1998 Act"), or

(c) any regulations made-

(i) under section 21(5) or (9) of that Act, or

(ii) under paragraph 10 of Schedule 2 or paragraph 5 of Schedule 8 to that Act;

and those provisions, so far as relating to transfers under them, shall in each case have effect subject to Schedule 10 to this Act.

(1A) However, nothing in-

(a) the provisions of that Schedule other than paragraph 2(4), or

(b) subsection (3) below,

applies in relation to any transfer agreement falling to be made under paragraph 4 or 7 of Schedule 21 to the 1998 Act or any corresponding provision of regulations under that Act.

(2) Schedule 10 to this Act has effect for the purpose of-

(a) dividing and apportioning property, rights and liabilities which fall to be transferred under any transfer to which this section applies by a transferor authority or body where that property has been used or held, or the rights or liabilities have been acquired or incurred, for the purposes of more than one school or other educational institution;

(b) excluding from transfer in certain circumstances property, rights and liabilities which would otherwise fall to be transferred under any such transfer;

(c) providing for identifying and defining the property, rights and liabilities which fall to be transferred under a transfer to which this section applies; and

(d) making supplementary and consequential provisions in relation to such transfers.

(3) In carrying out the functions conferred or imposed on them by that Schedule-

(a) the Education Transfer Council-

(i) shall, subject to subsection (4) below, not act on behalf of the transferor, the transferee or any other interested person, but

(ii) shall seek to ensure that all such persons' interests are protected; and

(b) it shall be the duty of the Council, so far as it is reasonably practicable for them to do so, to secure that each transfer to which this section applies is, so far as possible, fully effective on the date on which it takes effect under this Act or under or by virtue of the 1998 Act.

(4) Where the transferor under any such transfer is a local authority and in accordance with that Schedule anything falls to be or may be done by the Council for the purposes of or in connection with that transfer-

(a) it may not be done by the transferee; and

(b) in doing it the Council shall be regarded as acting on behalf and in the name of the transferee;

and in a case where the transferee is a body corporate established under this Act or the 1998 Act paragraph (b) above applies both in relation to things done before and in relation to things done after that body is established under this Act or the 1998 Act."

(3) For "the Board", wherever occurring in subsections (5) and (6) of section 198, there is substituted (in accordance with section 136(2) of this Act) "the Council".

"Division and apportionment of property etc.

3. For paragraph 1 of Schedule 10 to the 1988 Act (supplementary provisions with respect to transfers) substitute-

Division and apportionment of property etc.

1.–(1) Any property, rights and liabilities of a transferor authority held or used or subsisting-

   (a) for the purposes of more than one relevant institution; or
   (b) partly for the purposes of one or more relevant institutions and partly for other purposes of the transferor authority;

shall, where the nature of the property, right or liability permits, be divided or apportioned between the transferees, or (as the case may be) between the transferor authority and the transferee or transferees, in such proportions as may be appropriate.

(2) Any property, rights or liabilities of a transferor body shall, where the nature of the property, right or liability permits, be divided or apportioned between the transferees, or (as the case may be) between the transferor body and the transferee or transferees, in such proportions as may be appropriate.

(3) Where any estate or interest in land falls to be divided in accordance with either sub-paragraph (1) or sub-paragraph (2) above-

   (a) any rent payable under a lease in respect of that estate or interest; and
   (b) any rent charged on that estate or interest;

shall be correspondingly divided or apportioned so that each part is payable in respect of, or charged on, only one part of the estate or interest and the other part or parts are payable in respect of, or charged on, only the other part or parts of the estate or interest.

(4) Any such property, right or liability as is mentioned in sub-paragraph (1) or (2) above the nature of which does not permit its division or apportionment as so mentioned shall be transferred to the transferee (or to one or other of the transferees) or retained by the transferor authority or body according to-

   (a) in the case of an estate or interest in land, whether on the transfer date the transferor authority or body or the transferee (or one or other of the transferees) appears to be in greater need of the security afforded by that estate or interest or, where none of them appears to be in greater need of that security, which of them appears on that date to be likely to make use of the land to the greater extent; or

(b) in the case of any other property or any right or liability, which of them appears on the transfer date to be likely to make use of the property or (as the case may be) to be affected by the right or liability to the greater extent;

subject (in either case) to such arrangements for the protection of the other person or persons concerned as may be agreed between the transferor authority or body and the relevant person or determined by the Secretary of State under paragraph 3 below.

(5) In this paragraph-

(a) "relevant institution" means-
 (i) any institution which a body corporate is established under this Act to conduct;
 (ii) any institution to which section 130 of this Act applies; and
 (iii) any maintained school;
(b) "the relevant person" means-
 (i) in a case where the transferor is a transferor authority, the Education Transfer Council;
 (ii) in a case where the transferor is a transferor body, the transferee;
(c) references to a transferor authority are references to a local authority who are the transferor for the purposes of any transfer to which this Schedule applies;
(d) references to a transferor body are references to any foundation body who are the transferor for the purposes of any transfer to which this Schedule applies;

and for the purposes of this sub-paragraph references to a maintained school or a foundation body have the same meaning as in the School Standards and Framework Act 1998."

Identification of property, rights and liabilities

4. For paragraph 2 of Schedule 10 to the 1988 Act substitute-

"Identification of property, rights and liabilities

2.–(1) It shall be the duty of the transferor and the relevant person, whether before or after the transfer date, so far as practicable to arrive at such written agreements, and to execute such other instruments, as are necessary or expedient to identify or define the property, rights and liabilities transferred to the transferee or retained by the transferor or for making any such arrangements as are mentioned in paragraph 1(4) above and as will-

(a) afford to the transferor and the transferee as against one another such rights and safeguards as they may require for the proper discharge of their respective functions; and

(b) make as from such date, not being earlier than the transfer date, as may be specified in the agreement or instrument such clarifications and modifications of the effect of the provision of this Act or of the 1998 Act (or any regulations made under it) under which the transfer is required on the property, rights and liabilities of the transferor as will best serve the proper discharge of the respective functions of the transferor and the transferee.

(2) Any such agreement shall provide so far as it is expedient-

(a) for the granting of leases and for the creation of other liabilities and rights over land whether amounting in law to interests in land or not, and whether involving the surrender of any existing interest or the creation of a new interest or not;

(b) for the granting of indemnities in connection with the severance of leases and other matters;

(c) for responsibility for registration of any matter in any description of statutory register.

(3) Except in a case where the transferor is a local authority, the Education Transfer Council shall-

(a) assist the transferor, the transferee and any other interested person in identifying or defining the property, rights and liabilities transferred to the transferee or retained by the transferor;

(b) advise such persons as to the terms of any agreement or instrument falling to be made under sub-paragraph (1) above;

(c) assist such persons to negotiate any such agreement or instrument and mediate in any such negotiations;

(d) prepare drafts of any such agreement or instrument; and

(e) assist the parties in executing and giving effect to any such agreement or instrument.

(4) If and to the extent that they are requested to do so by any person falling to make a transfer agreement under paragraph 4 or 7 of Schedule 21 to the 1998 Act or any corresponding provision of regulations under that Act, the Education Transfer Council shall exercise any one or more functions falling within sub-paragraph (3) above in relation to such an agreement, or an instrument made pursuant to such an agreement, as if it were an agreement or instrument falling to be made under sub-paragraph (1) above.

(5) Any transfer of any estate or interest in land under this paragraph or under paragraph 1 above (whether by virtue of an agreement or instrument entered into before or after the transfer date) shall be regarded as having taken place on the transfer date.

(6) In this paragraph-

"the 1998 Act" means the School Standards and Framework Act 1998; and "the relevant person" means-

- (a) in a case where the transferor is a local authority, the Education Transfer Council;
- (b) in a case where the transferor is not a local authority, the transferee."

Resolution of disputes

5. For paragraph 3 of Schedule 10 to the 1988 Act substitute-

"Resolution of disputes

3.–(1) The Education Transfer Council shall notify the Secretary of State if it appears to them that it is unlikely in the case of any matter on which agreement is required to be reached under paragraph 2(1) above that such an agreement will be reached.

(2) Where the Secretary of State has received a notification from the Council under sub-paragraph (1) above, he may, whether before or after the transfer date, give a direction determining that matter, and may include in the direction any provision which might have been included in an agreement under paragraph 2(1) above.

(3) Any property, rights or liabilities required by a direction under this paragraph to be transferred to the transferee shall be regarded as having been transferred to, and by virtue of this Act vested in, the transferee on the transfer date.

(4) The Secretary of State shall consult the transferor, the transferee and any other interested person before giving a direction under this paragraph.

(5) The Education Transfer Council shall give the Secretary of State such assistance and advice as he may require for the purpose of determining any matter under this paragraph."

Proof of title by certificate

6. In paragraph 5 of Schedule 10 to the 1988 Act, for "or of the Education Act 1996" substitute "or of the School Standards and Framework Act 1998".

Construction of agreements etc.

7. In paragraph 7 of Schedule 10 to the 1988 Act, for "or of the Education Act 1996", in both places, substitute "or of the School Standards and Framework Act 1998".

Third parties affected by vesting provisions

8. In paragraph 9 of Schedule 10 to the 1988 Act-

- (a) in sub-paragraph (6)(a), after "Board" insert "or (as the case may be) the transferee";

(b) in sub-paragraph (6)(b), for "or of the Education Act 1996" substitute "or of the School Standards and Framework Act 1998 (or any regulations made under it)"; and

(c) in sub-paragraph (9), after "Board" insert "or (as the case may be) the transferee".

Delivery of documents to transferee

9. In paragraph 10 of Schedule 10 to the 1988 Act, after "transfer" insert "under which the transferor is a local authority".

Amendment of references to Education Assets Board

10. For "the Education Assets Board" or "the Board", wherever occurring in Schedule 10 to the 1988 Act, there is substituted (in accordance with section 136(2) of this Act) "the Education Transfer Council" or "the Council" respectively.

> **Schedule 29**
> *This Schedule contains technical provisions relating to the functions of the Education Transfer Council (previously the Education Assets Board) to enable property transfers to be effected and disputes resolved.*

SCHEDULE 30

MINOR AND CONSEQUENTIAL AMENDMENTS

Children and Young Persons Act 1933 (c.12)

1. In section 1(7) of the (1996 c. 56.)Children and Young Persons Act 1933 (saving for right of parents etc. to administer corporal punishment), for "teacher, or other person" substitute "or (subject to section 548 of the Education Act 1996) any other person,".

Local Authorities (Goods and Services) Act 1970 (c.39)

2.–(1) Subject to sub-paragraph (2), in the Local Authorities (Goods and Services) Act 1970 (supply of goods and services by local authorities to public bodies) "public body" shall include any Education Action Forum established in an education action zone.

(2) The provision in sub-paragraph (1) shall have effect as if made by an order under section 1(5) of that Act (power to provide that a person shall be a public body for the purposes of the Act).

(3) An order under section 1(5) may accordingly vary or revoke the provisions of sub-paragraph (1) above as they apply to an Education Action Forum specified in the order.

Local Government Act 1972 (c.70)

3.–(1) Section 177 of the Local Government Act 1972 (provisions supplementary to sections 173 to 176) shall be amended as follows.

(2) In subsection (1), omit the words from the beginning to "committees),".

(3) After subsection (1) insert-

"(1A) Subsection (1) above has effect without prejudice to the operation of the following provisions of the School Standards and Framework Act 1998, namely-
(a) paragraph 3 of Schedule 4 (allowances for school organisation committees);
(b) paragraph 3 of Schedule 18 (allowances for exclusion appeals panels); and
(c) paragraph 5 of Schedule 24 (allowances for admission appeals panels)."

Local Government Act 1974 (c.7)

4.–(1) The Local Government Act 1974 shall be amended as follows.

(2) For section 25(5) (authorities subject to investigation by Local Commissioner) substitute-

"(5) Any reference to an authority to which this Part of this Act applies also includes a reference to-
(a) a school organisation committee constituted in accordance with section 24 of the School Standards and Framework Act 1998,
(b) an exclusion appeals panel constituted in accordance with Schedule 18 to that Act,
(c) an admission appeals panel constituted in accordance with Schedule 24 or paragraph 3 of Schedule 25 to that Act, and
(d) the governing body of any community, foundation or voluntary school so far as acting in connection with the admission of pupils to the school or otherwise performing any of their functions under Chapter I of Part III of that Act."

Sex Discrimination Act 1975 (c.65)

5. In section 22 of the Sex Discrimination Act 1975 (discrimination by bodies in charge of educational establishments), in the Table, in paragraph 1, for "governors" substitute "governing body".

6. In section 27 of that Act (exception for single-sex establishments turning co-educational), after subsection (1) insert-

"(1A) Without prejudice to subsection (1), a transitional exemption order may be made in accordance with paragraph 21 or 22 of Schedule 6 or paragraph 16 or 17 of Schedule 7 to the School Standards and Framework Act 1998 (transitional exemption orders for purposes of the Sex Discrimination Act 1975: England and Wales)."

Race Relations Act 1976 (c.74)

7. In section 17 of the Race Relations Act 1976 (discrimination by bodies in charge of educational establishments), in the Table, in paragraph 1, for "governors" substitute "governing body".

National Health Service Act 1977 (c.49)

8. In Schedule 1 to the National Health Service Act 1977 (additional provisions as to the medical inspection of pupils, etc.)-

    (a) in paragraph 3, for the words from "by which" to "grant-maintained schools" substitute "in respect of the schools (other than foundation, voluntary or foundation special schools) which they maintain or the governing bodies of foundation, voluntary or foundation special schools in respect of those schools"; and

    (b) in paragraph 4, after "1996" insert "or (as the case may be) the School Standards and Framework Act 1998".

Representation of the People Act 1983 (c.2)

9. The Representation of the People Act 1983 shall be amended as follows.

10. In section 95(2)(a) (schools and rooms for parliamentary election meetings), for "county schools voluntary schools and grant-maintained schools" substitute "community, foundation and voluntary schools".

11. In section 96(2)(a) (schools and rooms for local election meetings), for "county voluntary or grant-maintained school" substitute "community, foundation or voluntary school".

12. In Schedule 5 (use for parliamentary election meetings of rooms in school premises and meeting rooms), in paragraph 1(1), for "a grant-maintained school" substitute "a foundation or voluntary aided school".

Local Government Act 1986 (c.10)

13. In section 2A(4)(a) of the Local Government Act 1986 (prohibition on promoting homosexuality by teaching or publishing material), for the words from "a county" to the end substitute "a maintained school or maintained nursery school, within the meaning of the School Standards and Framework Act 1998;".

Education (No. 2) Act 1986 (c.61)

14. In section 49(3) of the Education (No. 2) Act 1986 (appraisal of performance of teachers)-

    (a) for paragraph (b) substitute-
        "(b) at any special school which is not so maintained but is for the time being approved by the Secretary of State under section 342 of the Education Act 1996 (approval of special schools);", and

    (b) omit paragraph (ba).

Local Government Act 1988 (c.9)

15. In Schedule 1 to the Local Government Act 1988 (defined activities open to competition), in paragraph 8(5), for the words from "county or" to "education authority;" substitute "community, foundation or voluntary schools or community or foundation special schools;".

Education Reform Act 1988 (c.40)

16. The Education Reform Act 1988 shall be amended as follows.

17. In section 218 (school and further and higher education regulations), for subsection (12) substitute-

    "(12) In this section (except in subsection (6)(d) or (6A) above) "school" means any school maintained by a local education authority or any special school not so maintained."

18. In section 221(1)(b) (avoidance of certain contractual terms), for "an aided or grant-maintained school;" substitute "a foundation, voluntary aided or foundation special school;".

19. In section 226(4) (services to schools in member States providing education to British children), for the words from "any county" to the end substitute "any community, foundation or voluntary school."

20. In Schedule 8 (provisions relating to the body to be known as the Education Transfer Council)-

    (a) omit paragraph 6(3); and
    (b) in paragraph 8-
        (i) in sub-paragraph (4), omit "given with the consent of the Treasury"; and
        (ii) in sub-paragraph (7), for "Treasury" substitute "Secretary of State".

Children Act 1989 (c.41)

21. In Schedule 9 to the Children Act 1989 (child minding and day care for young children), in paragraph 3(3), for the definitions of "assisted" and "maintained" substitute-

    " "assisted" has the same meaning as in the Education Act 1996;

    "maintained" has the same meaning as in the School Standards and Framework Act 1998; and".

Local Government and Housing Act 1989 (c.42)

22. In section 13(5) of the Local Government and Housing Act 1989 (voting rights of certain members of committees)-

    (a) after "is required" insert "either"; and
    (b) at the end insert "or pursuant to regulations under subsection (6) of that section."

Environmental Protection Act 1990 (c.43)

23. In section 98(2) of the Environmental Protection Act 1990 (definitions), for paragraphs (f) and (g) substitute-

"(f) any community, foundation or voluntary school;
(g) any community or foundation special school."

School Teachers' Pay and Conditions Act 1991 (c.49)

24. The School Teachers' Pay and Conditions Act 1991 shall be amended as follows.

25. In section 1 (establishment of review body on statutory conditions of employment)-
   (a) in subsection (5)-
      (i) in paragraph (b), for the words from "governors of" to "grant-maintained schools" substitute "governing bodies of foundation, voluntary and foundation special schools", and
      (ii) omit the words from "and, where" to "that subsection"; and
   (b) omit subsection (6).

26. In section 2 (orders relating to statutory conditions of employment)-
   (a) in subsection (1)(b), for the words from "governors of" to "grant-maintained schools" substitute "governing bodies of foundation, voluntary and foundation special schools";
   (b) omit subsection (2);
   (c) in subsection (3), for "by Her Majesty's Stationery Office" substitute "in accordance with the order";
   (d) in subsection (4)-
      (i) in paragraph (a), omit ", in the case of a grant-maintained school," and the words from "and provide" to the end,
      (ii) in paragraph (g), after "authorities" insert "or governing bodies of schools", and
      (iii) omit paragraph (h);
   (e) in subsection (5), omit the words from "and, where" to "(2) above"; and
   (f) in subsection (6)(a), omit the words from "or, in" to "such schools,".

27. In section 3A (special provisions for teachers on transfer of employment)-
   (a) for subsection (1) substitute-
   "(1) This section applies where-
      (a) a community, foundation or voluntary or community or foundation special school is established in place of an independent school in pursuance of proposals published under section 28 or 31 of the School Standards and Framework Act 1998, and
      (b) a school teacher employed to teach at that independent school becomes employed by the local education authority or (as the case may be) the governing body in accordance with the Transfer of Undertakings (Protection of Employment) Regulations 1981."; and

(b) in subsection (3), for "an aided school" substitute "a foundation, voluntary aided or foundation special school".

28.–(1) Section 5 (interpretation, etc.) shall be amended as follows.

(2) In subsection (1)-

(a) in the definition of "school teacher", for "voluntary or grant-maintained" substitute "foundation, voluntary aided or foundation special";

(b) in the definition of "school which has a delegated budget", for "Part II of the (1996 c. 56.) Education Act 1996" substitute "Part II of the School Standards and Framework Act 1998"; and

(c) for the words from "other expressions" to the end substitute "where any other expression used in this Act is defined for the purposes of the Education Act 1996 or the School Standards and Framework Act 1998, it shall have the same meaning in this Act as in that Act."

(3) For the sidenote substitute "Interpretation, orders and application of provisions of Education Acts."

Diocesan Boards of Education Measure 1991 (1991 No.2)

29. The Diocesan Boards of Education Measure 1991 shall be amended as follows.

30. In section 3 (transactions for which advice or consent of Board is required)-

(a) in subsection (1), for the words from "before making" to the end substitute "before-

(a) publishing proposals for any prescribed alteration to the school under section 28(2)(b) of the School Standards and Framework Act 1998;

(b) publishing proposals for the discontinuance of the school under section 29(2) of that Act;

(c) serving notice of an intention to discontinue the school under section 30(1) of that Act;

(d) publishing proposals for changing the category of the school under paragraph 2 or 3 of Schedule 8 to that Act; or

(e) making any application to, or entering into any agreement with, any body or person for or in connection with any disposal (whether by sale or otherwise) of the premises of the school or any part of them.";

(b) in subsection (2), for "an aided or special agreement school" substitute "a voluntary aided school";

(c) omit subsections (4) and (5); and

(d) in subsection (6)-

(i) omit "or (5)", and

(ii) for "the secretary of the governing body" substitute "the clerk to the governing body".

31. In section 7 (powers of Board to give directions to governing bodies)-
(a) for subsection (1) substitute-

"(1) Where the Board is satisfied that the governing body of a voluntary aided church school in the diocese in discharging, or failing to discharge, its functions so far as relating to-
(a) the making of any prescribed alteration to the school under Chapter II of Part II of the School Standards and Framework Act 1998, or
(b) the discontinuance of the school under that Chapter, or
(c) changing the school's category in accordance with paragraph 2 or 3 of Schedule 8 to that Act,

is acting in a manner which is not in the interests of that school or of church schools generally, the Board may, subject to subsection (1A) below, give directions to the governing body as to the discharge of those functions.

(1A) The Board may not, under subsection (1) above, give directions as to the publication of proposals under paragraph 2 or 3 of Schedule 8 to that Act which would prevent the publication of proposals for the school to become a foundation school.";
(b) in subsection (2), for "the secretary of the governing body" substitute "the clerk to the governing body";
(c) in subsection (3), for the words from the beginning of paragraph (a) onwards substitute-
"(a) publication of proposals for any prescribed alteration to the school under section 28(2)(b) of the School Standards and Framework Act 1998; or
(b) publication of proposals under paragraph 2 or 3 of Schedule 8 to that Act,

the Board may itself publish those proposals, and the provisions of that Act shall apply to anything done by the Board by virtue of this subsection as if it had been done by the governing body of the school.";
(d) omit subsection (5); and
(e) for the sidenote substitute "Powers of Board to give directions to governing bodies of voluntary aided church schools."

32.–(1) Section 10 (interpretation) shall be amended as follows.

(2) In subsection (1)-

(a) omit the definition of "Church of England voluntary school", and
(b) for the definition of "church school" substitute-
""church school" means a foundation or voluntary school which is a Church of England school as defined by section 142(1) of the School Standards and Framework Act 1998;".

(3) Omit subsection (2).

(4) For subsection (3) substitute-

"(3) Expressions used in this Measure which are also used in the School Standards and Framework Act 1998 shall, unless the context otherwise requires, have the same meaning as in that Act."

Further and Higher Education Act 1992 (c.13)

33. The Further and Higher Education Act 1992 shall be amended as follows.

34. In section 5(4) (administration of funds by councils), for "grant-maintained school" substitute "maintained school".

35. In section 21 (initial instruments and articles)-

(a) in subsection (1), omit-
(i) paragraph (a), and
(ii) "(b) in any other case,";
(b) in subsection (2), omit-
(i) "orders and",
(ii) in paragraph (a), "grant-maintained school or other", and
(iii) in paragraph (b), "grant-maintained schools or other"; and
(c) in subsection (3), for the words from "a grant-maintained" to "earlier enactment)" substitute "a maintained school, the governing body incorporated under Chapter III of Part II of the School Standards and Framework Act 1998".

36. For section 25 substitute-

"**25.**–(1) This section applies where a further education corporation is established to conduct an institution which, on the date the corporation is established, is a foundation or voluntary school belonging to the group of schools for which a foundation body acts under section 21 of the School Standards and Framework Act 1998.

(2) Regulations may make such provision as the Secretary of State considers necessary or expedient in connection with the transfer, in any such case, of property, rights and liabilities from the foundation body to the further education corporation.

(3) Regulations under subsection (2) may, in relation to any such transfer of property, rights or liabilities-
(a) modify any provision made by or under any of sections 23, 24, 36 and 38 of this Act and Schedule 5 to this Act;
(b) apply any such provision with or without modifications;
(c) make provision corresponding or similar to any such provision.

(4) In this section "foundation body" and "group of schools" have the same meaning as in the School Standards and Framework Act 1998."

37. In section 26 (transfer of staff to further education corporation)-

    (a) in subsection (1), omit "or was a grant-maintained school"; and
    (b) in subsection (6)-
       (i) for "that authority" substitute "references to that authority, and", and
       (ii) for paragraphs (b) and (c) substitute-
    "(b) in relation to a corporation established to conduct an institution which, on that date, was a foundation or voluntary aided school, references to the governing body of that school."

38. In section 28(2)(a) (designation of institutions as eligible for funds) after "school" insert "(other than one belonging to a group of schools for which a foundation body acts under section 21 of the School Standards and Framework Act 1998)".

39. In section 32 (transfer of property, etc., to designated institutions), after subsection (2) insert-

    "(2A)   In the case of an institution which when designated was a voluntary aided school, on the designation date-

       (a) all land and other property which, immediately before that date, was property of the governing body of the school incorporated under Chapter III of Part II of the School Standards and Framework Act 1998, and
       (b) all rights and liabilities of that body subsisting immediately before that date,

    shall be transferred to and, by virtue of this Act, vest in the governing body of the designated institution; and the governing body of the school shall be dissolved on that date."

40. In section 37 (attribution of surpluses and deficits)-

    (a) in subsection (1), for "section 103 of the Education Act 1996 (schemes for financing schools)" substitute "section 48 of the School Standards and Framework Act 1998 (LEAs' financial schemes)"; and
    (b) in subsection (7), in the definition of "budget share", for "Part II of the Education Act 1996" substitute "Part II of the School Standards and Framework Act 1998".

41. In section 44(1) (collective worship) for the words from "was a" to the end substitute "was-

    (a) (within the meaning of the (1996 c. 56.)Education Act 1996) a voluntary school, or
    (b) (within the meaning of the School Standards and Framework Act 1998) a foundation or voluntary school having a foundation established otherwise than under that Act."

42. In section 45(1) (religious education) for the words from "means" to the end substitute "has the same meaning as in section 44."

43. In section 47(2) (transfer of higher education institutions to further education sector) for the words from "any provision" to the end substitute "provision as to the initial name of the corporation as a further education corporation."

44. In section 48 (statutory conditions of employment)-

    (a) in subsection (1)(a), for "voluntary or grant-maintained" substitute "foundation or voluntary aided"; and

    (b) in subsection (2)(a), for "voluntary or grant-maintained" substitute "foundation or voluntary aided".

45. In section 58(3) (reorganisations of schools involving establishment of further education corporation), for paragraph (b) substitute-

    "(b) a prescribed alteration within the meaning of section 28 of the School Standards and Framework Act 1998 has been made to the school,".

46. In section 90 (interpretation)-

    (a) after subsection (3) insert-

    "(3A) In this Act references to a voluntary aided school are-

        (a) in relation to any time before the appointed day within the meaning of the (1996 c. 56.)School Standards and Framework Act 1998, references to a voluntary aided school within the meaning of the Education Act 1996; or

        (b) in relation to any time on or after that day, references to a voluntary aided school within the meaning of the 1998 Act."; and

    (b) in subsection (5), at end insert "and section 140(2) of the School Standards and Framework Act 1998 has effect for defining the expressions there mentioned."

Tribunals and Inquiries Act 1992 (c.53)

47. In paragraph 15 of Schedule 1 to the Tribunals and Inquiries Act 1992 (tribunals under general supervision of Council on Tribunals)-

    (a) for paragraphs (b) and (c) substitute-

    "(b) exclusion appeal panels constituted in accordance with Schedule 18 to the School Standards and Framework Act 1998 (c. 31);

    (c) admission appeal panels constituted in accordance with Schedule 24 or paragraph 3 of Schedule 25 to that Act;"; and

    (b) in paragraph (d), for "(c. 38)" substitute "(c. 57)".

Charities Act 1993 (c.10)

48. In section 3 of the Charities Act 1993 (the register of charities), after subsection (5A) (inserted by Schedule 3 to the Teaching and Higher Education Act 1998) insert-

    "(5B) In addition, in subsection (5) above-

        (a) paragraph (a) shall be read as referring also to-

            (i) any body to which section 23(1)(a) or (b) of the School Standards and Framework Act 1998 applies, and

(ii) any Education Action Forum established by virtue of section 10(1) of that Act; and

(b) paragraph (b) shall be read as referring also to any foundation to which section 23(3) of that Act applies;

but an order of the Commissioners, or regulations made by the Secretary of State, may provide that section 23(3) of that Act shall cease to apply to any such foundation as is mentioned in that provision or to any such foundation of a description specified in the order or regulations."

49. In section 79(9) of that Act (parochial charities), for the words from "voluntary or" to the end substitute "foundation or voluntary school within the meaning of the School Standards and Framework Act 1998."

Welsh Language Act 1993 (c.38)

50. In section 6(1) of the Welsh Language Act 1993 (meaning of "public body"), for paragraph (l) substitute-

"(l) the governing body of a community, foundation or voluntary school or a community or foundation special school (within the meaning of the School Standards and Framework Act 1998);".

Value Added Tax Act 1994 (c.23)

51. In Schedule 9 to the Value Added Tax Act 1994 (exemptions), in paragraph (a) of Note (1) to Group 6 (education)-

(a) in sub-paragraph (iii), for the words from "a county" to "Education Act 1996" substitute "a community, foundation or voluntary school within the meaning of the (1996 c. 56.)School Standards and Framework Act 1998, a special school within the meaning of section 337 of the Education Act 1996"; and

(b) omit sub-paragraphs (v) and (vii).

Education Act 1994 (c.30)

52. The Education Act 1994 shall be amended as follows.

53. In section 11A (general duty of Secretary of State with respect to training), omit "grant-maintained schools,".

54. In section 12 (power of schools to provide courses of initial teacher training)-

(a) in subsection (1), for "any county, voluntary or maintained special school or of any grant-maintained school" substitute "any community, foundation or voluntary or community or foundation special school";

(b) omit subsections (4) and (5); and

(c) in subsection (6), for the words from "purposes of" onwards substitute "purposes of Chapter IV of Part II of the School Standards and Framework Act 1998 (financing of maintained schools), as being undertaken for the purposes of the school."

Employment Rights Act 1996 (c.18)

55. In section 134(1) of the Employment Rights Act 1996 (teachers in aided schools), for the words from "an aided school" to "1996" substitute "a foundation, voluntary aided or foundation special school is dismissed by the governing body of the school in pursuance of a requirement of the local education authority under section 55(5) of the School Standards and Framework Act 1998".

Nursery Education and Grant-Maintained Schools Act 1996 (c.50)

56. In section 4(1) of the Nursery Education and Grant-Maintained Schools Act 1996 (children with special educational needs), for the words from "(except where" to the end substitute "(except where a duty is already imposed under section 313(2) of the (1996 c. 56.)Education Act 1996 or section 123(1) of the School Standards and Framework Act 1998) to have regard to the provisions of the code of practice issued under section 313 (practical guidance in respect of the discharge of functions under Part IV of the Education Act 1996)."

Education Act 1996 (c.56)

57. The Education Act 1996 shall be amended as follows.

58. In section 1(2) (the stages of education), omit paragraph (b) and the "and" preceding it.

59. In section 5 (primary, secondary and middle schools)-

   (a) in subsection (3) for "section 49, 198(6) or 291" substitute "section 28(4) of the School Standards and Framework Act 1998", and
   (b) in subsection (5) for "sections 49, 198(6) and 291" substitute "section 28(4) of the School Standards and Framework Act 1998".

60. In section 6(2) (nursery schools and special schools), for the words from "and" onwards substitute "and (in the case of a school which is not maintained by a local education authority) is for the time being approved, as mentioned in section 337."

61. In section 9 (pupils to be educated in accordance with parents' wishes), for the words from "State," to "funding authorities" substitute "State and local education authorities".

62. In section 14 (functions of local education authorities in respect of provision of primary and secondary schools), omit subsection (5).

63. After section 15 insert-

   "15A.–(1) A local education authority may secure the provision for their area of full-time education suitable to the requirements of persons over compulsory school age who have not attained the age of 19, including provision for persons from other areas.

(2) Subsections (6) and (7) of section 14 shall apply in relation to functions under this section as they apply in relation to functions under that section."

64.–(1) Section 16 (power to establish, maintain and assist primary and secondary schools) is amended as follows.

(2) In subsection (1)-

(a) at the end of paragraph (a) insert "and", and
(b) omit paragraph (c) and the "and" preceding it.

(3) In subsection (2), for ", maintain and assist" substitute "and maintain".

(4) For the sidenote substitute "Power to establish and maintain primary and secondary schools."

65. In section 17(2) (powers in respect of nursery education), for "establish, maintain and assist" substitute "establish and maintain".

66. Omit sections 20 to 28 (the funding authorities).

67. In section 29 (provision of information by local education authorities)-

(a) omit subsection (2), and
(b) in subsection (3), omit the words "and the funding authority".

68. Omit section 30 (provision of information by funding authorities).

69. Part II (schools maintained by local education authorities) shall be omitted.

70. Part III (grant-maintained schools) shall be omitted.

71. In section 312 (definitions for purposes of Part IV)-

(a) in subsection (4)(a) omit "or grant-maintained schools in their area"; and
(b) in subsection (5) for the definition of "maintained school" substitute-
""maintained school" means any community, foundation or voluntary school or any community or foundation special school not established in a hospital."

72. In section 313(1) (code of practice on special educational needs), for "maintained or grant-maintained schools, or grant-maintained special schools," substitute "maintained schools".

73. In section 315(2) (review of arrangements for special educational provision), for the words from "the funding" onwards substitute "the governing bodies of community, foundation and voluntary and community and foundation special schools in their area."

74.–(1) Section 317 (duties of governing body or local education authority in relation to pupils with special educational needs) shall be amended as follows.

(2) In subsection (1), for "a county, voluntary or grant-maintained school," substitute "a community, foundation or voluntary school,".

(3) In subsection (2), for "a county, voluntary or grant-maintained school," substitute "a community, foundation or voluntary school,".

(4) In subsection (3)-

    (a) in paragraph (a)-

        (i) for "county, voluntary and grant-maintained schools" substitute "community, foundation and voluntary schools", and

        (ii) omit ", the funding authority"; and

    (b) in paragraph (b), for the words from "the funding" onwards substitute "the governing bodies of community, foundation and voluntary schools."

(5) In subsection (4), for "a county, voluntary or grant-maintained school" substitute "a community, foundation or voluntary school".

(6) In subsection (5), for "each county, voluntary, maintained special or grant-maintained school" substitute "each community, foundation or voluntary or community or foundation special school".

(7) In subsection (6), for "each county, voluntary or grant-maintained school" substitute "each community, foundation or voluntary school".

(8) In subsection (7), for the words from "the articles" onwards substitute "section 42 of the School Standards and Framework Act 1998."

75.–(1) Section 318 (provision of goods and services in connection with special educational needs) shall be amended as follows.

(2) In subsection (1)-

    (a) in paragraph (a), for "county, voluntary or grant-maintained schools" substitute "community, foundation or voluntary schools", and

    (b) in paragraph (b), for "maintained or grant-maintained special schools" substitute "community or foundation special schools".

(3) In subsection (2), for the words from "this section" to "in any other area" substitute "this section to the governing bodies of community, foundation or voluntary schools or community or foundation special schools in any other area".

(4) For subsection (3) substitute-

    "(3) A local education authority may supply goods and services to any authority or other person (other than a governing body within subsection (1)) for the purpose only of assisting them in making for any child to whom subsection (3A) applies any special educational provision which any learning difficulty of the child calls for.

    (3A) This subsection applies to any child-

        (a) who is receiving relevant nursery education within the meaning of section 123 of the School Standards and Framework Act 1998, or

(b) in respect of whose education grants are (or are to be) made under section 1 of the Nursery Education and Grant-Maintained Schools Act 1996."

76. In section 321(3) (general duty of local education authority towards children for whom they are responsible)-

(a) in paragraph (a), for the words from "maintained" onwards substitute "maintained school", and

(b) for paragraph (b) substitute-

"(b) education is provided for him at a school which is not a maintained school but is so provided at the expense of the authority,".

77. In section 324 (statement of special educational needs)-

(a) in subsection (5)(b), for "maintained, grant-maintained or grant-maintained special school" substitute "maintained school"; and

(b) after subsection (5) insert-

"(5A) Subsection (5)(b) has effect regardless of any duty imposed on the governing body of a school by section 1(6) of the School Standards and Framework Act 1998."

78. In section 327 (access for local education authority to certain schools), for subsection (b) substitute-

"(b) in pursuance of the statement education is provided for the child at a school maintained by another local education authority."

79. Omit section 330 (assessment of education needs at request of governing body of grant-maintained school).

80. For section 337 substitute-

"Special schools.

337.–(1) A school is a special school if it is specially organised to make special educational provision for pupils with special educational needs.

(2) There are the following categories of special school-

(a) special schools maintained by local education authorities, comprising-

(i) community special schools, and

(ii) foundation special schools; and

(b) special schools which are not so maintained but are for the time being approved by the Secretary of State under section 342."

81. Omit sections 338 to 341 (establishment of maintained and grant-maintained special schools).

82. For section 342 substitute-

"**Approval of non-maintained special schools**

342.–(1) The Secretary of State may approve under this section any school which-

    (a) is specially organised to make special educational provision for pupils with special educational needs, and

    (b) is not a community or foundation special school,

and may give his approval before or after the school is established.

(2) Regulations may make provision as to the requirements which are to be complied with as a condition of approval under subsection (1) above.

(3) Any school which was a special school immediately before 1st April 1994 shall be treated, subject to subsection (4) below, as approved under this section.

(4) Regulations may make provision as to-

    (a) the requirements which are to be complied with by a school while approved under this section, and

    (b) the withdrawal of approval from a school (including approval treated as given under subsection (3)) at the request of the proprietor or on the ground that there has been a failure to comply with any prescribed requirement.

(5) Without prejudice to the generality of subsections (2) and (4), the requirements which may be imposed by the regulations include requirements-

    (a) which call for arrangements to be approved by the Secretary of State, or

    (b) as to the organisation of any special school as a primary school or as a secondary school.

(6) Regulations shall make provision for securing that, so far as practicable, every pupil attending a special school approved under this section-

    (a) receives religious education and attends religious worship, or

    (b) is withdrawn from receiving such education or from attendance at such worship in accordance with the wishes of his parent."

83. Omit sections 343 to 346 (government etc. of special schools).

84. In section 348 (provision of special education at non-maintained schools), for subsection (3) substitute-

"(3) In this section "maintained school" means a school maintained by a local education authority."

85. In section 350 (definitions for purposes of Part V), for subsection (1) substitute-

"(1) In this Part "maintained school" means-

    (a) any community, foundation or voluntary school; or

    (b) except where otherwise stated, any community or foundation special school not established in a hospital."

86. In section 352(1)(a) (basic curriculum for maintained schools), for "sections 376 to 381" substitute "Schedule 19 to the School Standards and Framework Act 1998".

87. In section 356 (establishment of the National Curriculum by order)-

    (a) in each of subsections (4) and (8), for "by Her Majesty's Stationery Office" substitute "as specified in the order"; and
    (b) in subsection (5)(a)(ii), omit the words "(except in the case of grant-maintained schools)".

88. In section 357 (implementation of National Curriculum in schools), omit subsection (2).

89. In section 362 (National Curriculum: development work and experiments)-

    (a) in subsection (3), for "a county, controlled or maintained special school" substitute "a community, voluntary controlled or community special school", and
    (b) in subsection (4), for "a grant-maintained, aided or special agreement school" substitute "a foundation, voluntary aided or foundation special school".

90. In section 366 (information concerning directions under section 365)-

    (a) in subsection (1)(b), omit the words from "where" to "special school,";
    (b) in subsection (4), for "a county, voluntary or maintained special school" substitute "a maintained school";
    (c) omit subsection (5); and
    (d) in subsection (6), for "subsection (1), (4) or (5)" substitute "subsection (1) or (4)".

91. Omit sections 370 to 374 (functions of local education authority etc. in relation to curriculum).

92. Omit sections 376 to 389 (religious education and worship).

93. In section 390 (constitution of advisory councils), for subsection (2) substitute-

    "(2) The council shall consist of such groups of persons appointed by the authority as representative members ("representative groups") as are required by subsection (4)."

94.–(1) Section 391 (functions of advisory councils) shall be amended as follows.

(2) In subsection (1), for paragraph (a) substitute-

    "(a) to advise the local education authority on such matters connected with-
        (i) religious worship in community schools or in foundation schools which (within the meaning of Part II of the School Standards and Framework Act 1998) do not have a religious character, and

     (ii) the religious education to be given in accordance with an agreed or other syllabus in accordance with Schedule 19 to that Act,

as the authority may refer to the council or as the council may see fit, and".

(3) Omit subsections (8) and (9).

95. In section 392 (advisory councils: supplementary provisions), omit subsection (4).

96. Omit section 393 (duty to constitute new standing advisory council).

97.–(1) Section 394 (determination of cases in which requirement for Christian worship is not to apply) shall be amended as follows.

(2) In subsection (1)-

    (a) in paragraph (a), for "county school" substitute "community school";
    (b) for paragraph (b) substitute-
        "(b) any foundation school which has not been designated under section 69(3) of the School Standards and Framework Act 1998 by the Secretary of State as having a religious character,"; and
    (c) for "section 386(2)" substitute "paragraph 3(2) of Schedule 20 to the School Standards and Framework Act 1998 (requirement for Christian collective worship)".

(3) In subsection (4), for "section 387" substitute "paragraph 4 of Schedule 20 to the School Standards and Framework Act 1998 (disapplication of requirement for Christian collective worship)".

(4) In subsection (8), for "a school which becomes a grant-maintained school" substitute "a community school which becomes a foundation school (by virtue of section 35 of, and Schedule 8 to, the School Standards and Framework Act 1998)".

98. In section 395(1) (review of determinations under section 394), for "section 386(2)" substitute "paragraph 3(2) of Schedule 20 to the School Standards and Framework Act 1998".

99. In section 396(1) (power of Secretary of State to direct council to revoke determination or discharge duty), for "section 386(2)" substitute "paragraph 3(2) of Schedule 20 to the School Standards and Framework Act 1998".

100. In section 399 (determination of question whether religious education in accordance with trust deed), for "a voluntary or grant-maintained school" substitute "a foundation or voluntary school".

101. In section 402(6) (obligation to enter pupils for public examinations), for "a maintained special school" substitute "a community or foundation special school".

102. In section 403(2) (sex education: manner of provision), for "a maintained special school" substitute "a community or foundation special school".

103. In section 404 (sex education: statements of policy)-

  (a) in subsection (2), for "a maintained special school" substitute "a community or foundation special school"; and

  (b) omit subsection (3).

104. In section 406(3) (political indoctrination), for "a maintained special school" substitute "a community or foundation special school".

105. In section 407(2) (duty to secure balanced treatment of political issues), for "a maintained special school" substitute "a community or foundation special school".

106. In section 408 (provision of information)-

  (a) omit subsection (1)(b);

  (b) in subsection (2)(d), for "pupils at such categories of school" substitute "such classes or descriptions of pupils";

  (c) omit subsection (3); and

  (d) in subsection (4)-

  (i) omit paragraphs (b) and (c); and

  (ii) in paragraph (d), for "389" substitute "390".

107. In section 409 (complaints and enforcement: maintained schools)-

  (a) in subsection (1), for "of aided schools and of special agreement schools," substitute "of foundation and voluntary aided schools,";

  (b) in subsection (2), for the words from "any county" to "special school" substitute "any community, foundation or voluntary school maintained by the authority or any community or foundation special school";

  (c) in subsection (3)(b), omit "other than grant-maintained schools"; and

  (d) for the sidenote substitute "Complaints and enforcement: maintained schools."

108. For the cross-heading "SCHOOL ADMISSIONS" preceding section 411 substitute-

"ADMISSION, REGISTRATION AND WITHDRAWAL OF PUPILS"

109. Omit sections 411 to 432 (admission of pupils: general).

110. Omit section 433(4) (time for admission of pupils: admission for nursery education).

111. In section 434(4)(c) (registration of pupils: returns)-

  (a) at the end of sub-paragraph (i) insert "and"; and

  (b) omit sub-paragraph (ii).

112. Omit section 436 (effect of admission for nursery education).

113. In section 437 (school attendance orders)-

  (a) in each of subsections (5) and (6), omit "or grant-maintained"; and

(b) in subsection (8), for the definition of "maintained school" substitute-
"""maintained school" means any community, foundation or voluntary school or any community or foundation special school not established in a hospital; and".

114. In section 438 (choice of school: child without statement of special educational needs)-

(a) for subsection (4)(a) substitute-
"(a) within the period mentioned in subsection (3) the parent applies for the child to be admitted to a school maintained by a local education authority and, where that authority are not the authority by whom the notice was served, notifies the latter authority of the application, and";
(b) for subsection (5) substitute-
"(5) If-
(a) within the period mentioned in subsection (3), the parent applies to the local education authority by whom the notice was served for education to be provided at a school which is not a school maintained by a local education authority, and
(b) the child is offered a place at the school and the authority are required by virtue of regulations under section 18(3) to pay the fees payable in respect of the education provided for him at the school,

that school shall be named in the order."; and
(c) in subsection (6)(a)(i), omit "and is not a grant-maintained school".

115.-(1) Section 439 (specification of schools in notices under section 438(2)) shall be amended as follows.

(2) In subsection (2), for the words from "fixed" to "as the number" substitute "fixed in accordance with section 93 of the School Standards and Framework Act 1998 (fixing admission numbers) as the number".

(3) In subsections (3), (5) and (6), omit "or grant-maintained" wherever occurring.

(4) After subsection (4) insert-

"(4A) A local education authority shall not specify a school in a notice under section 438(2) if the admission of the child concerned would result in prejudice of the kind referred to in section 86(3)(a) of the School Standards and Framework Act 1998 (parental preferences) by reason of measures required to be taken as mentioned in subsection (4) of that section."

116. In section 440 (amendment of order at request of parent: child without statement of special educational needs)-

(a) in subsection (2)(a), omit "or grant-maintained school";
(b) in subsection (3), for paragraphs (a) and (b) substitute-

"(a) the parent applies to the authority for education to be provided for the child at a school which is not a school maintained by a local education authority and which is different from the school named in the order,

(b) the child is offered a place at the school and the authority are required by virtue of regulations under section 18(3) to pay the fees payable in respect of the education provided for him at the school, and"; and

(c) in subsection (4)(a), omit "and is not a grant-maintained school".

117. In section 444(4)(b) (offence: failure to secure regular attendance at school of registered pupil), omit the words "or the funding authority".

118. Omit section 448 (exemption where child becomes five during term).

119. For section 449 and the cross-headings preceding it substitute-

"Chapter III

Charges in connection with education at maintained schools

Preliminary

449. In this Chapter "maintained school" means any school maintained by a local education authority."

120. In section 451 (prohibition of charges for provision of education)-

(a) in subsection (1), omit "Subject to subsection (5)",

(b) in subsection (3)(b), for the words from "or 384" onwards substitute "(implementation of National Curriculum) or section 69 of the School Standards and Framework Act 1998 (duty to secure due provision of religious education).",

(c) in subsection (4)(b), for "384" substitute "section 69 of the School Standards and Framework Act 1998", and

(d) omit subsection (5).

121. In section 456(1) (regulation of permitted charges), omit the words from ", other than" to "section 231(8)".

122. In section 457 (charges and remissions policies)-

(a) in subsection (1), omit the words from "This subsection" onwards; and

(b) in subsection (3), omit "other than a grant-maintained school".

123. In section 458 (charges for board and lodging at boarding schools)-

(a) in subsection (1)-
  (i) for the words from "pupil concerned" to "charges" substitute "pupil concerned, to the local education authority, charges", and
  (ii) omit "or governing body";

(b) in subsection (2)-
  (i) omit paragraph (a), and

(ii) in paragraph (b), for "for his area" substitute "for that pupil's area";

(c) omit subsection (3); and

(d) in subsection (4)(b), omit "or to the governing body of a grant-maintained school".

124. In section 463 (meaning of "independent school")-

(a) at the end of paragraph (b) insert "or"; and

(b) omit paragraph (c) and the "or" preceding it.

125. In section 484 (grants for education support and training)-

(a) in subsection (1), for "grants for education support and training," substitute "education standards grants,";

(b) in subsections (3) and (4), for "any grant for education support and training" substitute "any education standards grant"; and

(c) for the sidenote substitute "Education standards grants."

126. In section 489 (conditions as to payment of grants under sections 484 to 488), in subsection (2)(a) for "grant for education support and training," substitute "education standards grant,".

127. In section 490(1) (grants in respect of special provision for ethnic minorities), omit paragraph (a).

128. For section 494 substitute-

"**494.**–(1) Subsection (2) applies where a pupil is permanently excluded from any school maintained by a local education authority ("the old authority") and, in the financial year in which the exclusion first takes effect, he is subsequently provided with education by another local education authority ("the new authority"), whether at a school maintained by that authority or otherwise than at school.

(2) The old authority shall pay to the new authority, in connection with the provision of education for that pupil in that financial year, such amount, if any, as is payable in accordance with regulations.

(3) Where a pupil is permanently excluded from any school maintained by a local education authority and, in the financial year in which the exclusion first takes effect, the following events subsequently occur-

(a) he is first provided by another local education authority ("the intermediate authority") with education in a pupil referral unit or otherwise than at school, and

(b) at any time afterwards he is provided with education by a local education authority other than the intermediate authority ("the last authority"), whether at a school maintained by that authority or otherwise than at school, then, in connection with the provision of the education mentioned in paragraph (b), subsection (2) shall apply to the intermediate authority and the last authority as if they were an old authority and a new authority respectively.

(4) Any dispute as to whether any local education authority are entitled to be paid any amount under this section by any other such authority shall be determined by the Secretary of State.

(5) Regulations may prescribe the time when the permanent exclusion of a pupil is to be regarded as taking effect for the purposes of this section."

129. In section 496 (power of Secretary of State to prevent unreasonable use of functions), in subsection (2)-

(a) at the end of paragraph (a) insert "and"; and
(b) for paragraphs (b) and (c) substitute-
  "(b) the governing body of any community, foundation or voluntary school or any community or foundation special school."

130. In section 497 (general default powers of the Secretary of State), in subsection (2)-

(a) at the end of paragraph (a) insert "and"; and
(b) for paragraphs (b) and (c) substitute-
  "(b) the governing body of any community, foundation or voluntary school or any community or foundation special school."

131. In section 498 (powers of Secretary of State where no properly constituted governing body), for subsection (2) substitute-

"(2) This section applies to any community, foundation or voluntary school or any community or foundation special school."

132. Omit sections 500 to 505 (rationalisation of school places).

133. In section 509 (provision of transport etc.)-

(a) omit subsection (5)(a); and
(b) for subsection (6) substitute-
  "(6) Regulations may require a local education authority to publish, at such times and in such manner as may be prescribed, such information as may be prescribed with respect to the authority's policy and arrangements relating to the making of-
    (a) provision under this section for persons attending institutions mentioned in subsection (1)(c) or (d) who are over compulsory school age and have not attained the age of 19; or
    (b) provision under section 509A (travel arrangements for children receiving nursery education otherwise than at school)."

134. In section 510 (provision of clothing)–

    (a) in subsection (1)(a) and (c), omit "or at a grant-maintained school" wherever occurring;

    (b) in subsection (3)(a), omit "or a grant-maintained school";

    (c) in subsection (4)(a), omit ", at a grant-maintained school"; and

    (d) in subsection (5)(a), omit "grant-maintained school or".

135. In section 514 (provision of board and lodging otherwise than at school), in subsection (1)(a), for the words from "particular" onwards substitute "particular community, foundation or voluntary or community or foundation special school, but".

136. In section 515(2) (provision of teaching services for day nurseries), for "voluntary school" substitute "foundation or voluntary school".

137. Omit section 516 (supply by LEA of goods and services to grant-maintained schools).

138. Omit section 517 (payment of fees at schools not maintained by a local education authority).

139.–(1) Section 519 (allowances for governors, etc.) shall be amended as follows.

(2) In subsection (1), for the words from "travelling" to "section 115);" substitute "such allowances as may be prescribed to governors of–

    (a) any community, foundation or voluntary school or community or foundation special school which does not have a delegated budget (within the meaning of Part II of the School Standards and Framework Act 1998);".

(3) In subsection (3), for "travelling and subsistence allowances" substitute "such allowances as may be prescribed".

(4) After subsection (6) add–

    "(7) Regulations may impose a limit on the amount which may be paid by way of any allowance under this section."

140. Omit section 520(3) (medical inspection and treatment of pupils: grant-maintained schools excluded).

141. In section 521 (examination of pupils for cleanliness), in subsection (4), omit paragraph (b) and the "and" preceding it.

142. In section 524 (removal of pupil at direction of medical officer)–

    (a) in subsection (1), for "excluded" substitute "suspended";

    (b) omit subsection (3)(b) and the "or" preceding it; and

    (c) for the sidenote substitute "Suspension of a pupil pending examination or cleansing."

143. In section 525 (offence of neglecting the cleanliness of a pupil), in subsection (3), omit "or a grant-maintained school".

144. In section 527A (local education authority plans for children with behavioural difficulties), as inserted by section 9 of the Education Act 1997, for subsection (7) substitute-

"(7) In this section "relevant school", in relation to a local education authority, means a school maintained by the authority (whether situated in their area or not)."

145. In section 529 (power to accept gifts on trust for educational purposes)-

(a) in subsection (2) for the words from "section 35(1)" onwards substitute "section 28 of the School Standards and Framework Act 1998 as an intention to establish a new community school (so that proposals for that purpose shall be published as required by that section); and Schedule 6 to that Act (statutory proposals: procedure and implementation) shall apply accordingly."; and

(b) in subsection (3) for "a county school" substitute "a community school".

146. In section 530 (compulsory purchase of land)-

(a) in subsection (2) for "voluntary school" substitute "foundation, voluntary or foundation special school"; and

(b) in subsection (3) for the words from "under" onwards substitute "under paragraph 18 of Schedule 6 to the School Standards and Framework Act 1998 (power to give assistance to governing body of voluntary aided school in carrying out statutory proposals)."

147. In section 531(2) (acquisition of land by agreement) for "voluntary school" substitute "foundation, voluntary or foundation special school".

148. In section 533 (duties of governing bodies of maintained schools with respect to provision of school meals etc.)-

(a) in subsection (2), for "a voluntary" substitute "any such"; and

(b) in subsection (3), after "Part II" insert "of the School Standards and Framework Act 1998".

149. Omit section 534 (duties of governing bodies of grant-maintained schools with respect to school meals).

150. In section 535(1) (provision of teaching services for day nurseries), for "a county or voluntary primary school" substitute "a community, foundation or voluntary primary school".

151. Omit section 536 (medical inspection and treatment of pupils at grant-maintained schools).

152. In section 537 (power of Secretary of State to require information from governing bodies etc.)-

(a) for subsection (1) substitute-

"(1) The Secretary of State may by regulations make provision requiring-

(a) the governing body of every school which is-

(i) maintained by a local education authority, or

(ii) a special school which is not maintained by such an authority, and

(b) the proprietor of every independent school,

to provide such information about the school as may be prescribed."; and

(b) in subsection (7)(a), omit "or which is a grant-maintained school".

153. For section 537A substitute-

"537A.–(1) Regulations may make provision requiring-

(a) the governing body of every school which is-

(i) maintained by a local education authority, or

(ii) a special school which is not maintained by such an authority, and

(b) the proprietor of every independent school,

to provide to the relevant person such individual pupil information as may be prescribed.

(2) In subsection (1) "the relevant person" means one or more of the following-

(a) the Secretary of State, and

(b) any prescribed person.

(3) Where any person within paragraph (b) of subsection (2) receives information by virtue of subsection (1), the Secretary of State may require that person to provide any such information-

(a) to him, or

(b) to any prescribed person.

(4) The Secretary of State may provide any individual pupil information-

(a) to any information collator,

(b) to any prescribed person, or

(c) to any person falling within a prescribed category.

(5) Any information collator-

(a) may provide any individual pupil information-

(i) to the Secretary of State,

(ii) to any other information collator, or

(iii) to the governing body or proprietor of the school attended by the pupil or pupils to whom the information relates; and

(b) may, at such times as the Secretary of State may determine, provide such individual pupil information as may be prescribed-

(i) to any prescribed person, or

(ii) to any person falling within a prescribed category.

(6) Any person holding any individual pupil information (other than the Secretary of State or an information collator) may provide that information to-

(a) the Secretary of State,

(b) any information collator, or

(c) any prescribed person.

(7) No information received under or by virtue of this section shall be published in any form which includes the name of the pupil or pupils to whom it relates.

(8) Regulations under this section may provide that, in such circumstances as may be prescribed, the provision of information to a person other than the Secretary of State is to be treated, for the purposes of any provision of such regulations or this section, as compliance with any requirement imposed by or by virtue of any such provision and relating to the provision of information to the Secretary of State.

(9) In this section-

"individual pupil information" means information relating to and identifying individual pupils or former pupils at any school within subsection (1), whether obtained under subsection (1) or otherwise;

"information collator" means any body which, for the purposes of or in connection with the functions of the Secretary of State relating to education, is responsible for collating or checking information relating to pupils."

154. In section 538 (provision of information to Secretary of State by governing bodies of maintained schools), for "a county, voluntary or maintained special school" substitute "a community, foundation or voluntary school or a community or foundation special school".

155. Omit section 539 (provision of information by governing body of grant-maintained schools).

156. In section 540 (distribution of information about schools providing a secondary education), for subsection (2) substitute-

"(2) In this section "school" means-

(a) any community, foundation or voluntary school, or

(b) any community or foundation special school (which is not established in a hospital)."

157. In section 541 (distribution of information about further education institutions), for subsection (4) substitute-

"(4) In this section "school" means-

(a) any community, foundation or voluntary school, or

(b) any community or foundation special school (which is not established in a hospital)."

158. In section 542 (prescribed standards for school premises)-

(a) in subsection (1), omit "and of grant-maintained schools";

(b) omit subsection (3); and

(c) in subsection (4), for "subsections (2) and (3) have" substitute "subsection (2) has".

159. In section 543 (relaxation of prescribed standards in special cases)-

(a) in subsection (1), for "or (4)" substitute ", (4) or (4A)"; and

(b) after subsection (4) insert-

"(4A) This subsection applies, in relation to any playing fields used by the school for the purposes of the school, if the Secretary of State is satisfied that, having regard to other facilities for physical education available to the school, it would be unreasonable to require conformity with any prescribed requirement relating to playing fields.

In this subsection "playing fields" has the same meaning as in section 77 of the School Standards and Framework Act 1998 (control of disposals or changing use of school playing fields)."

160. In section 544 (approval etc. of school premises and boarding houses)-

(a) in subsection (1), omit the words from "(or," to "authority)"; and

(b) in subsection (3)-

(i) at the end of paragraph (a) insert "and", and

(ii) omit paragraph (b).

161. In section 545(2) (exemption from building byelaws of approved buildings), omit paragraph (b) and the "or" preceding it.

162. In section 546(2) (control of potentially harmful materials and apparatus in schools)-

(a) at the end of paragraph (a) insert "and"; and

(b) omit paragraph (b).

163. In section 547 (nuisance or disturbance on school premises)-

(a) in subsection (2), omit paragraph (b) and the "or" preceding it;

(b) in each of subsections (4) and (7), for "an aided, special agreement or grant-maintained school" substitute "a foundation, voluntary aided or foundation special school"; and

(c) in each of subsections (5) and (8), for "a voluntary or grant-maintained school" substitute "a foundation, voluntary or foundation special school".

164. Omit sections 549 and 550 (provisions about corporal punishment).

165. In section 550B(2) (detention), as inserted by section 5 of the (1997 c. 44.) Education Act 1997, omit "(b) a grant-maintained or grant-maintained special school;".

166. In section 551(2) (regulations as to duration of school day etc.)-

(a) at the end of paragraph (a) insert "and"; and

(b) omit paragraph (b).

167. Omit section 552 (transitional exemption orders for purposes of Sex Discrimination Act 1975).

168.–(1) Section 554 (power to make new provision as to use of endowments) shall be amended as follows.

(2) For subsection (1) substitute-

"(1) This section applies where-

(a) in relation to any time before the appointed day, the premises of a voluntary or grant-maintained school (within the meaning of this Act) have ceased to be used for such a voluntary or (as the case may be) grant-maintained school; or

(b) in relation to any time on or after the appointed day-

(i) the premises of a foundation or voluntary school (within the meaning of the School Standards and Framework Act 1998) have ceased to be used for such a foundation or (as the case may be) voluntary school; or

(ii) in the opinion of the Secretary of State it is likely such premises will cease to be so used;

and in this subsection "the appointed day" has the meaning given by section 20(7) of the School Standards and Framework Act 1998."

(3) In subsection (3)-

(a) for paragraph (a) substitute-

"(a) that the school was or has been maintained as a voluntary or grant-maintained school (within the meaning of this Act) or as a foundation or voluntary school (within the meaning of the School Standards and Framework Act 1998) since 1st April 1945 (the date when Part II of the Education Act 1944 came into force); and "; and

(b) in paragraph (b), for "(or any corresponding earlier enactment)", substitute "of this Act (or any corresponding earlier enactment) or paragraph 3 or 4 of Schedule 19 to the School Standards and Framework Act 1998".

(4) For subsection (4)(b) substitute-

"(b) where religious education in accordance with such tenets is shown to have been given to any pupils at-

(i) a controlled school (within the meaning of this Act),

(ii) a grant-maintained school (within the meaning of this Act) which was a controlled school immediately before it became a grant-maintained school, or

(iii) a foundation or voluntary controlled school with a religious character (within the meaning of Part II of the School Standards and Framework Act 1998),

the religious education shall be taken to have been given to them at the request of their parents, unless the contrary is shown."

169. In section 556(2) (content of orders under section 554)-

(a) in paragraph (a), for "voluntary schools or grant-maintained schools" substitute "foundation schools or voluntary schools"; and

(b) in paragraph (b), for "voluntary" onwards substitute "school at the premises referred to in section 554(1)."

170. In section 557(9) (adoption of statutory trusts), in the definition of "relevant school" for "a voluntary school or a grant-maintained school" substitute "a foundation or voluntary school".

171. In section 559 (power of local education authorities to prohibit or restrict employment of children)-

(a) in subsection (1), for "county" substitute "community, foundation"; and

(b) in subsection (2), for "county" substitute "community, foundation".

172. In section 563(3) (educational records)-
(a) at the end of paragraph (a) insert "and"; and
(b) omit paragraph (b).

173. In section 566(1)(b) (evidence: documents), for "a county or voluntary school" substitute "a maintained school".

174. Omit section 567 (stamp duty).

175. In section 568 (orders)-

(a) for subsection (2) substitute-
"(2) For the purposes of subsection (1) "the excepted provisions" are-
section 349;
sections 468, 471(1) and 474;
section 489(3);
section 497; and
section 545.";
(b) in subsection (3), omit "section 517(6),"; and
(c) omit subsection (5)(b) and the "or" preceding it.

176. In section 569 (regulations)-

(a) in subsection (2), for "section 480 or 492 or paragraph 1(4) of Schedule 20," substitute "section 492,"; and

(b) in subsection (3), for "section 480 or 492 or paragraph 1(4) of Schedule 20" substitute "section 492".

177. In section 570 (revocation and variation of certain orders and directions)-

(a) in subsection (1)-

    (i) at the end of paragraph (a) insert "or", and

    (ii) omit paragraph (b); and

(b) in subsection (2), omit ", the funding authority".

178. In section 573 (meaning of expressions relating to alteration etc. of premises or character of schools)-

(a) in subsection (2), omit the words from "and "alterations"" onwards; and

(b) omit subsections (4) to (6).

179. Omit section 575 (meaning of expressions relating to employment).

180. In section 576 (meaning of "parent")-

(a) in subsection (1), for "the provisions mentioned in subsection (2)" substitute "section 499(8)"; and

(b) omit subsection (2).

181. Omit section 577 (minor authorities).

182. In section 578 (meaning of "the Education Acts"), insert at the appropriate place- "the School Standards and Framework Act 1998".

183. In section 579 (general interpretation)-

(a) in subsection (1)-

    (i) at the appropriate place insert- ""assist", in relation to any school, institution or university, shall be construed in accordance with subsections (5) to (7) below;",

    (ii) omit the definitions of "the appropriate further education funding council", "exclude", "governing body" (and "governors"), "the local education authority", "reception class" and "relevant age group",

    (iii) in the definition of "proprietor", for "a county, voluntary or grant-maintained school," substitute "a community, foundation or voluntary or community or foundation special school,", and

    (iv) for the definition of "trust deed" substitute- ""trust deed" includes any instrument (other than an instrument of government) regulating the constitution of the school's governing body or the maintenance, management or conduct of the school;"; and

(b) omit subsection (3).

184. In Schedule 1 (pupil referral units)-

(a) in paragraph 6-

    (i) for sub-paragraphs (1) and (2) substitute- "(1) In relation to every pupil referral unit, the local education authority, the management committee (where applicable) and the teacher in charge shall exercise their functions with a view to securing that the curriculum for the unit satisfies the requirements of section 351(1) (balanced and broadly based curriculum).

(2) Regulations may make provision for the determination and organisation of the curriculum in relation to every pupil referral unit, including provision as to making, and keeping up to date, a written statement of the policy in relation to that curriculum for the unit; and such regulations may require-

    (a) the local education authority, the management committee (where applicable), or the teacher in charge to exercise, or

    (b) such of them as may be prescribed to collaborate with each other in exercising,

such functions in relation to the curriculum as may be prescribed.", and

    (ii) in sub-paragraph (3)(a), for "or under any enactment referred to in sub-paragraph (2)" substitute "sub-paragraph (1) or (2)";

(b) omit paragraphs 12 and 13; and

(c) in paragraph 15(2)(c) omit the words "(including grant-maintained schools)".

185. Schedules 2 to 25A shall be omitted.

186.–(1) Schedule 27 (making and maintenance of statements under section 324) shall be amended as follows.

(2) In paragraph 3-

    (a) in sub-paragraph (1), for "the maintained, grant-maintained or grant-maintained special school" substitute "the maintained school"; and

    (b) in sub-paragraph (4), for "any maintained, grant-maintained or grant-maintained special school" substitute "any maintained school".

(3) In paragraph 8(1)(a), for "a maintained, grant-maintained or grant-maintained special school" substitute "a maintained school".

187. Schedule 28 (government and conduct of grant-maintained special schools) shall be omitted.

188. In Schedule 31 (agreed syllabuses of religious education), omit paragraphs 11 and 15.

189. The following provisions shall be omitted-

    (a) Schedule 32 (reduction of standard number for admission of pupils);

    (b) Schedule 33 (admission appeals);

    (c) Schedule 33A (children to whom section 411A(2) applies: appeals by governing bodies);

    (d) Schedule 33B (restrictions on admissions to grant-maintained schools);

    (e) in Schedule 37 (consequential amendments), paragraphs 9, 27, 33, 37(a), 41, 42(4)(b), 75, 82(1)(b) and the "and" preceding it, 82(2)(a), 82(2)(c) and the "and" preceding it, 82(3), 96(2), 97, 102, 103, 104(3), 105 to 108, 110(2) and (3)(a), 122 and 125(c) and (d);

    (f) in Schedule 39 (transitional provisions and savings), paragraphs 2(3) and 15; and

    (g) Schedule 40 (transitory provisions).

School Inspections Act 1996 (c.57)

190. The School Inspections Act 1996 shall be amended as follows.

191.–(1) Section 10 (inspection of certain schools by registered inspectors) shall be amended as follows.

(2) In subsection (3)-

(a) omit "(4) or";

(b) for paragraph (a) substitute-

"(a) community, foundation and voluntary schools;";

(c) omit paragraph (b);

(d) for paragraph (c) substitute-

"(c) community and foundation special schools;"; and

(e) for paragraph (d) substitute-

"(d) special schools which are not community or foundation special schools but are for the time being approved by the Secretary of State under section 342 of the Education Act 1996 (approval of special schools);".

(3) Omit subsection (4).

(4) For subsection (4B) substitute-

"(4B) In subsection (4A) a "closing school" means-

(a) a community, foundation or voluntary or community or foundation special school in respect of which proposals to discontinue the school have been approved, adopted or determined under Schedule 6 or 7 to the School Standards and Framework Act 1998;

(b) a foundation or voluntary school in respect of which the governing body have given notice of discontinuance under section 30 of that Act;

(c) a community, foundation or voluntary or community or foundation special school in respect of which the Secretary of State has given a direction to discontinue the school under section 19 or 32 of that Act;

(d) a city technology college or city college for the technology of the arts in respect of which notice of termination of an agreement made under section 482 of the Education Act 1996 has been given;

(e) a special school which is not a community or foundation special school but which is for the time being approved by the Secretary of State under section 342 of the Education Act 1996 and which the proprietor has decided to close; or

(f) an independent school falling within subsection (3)(e) which the proprietor has decided to close."

192.–(1) Section 11 (application of provisions for inspections) shall be amended as follows.

(2) In subsection (2), for the words from "county" onwards substitute "community, foundation or voluntary or community or foundation special schools."

(3) In subsection (4)-

    (a) in the definition of "appropriate appointing authority", for "aided or special agreement school" substitute "voluntary aided"; and

    (b) for the definition of "appropriate authority" substitute-

        ""appropriate authority" means in relation to a community, foundation or voluntary or community or foundation special school, the school's governing body or, if the school does not have a delegated budget within the meaning of section 49 of the School Standards and Framework Act 1998, the local education authority."

(4) In subsection (5)-

    (a) in paragraph (a), for "paragraph (e)," substitute "paragraph (d), (e),"; and

    (b) in paragraph (b), omit "whose governing body does not have a delegated budget".

193. In section 15(3)(b) (timing of inspections), for "a county, voluntary or maintained special school" substitute "a community, foundation or voluntary or community or foundation special school".

194.–(1) Section 16 (destination of reports) shall be amended as follows.

(2) In subsection (1)-

    (a) in paragraph (a), omit the words from "and, if" to "of State"; and

    (b) in paragraph (b), for "a county, voluntary or maintained special school" substitute "a community, foundation or voluntary or community or foundation special school".

(3) In subsection (3)-

    (a) in paragraph (c)-

        (i) for "a county, voluntary or maintained special school" substitute "a community, foundation or voluntary or community or foundation special school", and

        (ii) at the end insert "and"; and

    (b) omit paragraphs (e) and (f).

195.–(1) Section 17 (special measures by appropriate authority) shall be amended as follows.

(2) In subsection (3)-

    (a) in paragraph (b)-

        (i) for "a county, voluntary or maintained special school" substitute "a community, foundation or voluntary or community or foundation special school", and

        (ii) at the end add "and"; and

    (b) omit paragraph (c).

(3) In subsection (4), for "a county, voluntary or maintained special school" substitute "a community, foundation or voluntary or community or foundation special school".

(4) Omit subsection (5)(b) and (c).

(5) In subsection (7), for the words from "referred to" to "the case may be," substitute "under section 42 of the School Standards and Framework Act 1998 (governors' reports),".

196.–(1) Section 18 (additional special measures by local education authority) shall be amended as follows.

(2) In subsection (1)(a), for "a county, voluntary or maintained special school" substitute "a community, foundation or voluntary or community or foundation special school".

(3) In subsection (2)(b), for "an aided or special agreement school" substitute "a voluntary aided school".

197. In section 20(3) (destination of reports)-
    (a) in paragraph (a), for "a maintained or grant-maintained special school" substitute "a community or foundation special school"; and
    (b) omit "the funding authority, or".

198. In section 21(4) (special measures by appropriate authority)-
    (a) in paragraph (a), for "a maintained or grant-maintained special school" substitute "a community or foundation special school"; and
    (b) omit "the funding authority, or".

199.–(1) Section 23 (inspection of religious education) shall be amended as follows.

(2) For subsection (1) substitute-

"(1) It shall be the duty of the governing body of any voluntary or foundation school, which has been designated under section 69(3) of the School Standards and Framework Act 1998 by the Secretary of State as having a religious character, to secure that-
    (a) denominational education given to any pupils, and
    (b) the content of the school's collective worship (required by section 70 of that Act),

are inspected under this section."

(3) Omit subsections (2) and (3).

(4) In subsection (4)(ii), for "section 385 of that Act" substitute "section 70 of the School Standards and Framework Act 1998".

(5) In subsection (5)(a), for "a controlled school" substitute "a voluntary controlled school".

(6) In subsection (8)-

(a) in paragraph (a), omit "if the inspection is conducted by virtue of subsection (1),"; and

(b) in paragraph (b), omit "if the inspection is conducted by virtue of subsection (2),".

200. Omit the following sections-

(a) sections 26 to 30 (miscellaneous powers over schools requiring special measures);

(b) sections 31 to 41 (education associations); and

(c) section 44 (stamp duty on transfer under section 38 or 39).

201. In section 45 (orders and regulations)-

(a) in subsection (1), omit the words "(except an order under section 38)"; and

(b) in subsection (2), omit the words "(except an order under section 31, 33, or 39)".

202.–(1) Section 46(1) (interpretation) shall be amended as follows.

(2) In the definition of "Church in Wales school" etc, for "section 311(1)" onwards substitute "section 142 of the School Standards and Framework Act 1998;".

(3) In the definition of "delegated budget", for "section 116" onwards substitute "section 49 of the School Standards and Framework Act 1998;".

(4) Omit the definition of "the transfer date".

203. In paragraph 1 of Schedule 3 (inspections under section 10), for the definition of "appropriate authority" substitute-

""appropriate authority" means-

(a) in relation to a community, foundation or voluntary or community or foundation special school, the school's governing body or, if the school does not have a delegated budget within the meaning of section 49 of the School Standards and Framework Act 1998, the local education authority;

(b) in relation to a maintained nursery school, the local education authority;

(c) in the case of a school falling within paragraph (d), (e), (f) or (g) of section 10(3), the proprietor of the school;".

204. In paragraph 3 of Schedule 4 (inspections of denominational education)-

(a) in sub-paragraph (2), for the words from "governors and" to "and to such" substitute "governors, to the local education authority and to such", and

(b) in sub-paragraph (5), for the words from "means" onwards substitute "means the governors' report under section 42 of the School Standards and Framework Act 1998."

205. Schedule 5 (education associations) shall be omitted.

206. In Schedule 6 (consequential amendments), omit paragraph 7.

Education Act 1997 (c.44)

207. The Education Act 1997 shall be amended as follows.

208. Omit the following provisions-

(a) sections 2 and 3 (school discipline);
(b) sections 6 to 8 (exclusion of pupils);
(c) Part III (school admissions).

209. In section 15 (baseline assessments: interpretation), in the definition of "maintained primary school", for paragraphs (a) to (c) substitute-

"(a) a community, foundation or voluntary school, or

(b) a community or foundation special school (other than one established in a hospital),".

210. In section 16(5) (adoption of baseline assessment schemes), for "a school which is maintained by a local education authority," substitute "a maintained primary school,".

211. In section 17 (assessment of pupils)-

(a) in subsection (5), for paragraph (b) substitute-
"(b) the local education authority by whom the school is maintained,"; and
(b) in subsection (7)(a), omit the words from "(except" to "school)".

212. In section 18 (regulations for Chapter I of Part IV)-

(a) in subsection (1)(b), omit the words from "(except" to "school)"; and
(b) in subsection (2)(a), omit the words from "(in" to "school)".

213. In section 19 (school performance targets), for subsection (3) substitute-

"(3) In this section "maintained school" means-

(a) a community, foundation or voluntary school, or
(b) a community or foundation special school (other than one established in a hospital)."

214. In section 23 (functions of Qualifications and Curriculum Authority)-

(a) in subsection (3), for the words from "receiving nursery" onwards substitute "under compulsory school age."; and
(b) in subsection (5), in the definition of "maintained school", for paragraphs (a) to (c) substitute-
"(a) any community, foundation or voluntary school, and
(b) any community or foundation special school."

215. In section 29(3) (functions of Qualifications, Curriculum and Assessment Authority for Wales), for the words from "receiving nursery" onwards substitute "under compulsory school age."

216. In section 42 (miscellaneous amendments relating to school inspections), omit the words "and the Nursery Education and Grant-Maintained Schools Act 1996".

217. In section 43(2) (provision of careers education)-

(a) for paragraph (a) substitute-
    "(a) community, foundation and voluntary schools;";
(b) omit paragraph (b); and
(c) for paragraph (c) substitute-
    "(c) community or foundation special schools (other than those established in hospitals);".

218. Omit section 50 (recoupment by local education authority of costs of teachers' premature retirement).

219. In section 52 (commencement of compulsory school age), omit subsections (4) and (5)

220. In section 57 (minor and consequential amendments, repeals etc), omit subsections (2) and (3).

221. In section 58(4) (commencement) omit "section 50,".

222. Omit the following provisions-

(a) Schedules 1 to 3;
(b) in Schedule 6, paragraph 5.

223. In Schedule 7 (minor and consequential amendments), omit paragraphs 15 to 22, 25, 31 to 35, 40 and 45 to 51.

Education (Schools) Act 1997 (c.59)

224. In section 2 of the Education (Schools) Act 1997 (transitional arrangements for existing assisted pupils), after subsection (6) add-

"(7) Nothing in subsection (1) shall be taken as prejudicing the operation of any regulations under section 3 by virtue of which assisted places authorised to be provided under that subsection by a former participating school may instead be so provided by another such school or a new school created on the merger of such a school with another school."

Audit Commission Act 1998 (c.18)

225. In section 36(3) of the Audit Commission Act 1998 (studies at request of educational bodies)-

(a) for the words from "corporation, a" to "school" substitute "corporation or further education corporation", and
(b) in paragraph (b), omit "or governing body".

Schedule 30
This Schedule makes a large number of minor and consequential amendments to existing legislation required in the light of the changes made by the Act. It consists very largely of changes of nomenclature in that earlier legislation and the removal of references to grant maintained schools. There is a significant change in relation to the provision of information under S. 537A of the Education Act 1996 which now provides for information to be provided to an "information collator", a new body having general responsibility for collating and checking information relating to pupils. This will enable a national pupil databank to be established with pupils having individual identifying numbers.

SCHEDULE 31

REPEALS

Chapter or number	Short Title	Extent of repeal
1958 c. 51.	Public Records Act 1958.	In Schedule 1, in Part II of the Table at the end of paragraph 3, the entry relating to the Schools Funding Council for Wales.
1963 c. 33.	London Government Act 1963.	Section 31.
1972 c. 11.	Superannuation Act 1972.	In Schedule 1, the entries relating to the Funding Agency for Schools and the Schools Funding Council for Wales.
1972 c. 70.	Local Government Act 1972.	In section 134(1) and (2), the words "or of a grant-maintained school". In section 177(1), the words from the beginning to "committees),".
1974 c. 7.	Local Government Act 1974.	In Schedule 5, paragraph 5(1).

Chapter or number	Short Title	Extent of repeal
1975 c. 24.	House of Commons Disqualification Act 1975.	In Part III of Schedule 1, the entries "Any member of an education association in receipt of remuneration", "Any member of the Funding Agency for Schools in receipt of remuneration", and "Any member of the Funding Council for Wales in receipt of remuneration".
1975 c. 65.	Sex Discrimination Act 1975.	In sections 22, in the Table, paragraph 3A. Section 23C. In section 25, in subsections (2) and (4), ", 23C"; and in subsection (6), in paragraph (c)(i) "3A" and paragraph (e). In Schedule 2, paragraph 1.
1976 c. 74.	Race Relations Act 1976.	In section 17, in the Table, paragraph 3A. Section 18C. In section 19, in subsections (2) and (4) ", 18C" wherever occurring and in subsection (6), in paragraph (c)(i) "3A" and paragraph (e).
1977 c. 49.	National Health Service Act 1977.	In section 5, in subsections (1)(a) and (1A)(a) the words "or at grant-maintained schools".
1980 c. 44.	Education (Scotland) Act 1980.	In section 75A(9A), the word "and" immediately preceding paragraph (b).
1981 c. 67.	Acquisition of Land Act 1981.	In section 17(4), paragraphs (ab) and (ac).
1983 c. 2.	Representation of the People Act 1983.	In Schedule 1, in paragraph 22(1)(i) the words "a grant-maintained school".

Chapter or number	Short Title	Extent of repeal
1984 c. 55.	Building Act 1984.	In section 4(1)(a), in paragraph (ii) the words "under section 39 or 44 of the Education Act 1996 or" and paragraphs (iii) and (iv).
1986 c. 61.	Education (No. 2) Act 1986.	Section 49(3)(ba).
1988 c. 40.	Education Reform Act 1988.	Sections 166 and 167. In section 197(7), the words "or grant-maintained". In section 236(1), the entry relating to section 219. In Schedule 8, paragraph 6(3) and in paragraph 8(4) the words "given with the consent of the Treasury". In Schedule 12, paragraphs 11, 13, 15, 16, 18 to 22, 30, 31 and 36.
1989 c. 41.	Children Act 1989.	In Schedule 9, in paragraph 3, sub-paragraph (1)(f), and in sub-paragraph (3) the definition of "grant maintained".
1991 c. 49.	School Teachers' Pay and Conditions Act 1991.	In section 1, in subsection (5) the words from "and, where" to "that subsection" and subsection (6). In section 2, subsection (2), in subsection (4), in paragraph (a) the words ", in the case of a grant-maintained school," and the words from "and provide" to the end and paragraph (h), in subsection (5) the words from "and, where" to "(2) above" and in subsection (6)(a) the words from "or, in" to "such schools,".

Chapter or number	Short Title	Extent of repeal
1991 No. 2.	Diocesan Boards of Education Measure 1991.	In section 3, subsections (4) and (5) and in subsection (6), the words "or (5)". Section 5. Section 6(2). Section 7(5). Section 9. In section 10, in subsection (1) the definition of "Church of England voluntary school" and subsection (2).
1992 c. 13.	Further and Higher Education Act 1992.	In section 2(6), the words "grant-maintained schools,". In section 16, in subsection (2), the words "or any grant-maintained school" wherever occurring, and in subsection (3)(a) the words "or is a grant-maintained school". In section 21, in subsection (1) paragraph (a) and the words "(b) in any other case,", and in subsection (2) the words "orders and", "grant-maintained school or other" and "grant-maintained schools or other". In section 26(1), the words "or was a grant-maintained school". In section 54(1)(b), the words "grant-maintained school,". In Schedule 8, paragraphs 61 to 64.
1993 c. 10.	Charities Act 1993.	In Schedule 2, paragraph (d).
1994 c. 23.	Value Added Tax Act 1994.	In Schedule 9, Group 6, Note (1), paragraph (a)(v) and (vii).

Chapter or number	Short Title	Extent of repeal
1994 c. 30.	Education Act 1994.	In section 11A, the words "grant-maintained schools,". Section 12(4) and (5). Section 18(1)(a).
1995 c. 50.	Disability Discrimination Act 1995.	Section 19(6)(c) and (d).
1996 c. 18.	Employment Rights Act 1996.	In section 50(9)(b) the words "grant-maintained school,".
1996 c. 50.	Nursery Education and Grant-Maintained Schools Act 1996.	Section 5. Schedule 1.
1996 c. 56.	Education Act 1996.	In section 1(2), paragraph (b) and the word "and" preceding it. Section 14(5). In section 16(1), paragraph (c) and the "and" preceding it. Sections 20 to 28. In section 29, subsection (2) and in subsection (3) the words "and the funding authority". Section 30. Part II Part III. In section 312(4)(a), the words "or grant-maintained schools in their area". In section 317(3)(a), the words ", the funding authority". Section 330. Sections 338 to 341. Sections 343 to 346. In section 356(5)(a)(ii), the words "(except in the case of grant-maintained schools)". Section 357(2).

Chapter or number	Short Title	Extent of repeal
1996 c. 56. –*Contd.*	Education Act 1996. –*Contd.*	In section 366, in subsection (1)(b) the words from "where" to "special school," and subsection (5).
		Sections 370 to 374.
		Sections 376 to 389.
		Section 391(8) and (9).
		Section 392(4).
		Section 393.
		Section 404(3).
		In section 408, subsections (1)(b), (3) and (4)(b) and (c).
		In section 409(3)(b), the words "other than grant-maintained schools".
		Sections 411 to 432.
		Sections 433(4).
		Section 434(4)(c)(ii).
		Section 436.
		In section 437, in subsections (5) and (6) the words "or grant-maintained" wherever occurring.
		In section 438(6)(a)(i), the words "and is not a grant-maintained school".
		In section 439, in subsections (3), (5) and (6) the words "or grant-maintained" wherever occurring.
		In section 440, in subsection (2)(a) the words "or grant-maintained school" and in subsection (4)(a) the words "and is not a grant-maintained school".

Chapter or number	Short Title	Extent of repeal
1996 c. 56. –*Contd.*	Education Act 1996. –*Contd.*	In section 444(4)(b), the words "or the funding authority". Section 448. In section 451, in subsection (1) the words "Subject to subsection (5)," and subsection (5). In section 456(1), the words from ", other than" to "section 231(8)". In section 457, in subsection (1) the words from "This subsection" onwards and in subsection (3) the words "other than a grant-maintained school". In section 458, in subsection (1) the words "or governing body", subsections (2)(a) and (3), and in subsection (4)(b) the words "or to the governing body of a grant-maintained school". In section 463, paragraph (c) and the "or" preceding it. Section 490(1)(a). Sections 500 to 505. Section 509(5)(a). In section 510, in subsection (1)(a) and (c) the words "or at a grant-maintained school" wherever occurring; in subsection (3)(a) the words "or a grant-maintained school"; in subsection (4)(a) the words ", at a grant-maintained school"; in subsection (5)(a) the words "grant-maintained school or". Sections 516 and 517. Section 520(3).

Chapter or number	Short Title	Extent of repeal
1996 c. 56. *–Contd.*	Education Act 1996. *–Contd.*	In section 521(4), paragraph (b) and the "and" preceding it. In section 524(3), paragraph (b) and the "or" preceding it. In section 525(3), the words "or a grant-maintained school". Section 534. Section 536. In section 537(7)(a), the words "or which is a grant-maintained school". Section 539. In section 542, in subsection (1) the words "and of grant-maintained schools" and subsection (3). In section 544, in subsection (1) the words from "(or," to "authority)" and subsection (3)(b). In section 545(2), paragraph (b) and the "or" preceding it. Section 546(2)(b). In section 547(2), paragraph (b) and the "or" preceding it. Sections 549 and 550. In section 550B(2), the words "(b) a grant-maintained or grant-maintained special school;". Section 551(2)(b). Section 552. In section 560(6), the words "or the governing body of a grant-maintained school". Section 563(3)(b). Section 567. In section 568, in subsection (3) the words "section 517(6)" and subsection (5)(b) and the "or" preceding it.

Chapter or number	Short Title	Extent of repeal
1996 c. 56. *—Contd.*	Education Act 1996. *—Contd.*	In section 570, subsection (1)(b) and in subsection (2) the words ", the funding authority". In section 573, in subsection (2) the words from "and "alterations"" onwards, and subsections (4) to (6). Section 575. Section 576(2). Section 577. In section 579, in subsection (1) the definitions of "the appropriate further education funding council", "exclude", "governing body" (and "governors"), "the local education authority", "reception class" and "relevant age group" and subsection (3). In Schedule 1, paragraphs 12 and 13 and in paragraph 15(2)(c) the words "(including grant-maintained schools)". Schedules 2 to 25A. Schedule 28. In Schedule 31, paragraphs 11 and 15. Schedules 32 to 33B. In Schedule 37, paragraphs 9, 27, 33, 37(a), 41, 42(4)(b), 75, 82(1)(b) and the "and" preceding it, 82(2)(a), 82(2)(c) and the "and" preceding it, 82(3), 96(2), 97, 102, 103, 104(3), 105 to 108, 110(2) and (3)(a), 122 and 125(c) and (d). In Schedule 39, paragraphs 2(3) and 15. Schedule 40.

Chapter or number	Short Title	Extent of repeal
1996 c. 57.	School Inspections Act 1996.	In section 9(3)(a), the words "are exceptional and".
		In section 10, in subsection (3) the words "(4) or" and paragraph (b) and subsection (4).
		In section 11(5)(b), the words "whose governing body does not have a delegated budget".
		In section 16, in subsection (1)(a) the words from "and, if" to "of State" and subsection (3)(e) and (f).
		Section 17(3)(c) and (5)(b) and (c).
		In section 20(3), the words "the funding authority, or".
		In section 21(4), the words "the funding authority, or".
		In section 23, subsections (2) and (3) and in subsection (8), in paragraph (a) the words "if the inspection is conducted by virtue of subsection (1)," and in paragraph (b) the words "if the inspection is conducted by virtue of subsection (2),".
		Section 44.
		In section 45, in subsection (1) the words "(except an order under section 38)" and in subsection (2) the words "(except an order under section 31, 33, or 39)".
		In section 46(1), the definition of "the transfer date".
		Schedule 5.
		Schedule 6, paragraph 7.
1997 c. 44.	Education Act 1997.	Sections 2 and 3.
		Sections 6 to 8.

Chapter or number	Short Title	Extent of repeal
1997 c. 44. *—Contd.*	Education Act 1997. *—Contd.*	In section 17(7)(a), the words from "(except" to "school)". In section 18, in subsection (1)(b) the words from "(except" to "school)" and in subsection (2)(a) the words from "(in" to "school)". In section 42, the words "and the Nursery Education and Grant-Maintained Schools Act 1996". Section 43(2)(b). Section 50. Section 52(4) and (5). Section 57(2) and (3). In section 58(4), "section 50,". Schedules 1 to 3. In Schedule 6, paragraph 5. In Schedule 7, paragraphs 15 to 22, 25, 31 to 35, 40 and 45 to 51.
1997 c. 59.	Education (Schools) Act 1997.	Section 6(1). In section 7, in subsection (3)(a) "section 6(1)", and in subsection (4)(a) "(1) and".
1998 c. 18.	Audit Commission Act 1998.	In section 36, in subsection (1) the entries relating to the Funding Agency for Schools, the Schools Funding Council for Wales and the governing body of a grant-maintained school, and in subsection (3)(b) the words "or governing body". In Schedule 3, paragraphs 25 and 32.

Schedule 31
This Schedule lists in tabular form the repeals to existing legislation required as a result of the new Act.

SCHEDULE 32

TRANSITIONAL PROVISIONS AND SAVINGS

PART I FUNDING

Interpretation

1. In this Part of this Schedule-

"the 1996 Act" means the Education Act 1996;

"the appointed day", in relation to any provision of this Schedule, means such day as may be appointed for the purposes of that provision by an order made by the Secretary of State.

Continued operation of GMS grants provisions

2.–(1) Subject to the provisions of this paragraph, the GMS grants provisions shall continue to have effect on and after the appointed day in relation to-

(a) any payments of maintenance grant under section 244 or 250 of the 1996 Act in respect of any financial year (or part of such a year) beginning before that day; and

(b) any payments of capital or special purpose grants under section 245, 246, 251 or 252 of that Act made before that day.

(2) Regulations may provide-

(a) for any functions of the funding authority under the GMS grants provisions-
  (i) to be discharged instead by the Secretary of State as from a date specified in the regulations, or
  (ii) to be discharged instead by local education authorities as from the appointed day (either subject to obtaining the Secretary of State's consent or otherwise); and

(b) for any of those provisions to have effect, for any purposes specified in the regulations, with such modifications as are so specified.

(3) Regulations under sub-paragraph (2) shall not authorise a local education authority to impose any requirement under section 247(1) of that Act (as it has effect by virtue of sub-paragraph (1)); but the Secretary of State may by order-

(a) impose such a requirement; or

(b) waive or remove such a requirement even though a local education authority is by such regulations also authorised to do so.

(4) In this paragraph "the GMS grants provisions" means sections 244 to 254 and 256 to 258 of the 1996 Act and any regulations in force under any of those provisions immediately before the appointed day.

Existing loans

3.–(1) Any loan made under section 255 of the 1996 Act (loans to governing bodies) shall not be affected by the repeal of that section by this Act.

(2) Where such a loan was made by the funding authority, any rights or liabilities of the authority in respect of the loan shall become rights or liabilities of the Secretary of State on the appointed day.

Grants by Secretary of State in respect of planned expenditure

4.–(1) Regulations may provide for the payment by the Secretary of State of grants to-
  (a) the governing bodies of schools to which this paragraph applies, or
  (b) local education authorities,

in respect of relevant expenditure incurred or to be incurred by them.

(2) Regulations under this paragraph may-
  (a) in relation to grants made to the governing bodies of any such schools, make provision corresponding to sub-paragraphs (6) and (7) of paragraph 5 of Schedule 3; and
  (b) in relation to grants made to the governing bodies of voluntary aided schools, make in addition provision corresponding to sub-paragraphs (8) to (10) of paragraph 5 of that Schedule.

(3) This paragraph applies to a school if immediately before the appointed day-
  (a) the school was a grant-maintained or grant-maintained special school within the meaning of the 1996 Act, or
  (b) proposals for the establishment of the school fell to be implemented in accordance with section 215 of that Act.

(4) Each of the following provisions of Schedule 22, namely-
  (a) paragraph 1(1)(d),
  (b) paragraph 2(1)(d), and
  (c) paragraph 3(1)(e),

shall (subject to sub-paragraph (5) below) apply in relation to any grant made by virtue of this paragraph as if it were such a grant as is mentioned in that provision.

(5) Sub-paragraph (4) does not apply to any grant made by virtue of this paragraph to the governing body of a voluntary aided school.

(6) In this paragraph "relevant expenditure" means such expenditure (being expenditure arising out of an obligation incurred or decision made before the appointed day) as may be prescribed.

Deferment of governing body's right to delegated budget

5.–(1) A maintained school falling within section 49(1) shall not have a delegated budget as from the day on which section 49 comes into force if-

(a) the governing body's right to a delegated budget has been suspended under section 117 of the Education Act 1996 (suspension of financial delegation for mismanagement etc.) or section 28 of the School Inspections Act 1996 (suspension of right to delegated budget); and

(b) that suspension has not been previously revoked with effect from that or any earlier day.

(2) Such a school shall, however, have a delegated budget as from the day with effect from which that suspension is revoked.

(3) The Secretary of State may by order determine that a relevant school shall not have a delegated budget as from the day on which section 49 comes into force where he considers that it would not be expedient for the school to have such a budget as from that day for reasons connected with-

(a) the financial position, or

(b) the financial management,

of the school.

(4) Where the Secretary of State makes an order under sub-paragraph (3) in relation to a school-

(a) for the purposes of Part II of this Act the right of the governing body to a delegated budget shall be treated as if it had been suspended by the local education authority under paragraph 1 of Schedule 15 on the day on which section 49 comes into force;

(b) paragraphs 2 to 4 (but not 3(1)(a)) of that Schedule shall apply to any such suspension; and

(c) the school shall have a delegated budget as from the day with effect from which that suspension is revoked.

(5) Any reference in any of sections 54 to 57 to any suspension of a school's delegated budget under Schedule 15 includes a reference to-

(a) any suspension of a school's delegated budget by virtue of sub-paragraph (1); and

(b) (in accordance with sub-paragraph (4)), any such suspension by virtue of sub-paragraph (3).

(6) Where the day on which section 49 comes into force is earlier than the day appointed under section 20(7) any reference in this paragraph to a maintained school is a reference to a school which is (within the meaning of the (1996 c. 56.) Education Act 1996)-

(a) a school maintained by a local education authority, or

(b) a grant-maintained or grant-maintained special school,

and to which section 49 applies in accordance with regulations under section 144(1).

(7) In this paragraph-

    (a) "relevant school" means a maintained school which immediately before the day on which section 49 comes into force was a grant-maintained or grant-maintained special school within the meaning of the (1996 c. 56.)Education Act 1996; and

    (b) references to a school having a delegated budget or to a governing body's right to such a budget shall be construed in accordance with section 49(7).

PART II OTHER PROVISIONS

Limit on class sizes

6.–(1) The transitional provision which may be made for the purposes of section 1 by regulations under section 144(1) includes provision with respect to any relevant time-

    (a) for disapplying to any extent in relation to existing maintained schools (whether or not subject to compliance with any prescribed requirements) section 411(6), 416(1) or 426(1) of the Education Act 1996 (provisions about admission numbers);

    (b) for otherwise modifying any of the provisions (whether statutory provisions or articles of government) which are relevant to the determination or publication of the arrangements-

        (i) for the admission of pupils to such schools, or

        (ii) for appeals by parents against decisions taken in relation to the admission of pupils to such schools,

    or to the procedure relating to such appeals;

    (c) for requiring or authorising bodies responsible for determining such arrangements to determine and publish fresh arrangements, subject to such consultation as may be prescribed, where arrangements previously determined (or previously determined and published) by them are to any extent inconsistent with the provisions mentioned in paragraph (b) as they have effect in accordance with the regulations.

(2) Regulations made in pursuance of paragraph (b) of sub-paragraph (1) may, in particular, modify the provisions mentioned in that paragraph so that they apply in relation to existing maintained schools with the addition of provisions whose purposes correspond to those of any of paragraphs 6(5), 10(5) and 11 of Schedule 23 to this Act.

(3) In this paragraph-

"existing maintained school" means-

    (a) any county or voluntary school, or

    (b) any grant-maintained school,

within the meaning of the (1996 c. 56.) Education Act 1996;

"relevant time", in relation to an existing maintained school, means any time after the coming into force of regulations under section 1 by virtue of which any limit on class sizes is to apply, or be varied, in relation to the school.

School Teachers' Pay and Conditions Act 1991

7. The amendment made by section 13 of this Act shall not affect the operation of section 3 of the School Teachers' Pay and Conditions Act 1991, as in force immediately before that amendment comes into force, in relation to any order made under section 3 of that Act which-

    (a) is then in force; and

    (b) relates to a grant-maintained school which becomes a foundation or voluntary aided school on the appointed day in accordance with Schedule 2 to this Act;

and any such order may be varied or revoked accordingly.

Orders for purposes of section 20(5)

8. The Secretary of State may only make an order under section 20(5) where he considers it appropriate to do so on an application made for the purpose by-

    (a) the former maintaining authority (within the meaning of that provision), or

    (b) the local education authority in whose area the school in question will be situated immediately before the appointed day,

and received by him not later than 30th November 1998.

Notice by trustees to terminate former voluntary school's occupation of land

9.–(1) This paragraph applies where-

    (a) at any time before the appointed day, whether before or after the date on which this Act is passed, any trustees (being entitled to do so) have given to the governing body of a former voluntary school a notice which is effective to terminate, on or after that day, the school's occupation of any land held by the trustees for the purposes of the school; and

    (b) the termination of the school's occupation of that land would have the result that it was not reasonably practicable for the school to continue to be conducted at its existing site.

(2) Paragraph 8(2) of Schedule 22 shall apply in relation to the land to which such a notice relates as it applies in relation to the land to which a notice falling within section 30(10) relates.

(3) Section 30(12) and (13) shall apply, with any necessary modifications, for the purposes of sub-paragraph (1)(b) as they apply for the purposes of section 30(10)(b).

(4) In this paragraph "former voluntary school" means-

(a) any voluntary school, or

(b) any grant-maintained school which was a voluntary school immediately before becoming grant-maintained or was established by promoters,

within the meaning of the Education Act 1996, which on the appointed day becomes a foundation or voluntary school within the meaning of this Act.

Transfer of sites provided under sections 60 and 61 of the Education Act 1996

10.–(1) This paragraph applies where-

(a) before the appointed day a site was provided for a school by a local education authority under section 60 or 61 of the (1996 c. 56.)Education Act 1996 (obligation of LEAs to provide new sites and buildings for voluntary schools); but

(b) no conveyance was made in respect of that site under section 60(2) or (as the case may be) section 61(2) of that Act before that day.

(2) Where the site was provided under section 60 of that Act, sub-paragraphs (3) to (11) (but not (7)(b)) of paragraph 2 of Schedule 3 to this Act shall apply in relation to the provision of that site as if it had been provided under sub-paragraph (1) of that paragraph.

(3) Where the site was provided under section 61 of that Act, sub-paragraphs (3) to (9) of paragraph 4 of Schedule 3 to this Act shall apply in relation to the provision of that site as if it had been provided under sub-paragraph (1) of that paragraph.

Schedule 32
This Schedule contains transitional provisions necessary to ensure that existing arrangements continue into the new framework. There is a very wide provision for regulations to be made to ensure this.

Index

Printed in the United Kingdom by The Stationery Office Limited
J0092675 12/99 451563 19585